P9-ASM-732

Formulaic Language and the Lexicon

A considerable proportion of our everyday language is 'formulaic'. It is predictable in form and idiomatic, and seems to be stored in fixed, or semi-fixed, chunks. This book explores the nature and purposes of formulaic language and looks for patterns across the research findings from the fields of discourse analysis, first language acquisition, language pathology and applied linguistics. It gradually builds up a unified description and explanation of formulaic language as a linguistic solution to a larger, nonlinguistic, problem, the promotion of self. The book culminates in a new model of lexical storage, which accommodates the curiosities of non-native and aphasic speech. It proposes that parallel analytic and holistic processing strategies are able to reconcile, on the one hand, our capacity for understanding and producing novel constructions using grammatical knowledge and small lexical units and, on the other, our use of prefabricated material which, although less flexible, also requires less processing. The result of these combined operations is language that is fluent and idiomatic, yet crafted for its referential and communicative purpose.

Dr. Alison Wray is a Senior Research Fellow at the Centre for Language and Communication Research, Cardiff University, Wales. She is the author of *The Focusing Hypothesis: The Theory of Left Hemisphere Lateralised Language Re-Examined* (1992) and the coauthor of *Projects in Linguistics: A Practical Guide to Researching Language* (1998).

hdmv

Formulaic Language and the Lexicon

ALISON WRAY

Cardiff University, UK

CAMBRIDGE
UNIVERSITY PRESS

CARL CAMPBELL BRIGHAM LIBRARY
EDUCATIONAL TESTING SERVICE
PRINCETON, NJ 08541

CAMBRIDGE UNIVERSITY PRESS
Cambridge, New York, Melbourne, Madrid, Cape Town, Singapore, São Paulo

Cambridge University Press
The Edinburgh Building, Cambridge CB2 2RU, UK

Published in the United States of America by Cambridge University Press, New York

www.cambridge.org
Information on this title: www.cambridge.org/9780521773096

© Cambridge University Press 2002

This publication is in copyright. Subject to statutory exception
and to the provisions of relevant collective licensing agreements,
no reproduction of any part may take place without
the written permission of Cambridge University Press.

First published 2002
This digitally printed first paperback version 2005

A catalogue record for this publication is available from the British Library

Library of Congress Cataloguing in Publication data
Wray, Alison.
Formulaic language and the lexicon / Alison Wray.
    p.   cm.
Includes bibliographical references and index.
ISBN 0-521-77309-1
1. Lexicology – Methodology.   2. Linguistic analysis (Linguistics)   3. Language
acquisition.   4. Aphasia.   I. Title.
P326 .W73   2001
413′.028 – dc21

                                                                2001025455

ISBN-13 978-0-521-77309-6 hardback
ISBN-10 0-521-77309-1 hardback

ISBN-13 978-0-521-02212-5 paperback
ISBN-10 0-521-02212-6 paperback

Contents

List of Figures and Tables   *page* vii

Preface and Acknowledgements   ix

Part I. What Formulaic Sequences Are

1 The Whole and the Parts   3

2 Detecting Formulaicity   19

3 Pinning Down Formulaicity   44

Part II. A Reference Point

4 Patterns of Formulaicity in Normal Adult Language   69

5 The Function of Formulaic Sequences: A Model   93

Part III. Formulaic Sequences in First Language Acquisition

6 Patterns of Formulaicity in Child Language   105

7 Formulaic Sequences in the First Language Acquisition
   Process: A Model   128

Part IV. Formulaic Sequences in a Second Language

8 Non-native Language: Overview   143

9 Patterns of Formulaicity in Children Using a
   Second Language   150

10 Patterns of Formulaicity in Adults and Teenagers Using a
   Second Language   172

11 Formulaic Sequences in the Second Language Acquisition
    Process: A Model   199

Part V. Formulaic Sequences in Language Loss

12 Patterns of Formulaicity in Aphasic Language   217

13 Formulaic Sequences in Aphasia: A Model   247

Part VI. An Integrated Model

14 The Heteromorphic Distributed Lexicon   261

Notes   283
References   301
Index   327

Figures and Tables

Figures

1.1.	Advice on using prefabricated chunks of text	*page* 6
1.2.	Terms used to describe aspects of formulaicity	9
2.1.	Hickey's "Conditions for formula identification"	40
3.1.	Hudson's "Levels of interaction in fixedness"	61
3.2.	Van Lancker's "Subsets of nonpropositional speech and their common properties, presented on a hypothetical continuum from most novel to reflexive"	64
4.1.	Formulaic structure of part of the New Zealand weather forecast	80
4.2.	A comparison of the structure of the first half of three Shipping Forecasts from the British Meteorological Office	80
4.3.	Comparison of a BBC Radio 4 weather forecast with one 24 hours earlier and another one hour later	82
4.4.	Kuiper and Flindall's "Greeting formulae of individual checkout operators"	86
5.1.	The functions of formulaic sequences	97
5.2.	Schema for the use of formulaic sequences in serving the interests of the speaker	98
6.1.	Uses of *no* in a two year old	120
6.2.	Predicted fate of different types of analytic and holistic language	123
6.3.	Agendas and responses of the young child	125
7.1.	The balance of holistic and analytic processing from birth to adulthood	133

9.1. Distribution of child L2 studies in Table 9.1, by age 152
11.1. The creation of the lexicon in first language acquisition
(including the effect of literacy) 207
11.2. The creation of the lexicon in classroom-taught L2 (after
childhood) 208
12.1. Code's "Preliminary model of initial and subsequent
production of aphasic lexical and nonlexical speech
automatisms" 234
13.1. Normal production using a distributed lexicon 249
14.1. Notional balance of three types of lexical unit (formulaic
sequence) in distribution: The Heteromorphic Distributed
Lexicon model 263

Tables

3.1. Howarth's collocational continuum 63
4.1. Formulaic sequences as devices for situation manipulation 89
9.1. Studies of formulaic sequences in young children
acquiring L2 in a naturalistic environment 151
10.1. Studies examining formulaic sequences in adults
acquiring L2 'naturally' 174
10.2. Studies examining formulaic sequences in adults and
teenagers acquiring L2 in the classroom 178

Preface and Acknowledgements

This book began with a mystery. I had been reading about formulaic language in the context of language proficiency, and had been struck by three observations made in the literature. The first was that native speakers seem to find formulaic (that is, prefabricated) language an easy option in their processing and/or communication. The second was that in the early stages of first and second language acquisition, learners rely heavily on formulaic language to get themselves started. The third observation, however, seemed to fly in the face of the first two. For L2 learners of intermediate and advanced proficiency, the formulaic language was the biggest stumbling block to sounding nativelike. How could something that was so easy when you began with a language, and so easy when you were fully proficient in it, be so difficult in between?

I set myself the challenge of finding out, and focussed on two possibilities, both of which I now judge to be true. One was that the formulaic language described in the various areas of study was not quite the same thing in each case. The second was that there was some other key to understanding the nature of formulaic language, one which would be difficult to spot by looking only at the different types of data in isolation. The common link between formulaic language across different speakers might even not be linguistic at all.

Very little attempt had been made up till then to draw together what was known about formulaic language in the native adult population, first language acquisition, second language acquisition of all types, and language pathology. A critical synthesis was a prerequisite for getting a sense of how they differed, and what they had in common. The second stage was developing a theoretical model – or rather a series of models – which would account for the similarities and differences. At first, I imagined that a single journal article would be adequate to tell the story, but it was soon very evident that much more space was needed.

The result was this book. The "big picture" that I present, will, I hope, provide useful ideas for others to explore. However, it will undoubtedly disappoint some. Those still wedded to the idea that lexis, grammar, interaction and discourse structure can be understood in mutual isolation will be frustrated by my proposal that language knowledge and language use are highly sensitive to the moment-by-moment influences of mind and environment, so that we are able to switch with ease between processing modes to match the requirements of efficiency and accuracy in message delivery and comprehension. And those who place their faith in frequency counts as the only valid arbiter of formulaicity will not welcome my call for the reinstatement of native-speaker intuition as the best witness to the part of our lexicon which we use with most creative flexibility.

The models which I propose are a beginning. My aim is to stimulate debate across the relevant disciplines and subdisciplines and to encourage research within each area to take into account what the others have to offer. The goal is a full integration of the wealth of insights currently imprisoned within each field, and this book is a first attempt at such an integration. The detail may be challenged – indeed, I hope it will be – but the inclusive approach to explaining what language is and how we manage it is, I believe, here to stay.

A great many people have been generous with their time, advice and material during the preparation of this book. I am particularly grateful to the following:

Ellen and Naomi Visscher and Hannah and Jane Soilleux for data in Chapter 6; Reg Fletcher of The Kellogg Company, Catherine Coleman of the American Advertising Museum and Kate Maxwell of J. Walter Thomson, who all chased after information about the Rice Krispies advertising campaign on my behalf; Gwen Awbery, Ellen Schur and Anne Thalheim, who advised me on the translation of data and/or quotes from Welsh, Hebrew and French, respectively; Gill Brown, Paul Meara and his Vocabulary Acquisition Research Group at the University of Wales Swansea, Andy Pawley, David Tuggy, Renee Waara, Dave Willis and Jane Willis, with all of whom I have discussed one or more of the ideas presented in the book; Chris Butler, Chris Code, Kon Kuiper, Mick Perkins, Norman Segalowitz, Mike Stubbs and two anonymous readers, who were kind enough to read drafts of all or parts of the book and who provided detailed and challenging comments. I should emphasize that they do not necessarily endorse the views expressed in this book, and any inaccuracies or misunderstandings expressed in it are entirely my responsibility. Finally, I want to thank Mike Wallace for his consistent support, interest and good humour during what has been a mighty project.

Alison Wray
Cardiff, June 2001

PART I

WHAT FORMULAIC SEQUENCES ARE

1

The Whole and the Parts

'Twelve-inches-one-foot.   Three-feet-make-a-yard.   Fourteen-pounds-make-a-stone. Eight-stone-a-hundred-weight'. . . . Unhearing, unquestioning, we rocked to our chanting, hammering the gold nails home. 'Twice-two-are-four. One-God-is-Love. One-Lord-is-King. One-King-is-George. One-George-is-Fifth . . .' So it was always; had been, would be for ever; we asked no questions; we didn't hear what we said; yet neither did we ever forget it.

Laurie Lee: *Cider with Rosie.* Penguin:53–4

She would go and smile and be nice and say 'So kind of you. I'm so pleased. One is so glad to know people like one's books'. All the stale old things. Rather as you put a hand into a box and took out some useful words already strung together like a necklace of beads.

Agatha Christie: *Elephants Can Remember.* Pan:12

Introduction

In a series of advertisements run on British TV early in 1993 by the breakfast cereal manufacturer Kellogg, people were asked what they thought Rice Krispies were made of, and expressed surprise at discovering that the answer was rice.[1] Somehow they had internalized this household brand name without ever analyzing it into its component parts. It was as if the name of the product had taken on a life of its own, and required no more reference back to its 'meaning' than do words of foreign origin such as *chop suey* ('mixed bits') and *spaghetti* ('little cords'). But how could this come about in the case of a name which, although oddly spelled, so transparently refers to crisp rice? In actual fact, overlooking the internal composition of names is a far more common phenomenon than we might at first think. Many personal names have 'meanings' which we simply ignore: we do not expect someone called 'Verity Baker' to be a truthful bread maker, or someone called

'Victor Cooper' to win barrel-making competitions.[2] Since interpreting such names in a literal way would be a distraction, it is actually very useful that we can choose the level at which we stop breaking down a chunk of language into its constituent parts. Nor is it just names that we treat in this way. We also overlook the internal composition of a great many words. Although there is a historical reason why a ladybird is so called, there is no more sense in decomposing the word than there is in falsely breaking down *carpet* into 'car' and 'pet'.

If this phenomenon were restricted to proper names and single words, it would be remarkable enough. But this is just the thin end of the wedge, for we are also able to treat entire phrases, clauses, and even lengthy passages of prose in this way. Just as with the name *Rice Krispies*, which, in effect, means both 'crisp rice' and 'common breakfast cereal of indeterminate composition', the result is often, though not always, two layers of meaning. If you break the phrase up, it means one thing, but if you treat it whole, in its accustomed way, it possesses a meaning that is something other than, or in addition to, its constituent parts. Idioms are a clear example of this. The phrase *pull someone's leg* has a literal, if rather improbable, meaning, which involves a person, the person's leg, and the action of pulling. But the phrase as a whole has the meaning 'tease', and it is difficult, in that interpretation, to work out why there is any reference to legs or pulling at all.

Words and word strings which appear to be processed without recourse to their lowest level of composition are termed *formulaic*, and they are the focus of this book. They are interesting because their widespread existence is an embarrassment for certain modern theories of linguistics, which have unashamedly pushed them aside and denied their undoubted significance. In exploring the way in which formulaicity contributes to our management of linguistic communication, we shall address such questions as: Just how common is formulaic language? What forms can it take? What is it used for? What role does it play in our production and comprehension of normal discourse? How is it to be accommodated within linguistic theory? How do first language learners acquire it? Why is it so problematic for second language learners? What happens to it when someone loses language capabilities through brain damage? And what role might it play in the general and linguistic recovery of such individuals?

In the course of the book, we shall see that research on formulaic language has lacked a clear and unified direction, and has been diverse in its methods and assumptions. Both within and across subfields such as child language, language pathology and applied linguistics, different terms have been used for the same thing, the same term for different things, and entirely different starting places have been taken for identi-

fying formulaic language within data. As a result, little headway has been
made in spotting larger, more general patterns, and no attempt has been
made before, to compare and contrast the full range of findings and to
reconcile them within a single theoretical account.

The momentum of the book is towards a unified description and
explanation of formulaic language and its status relative to the lexicon.
Parts I and II culminate in the assertion that recognizing the role of formulaicity is fundamental to understanding the freedoms and constraints
of language as a formal and functional system. Specifically, it is proposed
that formulaic language is more than a static corpus of words and phrases
which we have to learn in order to be fully linguistically competent.
Rather, it is a dynamic response to the demands of language use, and, as
such, will manifest differently as those demands vary from moment to
moment and speaker to speaker. This hypothesis, developed with reference to what is known about formulaicity in the language of adult native
speakers, is then tested through a comprehensive survey of findings in
the published research of three other fields: first language acquisition
(Part III), second language acquisition (Part IV) and aphasia (Part V).
For each area of research, individual descriptive and explanatory models
are developed, and these are drawn into a unified model in Part VI.

Setting the Scene

The Shape of Formulaicity

It is something of a joke amongst those who write for a living that it is
possible to construct plausible text out of prefabricated chunks (Figure
1.1). The humour of such examples resides in our recognition that "just
as we are creatures of habit in other aspects of our behavior, so apparently are we in the ways we come to use language" (Nattinger &
DeCarrico 1992:1). Despite Pinker's (1994:90ff) assertion that using
prefabricated chunks of language is a peripheral pursuit that tells us
nothing about real language processing, there is plenty of evidence to
the contrary. For, in our everyday language, "the patterning of words and
phrases . . . manifests far less variability than could be predicted on the
basis of grammar and lexicon alone" (Perkins 1999:55–56). There are
words and phrases that we are likely to say when we see a particular
friend, or find ourselves in a certain situation (Coulmas 1981). If we tell
the same story, or deliver the same lecture, more than once, we will soon
find that whole ideas are expressed in the same chunks of language each
time (Peters 1983:80, 109). We may re-echo a form of words that we used
earlier, or which someone else has just used (Pawley & Syder 2000:178).
In the context of 'collocation' we find that some words seem to belong

To pad out a report or an essay which is short on words without having to do any original thinking simply take one phrase from each column and join them as a sentence.

I	II	III	IV
On the other hand	the realization of preset programme assignments	compels us to reanalyze thoroughly the forms	of existing administrative and financial conditions.
Similarly	the scope of staff schooling	requires the explicit formulation and definition	of further directions of development.
However, we must not forget that	permanent growth volume and the range of our activities	helps in the preparation and realization	of the system of universal participation.
The weight and meaning of these problems does not need justification as	the current structure of organizations	safeguards the involvement of a wider group in the forming	of participants' attitudes in the face of the tasks set by organizations.
Richly diversified experiences and	the new model of organizational activity	fulfils important tasks in the elaboration	of new propositions.
The concern of the organization, in particular	further development of various forces of activity	enables the creation, to some extent,	of the directions of progressive education.
Higher ideological assumptions, and also	permanent safety of our activities in information and propaganda	is causing appreciation of the scale of importance	of needs-related systems.
In this way	consultation with active members	presents an interesting verification test	of appropriate conditions of activation.
Broadly speaking,	any alternative approach to the questions	draws after itself the initiation and modernization processes	of the model's development.

Figure 1.1. Advice on using prefabricated chunks of text (origin unknown).

together in a phrase, while others, that should be equally good, sound odd. For instance, Biber, Conrad and Reppen (1998) report that, in a 2.7 million word corpus of academic prose, *large number* was more than five times more common than *great number* (48.3 per million versus 8.9 per million).[3]

Whether these preferred strings are actually stored and retrieved as a unit or simply constructed preferentially, it has been widely proposed that they are handled, effectively, like single "big words" (Ellis 1996:111). They are "single choices, even though they might appear to be analysable into segments" (Sinclair 1991:110). Some are fully fixed in form (e.g., *Fancy seeing you here; Nice to see you*) and can bypass the entire grammatical construction process (Bateson 1975:61). Others, termed *semi-preconstructed phrases*, such as NP_i *set* + TENSE $POSS_i$ *sights on (V)* NP_j, require the insertion of morphological detail and/or open class items, normally referential ones (giving, for instance, *The teacher had set his sights on promotion; I've set my sights on winning that cup*).

A Long-Recognized Phenomenon

Observations of unexpected levels of fixedness in language can be traced back to the mid-nineteenth-century writings of John Hughlings Jackson, whose interest was in the ability of aphasic patients fluently to utter rhymes, prayers, routine greetings and so on, even though they had no ability to construct novel utterances (see Chapter 12). Half a century later, Saussure (1916/1966) talked of "synthesizing the elements of [a] syntagm into a new unit . . . [such that] when a compound concept is expressed by a succession of very common significant units, the mind gives up analysis – it takes a short cut – and applies the concept to the whole cluster of signs, which then becomes a simple unit" (p. 177). Jespersen (1924/1976) observed that "a language would be a difficult thing to handle if its speakers had the burden imposed on them of remembering every little item separately" (p. 85). He characterized the *formula* as follows:

[it] may be a whole sentence or a group of words, or it may be one word, or it may be only part of a word, – that is not important, but it must always be something which to the actual speech instinct is a unit which cannot be further analyzed or decomposed in the way a free combination can. (p. 88)

Bloomfield (1933) observed that "many forms lie on the border-line between bound forms and words, or between words and phrases" (p. 181). According to Firth (1937/1964), "when we speak . . . [we] use a whole sentence . . . the unit of actual speech is the holophrase" (p. 83). Firth considered it central to characterizing communication within a speech community to identify and list the "usual collocations" (1957/1968:180ff). Hymes (1962/1968) proposed that "a vast portion of verbal behavior . . . consists of recurrent patterns, of linguistic routines . . . [including] the full range of utterances that acquire conventional significance for an individual, group or whole culture" (pp. 126–127). Bolinger (1976) asserted that "our language does not expect us to build everything starting with lumber, nails, and blueprint, but provides us with an incredibly large number of prefabs" (p. 1), and Charles Fillmore (1979) argued that "a very large portion of a person's ability to get along in a language consists in the mastery of formulaic utterances" (p. 92).

However, insofar as these descriptions applied beyond the realm of the noncomponential idiom, they became increasingly marginalized as Chomsky's approach to syntactic structure gained prominence. Only with the new generation of grammatical theories, based on performance rather than competence (see later), has the idea of holistically managed chunks of language been slowly reinstated, and its implications recognized.

Terminology

Figure 1.2 lists some of the terms which can be found in the literature to describe a larger or smaller part of the set of related phenomena that we shall be examining in this book. While there is undoubtedly a certain measure of conceptual duplication, where several words are used to describe the same thing, it is also evident that some of the terms shared across different fields do not mean entirely the same thing in all instances. The label used by a given commentator may reflect anything from the careless appropriation of a nontechnical word to denote a specific meaning, to the deliberate selection of a particular technical term along with all its preexisting connotations. Overall, we must exercise some doubt about the likelihood that "while labels vary, it seems that researchers have very much the same phenomenon in mind" (Weinert 1995:182), for we shall see in Chapter 3 that this large and unwieldy set of types has been carved up and categorized in innumerable ways, all of which have something useful to say, but none of which seems fully to capture the essence of the wider whole.

Because of this plethora of terms, and the individual ways in which they are implicitly or explicitly defined,[4] we encounter a certain difficulty in wanting to refer to findings within and across research areas without appearing to impose one or another theoretical position. The survey which will unfold in the course of the book is intended to cast a fresh

amalgams – automatic – chunks – clichés – co-ordinate
constructions – collocations – complex lexemes – composites –
conventionalized forms – F[ixed] E[xpressions] including I[dioms]
– fixed expressions – formulaic language – formulaic speech –
formulas/formulae – fossilized forms – frozen metaphors – frozen
phrases – gambits – gestalt – holistic – holophrases – idiomatic –
idioms – irregular – lexical simplex – lexical(ized) phrases –
lexicalized sentence stems – listemes – multiword items/units –
multiword lexical phenomena – noncompositional –
noncomputational – nonproductive – nonpropositional –
petrifications – phrasemes – praxons – preassembled speech –
precoded conventionalized routines – prefabricated routines and
patterns – ready-made expressions – ready-made utterances –
recurring utterances – rote – routine formulae – schemata –
semipreconstructed phrases that constitute single choices –
sentence builders – set phrases – stable and familiar expressions
with specialized subsenses – stereotyped phrases – stereotypes –
stock utterances – synthetic – unanalyzed chunks of speech –
unanalyzed multiword chunks – units

Figure 1.2. Terms used to describe aspects of formulaicity.

eye over the range of accounts and data, in order to establish the larger
pattern into which they all fit. What is needed, then, is a term which does
not carry previous baggage, and which can be clearly defined. The neutral
term *formulaic language* is too commonly used in the literature to be
free of such associations. In its place, therefore, we shall use *formulaic
sequence*.[5] The word *formulaic* carries with it some associations of 'unity'
and of 'custom' and 'habit', while *sequence* indicates that there is more
than one discernible internal unit, of whatever kind. As we shall see,
there are good reasons for avoiding any implication that these internal
units must be words. Our working definition of the *formulaic sequence*
will be as follows:

*a sequence, continuous or discontinuous, of words or other elements, which is, or
appears to be, prefabricated: that is, stored and retrieved whole from memory at
the time of use, rather than being subject to generation or analysis by the language
grammar.*[6]

It is clear from this definition that the term aims to be as inclusive as
possible, covering any kind of linguistic unit that has been considered
formulaic in any research field.[7] The intention is to make reference
easier, not to constrain the discussion, so, despite the features of the
definition, the term will have to be used fairly loosely as a coverall. In
particular, although our starting place is a recognition that there is

something about a formulaic sequence that makes it appear to be unitary, we shall also cover accounts which do not embrace, or do not require, holistic storage, including purely frequency-based descriptions. At times, especially in Chapters 11 and 13, we shall be focussing on the ability of morphemes and polymorphemic words to count as formulaic sequences. In such contexts, we shall need to differentiate between types of formulaic sequence and the terms *formulaic word string, formulaic word* and *morpheme* will be used.

Selecting a Theoretical Reference Point

"Linguists seem to underestimate the great capacity of the human mind to remember things while overestimating the extent to which humans process information by complex processes of calculation rather than by simply using prefabricated units from memory" (Lamb 1998:169). It will be proposed in this book that although we have tremendous capacity for grammatical processing, this is not our only, nor even our preferred, way of coping with language input and output. In particular, it will be argued that much of our entirely regular input and output is not processed analytically, even though it could be. Clearly, in order to explore this idea, it is necessary to engage with at least one established model of grammatical processing. Several recent models intrinsically accommodate some or all aspects of formulaicity, including Cognitive Grammar (e.g., Langacker 1987, 1991), Construction Grammar (e.g., Fillmore, Kay & O'Connor 1988; Michaelis & Lambrecht 1996; Tomasello & Brooks 1999), the Emergent Lexicon (Bybee 1998), Lexical-Functional Grammar (Bresnan 1982a, 1982b), the Cardiff Grammar, a version of Systemic Functional Grammar (e.g., Tucker 1998), and Pattern Grammar (Hunston & Francis 2000). However, to adopt one of these for our current purposes would be premature, since their very tolerance of formulaicity means that they will not challenge the core assumptions about its nature which this book seeks to tease out and examine. Rather, we need a model which directly opposes those assumptions, so that every claim about what formulaicity is and why it exists has to be fully justified.

The theoretical positions least sympathetic to formulaicity as a principle feature of language structure are the ones which propose a single grammatically based processing system. Within those, it is Chomsky's (1965) claim, that we have a greater understanding of language structure than we could possibly construe only from the observation of input, which remains the most difficult to defeat. Therefore, the argument of this book will be directed against the traditional generative account of syntax, in which language structure is founded on abstract universal and local rules. The Chomskian position offers the clearest contrast to the whole notion of circumstantial associations between words, is least tolerant of internally complex units, and holds itself separate from performance and pragmatics, the two axes of the model of formulaicity developed here. There is also a particular advantage in pitching what will be a model of part-analytic, part-holistic processing against a purely analytic one. It invites us to construe the analytic grammatical system and the holistic formulaic one as essentially separate. Now this may well not be desirable in the end, but it will make much clearer the path of the argument.

It would be short-sighted simply to ignore the alternative theories, however, especially since they may offer plausible solutions to the problem of how formulaicity is to be accommodated within a productive knowledge of grammar.[8] So we shall return to the question of theoretical models of grammatical structure and processing in Chapter 14, when we shall be able to assess more directly the demands that the existence of formulaicity makes on explanatory adequacy.

Formulaicity and Our Capacity for Novelty

The reason why formulaicity has been somewhat overlooked in the last few decades is that, from the standard perspective of how linguistic systems must be designed, it does not sit easily with our capacity for novel expression. Novelty in language, or rather the potential for it, has lain at the centre of modern linguistic theory for several decades: "an essential property of language is that it provides the means for expressing indefinitely many thoughts and for reacting appropriately in an indefinite range of new situations" (Chomsky 1965:6).

Chomsky's observations about our inherent capacities to generate and to understand sentences that we have never encountered before are fundamental and entirely valid. But the significance of this capability has been considerably overstated, relative to our actual use of language on a minute-by-minute basis:

native speakers do *not* exercise the creative potential of syntactic rules to anything like their full extent, and . . . indeed, if they did so they would not be accepted as exhibiting nativelike control of the language. The fact is that only a small proportion of the total set of grammatical sentences are nativelike in form – in the sense of being readily acceptable to native informants as ordinary, natural forms of expression, in contrast to expressions that are grammatical but are judged to be 'unidiomatic', 'odd', or 'foreignisms'. (Pawley & Syder 1983:193)

In order to understand the significance of this fundamental misalignment of positions, we need to consider just what 'novelty' is in this context, and how it can be reconciled with the repetitiveness of much of our everyday language.

Novelty

Poetry is a clear case in which the writer's success in achieving a particular effect often relies on novel juxtapositions of ideas: *The shrill, demented choirs of wailing shells; Young death sits in a café smiling; With Time's injurious hand crush'd and o'erworn; You are his repartee.*[9] Our capacity to interpret such strings has reasonably been taken as evidence that we possess a flexible lexicon and grammar which enable us to find meaning in combinations of words we have not encountered before.[10] That capacity is particularly useful when, for instance, word classes are changed (e.g., *he sang his didn't he danced his did*),[11] or unaccustomed morphological relations are created (e.g., *and you and I, light-tender-holdly, ached together in bliss-me-body*).[12] However, in most cases 'novelty' is much less a question of doing things with grammar than juxtaposing new ideas in commonplace grammatical frames. So, although the sentence *there's a man-eating tiger on the sugar lump* is novel both in the sense that it is unlikely to have been encountered before, and also in that it expresses a new idea, this effect is created by the juxtaposition of the referential subject matter, not by any grammatical creativity. Most of our language, then, is novel in a rather uninteresting way (cf. Schmidt & Frota 1986:309–310). Yet because there is the possibility that we will encounter the more challenging kind of novelty that poetry, and speaker errors, bring, we need to be equipped to deal with it.

This capacity for handling novelty, both ideational and grammatical, is sufficient to rule out the possibility that language knowledge consists *only* of a set of prefabricated phrases and sentences memorized from previous encounters with them (Bloom 1973:17). Whatever determines our preferences for certain phrases – their storage in prefabricated form, or something else – the most that we could argue is that this process *co-exists* with our ability to create and understand entirely novel strings. Although we customarily say, *Hi, how are you doing?* or some other idiomatic greeting on meeting a friend, there is nothing at all to stop us saying, *What a pleasant event it is to see you. Tell me, how is your life progressing at the moment?* The real issue is whether it is, or isn't, possible to account for real language data *without* invoking prefabrication.

The Theoretical Significance of Formulaic Sequences

Until quite recently, only two arguments really challenged the Chomskian claim that the language of normal adult native speakers is fully generated at the time of production and fully analyzed in comprehension. The first was that idioms cannot be so processed, if they are to render their real meaning (e.g., Chafe 1968; Jackendoff 1997; Lyons 1968:177ff; Weinreich 1969). The only way to decode and encode an expression like *pig in a poke* is to have a direct link from its phonological or graphemic form to its meaning. It is, as Kiparsky put it, "a ready-made surface structure" (Watkins 1992:392). However, since the idioms are a small set, it was relatively easy to propose that they are an awkward exception, and need to be listed whole in the lexicon. There were no major further implications to this. The second argument was the one which we have seen illustrated above from Pawley and Syder (1983): not all possible grammatical sentences occur with equal frequency or are judged equally idiomatic by native speakers. This observation, along with explanations of it, has been made many times over the last few decades, but had little impact on the theoretical stance of the powerful syntax fraternity, because it seemed focussed on the circumstantial practice of real speakers, whereas "[a] grammar of a language purports to be a description of the ideal speaker-hearer's intrinsic competence" (Chomsky 1965:4). Since there is no gain-saying the fact that an "ideal speaker-hearer" of standard English is entirely capable of constructing, and understanding, a sentence such as *The captain has illuminated the seatbelt sign as an indication that landing is imminent*,[13] it could reasonably be viewed as irrelevant that, in actual fact, a native speaker probably never would construct such a sentence because one or more other ways would tend to come to mind first, such as *The captain has put the seatbelt sign on, which means we're about to land*.

The mighty resilience of the Chomskian position relates to its avoidance of any engagement with what people actually say, or which grammatically possible constructions of their language they might find more difficult to encode and/or decode than others. For as long as the unease with this mismatch of theory and data was primarily reliant on small samples and armchair intuition, 'idiomaticity' could be kept at arm's length and relegated to the 'lesser' fields of sociolinguistics and pragmatics. However, that is now no longer the case.

Corpus linguistics has upped the ante for the traditional accounts, revealing formulaicity, in its widest sense, to be all-pervasive in language data (see Chapter 2). Whereas it was previously possible to imagine that words combined fairly freely, their restrictions attributable to context and pragmatics, and to easily definable social signalling, it is now clear that, once you actually map out the patterns of distribution for words, no such piecemeal and superimposed explanation is possible. Words belong with other words not as an afterthought but at the most fundamental level. John Sinclair, a central figure in the development of techniques in corpus linguistics and their application to the practical task of dictionary-writing, and the first to uncover the full extent of word patterning, firmly believes that any plausible description of normal language must take this "unrandomness" (Sinclair 1991:110) in the distribution of words into account.

Explaining 'unrandomness' requires a model of linguistic knowledge which preferentially associates some regular combinations of words relative to others, and this creates a fundamental problem for generative grammar. It would be, at the very least, inelegant for such models to have any sizeable store of complex as well as simple items, and total anathema if such items were actually regular in form and meaning, consisting of predictable subcomponents. This is because two central requirements of these accounts of language are explanatory *simplicity* (Hjelmslev 1943/1969:18) and streamlined modelling of mental storage and processing. This means that the language descriptions are directed towards the potential for the free combination of minimal units, subject to the constraints of general principles and of local co-occurrence restrictions (Marantz 1995:352; Webelhuth 1995a:9). Chomsky's Minimalist Program is a case in point, identifying operations that represent 'least effort' as the preferred ones, with other, more effortful ones termed 'last resort'; the procedural rule is that of "a striving for the cheapest or minimal way of satisfying principles" (Marantz 1995:353).

Two Systems

Sinclair's (1987, 1991) explanation of 'unrandomness' is that we handle linguistic material in two different ways. The *open choice principle* results in the selection of individual words, and gives us the same kind of creative leeway as the Chomskian account. The *idiom principle* brings about the selection of two or more words together, on the basis of their previous and regular occurrence together (Sinclair 1991:110f). Sinclair proposes that

the first mode to be applied is the idiom principle, since most of the text will be interpretable by this principle. Whenever there is good reason, the interpretive process switches to the open-choice principle, and quickly back again. Lexical choices which are unexpected in their environment will presumably occasion a switch. (1991:114)

Wray (1992) also proposes a dual-systems solution. Analytic processing entails the interaction of words and morphemes with grammatical rules, to create, and decode, novel, or potentially novel, linguistic material. Holistic processing relies on prefabricated strings stored in memory. The strategy preferred at any given moment depends on the demands of the material and on the communicative situation, and so, importantly, holistic processing is not restricted to only those strings which *cannot* be created or understood by rule, such as idioms. It can also deal with linguistic material for which grammatical processing would have rendered exactly the same result.

The explanatory power of dual-processing systems accounts is considerable (see, for instance, Erman & Warren 2000). Neither a grammar-only nor a formula-only model can accommodate both the linguistic competence of the "ideal speaker listener" (Chomsky 1965:3) and the idiomaticity associated with a preference for some grammatical strings over others.[14] The grammar on its own will overgenerate acceptable strings, relative to what sounds nativelike (Pawley & Syder 1983), while prefabricated units offer only a restricted range of forms and meanings, and so are of little use when dealing with something novel.[15] But between them, they can explain both novelty and idiomaticity.

At first glance, a dual-systems model is inelegant because it means that there is multiple representation of linguistic items (e.g., Bolinger 1975:297; Peters 1983:3–4). Accounts concur that prefabricated strings must run into many thousands (Jackendoff 1997:155–156; Van Lancker 1987:56), and, as corpus studies show, they will contain many of the same words in different formulations. However, although a dual-systems account lacks the particular elegance of a streamlined model, that is of no significance if, in the light of all the available evidence, it becomes clear that a single-system model is implausible. Occam's Razor invites us to select the most elegant of the *possible* explanations. As Langacker (1987) points out, "the principle of economy must be interpreted in relation to other considerations, in particular the requirement of factuality: true simplicity is not achieved just by omitting relevant facts" (p. 41). In any case, as we shall see now, storing often-used word strings whole constitutes, in itself, an alternative type of efficiency.[16]

Formulaic Sequences and Processing Pressures

A given communicative situation will tax one's resources, with the result that a demand placed on the individual may actually exceed the resources available. For example, understanding a spoken message in a noisy room or during an emotionally charged exchange will normally make greater demands on the listener than will a casual conversation. If the demands are too great, then the individual will not be able to engage in all the complex processing that the situation requires. (Segalowitz 1997:105)

In this light, it seems reasonable that "the main reason for the prevalence of formulaicity in the adult language system appears to be the simple processing principle of economy of effort" (Perkins 1999:56). This economy occurs because it gives us access to "ready-made frameworks on which to hang the expression of our ideas, so that we do not have to go through the labor of generating an utterance all the way out from 'S' every time we want to say something" (Becker 1975:17). If Becker is right, then it suggests that some aspects of our processing ability can fail to match the power of our analytical grammar.[17] In one respect, this has been long accepted in syntactic theory. Recursivity permits multiple self-embedding, including centre-embedding, as with Chomsky's (1965) example *the man who the boy who the students recognized pointed out is a friend of mine* (p. 11), but our limited memory makes it difficult to hold all the unfinished structures in an orderly way until they are resolved (Miller & Chomsky 1963:473ff; Yngve 1961). Centre-embedding is rare (though, as Sampson 1996 argues, perhaps not as rare as many have claimed), but much more common constructions can also create processing problems in certain situations. Some kinds of input are substantially more difficult to follow than others, and if, as later argument will suggest, our output has to be fluent in order to be successful in its impact, then the dysfluency which producing complex constructions can lead to will be dispreferred, in favour of, for example, chaining together short, self-contained strings (Pawley & Syder 1983).

As mentioned previously, one explanation for the shortfall between grammatical capability and on-line processing capability is limitations in short-term memory. Others are biologically or chemically imposed limitations on processing speed (e.g., Crick 1979:134), competition for the focus of attention (Pawley & Syder 2000:196; Wray 1992), and limited facility with switching the focus of attention (Segalowitz 2001). Miller (1956), Bower (1969) and Simon (1974) have shown how chunking information into single complex units increases the overall quantity of material that can be stored in short-term or working memory. Ellis and Sinclair (1996) note that a person's phonological working memory span correlates with his or her language learning capacity.[18] This links short-term memory to the question of processing speed:

It would be physiologically impossible for us to produce speech with the ra-
pidity and proficiency that we are able to if we had to plan and perform each
segment individually. Speech appears to be under a mixture of closed-loop and
open-loop control. . . . In closed-loop control, speech is feed-back-controlled,
segmentally planned and executed. Under open-loop control whole chunks
are holistically planned and automatically produced. The speed and fluency of
normal speech production from a neuromuscular system under physiological and
mechanico-inertial constraints, means that a significant amount of automaticity
is required for speech to proceed. (Code 1994:139–140)

It seems to be in our interests to be fluent, and "it is our ability to use lexical phrases ... that helps us speak with fluency" (Nattinger & DeCarrico 1992:32). The advantage of fluency[19] seems to be in "permitting speakers (and hearers) to direct their attention to the larger structure of the discourse, rather than keeping it focused narrowly on individual words as they are produced" (ibid.). Thus, it is advantageous for us to be able to exercise flexibility, by trading off processing effort against novelty (Kuiper 1996:96ff; Oppenheim 2000).

The dual-system model proposed here has much in common with that of Wray (1992), but is also different in some important ways. Wray (1992) suggests that holistic processing, associated with the right hemisphere of the brain, may be preferred for all commonplace linguistic material up to clausal level, through the recognition of familiar frames, while the analytic mechanisms (left hemisphere) focus on the juxtaposition of propositions, and on troubleshooting when dysfluencies, errors or unexpected structures interrupt routine decoding. This emphasis divides grammatical abilities between the two systems. In our current model, the formulaic system will not entail any grammatical processing, only lexical retrieval, though the internal complexity of the units retrieved may give the impression that grammatical construction has taken place. In this respect, it has more in common with Becker's (1975) formulation:

We start with the information we wish to convey and the attitudes toward that information that we wish to express or evoke, and we haul out of our phrasal lexicon some patterns that can provide the major elements of this expression ... Then the problem is to stitch these phrases together into something roughly grammatical, to fill in the blanks with the particulars of the case in hand, to modify the phrases if need be, and if all else fails to generate phrases from scratch to smooth over the transitions or fill in any remaining conceptual holes. (p. 28)

The flexibility afforded by novel construction will be sacrificed both in routine interaction, where it is not needed, and also where processing pressures are abnormally high, such as when a person is trying to concentrate on something else while speaking, like listening to the radio or negotiating a difficult junction on the road. In those cases, very little nonformulaic language may be produced, and even filling open class slots may be achieved using default pronouns and fillers like *thing* and *whatchamacallit* rather than searching for the appropriate lexical item. In the case of comprehension, focussing on difficult ideas will encourage the hearer or reader to use context and pragmatics to help identify where the novelty (if any) of the message lies, and take shortcuts in decoding the packaging around it, by identifying blocks of material as formulaic. Because such material will not be subjected to full linguistic analysis, errors such as semantic incongruities, agreement errors, slips of the tongue and typos, will often go unnoticed (see Wray 1992:chap. 1).

Conclusion

We have seen that the advantage of the analytic system, which creates grammatical strings out of small units by rule, is its flexibility for novel expression and the interpretation of novel and unexpected input. The advantage of the holistic system is that it reduces processing effort. It is more efficient and effective to retrieve a prefabricated string than create a novel one. In adult speakers (though not necessarily in children – see Chapter 7), the relative balance of the two systems in operation appears to be in favour of the holistic, for we prefer a pragmatically plausible interpretation over a literal one, and we seem able to use with ease formulaic sequences whose internal form we have, apparently, never engaged with. The use of the holistic system extends much farther than just that small subset of idioms which could not be handled any other way, and, on a moment-by-moment basis, "the fact that we can analyze does not necessarily mean that we do" (Bolinger 1975:297). As Widdowson (1989) observes:

communicative competence is not a matter of knowing rules for the composition of sentences and being able to employ such rules to assemble expressions from scratch as and when occasion requires. It is much more a matter of knowing a stock of partially pre-assembled patterns, formulaic frameworks, and a kit of rules, so to speak, and being able to apply the rules to make whatever adjustments are necessary according to contextual demands. Communicative competence in this view is essentially a matter of adaptation, and rules are not generative but regulative and subservient. This is why the Chomsky concept cannot be incorporated into a scheme for communicative competence. (p. 135)

In Chapters 4 and 5, we shall use evidence from the language of adult native speakers to assess the plausibility of processing constraints as a full explanation for formulaicity. But first we turn to the interrelated procedural issues of identifying formulaic sequences in text and pinning down just what it is that makes them formulaic.

2

Detecting Formulaicity

Introduction

Of two constructions made according to the same pattern, one may be an ad hoc construction of the moment and the other may be a repetition or reuse of one coined long ago. . . . This may be reflected in a number of ways other than that of their grammatical structure, which is presumed constant. They may be characterized by different internal entropy profiles. They may have different text frequencies. They may have different latency patterns, these being reflected in observably different timing patterns and in differences in the introduction of hesitation pauses. (Lounsbury 1963:561)

In this chapter, we shall consider how various features associated with formulaic sequences might be used to help identify them, and in Chapter 3 we shall review approaches to definition. It might seem rather odd to do things in this order, since identifying something obviously relies on how you define it. However, the relationship between definition and identification is circular: in order to establish a definition, you have to have a reliable set of representative examples, and these must therefore have been identified first.[1] In actual fact, in the case of formulaic sequences, identification relies less on formal definitions than the definitions rely on identification, and that tips the balance in favour of dealing with the two in this order. We do, of course, have our working definition of formulaic sequences (Chapter 1) to guide us. Because it focusses on the manner of storage – an internal and notional characteristic, rather than external and observable – this definition is deliberately inclusive and should not force the exclusion of any linguistic material for which any kind of argument can be made for inclusion.

We shall find, in the course of this review, that there are two basic ways in which formulaic sequences can be collected. One is to use an experiment, questionnaire or other empirical method to target the production of formulaic sequences (as defined by the study in question) as data. The other is to collect general or particular linguistic material and then hunt through it in some more or less principled way, pulling out strings which, according to some criterion or group of criteria, can justifiably be held up as formulaic.[2] We shall focus mostly on the latter approach here, since it is the isolation of formulaic sequences from standard data sets that is most consistently problematic and subject to variation. We begin with the least scientific, but most commonly used, method of extraction: intuition.

Intuition and 'Shared Knowledge'

There is a close link between formulaicity and idiomaticity,[3] though whether it is a causal link or just one of association is open to debate. Idiomaticity, in turn, can only be defined in terms of the intuition of members of the relevant speech community: an expression is idiomatic if it 'sounds right', and is "regularly considered by a language community as being a unit" (Moon 1997:44). Researchers, as members of their speech community, often are the self-appointed arbiters of what is idiomatic or formulaic in their data (e.g., Erman & Warren 2000). Even where some other measure is primarily in use, intuition still tends to guide the design of experiments, the interpretation of results and the choice of examples used in the published reports. However, intuition is generally treated with suspicion in scientific research, since it is obstinately independent of other kinds of observation.

Objections to Intuition

Chomsky's reason for discounting intuition was that the processes of interest to the theoretical linguist are too deeply embedded for introspection:

Any interesting generative grammar will be dealing, for the most part, with mental processes that are far beyond the level of actual or even potential consciousness; furthermore, it is quite apparent that a speaker's reports and viewpoints about his behavior and his competence may be in error. Thus a generative grammar attempts to specify what the speaker actually knows, not what he may report about his knowledge. (Chomsky 1965:8)

Despite this clear assertion, Chomsky's theories have consistently made intuitive pronouncements about what is and is not grammatical, often to the consternation of those who disagree about particular classes of example, or who do not believe that one person's grammaticality judgement has anything to say about another person's grammar.

It is now a contention of several theories that the entire notion of a central grammatical system for the individual is erroneous, and that "grammatical knowledge [is] more like a collection of know-hows to deal with various contingencies" (Grace 1995:1). Ironically, this tends to place intuition back at the centre of things, as a legitimate expression of, and potential external means of observing, the piecemeal knowledge accumulated through our many encounters with language in use, in the absence of a coherent or common grammar. It is, then, a matter of theoretical conviction whether intuition is regarded as the ultimate arbiter in reflecting the 'true state of affairs', or an unwelcome distraction from it.

A quite different objection to intuition as a way of judging linguistic structure comes from corpus research. Before the advent of the technology for searching large corpora, it was generally assumed that our intuitions about language were basically accurate, so it seemed to make little difference whether you found an illustrative example in real text or made one up. However, corpus research has revealed that "human intuition about language is highly specific, and not at all a good guide to what actually happens when the same people actually use the language" (Sinclair 1991:4). Thus, Sinclair argues that intuition is only useful for gaining insights into the nature of intuition itself, not the nature of language (ibid.). Corpora are viewed as "the only reliable authority", challenging us "to abandon our theories at any moment and posit something new on the basis of the evidence" (Francis 1993:139). One consequence of this position has been a fundamental challenge to assumptions about the validity of standard grammatical models based on intuitive judgements. Specifically:

[n]ative speakers have no reliable intuitions about . . . statistical tendencies [in lexical distribution]. Grammars based on intuitive data will imply more freedom of combination than is in fact possible. . . . Every sense or meaning of a word has its own grammar: each meaning is associated with a distinct formal patterning. Form and meaning are inseparable. (Stubbs 1993:17)

Nevertheless, we shall see later in this chapter that the frequency counts which corpus research provides are a mixed blessing in the context of identifying all, and only, the formulaic sequences of a language.

Native-Speaker Intuition in SLA Research

While research focussed on the knowledge of native speakers can afford the luxury of agonizing about the status of intuition, second language acquisition research is generally less squeamish, since there is a far more pressing problem: *non*-native speaker intuition, or the lack of it. In a context of trying to ascertain precisely what it is about learner output that makes it 'incorrect', heavy reliance is generally placed on the intuitive judgement of native speakers. After all, the learner is, at some level, aspiring to precisely those insights which a native speaker has, irrespective of what grammatical theories or frequency counts may say about them (Cornell 1999:5).

The problem with identifying formulaic sequences in the second language acquisition context, then, has less to do with *whether* native speaker intuition is drawn upon, than how. There is a strong temptation to be unashamedly unscientific; for example, "we eventually listed a number of expressions that we intuitively regarded as formulas" (Bahns, Burmeister & Vogel 1986:700). Preferable, on balance, is using a panel of independent judges, since there should be a certain resilience in a consensus achieved in this way. All the same, there can be a wide variation in the overall number of sequences spotted by different judges (Jane Willis, personal communication). Foster (2001) has attempted to formalize the procedures and make them as reliable as possible, using seven native speaker judges, "all university teachers of Applied Linguistics with many years experience in English as a foreign language" (p. 83).[4] Their instructions were "without consulting anyone else, to mark any language which they felt had not been constructed word by word, but had been produced as a fixed 'chunk', or as part of a sentence 'stem' to which some morphological adjustments or lexical additions had been required" (p. 83). Foster then applied an exclusion threshold according to which only chunks identified by at least five of the seven judges were counted in her analysis. Foster's report of how the judges handled their task clearly shows that intuition is a slippery customer, eliciting a complex mixture of confidence and doubt in the mind of the conscientious judge:

According to the written comments of all seven informants, theirs was not an easy task. Lapses of concentration with reading meant missing even obvious examples of prefabricated language, so progress was slow and exhausting. All seven reported difficulty in knowing where exactly to mark boundaries of some lexical chunks and stems as one could overlap or even envelop another. Nevertheless, after a certain amount of self-imposed revision, each reported feeling reasonably confident with their coding. (p. 84)

Inherent Problems with Intuition

Foster's method represents a significant milestone in this highly problematic area of identifying formulaic sequences in text, and although there are arguably 'better' solutions for each of the difficulties inherent in relying on intuition, we shall see that each of those solutions also brings its own further problems by very dint of its failure to anchor onto intuition. Specifically, the weaknesses of even Foster's relatively robust analytic method are endemic:

- It has to be restricted to small data sets. Foster used only one third of her 60,000 word data set, as asking the judges to deal with any more would have been impractical. In contrast, frequency-based computer searches can handle corpora of any size.
- There is no way to avoid inherent inconsistency within the range of judgements made by an individual, because of factors such as tiredness and unintended alterations in the judgement thresholds across time. Computers do not suffer from such problems.
- There is a danger of significant variation between judges. Foster alleviated this problem by using a high threshold of consensus, and by selecting individuals with similar backgrounds. She also gave them all the same instructions. However, the very need for several judges rather than one is because there are risks of error that computers are not subject to.
- There is no guarantee that formulaic sequences have firm borders in the sense that we have come to expect in the context of phrase structure analysis, so, even if all judges were actually operating identical criteria, for any given string there may not be one single answer to find. A computer analysis would not operate any kind of variable or discretionary judgement, and would have to be preset to find particular things. As we shall see, while this is an advantage if you already know how to identify the thing you are looking for, it is a potential disadvantage if you do not, since a clear-cut analysis will be unable to point up the areas of doubt.
- As Chomsky observes (see earlier), the application of intuition makes subjective externalized insights valid, at the expense of any knowledge we may have that is not available at the surface level of our awareness. A computer program will identify, without favour, all the patterns that it is set up to find. However, as we shall see, that still leaves the onus on the researcher to explain the patterns that appear to run counter to our intuition, and if no explanation can be found, they are likely to be discarded as noise.

Shared Knowledge As a Basis for Identification

'Shared knowledge' is another aspect of intuition that we can briefly explore here. It is important because it pervades the literature and is the very basis of how researchers come to share a sense of what constitutes a formulaic sequence. The following example[5] is a useful starting point. The author is making a point about the ubiquity and naturalness of formulaic sequences, by deliberately incorporating as many as possible into his text and highlighting their presence:

/In-a-nutshell/   it-is-important-to-note-that/   a-large-part-of-communication /makes-use-of-/   fixed-expressions./As-far-as-I-can-see/   for-many-of-these-at-least/ the-whole-is-more-than-the-sum-of-its-parts./ The meaning of an idiomatic expression cannot be deduced by examining the meanings of the constituent lexemes. /On-the-other-hand/ there-are-lots-of phrases that/ although they can be analyzed using normal syntactic principles/ nonetheless/ are not created or interpreted that way./ Rather, /they are picked-off-the-shelf/ ready-made/ because they-say-what-you-want-to-say./ /I-don't-think-I'm-going-out-on-a-limb-here./ However /it-is-appropriate-to-say-at-this-point/ that-much-work-remains-to-be-done./ (Ellis 1996:118–119)

This represents a kind of insider joke, which is based upon the expectation of shared knowledge between writer and reader – the use of formulaic sequences to talk about formulaic sequences. In the wider world, the same expectation of shared knowledge makes possible the shortening of well-known idioms, as in *a stitch in time* and *sleeping like the proverbial*, and can also be a source of humour, as with the interpretation of the clause *I hold your hand in mine* in Tom Lehrer's song:

> *I hold your hand in mine, dear, I press it to my lips,*
> *I take a healthy bite from your dainty fingertips.*
> *My joy would be complete, dear, if you were only near,*
> *But still I keep your hand as a precious souvenir.*[6]

Such humour juxtaposes 'shared knowledge' with semantic transparency to provide two readings of the same string. Often, however, transparency and shared knowledge are not closely allied. Clearly, any string that is formulaic for, say, the speaker, but not for the hearers, will simply not be understood unless it is transparent (Peters 1983:81), while sequences which a whole community stores holistically can be much more irregular and opaque, since all the hearers possess a form-meaning mapping already. "In fact, the very opacity of certain expressions can be used as a sort of verbal fence to include certain hearers who have the knowledge to decode the expressions and to exclude those others who lack that knowledge" (ibid.). As a result, shared knowledge can be the badge of belonging to a speech community, and not possessing that knowledge can be a mark of social exclusion (see Chapters 4 and 5). Returning to the question of how formulaic sequences can be identified in text, shared knowledge means that, for members of the same speech community, it might be possible to use, as a measure of formulaicity, the extent to which a word string, started by one person, can be reliably completed by others, without any of the deviation in form that the application of creative processes would predict (Van Lancker 1987:56). However, such a measure would only be suitable for the subset of formulaic sequences which are not dependent on current interactional demands (see Chapter 5). Furthermore, it would run into problems where there is natural variation in the format of formulaically delivered messages (Chapter 4).

Frequency

In corpus linguistics, computer searches are conducted to establish the patterns of distribution of words within text. This is done on the basis of frequency counts, which reveal which other words a given target word most often occurs with. These patterns of collocation turn out to be far from random. For instance, Hunston and Francis (2000) show how the word 'matter' characteristically occurs in the pattern '*a matter of V-ing*' (e.g., *a matter of developing skills; a matter of learning . . . ; a matter of becoming able to . . .*) (p. 2). It is structures like '*a matter of V-ing*' that, in the wider literature, are characteristically proposed to be formulaic 'frames' (see Chapter 3). Furthermore, if you take a word string which is indisputably formulaic, such as *happy birthday* or *high time*, it can be searched for through a large corpus and shown to have a frequency consistent with the intuition that it is common as well as idiomatic (we shall unpack this assertion later). Both these associations invite us to see frequency as a salient, perhaps even a determining, factor in the identification of formulaic sequences. It seems, on the surface, entirely reasonable to use computer searches to identify common strings of words, and to establish a certain frequency threshold as the criterion for calling a string 'formulaic'. The reasoning, of course, is that the more often a string is needed, the more likely it is to be stored in prefabricated form to save processing effort, and once it is so stored, the more likely it is to be the preferred choice when that message needs to be expressed. Since the preferential selection of the prefabricated form will actually suppress the frequency with which any other possible expression of the same message is selected, the contrast in frequency should be clear. The process of identifying formulaic sequences should, then, be unproblematic, because "their normality is a function of their occurrence as holistic units. So it becomes a relatively straightforward matter to list them as an inventory" (Widdowson 1990:92). The advantage of relying on computer searches for the identification of formulaic sequences would seem enormous:

The retrieval systems, unlike human beings, miss nothing if properly instructed – no usage can be overlooked because it is too ordinary or too familiar. The statistical evidence is helpful, too, because it distinguishes the commoner patterns of usage, which occur very frequently indeed, from the less common usage, which occurs very infrequently. (Sinclair & Renouf 1988:151)

Sinclair and Renouf go on to observe that "no description of usage should be innocent of frequency information" (p. 152). However, they distance themselves from the idea that frequency is the *only* factor relevant to capturing patterns of usage (ibid.), and their caution is well placed. There are several reasons for taking care when applying frequency information to the identification of formulaic sequences.

Procedures

Using computer searches to identify formulaic sequences might seem to be a simple matter. The researcher must decide what will count and what will not, and set up the search accordingly. For instance, it is possible to search for co-occurrences of two or more words, either adjacent or up to a specified distance apart – the optimal distance for two words seems to be up to four intervening words (Sinclair 1998:15). When searching for multiword strings, decisions have to be made about how big the strings should be, and how frequent an association has to be in order to count.[7] Such frequency thresholds are inevitably arbitrary, and, in practical terms, are chosen on the basis of the size of the corpus, the desired quantity of data and the size of the chunks being sought, since "the length of the recurrent word combinations is inversely related to their frequency" (DeCock, Granger, Leech & McEnery 1998:71). In their study, for instance, DeCock et al. searched for two-word chunks with a frequency greater than nine occurrences, three-word chunks occurring more than four times, four-word chunks more than three times and five-word chunks more than twice, using two independent corpora of around 63,000 and 80,500 words, respectively.

However, frequency counts are still somewhat overpowerful, and while some effort can be made in honing them to provide all and *only* the items of interest (Clear 1993:275), additional decisions have to be made post hoc, about which of the identified associations to discard. For example, where the search tools ignore major constituent and sentence boundaries, changes of speaker, false starts, and so on, it may be decided to apply structural criteria (Butler 1997:62) and eliminate those which are "phraseologically uninteresting" (Altenberg 1990:133). In addition, spoken corpora tend to contain transcriptions of hesitation phenomena such as *erm* and *er*, and the researcher must decide whether these are to count as words (e.g., DeCock et al. 1998:73). Finally, it is often clear from looking at a particular example that there is nothing intrinsically interesting about it, as with *gol, gol, gol, gol, gol,* from Butler's (1997) Spanish corpus, presumably shouted by a sports commentator when a goal was scored in a football match (p. 69).

Thus, while it might seem sensible simply to count everything, it is often intuitively clear that some patterns are more important and relevant than others. However, ad hoc intuitive decisions (such as those used by Nattinger & DeCarrico 1992:20, for instance) have the potential to bring about the same problems as we identified in the last section. Foremost of these, of course, is the undermining of the very value of a computer search, namely, the avoidance of subjective judgement. We neither fully understand the nature and causes of formulaicity, nor have any entirely satisfactory alternative means of identifying examples. It is, then, premature to be deciding which patterns of words are and are not relevant.

Further problems regarding the procedures of frequency counts can be identified. Firstly, corpora are probably unable to capture the true distribution of certain kinds of formulaic sequences. Indisputably, what they offer is considerably better than anything we had before. However, the selectiveness of small corpora may exclude certain types of common, but less easily gathered or analyzed, material (see, for instance, Butler's 1997:64 criticism of his own corpus). 'Fifteen minutes of fame' expressions,[8] which become very popular in a limited context for a short time, perhaps as a result of a news item or a TV series, are also a problem. Corpora will, characteristically, either entirely miss such examples, or overrepresent them, according to the input material. Meanwhile, the very breadth of a large corpus, drawing from a wide range of different types of source text (e.g., Moon 1998a:48), means that it is not likely to be representative of the rather narrower linguistic experience of any one individual. It is probably fair to suggest that the research tends to hope that the patterns in the corpus actually do reflect those of individual speakers, since it might be difficult to justify the study of language as an external phenomenon if this did not offer useful insights into language as an internal, personal phenomenon. But presumably only relatively few people regularly read both tabloid and broadsheet newspapers and listen to both pop quizzes and heavy current affairs programmes on the radio – the sorts of data that are thrown together in a corpus. Finally, as Butler (1997:69) points out, corpora which combine spoken and written data are almost certainly fudging important distinctions which are revealed by their separate analysis.

The second problem is that the tools used in corpus analysis are no more able to help decide where the borders between formulaic sequences fall than native speaker judges are. Altenberg (1990) shows how even a simple word string like *thank you* creates difficulties, since, besides occurring entirely alone, it is also found in longer strings such as *thank you very much, thank you very much indeed* and *thank you bye* (p. 136). Are these different strings? Is the basic string *thank you* and the rest unimportant? Or is one string embedded in another? These questions cannot be answered without the application of common sense and a clear idea of the direction of one's research: the latter automatically creates bias in the interpretation of the raw data.

Measurements

Further difficulties in relating frequency counts to the reliable identification of formulaic sequences arise when we consider just what we are trying to measure, and how. One of the most striking general observations is that there are vast discrepancies across studies, regarding the proportion of language that is viewed as formulaic. To take just a few examples, Altenberg (1990) states that "roughly 70% of the running words in the London-Lund Corpus[9] form part of recurrent word combinations of some kind" (p. 134), and by 1998 he has increased this estimate to 80% (p. 102). Moon (1998a), on the other hand, estimates that only between 4% and 5% of the Oxford Hector Pilot Corpus of over 18 million words were parts of the FEIs (fixed expressions including idioms) which she was studying. Butler (1997) identifies repeated phrases as 12.5% of the spoken part of his corpus of Spanish (total 10,000 words), 9% and 8.2% of two transcribed interviews (each 14,000 words), and 5% of the written corpus (57,500 words). Why are there such enormous differences? As we might expect, the devil is in the detail. Altenberg applied a low threshold, counting "any continuous string of words occurring more than once in identical form" (1998:101), though this, of course, will only pick up discontinuous sequences insofar as they possess two consecutive words.[10] Butler's threshold was higher: strings had to be at least three words long, and occur at least 10 times (1997:66). Moon's criterion was different again. She did not do an open-ended search at all, but rather checked the corpus for occurrences of a preestablished list of 6,776 strings recognized as expressions in the Collins Cobuild English Language Dictionary (Moon 1998a:45). Clearly, one lesson that this teaches us is that different studies are not easy to compare. But it also highlights the fundamental lack of agreement about precisely what deserves most attention and how to identify it.

Various suggestions have been made about how to establish ratio measures which will capture the essence of repetitive language. Bateson

(1975) proposes that a ratio of morphemes to praxons (formulaic sequences)[11] would differentiate a highly fused text (i.e., one with many formulaic sequences in it) from a less highly fused one (p. 63). This calculation works on the basis that the more novel the language in a text, the more different morphemes it will contain. While that assumption may be true in a very large data set, where the same formulaic sequences appear many times, in a small text there is likely to be too much message variety for the formulaicity to impact in this way. Church and Hanks's (1989) *association ratio* measures degrees of word association strength in corpora, by calculating the probability that two words will occur together (i.e., within a specified 'window' of continuous text), given their probability of occurring in the corpus overall (p. 77). Perkins (1994) has developed a method of "quantifying the extent to which a sample of language is repetitive or stereotyped by focusing on the reciprocal relationship between the frequency of occurrence and the degree of productivity of its component elements" (pp. 333–334). Although intended for small samples of disordered speech, the calculation seems suitable for large quantities of computer-analyzed data.

Ratio measures, including the rather problematic type-token ratio,[12] take account of the need to juxtapose the frequency with which a particular item occurs within a given pattern and its overall frequency in the corpus. This procedure reveals the flexibility of that item relative to its context. Some items have no flexibility at all, such as *kith*, which, according to Moon (1998a:78–79), occurs only in *kith and kin*, and *dint*, which is found only in *by dint of* (ibid.), while others, including the preposition class, are common both within and outside recognized expressions. However, even this measure can be misleading. The primary reason for any content word to be frequent is that its meaning is fragmented. Willis (1990) nicely illustrates this fact with reference to the word *way*, which he argues could usefully be a key vocabulary item in ESL teaching. This is not because *way* in the sense of 'minor road', or even 'direction', is particularly frequent, but because *way* figures in numerous expressions (e.g., *in a way, by the way, by way of, ways and means*) which, between them, propel the word virtually to the top of the frequency counts in a large corpus. In a standard dictionary, dozens of entries may be needed to capture all the different aspects of a word's meaning, and it is often difficult to judge just where to draw the line between one word having multiple, related meanings and there actually being two (or more) words which happen to be spelled and pronounced the same way.

Even the very notion of a separate meaning for a word becomes problematic. As Sinclair and Renouf (1988) observe, "the more frequent a word is, the less independent meaning it has, because it is likely to be acting in conjunction with other words, making useful structures or contributing to familiar idiomatic phrases" (p. 153; see also Sinclair 1991:113). In this, they consider that English may be somewhat unusual: "English makes excessive use, e.g., through phrasal verbs, of its most frequent words" (p. 155). It is, of course, self-evident that language makes most use of its most frequent words, and the key word in their statement is "excessive".

After all this, it could be argued that all such frequency-based measures are missing the mark. Undoubtedly, many word strings are indisputably formulaic, but not frequent (e.g., *The King is dead, long live the King*). Foster (2001) points out that "Even a corpus as large as The Bank of English at the University of Birmingham, now nearly three hundred million words, fails to show even a single example of many phrases that would be considered a normal part of any native speaker's repertoire" (p. 81). Amongst the idioms that Moon (1998a) failed to find in her 18-million-word corpus were *bag and baggage, by hook or by crook, kick the bucket, hang fire* and *out of practice*. Moon points out that there is no way of differentiating between a current expression which simply fails to occur in the corpus, and one that fails to occur because it is not in current usage. The problem is even worse when it comes to collocation: "even if words are individually quite frequent, collocations of these words may drop to zero in corpora as large as 100-million words" (Stubbs 2000).

This observation suggests that raw frequency is not an adequate measure of formulaicity. To capture the extent to which a word string is the preferred way of expressing a given idea (for this is at the heart of how prefabrication is claimed to affect the selection of a message form), we need to know not only how often that form can be found in the sample, but also how often it *could* have occurred. In other words, we need a way to calculate the occurrences of a particular message form as a proportion of the total number of attempts to express that message.[13] This can be clearly illustrated with the examples *happy birthday* and *many happy returns*. To find out that *happy birthday* occurs n times in a corpus, while *many happy returns* occurs only $n - x$ times, certainly tells us something about the relative frequency of those two expressions, but it is not until we know that, between them, these two expressions account for, say, 98% of the occasions when birthday wishes were conveyed, that we really understand the power of their formulaicity. In the case of Moon's analysis, then, what we cannot tell is whether *out of practice* failed to occur in the corpus because in every case of that idea being expressed, other ways of saying it were preferred, or because the idea never got expressed (and, if it had, *out of practice* is the string that would have been used). Some messages are much more common than others, and so it is a ratio of message to message-expression that will best help us to understand how some expressions of a given message are favoured over others.[14] There has not, to my knowledge, been any attempt to analyze and tag a corpus for utterance function in the way that we should require for the calculation of such ratios.

The Relationship Between Frequency and Formulaicity

We have already seen that, for various practical reasons, the frequency-based analyses conducted in corpus linguistics do not fully meet our needs when it comes to identifying formulaic sequences. There are further grounds for caution too. Firstly, a frequency count will not be able to differentiate between the occurrences of a configuration when it is formulaic and the same configuration as a novel juxtaposition of smaller units. For instance, *keep your hair on* is not formulaic when it means 'don't remove your wig', but it is formulaic in its meaning 'calm down'. Spotting the word string is the least of the problems here. Contextual and pragmatic cues[15] would be used to disambiguate a sentence like this, and frequency counts are not sensitive to such cues.

Secondly, just as there is evidence that a string generally agreed to be formulaic may or may not have a high frequency in even the largest of corpora, so it is also not possible to assert that all frequent strings are prefabricated. It can, it is true, be argued on theoretical grounds that, if a string is required regularly, it is likely to be stored whole for easier access (e.g., Becker 1975; Langacker 1986:19–20), but it does not have to be. In order to distinguish between frequent strings that were and were not prefabricated, we should therefore need an independent set of supplementary criteria. Possible candidates are reviewed in the remainder of this chapter.

Structure

Is it possible to identify formulaic sequences on the basis of their form? Several possible ways of doing so have been proposed. The most basic, and least useful in the context of researching the nature of formulaicity, is to define formulaic sequences as the set of multiword strings listed in a particular dictionary (e.g., Kerbel & Grunwell 1997; Moon 1998a, 1998b). More productive are criteria deriving from empirical investigation. Butler (1997), on the basis of his frequency-based exploration of Spanish text, notes that "the majority of the longer repeated sequences . . . begin with conjunctions, articles, pronouns, prepositions or discourse markers" (p. 76). This finding requires closer consideration. An intuitive examination of a piece of text may convince us that a sequence whose first fixed item is, say, a preposition, actually begins with a slot for an open class item, such as a noun or verb. For instance, the frame NP_i be-*TENSE* past *PRO$_i$-POSSESSIVE* sell-by date (e.g., *This cheese is past its sell-by date; Dad is past his sell-by date*) could be represented as *past PRO$_i$-POSSESSIVE sell-by date*, but since the subject NP is compulsorily co-indexed with the pronoun, it seems intrinsic to the whole. Because the content of an open class slot will vary, a corpus search alone will fail to recognize it as part of a recurrent sequence. Butler's observation only informs us that the first-occurring *invariable* word in a repeated sequence tends to be a function word or discourse marker, not that this word is necessarily the first word of the entire sequence.[16]

A further possible difficulty with form-based criteria for identification comes from the case of formulaic paradigms with no common lexical material. One example is the limerick, and another is the set of *Is the Pope a Catholic?* responses (Bouton 1988). Members of this set occur when a question is asked to which the answer is a definite 'yes' (e.g., *Do you like beer? – Is the Pope a Catholic?*), the response being another question to which the answer is obviously (or obviously intended to be) 'yes'. The speaker is free to offer any such response, with credit given for wit (e.g., *Do fleas like cats? Does a one-legged duck swim round in circles?*). With the absence of common lexical or morphological forms across the set members, the formulaicity resides in the context-structure interface rather than the form per se. This challenges the idea of a form-based criterion, for what, precisely, is being stored, when all the words can be novel?

However, one reasonable resolution is to argue that 'empty-frame' paradigms like this are not formulaic sequences at all. Normal prefabricated frames, with some fixed items and some gaps for open class items, lead to a genuine mix of routine and novelty, since the purpose of the novel items in the frame is to provide specific referentiality which tunes the string to the context. Thus, products of the frame are expressly *not* semantically interchangeable, so *if it's good enough for my sister, it's good enough for him* does not mean the same as *if they're good enough for a wedding reception, they're good enough for her party*, and so on. In contrast, the *Is the Pope a Catholic?* frame is not varied according to the needs of specific reference, but for other reasons. In fact, it is probably fair to say that any expectation of spontaneous variation in this structure is more a case of wishful thinking than reality. Much more likely is that any given individual has heard, or invented, one or two alternatives to *Is the Pope a Catholic?* which he or she can retrieve easily because they, like the original, are stored whole. In other words, the individual possesses a small set of synonymous phrases, and selects the one which seems most desirable for the occasion (the funniest, the least offensive, or whatever). If this is the case, then the lexicon is not storing the underlying structure, but the examples themselves. Just as this predicts, and in contrast to frames like *If PRO$_i$ BE good enough for NP$_j$ PRO$_i$ BE good enough for NP$_k$*, a speaker is *not* in a position to produce more and more novel examples of the Pope paradigm on request, but rather is restricted only to those which he or she already knows. The construction of a new one is a difficult and deliberate process. As such, the 'structural' characteristics have nothing to do with the lexicon, beyond their having been abstracted analytically by juxtaposing individual examples to see what made them similar. As for comprehension, the fact that, when we hear a new example of the *Is the Pope a Catholic?* paradigm, we recognize and appreciate it, owes more to precedent and pragmatics than the storage of an empty frame. Being novel, it will have to be analyzed, as any novel string is, and this will render two important pieces of information: its content is superficially irrelevant to the context and it is a yes-no question with an obvious 'yes' answer. Pragmatics will do the rest. If we are familiar with the genre,[17] the string will be identified as 'another of those *Is the Pope a Catholic?* expressions' and, if possible, stored whole for later use, since new examples are highly prized.

Compositionality

One way to identify formulaic sequences in text could be to examine their internal composition (something which will be explored more directly in Chapter 3). At the heart of this approach is the observation that a sequence of words, once it is formulaic, is subject to detachment from the effects of the live grammar and lexicon. The string is no longer obliged to be grammatically regular or semantically logical. Sequences become frozen, or fossilized, and as a result often retain words or grammatical forms which are no longer current in the language. For example, *if I were you* contains the subjunctive form of *be*, and *by dint of* features an obsolete lexical item. The meaning may also become detached from the literal. Thus, the two formulae *I couldn't care less* and *I could care less* mean the same thing, even though they appear to be opposites (Tannen & Öztek 1981:37). In extreme cases, the only way to guarantee understanding a noncompositional sequence is to have previously learned it whole.

For those who view formulaicity in language as a peripheral feature (e.g., Pinker 1994:149), the idea that formulaic sequences might be identified as nonliteral and noncanonical is appealing. At this end of the variability spectrum, there is little to choose between a morphological and an etymological analysis, and it is useful to use the criteria of semantic transparency and grammatical regularity as a measuring gauge. However, for our present purposes, an identification procedure of this kind will be too conservative, because it excludes the formulaic sequences that are entirely regular in form and transparent in meaning (Jespersen 1924/1976:84).

An alternative use of the transparency and regularity gauge might be in subcategorizing types of formulaic sequence. In other words, the feature ± idiom could be a defining variable in a typology of formulaic sequences along a continuum from fully bound to fully free. Howarth (1998a, 1998b), who engages in some detail with the best criteria for such a classification, argues convincingly against this, however, showing that is it more useful to separate out this variable from the main structure of the definition. He argues that fossilization, which creates the idiom, is determined not by predictable formal and semantic pressures, but by a range of independent criteria. For further discussion of the idiom as a type of formulaic sequence, see Chapter 3.

Fixedness

We shall see in Chapter 3 that there has been much discussion about the fixedness of formulaic sequences. One variable is the scope for the insertion of elements into a sequence. Pawley (1986) compares *first (and only) attempt with first (*and only) aid* (pp. 107–108), and shows how such insertions undermine the idiomatic nature of a formulaic expression. The phrase *lead up the garden path* is a figurative formulaic sequence, but *lead, happily singing, up the winding garden path*, even if figuratively interpreted, does not retain the particular meaning of the formula (ibid.: 108). For certain kinds of formulaic sequences this, and other possible tests of fixedness, could have a role, but it would be a limited one. We are so accustomed to playing with language, both formulaic and nonformulaic, that the dividing line between what does, and does not, offend the integrity of a sequence may not always be clear, particularly as what is a novel and jokey adaptation one day can be formulaic the next, if it is picked up and repeated a few times. A further difficulty is that only a small subset of formulaic sequences are entirely fixed: those which are not, legitimately permit insertions. Indeed, the fixedness criterion does not sit well with the existence of semi-fixed sequences, which contain slots for a variety of compulsory and optional material to be inserted.

Phonological Form

The identification of formulaic sequences on the basis of "phonological coherence" (Hickey 1993:32) is, of course, restricted to the spoken language, though written texts could reflect those characteristics to some extent, through punctuation and layout. Features such as overall fluency, intonation pattern and changes in speed of articulation are all potential pointers to a stretch of prefabricated material (Pawley & Syder 2000:173). The scope of phonological information to aid the identification of formulaic sequences is well illustrated in experiments by Van Lancker and her team. In a series of experiments, Van Lancker and Canter (1981) tested the hypothesis that hearers should be able to differentiate formulaic and nonformulaic sequences via subtle phonological cues deriving from the difference between holistic and analytic processing. Recordings were made of texts containing idiom and literal interpretations of strings such as *skating on thin ice* (in this case, one text was about a boy skating on a lake, the other about a man taking a risk). The sentences containing the relevant strings were removed from their context and played to subjects, who had to judge whether the intended meaning was figurative or literal, that is, whether the expression was a formulaic idiom or a novel string. They were unable to make such a differentiation above chance level, but in a second test, in which the readers had been asked to emphasize which meaning was intended, the average score was over 85% correct. In a follow-up study, Van Lancker et al. (1981) analyzed the phonological properties of the recordings, to identify the substance of the differences perceptible to the hearers. They found that the literal readings were of greater duration, because they contained more pauses and because the key lexical items were spoken more slowly. The literal readings also contained more pitch changes and more of the clusters of phonological information (pauses, pitch drops, etc.) associated with the marking of open junctures, "the phonetic phenomenon which signals linguistic (lexical or syntactic) boundaries" (Van Lancker et al. 1981:331). They were also more articulatorily precise (pp. 333–334). It follows, then, that particular phonological features might be used to help identify formulaic sequences.

Fluency

According to Pawley (1986), "pauses within lexicalized phrases are less acceptable than pauses within free expressions, and after a hesitation the speaker is more likely to restart from the beginning of the expression" (p. 107). It certainly seems a reasonable hypothesis that, if formulaic sequences are retrieved whole from memory (or at least with less recourse to on-line rule application and lexical retrieval than novel utterances), they should be produced more fluently than novel ones. For any given speaker, fluency is relative, of course, but it might be measured by comparing the number of words per unit time in different types of language production, or by counting the number of words between the pauses, as Pawley and Syder (2000), for instance, do.[18]

Various investigations of these variables have been conducted over the years (for one review, see Van Lancker 1987:99–100). Goldman-Eisler (1968) contrasted the spoken delivery of read texts previously prepared, with that of spontaneous speech. In the former, pauses occurred reliably at clause and sentence boundaries, while in spontaneous speech only 55% did, the remainder occurring in "non-grammatical places" (p. 14). Her interpretation of this is that, in prepared speech, we pause in the places which are most helpful to the hearer's decoding (pp. 12–13). This observation implies that in spontaneous speech other factors – presumably to do with planning – impede this attempt to help the hearer. Implicit support comes from Pawley and Syder's (1983) data from spontaneous interviews. They found that some speakers were able to mitigate the potential disruption of dysfluency by applying a 'one clause at a time constraint', the realization of which was 'clause-chaining' (pp. 202–203). They suggest that a speaker "strings together a sequence of relatively independent clauses, clauses which show little structural integration with earlier or later constructions" (p. 202). This strategy seems to alleviate the strains of both production and comprehension that are concomitant with a more interclausally integrated discourse:

The risks of syntactic breakdown are greater when using the integrating style. With the chaining style, a speaker can maintain grammatical and semantic continuity because his clauses can be planned more or less independently, and each major semantic unit, being only a single clause, can be encoded and uttered without internal breaks. To achieve the same degree of coherence using the integrating style the speaker generally must reduce his articulation rate and/or make more frequent clause-internal pauses. This choice is not much favoured by either speakers or listeners. (Pawley & Syder 1983:203–204)

To call the clause-internal pauses 'ungrammatical', as Goldman-Eisler does, tends to suggest that they are unprincipled; and this is what Pawley and Syder also seem to be implying. However, others have proposed that there is a pattern to them. Raupach (1984) believes that "pauses or hesitation phenomena such as drawls, repeats, false starts, etc." (p. 114) occur at the boundaries of formulaic sequences, so that "a formal approach to identifying formula units in spontaneous speech must, as a first step, list the strings which are not interrupted by unfilled pauses" (p. 116). If Goldman-Eisler's and Raupach's positions are compatible, it must be because formulaic sequences do not map onto the linguistic units of grammatical syntactic structure. It could be that both prepared and spontaneous speech consist of the fluent production of linguistic units punctuated by pauses, but those units are different in the two cases: they reflect grammatical constituent structure in the former, and formulaic sequences in the latter. The boundaries of formulaic sequences may well seem unprincipled, since the fixed parts of a formulaic frame seem able to be a subcomponent of a clause, or, conversely, a larger unit, that can span the boundary between two clauses without entirely containing either. The bizarreness of the patterns could be exacerbated if pauses can also occur before the insertion of an open class item into a specified slot *within* a sequence, and this would also somewhat complicate the process of identifying the boundaries.[19]

Work by Towell, Hawkins and Bazergui (1996) throws some light on how L2 learners' developing fluency skills may be reflected in their pause patterns. Investigating how L2 fluency was improved by living in the L2 environment, they collected pre- and post-residence spontaneous interviews with British advanced learners of French, and compared the speaking rate (syllables per minute), articulation rate (syllables per second), phonation:time ratio (percentage of time speaking as a ratio of the total time it took complete the message), and mean length of runs (mean number of syllables between pauses) (p. 91). They found that the increased fluency observed after residence was due neither to the speaker pausing less overall nor speaking faster, but to a greater length and complexity of the units produced between the pauses (pp. 112–113). As we shall see in Chapter 10, Towell et al.'s work raises an important issue regarding the nature of learning: it is extremely difficult to differentiate between, on the one hand, fluency brought about by the acquisition of more formulaic sequences, each relatively impervious to internal pausing, and, on the other, the process of 'proceduralization', in which there is simply an increase in the efficiency with which novel L2 utterances can be planned and delivered.

Stress and Articulation

Jespersen (1924/1976) sees stress as a key defining feature of formulaic sequences. Because a sequence is "felt and handled as a unit", he argues, it is not possible to pause between the component words or to stress them in an unaccustomed way (p. 83). It is consistent with this observation that the articulation within formulaic sequences might be less precise than in equivalent novel strings, since the strongest articulation occurs on stressed syllables (Brown 1990:46). Van Lancker et al. (1981) report many examples of a less precise articulation in the pronunciation of idioms, as compared with the identical strings with a literal meaning. The contrasts include, respectively, the absence, versus presence, of a glottal stop before an initial vowel (e.g., *an* ^(ʔ)*axe to grind*); a shorter, versus a longer, initial consonant (e.g., *it's r(:)otten to the core*); the presence, versus absence, of initial /h/ in unstressed words (e.g., *eating out of (h)er (h)and*); the use of [ɾ], versus [tʰ], in words such as *skating* and *eating* (the subjects were North American); shorter, more neutral vowels, versus longer, more distinct ones, in unstressed words such as *to, and, the*; and diphthongs reduced to monophthongs, versus clearly diphthongal (e.g., *ice* as [aːs] in the idiom and [aɪs] in the literal reading) (p. 334). These findings correspond with the patterns described by Bybee (1998). She examines the distribution of pronunciations of the word *don't* with a full vowel or with schwa. She views each occurrence of the schwa pronunciation as indicative of its occurrence within a larger multiword unit.

Peters (1983) considers how the young child, during acquisition, might use stress and articulation to identify salient strings. She proposes that the child segments previously unanalyzed sequences by taking note of their internal pattern of rhythm, intonation and stress, as well as the boundaries which are revealed through a speaker's repetition of fragments of the utterance. Plunkett (1993), in his investigation of how young children apply the principles of segmentation to stretches of language that they hear (see Chapter 6), uses reduced clarity of articulation as a means of identifying sequences which the child has learned formulaically (pp. 46–47).

Brown (1990) engages with the question of articulation from the point of view of practical approaches to second language teaching, but her observations seem to be pertinent to this discussion. She presents an enormous set of examples (1990:chap. 4), transcribed from radio broadcasts, of phrases occurring in fast, natural speech. They illustrate the range of consonant weakening and vowel reduction that can occur as a function of stress reduction. Brown makes no claims about the nature of the units most likely to display these features, nor about whether the boundaries of such units might be less likely to. And although it is tantalizingly striking that a great many of her examples seem, intuitively, to be formulaic (e.g., *last year; protest meeting; World Wild Life Fund; nothing stands still; who'd been on duty; as confused as ever; banned for life*), it could well be that this reflects no more than Brown's own intuitive decision about the most relevant and informative chunks to cite in order to make her points. It remains to be seen whether an in-depth study of the reduction phenomena identified by Brown would indeed suggest that formulaic sequences are as resilient to that pressure at their boundaries as they are subject to it internally. And, of course, this still does not free us from the perennial difficulty of how to separate out the process of identification from that of definition. As before, it will not be possible to demonstrate that certain phonological patterns are a feature of the boundaries of formulaic sequences until we have an independent way of identifying where those boundaries are.

Liaison in French

As Brown (1990:2) points out, for English, at least, there is a tendency to perceive the assimilation and elision that occur in the normal speech of native speakers as "'degenerate' and 'slovenly'". But in French a related phenomenon, liaison, is viewed as a sign of correctness. The basis of liaison is the phonological structure of French as CV-CV, so that, as a general rule, vowel-initial words 'borrow' the last consonant of a preceding word, and two adjacent vowels across a word boundary will be reduced to one (Bernac 1976:20–21). Bybee (1998) proposes that the distribution of liaison patterns in colloquial spoken French is indicative of the formulaic storage of the word strings so-joined. She treats them as "evidence for the size and nature of processing units [which] point to constructions rather than words as the minimal unit for storage and processing" (p. 432). In modern colloquial French, however, there is considerably less liaison than in formal and performance French, and this direction of change is contrary to what we would expect if the liaison feature marks formulaicity.[20]

Identification in Specific Data Types

One of the problems with identifying formulaic sequences is that adult native speakers are very proficient integrators of novel and prefabricated components, so the joins are not clear to see. Children, non-native speakers and those with linguistic disabilities, on the other hand, are less adept at this integration, and also may produce errors which are indicative of a string being, or not being, formulaic for them. Such patterns can be used to draw up criteria for identifying formulaic sequences in that kind of data. For first language acquisition, Hickey (1993) offers a set of conditions which a sequence either may, or must, display if it is to be identified as formulaic (Figure 2.1). Although some of Hickey's criteria are likely to apply beyond the forum of child language data (perhaps 2, 5, 6,

Condition 1:   The utterance is at least two morphemes long. (Necessary, graded)
Condition 2:   The utterance coheres phonologically. (Necessary)
Condition 3:   The individual elements of an utterance are not used concurrently in the same form separately or in other environments. (Typical, graded).
Condition 4:   The utterance is grammatically advanced compared to the rest of the child's language (i.e., the grammatical pattern is not represented with different words). (Typical, graded)
Condition 5:   The utterance is a community-wide formula, or one which occurs frequently in the parents' speech. (Typical, graded)
Condition 6:   The utterance is an idiosyncratic chunk. (Typical, graded)
Condition 7:   The utterance is used repeatedly in the same form. (Typical, graded)
Condition 8:   The utterance is situationally dependent. (Typical, graded)
Condition 9:   The utterance may be used inappropriately, either syntactically or semantically. (Typical, graded)

Figure 2.1. Hickey's "Conditions for formula identification". Reprinted from *Journal of Child Language*, vol. 20, T. Hickey, "Identifying formulas in first language acquisition", p. 32, copyright 1993, with permission from Cambridge University Press.

7 and 8), the rest are specific to the young child. In the case of clinical data, the identification of formulaic sequences is almost entirely driven by their exceptional nature. In effect, any output which is exceptional in terms of its length, fluency, grammatical accuracy and/or semantic integrity is likely to be viewed as formulaic, simply because it stands outside the characteristic capabilities of the individual for novel construction. If such language is viewed as having 'survived' the trauma unscathed, then it should be similar in nature to the formulaic language of nondisabled speakers. To that extent, at least, it is possible to use information from the field of language pathology to gain insights into the nature of formulaic sequences in the normal population. This, indeed, is how memorized texts such as rhymes and prayers first came to be identified as formulaic (see Chapter 12).

In second language research, there is more of a tendency to take presupposed norms of what is formulaic for the native speaker and to use them to identify formulaic sequences in the learner population, than to use the learners' output to shed light on the native speaker inventory. In particular, it is common for patterns of errors to be used to ascertain when the learner is creating a novel construction and when using a formulaic sequence (see Chapter 8). Scarcella (1979) had non-native speaker subjects complete phrases in cartoon captions which would, for a native speaker, be formulaic sequences. Using the responses of native speakers (which were consistent) as a baseline, she was able to judge whether the learner had mislearned a formulaic sequence, partially forgotten it, or approximated it using a novel construction. Biskup (1992) sought to explain learner errors in common collocations as the product of interference from equivalent forms in the native language. The use of errors for this kind of evaluation is complex, however. A formulaic sequence can feature "either . . . a more frequent than average correct production of a certain structure" if it has been learned unanalyzed, or "errors in structures that are otherwise correct" if it has been fused[21] after rule-based generation, and then fossilized (Bolander 1989:73). There is, however, one particular aspect of second language research which offers direct insights into formulaicity in the native language. It is code-switching.

The Case of Code-Switching

According to Weinreich (1963), "The ideal bilingual switches from one language to the other according to appropriate changes in the speech situation . . . but not in an unchanged speech situation and certainly not within a single sentence" (p. 73). Weinreich's observation notwithstanding, code-switching can and does occur within the sentence, as witnessed by examples such as German/English *Papa, wenn du das Licht ausmachst, then I'll be so lonesome* 'Daddy, if you put out the light, then I'll be so lonesome' (Leopold 1978:24) and Finnish/English *Missä se minun Hallowe'en pumpkin on?* 'Where is my Hallowe'en pumpkin?' (Linnakylä 1980:371).[22]

Most research on the location of the transition points from one language to the other has concentrated on constituent structure (see Mahootian 1996 for one approach and references to many others). Azuma (1996), for instance, claims that in natural code-switching, the transition occurs "at syntactically definable constituent boundaries" (p. 397). In Azuma's experiment, bilinguals were required to switch language in response to a tone, and the transition was found to adhere to constituent boundaries in almost all cases. Specifically, in 68% of cases where the tone occurred before the end of the sentence, the speaker continued in the pretone language for at least one more word before switching, and in only 5% of these instances was the unit so-created not a syntactic constituent (p. 406).

However, Backus (1999) proposes an alternative account of the transition in code-switching. He suggests that transitions between the two languages happen at the boundaries of formulaic sequences and that the

study of code-switching can therefore "help . . . to identify multimor-
phemic elements of a language that are accessed as unanalyzed (i.e.
lexical) units in speech" (p. 93). His position is that,

> if two or more EL[23] morphemes are used in c[ode] s[witching] and they form
> a conventional combination in the EL, then it would be too coincidental if the
> speaker had produced them as two or more independent switches, composition-
> ally building up the composite expression. It is very likely that the whole thing
> was retrieved from the EL lexicon as a unit. (p. 97)

Backus provides various examples and lines of argument in support of
his hypothesis, and forwards some explanations, based on attention and
semantic specificity, for the existence of counterevidence, particularly
'mixed code calques', in which part of a recognized combination of the
EL appears in the ML (p. 106). The overall effect of the evidence on his
hypothesis is to create the impression of unwelcome complexity, relative
to what seems at first glance a very appealing and plausible idea. We need
not enter here into a discussion of why that might be, but our later exploration of what may be motivating the selection of a formulaic sequence
over a novel construction does widen the scope for explaining the complexity of the patterns in code-switching, by introducing a range of interactional and memory-based processing constraints. Entertaining such
factors removes the explication of the phenomenon from the narrow
bounds of unit definition per se, avoiding the need to play constituent
structure and formulaic sequences off against each other.[24] What is of
central concern to us here, however, is whether, if Backus is right about
the nature of the inserted units, it is legitimate to use this feature of code-
switching as a means of identifying formulaic sequences, particularly
their boundaries.

   As always, the problem is independent verification. With enough
confidence in Backus's position, it would, of course, be possible simply
to define as formulaic units all EL strings found in an ML context. But
that would be fatuous, since it would overrule all other identificational
procedures and simply map the set of EL insertions onto the set of
formulaic sequences in the language. It would not be predictive, since
no string could be anticipated to appear as an EL unit, and thereby
identified as formulaic, until it had actually appeared as one. Backus fully
recognizes this, and proposes that the independent verification of
formulaicity be, at least for the purposes of testing the hypothesis, that
they are recognizable "conventional combinations in the EL" (p. 97).

   But this position, as before, brings us into circularity, since the whole
purpose of searching for means of identifying formulaic sequences is to
enable us to work out just what the set of 'conventional combinations'

is. We have seen that intuition is a much-used but somewhat unreliable tool, and that frequency counts and the other measures fail to capture the whole picture. The problem is that whatever formulaic sequences are, they are not sufficiently consistent in form (nor do they have a consistent function, as we shall see in the next chapter) for them to be pinned down. Unless we *can* pin them down, we cannot progress far towards formal criteria for identification because we cannot satisfactorily define the units that we wish to identify.

Conclusion

In our pursuit of one or more ways of reliably identifying formulaic sequences in text, we have reviewed the potential role of intuition, computer frequency counts, examinations of internal structure and phonological form, and insights from specific types of data. In all cases, we have found too little basis for separating off the establishment of a basic definition from the setting up of robust criteria for identification. In short, you can't reliably identify something until you have independent verification of what it is you are trying to identify. In every case, formulaicity seems to manifest too great a diversity of potential forms to submit to predictability beyond the most general and mundane level. Yet formulaicity does not seem to be just fundamentally general and mundane. It may simply be that identification cannot be based on a single criterion, but rather needs to draw on a suite of features. Alternatively, formulaicity may be governed by some unifying criterion that our efforts so far have failed to capture. In the next chapter, we shall take a different perspective, in an attempt to identify more exactly how satisfactory definitions might be made, since this is part of our problem.

3

Pinning Down Formulaicity

Introduction

We saw in the last chapter that the identification of formulaic sequences in text is extremely difficult, largely because of the absence of any single definition able to capture all the relevant features at once.[1] Various solutions to this problem are possible. One is to live with a definition that is, at some level, exclusive. This means that types of string which fall outside that definition are simply set aside, even if they seem to have something 'formulaic' about them. Many of the definitions that we shall review in this chapter do this either explicitly or implicitly. Another solution is to accept a fragmented definition or, to put it another way, establish a bundle of features, any or all of which a formulaic sequence may possess, but none of which is individually necessary. To date, this approach does not seem to be much adopted in definitions of formulaic sequences, perhaps because there is still a strong underlying belief that they are a single linguistic phenomenon (something that I shall dispute later). Two more favoured approaches are the closely related 'prototype' definition, in which an individual example of a formulaic sequence is identified with reference to one or more definitions which can apply strongly or weakly, and the 'continuum' type of definition, where subtypes of sequences are set along a scale from most to least formulaic. Finally, there is always the possibility of discarding all the definitions that rest on form, in favour of a different type of definition. This is the path that we shall ultimately take. First, though we must establish our starting point: the existing taxonomies, definitions and explanations.

Taxonomies

Classifications of formulaic sequences abound, and include those of Aijmer (1996), Alexander (1984, 1987, 1989), Becker (1975), Benson

44

(1985), Bolinger (1976), Coulmas (1979, 1994), Cowie (1988, 1994), Erman and Warren (2000), Hatch, Peck and Wagner-Gough (1979), Howarth (1998a), Hudson (1998), Keller (1981), Krashen and Scarcella (1978), Lattey (1986), Lewis (1993, 1997), Mel'čuk (1998), Moon (1992, 1997, 1998a), Nattinger and DeCarrico (1992), Scarcella (1979:80, 85), Van Lancker (1987) and Yorio (1980:434ff, 1989:56–57).[2] Classifications can be geared towards theoretical or practical ends, and occasionally both at once (e.g., Nattinger & DeCarrico 1992:ch. 3, reviewed later). Although both approaches can fall into similar problems with marshalling what is a very unruly set of related types of material, the tests of their success are rather different. A theoretically-driven taxonomy needs to justify itself with reference to an external model of what language is and how it works. In most cases, this is an assumption that the most creative language is assembled by rule from small components, so that there is a relationship between formulaicity and an absence of creativity. Just what that actually means is not always quite clear, however, since, as we saw in Chapter 1, most 'novelty' resides in the choice of lexical items, not in the structure of the utterance that contains them, and formulaic sequences are well able to contain slots that accept open class items, thus creating a novel message with little on-line creativity. The resilience of a theoretically-driven classification is tested by the identification of counterexamples, but some proposals, unfortunately, are so descriptively bland as to make no useful predictions about what may *not* manifest as formulaic. To be fair, however, the task is burdened by the apparently inexhaustible ability of a language continuously to throw up new formulaic sequences of all types, from soliloquies to gibberish – we shall see in later chapters that there is a mechanism, 'fusion', that can account for this.

Practically-driven taxonomies, on the other hand, do not need to be theoretically grounded or theoretically robust. They do, however, have to work for their intended purpose. Language teaching and dictionary writing, both for natives and non-natives, are two major contexts in which some sort of organization of types is found necessary. Teaching syllabuses like those of Lewis (1993), Nattinger and DeCarrico (1992) and Willis (1990)[3] are more or less obliged to address the issue of types of sequence, and even teaching materials dedicated to one small part of the whole (e.g., Milton & Evans 1998) have to decide what to include and what omit. In the field of lexicography, the practical difficulties of what and how to list are a major hurdle once the focus shifts from just one word at a time (see Pawley's 1996 exploration of this). To give just one example, it is often difficult to be consistent in decisions about which of the component words of a phrase should be viewed as the 'key' word for the listing. In many cases, the first word is a function word like *the* or *in*, and thereafter there may be two or more content words which seem equally salient to the identification of the whole. Each lexicography team must make a decision and then attempt to apply it consistently (see, for instance, Cowie & Mackin 1975:xviiff and 370ff).

Much pioneering work on accommodating multiword strings in dictionaries was carried out in the former Soviet Union in the 1950s and 1960s and this is, for Westerners, still a largely untapped resource (see Cowie 1998 for an overview of that work). In recent years, the new generation dictionaries based on the data from large corpora have led to the development, hand-in-hand, of pragmatic solutions to the difficulties of organization and presentation, and new theoretical models to explain the patterns (e.g., Sinclair 1991, 1998).

There would be little value in unpacking the large body of different taxonomies here, or in making an in-depth comparison (though see Hudson 1998:chap. 1 and Moon 1998a:chap. 1, who do). Rather, in what follows we shall identify the fundamental features of these taxonomies and use these as the focus of our further exploration.

What to Include

The value of a taxonomy must be that it facilitates a principled subcategorization that can be applied to real examples. Hudson (1998), however, concludes, on the basis of her survey of published accounts, that "an inherent shortcoming of these typologies is that the categories are neither discrete nor comprehensive" (p. 13). Furthermore, "many fixed expressions cannot be accommodated in any of the categories that have hitherto been defined" (p. 34). The exclusion from one taxonomy of some types included in others is commonplace, and often results from drawing on data from only one type of speaker. For instance, Fillmore (1979) is interested in 'formulaic expressions' that "are learned in close association with the situations in which their use is appropriate" (p. 92), and he specifically notes that this sets them apart from deliberately memorized texts such as rhymes and prayers. In contrast, these very 'automatic' word strings are central to the definition of formulaic language in aphasia (e.g., Van Lancker 1987); since both deliberately memorized strings and expressions with strong situational associations are highly resilient to severe language impairment (see Chapter 12), their different provenance appears immaterial in the context of aphasia. Another category of word string that is variously included and excluded from taxonomies is simple collocations (Howarth 1998a:25f). We shall see later that these hover at the edge of definitions of formulaicity, and thus need careful handling.

Internal Structure

Taxonomies are attractive because they promise a neat categorization. However, in order to be either useful or theoretically plausible, they must be internally consistent, with some sort of principled dependency between the classes they differentiate. Otherwise, they are no more than glorified lists. Also, there must be some clear way of keeping categories separate, and this is another failing that Hudson identifies as character-istic of most taxonomies (1998:13). Broadly speaking, taxonomies fore-ground one or more of four features of formulaic sequences: *form*, *function*, *meaning*, and *provenance*. The problem is that these features overlap, causing some muddying of the waters. For instance, Becker (1975) offers the following six-way division:

- polywords (e.g., *(the) oldest profession; to blow up; for good*)
- phrasal constraints (e.g., *by sheer coincidence*)
- meta-messages (e.g., *for that matter* . . . (message: 'I just thought of a better way of making my point'); . . . *that's all* (message: 'don't get flustered'))
- sentence builders (*(person A) gave (person B) a (long) song and dance about (a topic)*)[4]
- situational utterances (e.g., *how can I ever repay you?*)
- verbatim texts (e.g., *better late than never; How ya gonna keep 'em down on the farm?*) (adapted from Becker 1975:6–7).

Of these, the *polyword* and *phrasal constraint* categories are form-based, *meta-message* relates predominantly to meaning, *sentence builder* implies from its name a functional focus, though it is really a form category, *sit-uational utterance* is predominantly functional, and *verbatim text* reflects provenance.

Nattinger and DeCarrico (1992) attempt to legitimize the difficulty by speaking of *form-function* composites, a product of

a particular type of pragmatic competence, which takes specific strings generated by the syntactic component and assigns them functional meanings, so that these strings not only have syntactic shapes, but are capable as well of perform-ing pragmatic actions such as promising, complimenting, asserting, and so on. (p. 11)

Hudson (1998), whose basic taxonomy has three form-based criteria and one meaning-based criterion (pp. 8–9), divides her 'fixed expressions' into *independent utterances* and *subclausal units*:

> This structural division correlates strongly with functional differences. The independent clause type function primarily as socio-cultural or interpersonal expressions of social identity, relationship structuring or attitude marking. (p. 33)

Cross-associations such as these between form and function, and also between form, meaning and provenance, or between any other subsets, are probably nearer the truth than single-parameter categorizations, but their additional complexity also clouds the picture, with the assignment of items to one or another subcategory becoming difficult at times. In order to tease out the features considered central to formulaic sequences, we shall consider separately the four parameters identified above: form, function, meaning and provenance, evaluating dedicated taxonomies in their relevant context.

Features of Form

Categorizing formulaic sequences according to their form is, in some ways, a relatively simple job, but it lends itself rather better to purely descriptive accounts (e.g., Moon 1997:43ff) than to explanatory ones, with the result that the outcomes tend to be less consequential than those of other approaches. Nattinger and DeCarrico (1992:36ff) offer one attempt at a detailed form-only categorization, based to some extent on Becker's more muddled one described earlier. They take as their form criteria: (1) the *grammatical level* of the sequence type (word or sentence level); (2) whether it is *canonical* or not (i.e., conforms internally with the grammatical rules of the language, p. 33); (3) *variability*, which relates to whether or not it can be morphosyntactically adjusted (e.g., *as far as I/we/you know*) and/or subject to a finite set of alternatives (e.g., *see you ____*, which can be realized as *see you soon*, *see you later*, and *see you*); (4) *continuity*, where discontinuous strings have slots into which a word or phrase can be inserted. Unfortunately, Nattinger and DeCarrico are immediately plunged into contradictions and counterexamples,[5] and are required to label some types as "mostly", "often" or "somewhat" consistent with a form criterion (p. 45). Despite the superficial tidiness of the classification, it is clear that, at the very least, some subcategorization would be useful, formally to differentiate class members that have different scores on the key parameters. Alternatively, their difficulties could indicate that the very classification system is inadequate. Certainly, by their own admission, the contrast between 'phrasal constraints' and 'sentence builders' is a little artificial:

[A] lexical phrase can be classed differently depending on the filler it takes. *The*
____*er the* ____*er* is a phrasal constraint, whose slots take adjectives as fillers
(*the faster the better*), but when expanded to encompass clausal categories [e.g.,
the ____*er X, the* ____*er Y* as in *the sooner all this work is finished, the sooner
we will all be able to go home*], . . . it becomes a sentence builder. (p. 44)

All of this reminds us of the limitations of a descriptive taxonomy, where
it is all too easy for the categories to be determined by the terms, and
the terms by the categories. We shall see further examples of internal
subclassification of forms when we consider the relationship between the
formulaic sequence and the idiom and metaphor, in the later section on
meaning. For the present, we shall pursue our exploration of form under
three headings, each of which captures a theme from the approaches that
research has embraced. These headings are *irregularity*, *variability* and
collocation.

Irregularity

It is common for formulaic sequences to contain a word behaving in an
abnormal way, whether displaying grammatical irregularity or having an
unusual meaning. A normally intransitive verb may take an object, as in
to come a cropper (Flavell & Flavell 1992:7), and there may be limitations on the normal range of transformations or inflections (Verstraten
1992). For example, although it is possible to pluralize *beat about the bush*
or passivize *face the music* for particular effect, this is not what we
commonly do, and it destroys their formulaic status (Flavell & Flavell
1992:6). The effect of bypassing an examination of the internal composition of a string can be to protect the meaning from the normal
pressures of language change, leading, in some cases, to a sort of
'fossilization', by which antiquated words may be preserved (e.g., *long
live the King/Queen; curry favour; rather thee than me*), and a metaphorical meaning may become dominant relative to its literal one (e.g., *back
to square one*) or even entirely replace it (e.g., *go the whole hog*). Such
oddities seem to be a natural, but not a necessary, consequence of a
sequence becoming formulaic, and, although typical, irregularity is not
in itself a sufficient defining feature of formulaic sequences.

Variability

In Jespersen's (1924/1976) view, word strings could only count as 'formulas' if "no one can change anything in them" (p. 83). This extended to
not being able to alter the stress or put a pause between the words (ibid.).
This definition admits only the idioms and the memorized rhymes,
prayers, proverbs, quotations and so on, the kind of 'automatic' language

that, by remaining intact after aphasia, first drew attention to the whole phenomenon of formulaicity in the mid nineteenth century (see Chapter 12). The definition of 'formulas' has become increasingly inclusive since Jespersen's day, and our present interests must marginalize Jespersen's categories as the exception rather than the rule, since all other kinds of formulaic sequence are characteristically open to some variation in form.

Variability is a keystone of many form-based accounts of formulaicity (see, for instance, Sinclair 1987:321ff). At the simplest level, it is possible to distinguish between sequences that are entirely invariable, and those which are more flexible. We shall begin with the latter. Some variable sequences permit only a particular limited range of morphological possibilities (e.g., *it's been/it'll be/it's a devil of a job*). Others tolerate a small, specified set of alternative content words in one position (e.g., *a piece* or *slice of the action*; *show* or *teach* SOMEONE (or *know* or *learn*) *the ropes*). The rest have slots for open class items (e.g., *know* SOMETHING *like the back of* ONE'S *hand; give* SOMEONE *a piece of* ONE'S *mind*). Open class items are most often referential noun phrases, with pronouns particularly common. Sinclair (1987) illustrates how variability pervades phrases like *it's not in his nature to X*:

The word *it* is part of the phrase, and [so is] the verb *is*, though this verb can vary to *was* and perhaps can include modals. *Not* can be replaced by any 'broad' negative, including *hardly, scarcely*, etc. *In* is fixed but *his* can be replaced by any possessive pronoun and perhaps by some names with *'s. Nature* is fixed. (p. 321)

For a thorough review of variability in formulaic sequences, see Moon (1998a:chap. 6), from which many of the examples in this section are drawn.

Variability often seems rather ad hoc. The two idioms *kick the bucket* and *spill the beans*, for instance, seem similar: both consist of a transitive verb plus object noun phrase, and both have a metaphorical meaning which is not directly discernible from the words themselves. Yet, as Wood (1986:1) points out, passivization causes the loss of the idiom meaning in one (**the bucket was kicked*), but not the other (*the beans were spilled*). Hudson (1998) suggests that the failure for certain sequences to accept lexical or regular syntactic variation can mostly be explained in one of two ways. One is that meaning cannot be assigned to the individual words in the string, and this makes certain kinds of transformation meaningless. In *spill the beans*, it is easy to match the words and the metaphor: the 'beans' are the information, and it is 'spilled' when it is mentioned inappropriately. This connection makes possible variations like *how* *many more beans are there to spill?* and *she is a champion bean-spiller.* With *kick the bucket,* on the other hand, it is harder to connect individual meanings to each word, and this makes variation less useful. Similarly, as Hudson observes, "*red* in *red herring* will not be substituted by any other colour since the significance of redness in the expression is entirely opaque" (Hudson 1998:35; see also Weinreich's 1969:42 discussion of the same expression).

The other cause of low variability, according to Hudson, is syntactic function. Many sequences are, syntactically speaking, adverbs (e.g., *by and large; hook, line and sinker; all at once*). Others are fully self-contained units (e.g., *you bet; look before you leap*). In English, neither adverbs nor complete phrases are subject to variation: if we paraphrase these examples as the adverbs *mostly, completely, suddenly* and the expressions *yes* and *(be) careful,* they are all invariable. This observation leads Hudson (1998) to propose that formulaic sequences be defined *not* according to what they are like on the inside, but rather according to their effective grammatical role, as reflected in the way they embed into text: "Learners need to know not only the semantics, pragmatics and phonology of linguistic units, but also their grammatical roles. It is of lesser importance to distinguish fixed expressions according to their internal structure or composition" (p. 166).

In short, it seems reasonable to demystify the phenomenon of variability by noting that a lack of variability is, in the majority of cases, sanctioned by its grammatical role or by the absence of literal meaning. However, this is only a one-way effect. Plenty of formulaic sequences, by virtue of their grammatical role as, say, a noun or a verb, or their literal meaning, *could* be more variable than they actually are. The most extreme case of this relates to patterns in collocation.

Collocation

"Collocation is an aspect of lexical cohesion which embraces a 'relationship' between lexical items that regularly co-occur" (Carter 1988:163), or, as Firth put it, "You shall know a word by the company it keeps!" (1957/1968:179). It is far from being the case that all commentators see collocational associations as 'formulaic' in any useful sense at all. Whereas other types of formulaic sequence are entirely or partly fixed, so that there is a central internal stability, collocation is much more fluid. It is about tendencies and preferences only, as evidenced by common, but often far from exclusive, pairings of words, such as *hard work, hard luck, hard facts, hard evidence* (Sinclair 1987:322). Since there is the potential for so much variation, the idea that individual pairings are stored in the lexicon entails the existence of a very large store of such items, most of which could easily be constructed by rule via the open choice principle (see Chapter 1), upon which "the only restraint is grammaticalness" (Sinclair 1987:320).

However, Sinclair then demonstrates the much greater pervasiveness of collocation within the fabric of language. He notes, for instance, that "*set eyes on* . . . seems to attract a pronoun subject, and either *never* or a temporal conjunction like *the moment, the first time* and the word *had* as an auxiliary to *set*. How much of this is integral to the phrase?" (p. 321).

His subtle observations derive from corpus studies, in which the actual occurrences of a given word or word string can be tracked and quantified across large collections of text (see Chapter 2). Clearly, the job of classifying formulaic sequences into clear-cut types is much confounded by collocation, for, as Sinclair asks, how can we judge just what belongs to the phrase and what is outside, but in association with, it? How is one to accommodate *tendencies* to co-occur and long distance relations that are found *very often* and *in general*? One solution to this, and other problems with the varying flexibility of formulaic sequences, is to envisage a continuum, from entirely fixed to entirely free (see later). However, the preferred way forward for those centrally involved with collocation in large corpora is to discard the notion of 'meaning' as something nuclear, in favour of the Wittgensteinian conceptualization of meaning as 'use'. For example, Clear (1993) shows 18 different form-meaning patterns for *keep*, a word which "is quite frequent in any corpus of modern English, and which defies coercion into a tidy list of discrete, enumerable senses" (p. 272). This illustration demonstrates two maxims deriving from lexicogrammatical research: "meaning is not a constant across the inflected forms of a lemma" and "every sense or meaning of a word has its own grammar: each meaning is associated with a distinct formal patterning. Form and meaning are inseparable" (Stubbs 1993:17). For examples of the patterns of collocation uncovered by corpus research, see, for example, Altenberg (1993), Butler (1997, 1998, 1999), Cowie (1992:4–5), Hudson (1998), Sinclair (1987, 1991), and Stubbs (1995, 1997).

Function

Conventionalized forms . . . offer social support to deal with situations that are awkward or stressful . . . [and] make communication more orderly because they are regulatory in nature. They organize reactions and facilitate choices, thus reducing the complexity of communicative exchanges. They are group identifying. They separate those who belong from those who don't. (Yorio 1980:438)

A focus on function takes the position that formulaic sequences are "expressions whose occurrence is tied to more or less standardized communication situations" (Coulmas 1981:2–3). However, since the relationship between a linguistic form and its function is rather unpredictable, a function-based definition runs into as many problems as a purely form-based one. This is because, given that a language needs a conventionalized way of achieving a particular function, it is virtually impossible to predict precisely what form the linguistic unit used for that purpose will take. This, indeed, is the essence of Pawley and Syder's (1983) point about the difficulties non-native speakers can have in knowing which is the idiomatic way of expressing a particular idea: there are often lots of potential candidates, all of which could achieve the function perfectly well, but not all of which are equally acceptable as 'what we say'.

Because of this, definitions of formulaic sequences based on their function tend either to become the victim of complex subcategorizations by form, which can certainly impose an order but not one with any obvious independent usefulness, or else the formal specifications are set aside, leaving lists which just look as though they need organizing. A good example of the former type is Nattinger and DeCarrico's (1992) functional taxonomy (pp. 65ff). They create a basic three-way functional distinction, with the category labels *social interactions*, *necessary topics* and *discourse devices*. They go on to demonstrate (pp. 65ff) how each of their functional categories can be realized by each of the three forms *polywords*, *phrasal constraints* and *sentence builders* (they have amalgamated their previous fourth category, *institutionalized expressions* with *polywords*). They are also able to show that the same patterns are found in Chinese, Spanish and Russian. While this is a neat presentational device, it is not all that helpful. There is no particular value in knowing that any function can be realized by any form, since there is no way of predicting which will occur when. Yet there is an implication that the taxonomy will contribute to the learner's ability to master the principle of formulaic sequences in language.

Aijmer's (1996) approach pays less direct attention to the function-form relationship. She identifies three roles for the *conversational routines* in which she is interested. One type performs socio-interactional functions, such as thanking, requesting, offering and apologizing, and these form the major basis of her study. The routines in her second set have a role in discourse. Some of these indicate an orientation to the content (e.g., *I'll be frank; in my opinion; between us; as far is X is concerned*) (p. 222). Others mark the organization of the text. Sequences of this kind Aijmer divides into two subgroups, according to their scope.

Local markers are "cues to the relationship between adjacent utterances" (e.g., *believe it or not; as a matter of fact; if I might say so at this stage*) (p. 205). Global markers "mark elements of the macro-structure" (e.g., *to follow up [that statement]; to put you in the picture; wait till I tell you*) (ibid.). The third functional type which Aijmer (1996) identifies is *attitudinal routines* "which express the speaker's attitudes or emotions" (p. 2); however, she does not expand on this observation, nor investigate it in her study.

Cowie (1988) identifies two function-based roles. *Formulae* perform discourse and social roles, and so correspond with Aijmer's first two functions for her *conversational routines*. He observes that achieving the intended function for such sequences involves sensitivity on the part of speaker and hearer. For instance, *Do you know* signals surprise about the statement that follows, so correct usage of such a formula requires not only knowledge of its form but also of its position and the intonation pattern that is laid on it (p. 134). His other category, *composites*, falls outside Aijmer's coverage. *Composites* "function as constituents in sentences (as objects, complements, adjuncts, and so on) and contribute to their referential, or propositional meaning. They are lexical building-blocks . . ." (p. 134). In other words, Cowie recognizes that not all formulaic sequences can be directly associated with an interactional or discourse role, and that an inclusive account needs to accommodate the purely referential too. Moon (1992) similarly includes a category of *informational* fixed expressions (e.g., *in advance; by means of; two or three; all manner of; on the grounds that; white as a sheet; in a twist*) (p. 20). Besides this, she identifies three other categories: *evaluative*, "used by speakers/writers to communicate their evaluations to their hearers/ readers" (ibid.) (e.g., *a pain in the neck; beggars can't be choosers*); *situational* expressions, including greetings and apologies; and *hyperpropositional* expressions, which correspond to the 'discourse marker' categories of other commentators.

As to the relative frequency of formulaic sequences in these different roles, Butler (1997) notes that, in his five corpora, "the majority of the longer repeated sequences . . . serve interpersonal or textual rather than ideational functions" (p. 76). This seems to indicate that Cowie's and Moon's referential category may be peripheral to the general nature of formulaic sequences. However, there is still much work to be done on reconciling quantitative and qualitative assessments of formulaicity, and there may be other ways of deciding the importance of a function than the frequency with which individual exemplars occur (see Chapter 2). At the very least, we may note that the referential function seems in some way different in kind from the socio-interactional and discourse ones. In Chapter 5, the distinction will be accommodated by proposing two independent but intersecting functional frameworks.

In the context of the translatability of formulaic sequences, Coulmas (1979) considers how universal their functions are:

> some situations, such as, presumably, *greeting* or *leave-taking* may be universal; others may be common to some societies and language, e.g., *proposing to change from* v- *to* t- *forms of address;*[6] and still others may be restricted to one sole culture, as many rituals, customs, and habits probably are. (p. 245)

However, he notes that "what appears to be idiosyncratic in a close-up perspective may be recognized as belonging to a generic type on a more abstract level" (ibid.). Since the pragmatic variables of one society may differ from those of another, the choice of formulaic sequence in a give situation may be triggered in different ways:

> The time of day may be a determining factor in one society, and immaterial in another, where the season may be of much greater relevance. Likewise, place, sex, age, familiarity, rank, role relationship, social occasion, etc. may or may not be relevant to the selection of a given R[outine] F[ormula]. (pp. 245–246)

Coulmas goes on to identify a taxonomy of the variables in a situational frame, and tests it on the English formula *Congratulations!* and the Japanese near-equivalent *o-medetō gozaimasu* (p. 246ff). This enlightening comparison shows how cultures vary in their prioritization of, and required values for, key variables, such as age, rank, familiarity, elapsed time since the event referred to, nature of the event, previous mention of the event, style of expression, and concomitant gesture. In this light, it is clear that, for at least some formulaic sequences associated with social functions, the word-string itself is only part of the interaction, the remainder being achieved by other aspects of behaviour and by appropriacy of context. Indeed, in some cases the words, as words, are redundant, except as the means of achieving the act of 'phatic communion' (Malinowski 1923/1946:315).

Recognizing the major role of situation is a timely reminder that formulaic sequences rely for their effect on being appropriately received by the hearer as well as appropriately delivered by the speaker (see Chapters 4 and 5). In addition, some formulaic sequences, often referred to as 'scripts', actually entail more than one participant (see, for instance, Ellis 1984:57; Garvey 1977:43), and a deliberate exclusion of the second party would be seen as a powerful and indicative gesture of linguistic and/or social control (e.g., Schmidt 1983:156).

Meaning

Comparing classifications of formulaic sequences according to meaning
is a complex task, since there are several levels and perspectives.
Although rather too conservative for our ultimate needs, one classic
division found in the literature separates formulaic and nonformulaic
language according to semantic transparency. For instance, Van Lancker
(1987) states that

[p]ropositional utterances have full 'analyticity' – the meaning follows from an
analysis of the meaning of the component parts of the utterance. Familiar phrases
of all kinds – idioms, greetings, speech formulas, proverbs – have a meaning that
flows from the utterance *as a whole*. Analysis results in the *wrong* interpretation.[7]
(p. 55)

Van Lancker's definition of 'familiar phrases' suggests that she is happy
to amalgamate semantics and pragmatics. We shall consider both,
beginning with an exploration of the relationship between aspects
of semantics, as exemplified by the idiom and by metaphorical
expressions.

Idiom and Metaphor

For many, over the years, the archetypal formulaic sequence has been
an idiom[8,9] (Hudson 1998), a central definition of which relates to the
meaning of the whole being different to the sum of the parts (Cornell
1999; Flavell & Flavell 1992:6; Hudson 1998:13; Irujo 1986; McCarthy
1998; Nattinger & DeCarrico 1992:32–33; Williams 1994; Wood 1986).
Once again, features of form are intrinsic to most definitions. Wood's
(1986) definition of the 'true' idiom is "a complex expression which is
wholly non-compositional in meaning and wholly non-productive in
form" (p. 2). Flavell and Flavell (1992) state that idioms "break the
normal rules" (p. 6) either syntactically or semantically. Nattinger and
DeCarrico (1992) define idioms as "complex bits of frozen syntax, whose
meanings cannot be derived from the meaning of their constituents, that
is, whose meanings are more than simply the sum of their individual
parts" (p. 33). Williams (1994) uses the term *idiom* to refer to "any
defined unit whose definition does not predict all of its properties" (p.
8). Although he adds that idioms violate rules both of form and of interpretation (ibid.), he also states that "idioms obey the basic rules of form
in a language. For example, all idioms in English obey the 'head-initial'
setting of the head position parameter. On the other hand there are

unpredictable, language-particular exploitations of the formal possibilities" (p. 9). Williams's approach addresses the way in which idioms might challenge assumptions about underlying syntactic formulations. As such, it operates at a different level from most accounts, which deal only with surface forms.

The idiom gains its holistic meaning either by virtue of a null interpretation at the word-by-word level or by being metaphorical (Moon 1992; Yorio 1980). Some such idioms require general or etymological knowledge for the connection to be seen (e.g., *straight from the horse's mouth; sure as eggs is eggs; pig in a poke*), and, if that knowledge is absent, they are impenetrable at the word level, so, in effect, the metaphor works on the sequence as a whole. Nontransparent idioms must, by definition, be formulaic, as they could not be constructed from, nor usefully broken down into, their component parts. Others relinquish their holistic meaning by the application of a little common sense (e.g., *the autumn of one's life; lie low; let the cat out of the bag*), and it could, indeed, be argued that the meanings are not holistic in the narrow sense, since the metaphor is specific to the individual words.[10] For some commentators, this excludes such sequences from the definition of the idiom. However, Cowie (1988) argues that the common practice of viewing lack of transparency as the "essential defining feature" of the idiom is incorrect. Rather, he demonstrates that there is a continuum of direct interpretability, so that there are "very many semantically evolved composites which are still partially analysable" (p. 135). There is, he argues, no clear dividing line between what is transparent and what is nontransparent. Wood (1986) also recognizes a continuum of semantic compositionality, "shading by gradual degrees from total non-compositionality to fully regular combination" (p. v).

If the process of drift is gradual, we shall surely run into problems if we try to pin down whether a given string is, for a certain individual, composed of active or inactive constituents. Certainly there are phrases, as there are also words, which are easily recognized as relinquishing their literal meaning only under the auspices of etymological interest (as opposed to morphological necessity), but it might be difficult to ascertain whether, for many others, the dividing line is a hard and fast one from speech event to speech event, and just what underlies the state of being "on the brink of lexicalization" (Coulmas 1981:3). This basic difficulty arises from viewing formulaic sequences as 'set' rather than fluid. Fluidity allows for them to be componential on one occasion and entirely holistic on another, and this will be a key feature of the new account of formulaicity developed in the course of this book.

Pragmatic Meaning

Further evidence that strings with a literal, referential meaning can still be formulaic is that they can possess a second layer of pragmatic meaning. Cowie (1988) specifically differentiates *idioms*, which are "semantically specialized" (p. 133) from other fixed phrases that are "pragmatically specialized" (p. 132). At the lexical level, we find strings to which common agreement in the speech community has assigned a particular meaning that favours one of the possible interpretations of the words. A *hand-stand* could have been a structure placed at hand height for placing items on, just as a *hand-rail* is a bar at hand height. A *hand-cuff* could have been a blow with the hand, and a *hand-out* could have been a signal made by cyclists when turning a corner. We have, on originally hearing the string, construed the meaning using pragmatics, and then stored the form whole, rarely if ever examining it internally again.

Nattinger and DeCarrico (1992) have a quite specific idea about the relationship between formulaic and generated strings, which rests upon the notion that the former ('lexical phrases') have a pragmatic function:

> consider the lexical phrase frame *if I were* ____ (If I were you/the king/the president, etc.) versus an expression such as *if I were the one that she really wanted to talk to*. Whereas the first is a lexical phrase, the second is generated by regular rules of syntax. That is, the same lexical phrase can also be analyzed by the grammatical rules, and the two similar-appearing expressions would be handled differently in grammatical and pragmatic competence. *If I were you* exists as a phrasal constraint assigned a function (expression advice) by pragmatic competence, while the similar phrase *if I were you* can be produced by grammatical competence (*if* + S + V + O). . . . A further difference, of course, is that the latter expression does not have a particular associated function. (pp. 12–13)

This view excludes the semantically literal and grammatically regular string from inclusion as formulaic and does not allow for the possibility that the frame *if I were X* in *if I were the one that she really wanted to talk to* is *also* formulaic, and simply not marked for special pragmatic meaning.

Pragmatics is a dynamic function of language and is applied to the juxtaposition of a linguistic event and a situation, in order to make sense of their coincidence. As such, the interpretation of a formulaic sequence depends on when and how it is used (Coulmas 1979:241). Coulmas argues that there is only limited value in examining the descriptive meaning of formulaic sequences, which are predominantly defined by their expressive power. He goes on to say:

an adequate analysis of the meanings of R[outine] F[ormula]s depends heavily on a proper description of their respective situational contexts. Only knowledge of the relevant dimension of social situations (and their relative weight) guarantees an understanding of the meaning of formulae which are tied to them. (p. 242)

There is an interesting corollary of this. Just what is the 'meaning' that is stored *with* a formulaic sequence, if that meaning is so intimately derived from the situational context of its use? In Chapter 5 it will be proposed that there is little value in starting from a decontextualized definition of the formulaic sequence. Rather, with Coulmas, we shall ask what the situation is, and what meaning is to be expressed, and then ask which formulaic sequence is most likely to be selected for the job. In other words, the selection of a formulaic sequence will be viewed as a dynamic solution to a range of specific "problems" arising on line.

Provenance

'Provenance' is intended here to refer to the way that formulaic sequences come about, since this is often one of the ways in which they are defined. Peters (1983) defines what she terms the 'speech formula' as a "multi-morphemic phrase or sentence that, either through social negotiation or through individual evolution, has become available to a speaker as a single prefabricated item in her or his lexicon" (p. 2). Specifically, she proposes that we acquire our formulaic sequences in two ways: by encountering them in the speech of others and by creating them out of their component parts ('fusion'). Both types play a role in language acquisition (see Chapter 6), and both support the adult language too.

Sequences That Start Off Formulaic

While it is true that virtually any formulaic sequence that we encounter was once novel for someone, some will be so obviously formulaic that we can assume that everyone just learns them whole. For instance, *abracadabra* and *open sesame* are accepted as nonsense strings with a clear functional meaning. Other recognizably formulaic strings are memorized texts, such as rhymes, prayers, and lists, which come about precisely for the purpose of being passed on (see more about oral traditions in Chapter 4). However, for the majority of formulaic sequences in our input, we have a choice about what to do with them. We can adopt them as formulaic for ourselves, in which case we may never break them down. Or we can break them down and extract meaning from the individual parts.

Occasionally, problems will be encountered, particularly if a formulaic sequence is new in the variety. A good example of this is the phrase *take a rain check*, which has recently arrived in British English from the United States. In U.S. English this phrase means 'to postpone', since, at a ball game, a 'rain check', a compensatory ticket, is issued if the game is cancelled due to bad weather. British sport does not favour this practice (perhaps because it rains too often) and so the term 'rain check' is not known to most people. Thus, when the idiom is heard in American TV programmes and films, heavy pragmatic activity has had to go on. This has directed Britons towards what is, coincidentally, one of their major pastimes – looking out the window to check if it is raining. It is also normal British practice to decide only at the last minute whether to engage in an outdoor activity, because you never know what the weather will do. As a result, the logical interpretation, to the British mind, of *can we take a rain check?* uttered in the immediate context of declining an invitation, is not, as intended, that the event will simply happen later, but that the individuals in question should see how things turn out before they decide whether it happens at all. Thus, in the United Kingdom, *take a rain check* means 'see if it seems like a good idea when the time comes', not 'do it later'.

Sequences That Become Formulaic

How does a sequence become formulaic in the first place? This question needs to be answered slightly differently depending on whether it relates to the language as a whole or the language knowledge of an individual. We shall deal with the latter in Chapter 6, in the context of first language acquisition. As regards the former, Hudson (1998) offers a useful model of the circularity which sustains formulaicity within the language (Figure 3.1), and explains it as follows:

ad hoc expressions take on new meanings through pragmatic inferencing in the *discourse*. The development proceeds through semantic and phonetic reduction to a stage at which the contribution of the parts of the expression to the whole is beyond *conceptualization*, and the expression becomes fixed in its *realization*. At this third stage expressions are completely invariable although they might still comprise more than one orthographic word. (p. 2)

An example of this is the name of the British magazine *Radio Times*, established in the 1920s by the BBC to list its radio programmes. Over time, names can become formulaic (recall *Rice Krispies* in Chapter 1) and take on their own associations. In this case, the *Radio Times* developed an identity which extended well beyond its listings function, by

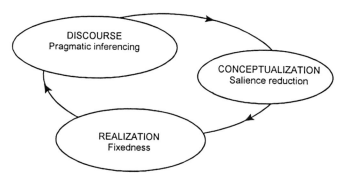

Figure 3.1. Hudson's "Levels of interaction in fixedness". Reprinted from *Perspectives on Fixedness: Applied and Theoretical* by J. Hudson, p. 2, copyright 1998, with permission from the author.

including features about the stars, and, in due course, television listings too, first of the BBC and ultimately of all the other major independent, satellite and cable channels too. The radio listings are now tucked away at the back, and many readers probably never even notice that they are there. Such readers might be surprised to have it pointed out to them that the title of the magazine actually contains the word *radio* at all. As Cowie (1988) puts it, "formal invariance over time [is] a major factor leading to a gradual reduction in the meaningfulness, or meaning, of component words" (p. 135).

Defining formulaic sequences according to their provenance, then, can focus both on strings of smaller units that have got stuck together (e.g., Bybee 1998; Langacker 1987), and on long strings with a complex meaning that have never got broken down (Hickey 1993:29). Ideally, an account of how formulaicity works should accommodate both of these, and show how they relate. As Cowie (1988) points out:

The two perspectives [of lexicology and psycholinguistics] are interrelated . . . by the reciprocal relationship which exists between expressions which are already recognized by a speech community (and so are likely to be recorded in dictionaries) and the speaker's predisposition to store specific word combinations for future use. On the one hand, the existence in a language such as English of very many institutionalized units perfectly serves the needs of adults (native speakers as well as foreign learners) who are predisposed to store and reuse units as much as, if not more than, to generate them from scratch. On the other hand, the widespread 'fusion' of expressions which appear to satisfy the individual's communicative needs at a given moment, and are later reused, is one means by which the public stock of formulae and composites is continuously enriched. (p. 136)

Continuum Models

The idea that formulaic sequences can best be described as lying along a continuum is quite widespread. However, care has to be taken, when evaluating and comparing them, to notice precisely what the basis of any given model is. The majority of continuum models deal with actual features of the linguistic material. For instance, Pawley and Syder (1983) focus on variability, speaking of a "novelty scale" (p. 205) from entirely novel to entirely memorized sequences. Between these lie "clauses [which] fall at various points along the cline . . . , consisting partly of new collocations of lexical items and partly of memorized lexical and structural material" (p. 205). Howarth (1998a) argues in similar vein: "It is essential to see the categories as forming a continuum from the most free combinations to the most fixed idioms, rather than discrete classes" (p. 35). However, some models focus on processing patterns. Givón (1989), for example, proposes an 'automaticity continuum' (p. 258). This is a "hierarchic, multi-level scale" from the most conscious to the most automatic processing. The more predictable a task, the more automated, while "the highest level of attention is assigned to . . . tasks that are *least* automated, being least predictable" (pp. 258–259). This processing continuum is not specific to language, but language production and comprehension are one reflection of it (pp. 261ff). Such different types of continua could be compatible, but need not be. Sinclair (1987), like Pawley and Syder, recognizes a continuum of variability, but his view of processing is that it is *not* characterizable as a continuum at all. His view is that there are two distinct ways of processing language, according to the 'open choice principle' and the 'idiom principle' (pp. 319–320). These are "incompatible with each other. There is no shading of one into another; the switch from one model to the other will be sharp" (p. 324).

As with taxonomies with clear-cut categories, a continuum model ideally needs to restrict itself to one mode of description, whether that be form, function, or whatever. Once again, however, we find that this is not always the case. Peters (1983), for instance, proposes a continuum which, by implication at least, relates usage and form. Her model is

[a] continuum between 'cultural formulas', which, judging from their invariance in form, are treated as units in a particular speech community (whether of two or a million persons), and 'idiosyncratic formulas', which may have a prefabricated status only for one particular speaker. (p. 3)

What she means is that some formulaic sequences are recognizable as such by everyone, while others will be formulaic for the speaker but not for the hearer. In actual fact, this is less of a continuum than a straight

Table 3.1. *Howarth's collocational continuum*

	Free combinations	Restricted collocations	Figurative idioms	Pure idioms
Lexical composites verb + noun	*blow a trumpet*	*blow a fuse*	*blow your own trumpet*	*blow the gaff*
Grammatical composites preposition + noun	*under the table*	*under attack*	*under the microscope*	*under the weather*

Reprinted from *Applied Linguistics*, vol. 19, P. Howarth, "Phraseology and second language proficiency", p. 28, copyright 1998, with permission from Oxford University Press and the author.

opposition, since there are no interim positions for the hearer: either the string is processed formulaically or it is not.

However, if we shift the focus away from what the hearer and speaker do on any given occasion to what their options are, the scale does indeed spread into one more suitable for a continuum model. It hinges on Peters's suggestion that the speaker has a choice about whether to treat the string formulaically or, like the hearer, as novel (p. 3). This is something which is only possible if the composition of the string is grammatically regular and semantically transparent. In contrast, formulaic sequences which the entire speech community knows, never have to be broken down, and so they do not need to be decomposable.

Cowie's (1988) continuum approach is superficially like that of Pawley and Syder (1983), because it hinges on formal criteria. However, he links increased fixedness of form with meaning change (p. 135), particularly a tendency for "the literal senses ... not [to] survive alongside their figurative ones in normal every day use ... [so that] for some speakers they may indeed be unrelatable" (p. 135). In the same vein, Howarth (1998a) proposes a continuum (Table 3.1)[11] which veers from form-based on the left to meaning-based on the right.

Unintentional confusions arise when an idea from one domain is applied to another. For instance, Nattinger and DeCarrico (1992:34–35) invoke Wood's (1986) semantic continuum as exemplary for their illustrations of a form-based one. Meanwhile, Van Lancker's continuum (Figure 3.2), first formulated in the early 1970s (see Bolinger 1976) but reproduced here from her 1987 paper, illustrates the nature of an inherently multidimensional description. Her terms include forms (*sentence stems, collocations, lists*, etc.), functions (*indirect requests, song lyrics and titles, pause fillers*, etc.) and meanings (*metaphors, idioms, proverbs*, etc.).

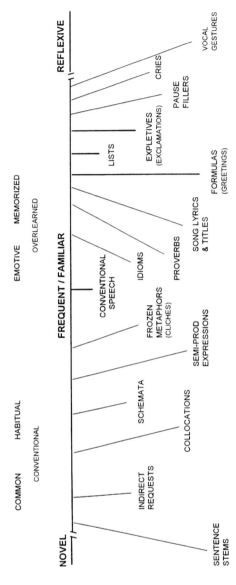

Figure 3.2. Van Lancker's "Subsets of nonpropositional speech and their common properties, presented on a hypothetical continuum from most novel to reflexive". Reprinted from "Nonpropositional speech: neurolinguistic studies" by D. Van Lancker, in *Progress in the Psychology of Language*, vol. 3 (A.W. Ellis, ed.), p. 56, copyright 1987, with permission from the author.

At the extreme, the continuum approach should imply that syntax, morphology and lexis are all degrees of the same thing (Nattinger & DeCarrico 1992:34), something which some grammatical models, such as Cognitive Grammar (e.g., Langacker 1986, 1995), easily accommodate, and which an inclusive definition of formulaic sequences must also entail (see Chapter 14).[12] Most models, including Van Lancker's, leave aside the novel language which is the domain of the open choice principle (Sinclair 1987, 1991) and focus only on degrees of fixedness within what is evidently fixed.

Summary

We have reviewed four themes which repeatedly appear at the heart of definitions of formulaic sequences. Of these, form is probably the most consistently addressed, followed by function. Meaning and provenance tend to be tacked on, as features pertaining to the others. Yet it is clear that all four are closely interrelated. It is provenance that explains the quirks of both form and meaning, and it is function and meaning which propel a sequence through the process from novel to formulaic. We have seen that a focus on form is able to capture some descriptive characteristics of formulaic sequences, but that the approach is weakened by unbalanced but ubiquitous formal characteristics which cut across the main categories, and/or deep-seated difficulties in excluding function, meaning and provenance from the finer points of the account. To extend form-based accounts beyond the descriptive would be to ask such questions as why the language tolerates this wide variation in fixedness and grammaticality. In particular, why are there grammatical strings that are also immutable (e.g., *a watched pot never boils, nice meeting you, how are you, give me a break*; Nattinger & DeCarrico 1992:40), when their analysis, which would be simple and uneventful, could so easily make their components available for open class substitutions? Peters's (1983) solution is to reverse the perspective entirely: it is not so much that not analyzing sequences brings about invariance, as that invariance prevents analysis (p. 11).[13] Since invariance is a function of customary use, and customary use is a function of interactional meaning, this, once more, draws the discussion out of the narrow bounds of form alone, and into the areas of function and meaning.

Continua are descriptively attractive, but entail more at an explanatory level than is always recognized. Specifically, it is not sufficient to be able to answer the question 'what will we have if we move a little to the right (or left) on the continuum line?', for there is also an implicit, and problematic, expectation of graduality in how the items are produced and understood. If one were to superimpose form-based, function-based, meaning-based and provenance-based continua, it would be clear that categories adjacent on one may be distant on another. For instance, two strings similar in their level of formal variability may have entirely different types of function, may be placed far apart on the meaning continuum, since one is literal and one is metaphorical or semantically noncompositional.

In the next few chapters, we shall see more evidence that formulaic sequences are not a single and unified phenomenon. From the context of specific types of data, we shall look more closely at form, function, usage, meaning and likely provenance, and use the amassed evidence to develop a different kind of account. In order to avoid getting caught back into the vicious circle between identification and definition, we shall look for independent evidence of what should and should not count as formulaic. We shall see that the neat definitions of this chapter, already creaking at the seams, are unable to cope with some of the specific features of particular data types, but that they are helpful in providing a baseline (or rather, several baselines) for evaluating a new kind of definition and explanation of formulaicity.

PART II

A REFERENCE POINT

4

Patterns of Formulaicity in Normal Adult Language

In Chapter 1, we saw that the practical purpose of using formulaic sequences appears to be that they reduce processing effort. As Kuiper (1996) puts it:

> Formulae make the business of speaking (and that of hearing) easier. I assume that when a speaker uses a formula he or she needs only to retrieve it from the dictionary instead of building it up from its constituent parts. (p. 3)

By saving on processing, the speaker is able to focus on other kinds of concomitant activity. These may be, for instance, evaluating the ideas contained in the present conversation (e.g., Wray 1992), or engaging in another, unrelated, activity. Jaffe (1978) illustrates the difficulties of the overload which can occur when trying to pay attention to too many things at once:

> While listening to a news broadcast on the radio, I began to tell an interesting story aloud. This 'split attention' task yielded an eerie experience. When I tried to speak fluently, the broadcast was reduced to gibberish, like the babble of peripheral conversation at a large cocktail party. It was unquestionably speech but was as meaningless as a poorly understood foreign language. Conversely, if I made a concerted effort to follow the gist of the newscast, my own speech became halting and repetitious and I lost the thread of my story. (p. 55)

Despite these observations, it will become clear in the course of this chapter that not all formulaic sequences can be satisfactorily explained in terms of their ability to reduce the processing load of the speaker. Therefore, we shall also be considering other roles which they might play.

The reason for focussing on the language of the adult native speaker at this stage is that it represents the end point of the long process of first language acquisition, the goal (or one possible goal) of second and foreign language learning, and the pre-trauma norm from which aphasic symptoms diverge. Thus, it will provide a clear point of reference for making later comparisons with the language of young children (Chapter 6), second language learners (Chapters 9 and 10) and aphasics (Chapter 12).

Evaluating the Formulaic Sequences of Adult Native Speakers

We have already seen in Chapters 2 and 3 that there is no simple way of categorizing formulaic sequences, either by form or function. In what follows, types of formulaic sequence will be grouped according to a particular common characteristic. This is not intended to imply a typological match. It is an organization of convenience, which will suitably reveal patterns in the data. Inevitably, some types of sequence will turn up in more than one category, but this is simply an indication of the kind of complexity that we are dealing with.

Sequences Remembered for Their Own Sake

Adult native speakers know a great many phrases, sentences and larger texts which they have memorized at some time in the past. These include rhymes, songs, prayers, quotations, lists and mnemonics. The days of the week, the times tables and so on, are learnt with a rhythm that supports their recall on demand. By memorizing the words, you end up knowing that a particular string 'sounds right' while other logical possibilities sound less familiar and so can be dismissed. In the case of the times tables there is an additional effect, that of replacing an otherwise arithmetical activity with a routine linguistic one.

Mnemonics add an extra twist, in that the material memorized is not the material that you actually want to remember, but a key to it. The idea is that the mnemonic is more memorable than the target material, and so is more likely to be recalled successfully. Mnemonics are useful for recalling sequences of similar items, such as the colours in the rainbow and the number of days in each month. Nonlinguistic material may be translated into linguistic form, because the semantic dimension of the word sequence, not present in the target material, helps prevent inaccuracies. For instance, the notes on the musical stave are remembered by means of sentences like *Every Good Boy Deserves Fun* and *Good Boys Deserve Fun Always*. Even an equation like $C/5 = (F - 32)/9$ (for converting between Centigrade and Fahrenheit) can be remembered with the help of a mnemonic like *Children over five are frequently taken away for rates (four eights) that are all above the highest single figure*. It is a common feature of such mnemonics that they can strike the casual reader as bizarre and *un*memorable, yet can stick in the mind of the learner for many years.

Also often memorized are quotations from literary works, including poems and speeches in a play. This may be so that they can be performed, quoted in exams, or just recalled at will for the pleasure of it. A less deliberate kind of memorization, but still aimed at providing access to information, occurs in the case of proverbs, the purpose of which is to anchor folk-truths.[1] Many proverbs are so well known that it is possible to cite a short form (e.g., *a stitch in time (saves nine); too many cooks (spoil the broth))* or replace the second half with an indication of the proverbial status of the string (e.g., *many hands, as they say; sleeping like the proverbial*). The shared knowledge of the established form also explains the humorous effect of incorrect completion (e.g., *People in glass houses shouldn't... run around naked; Don't bite the hand that... looks dirty; Happy is the bride who... gets all the presents; Children should be seen and not... spanked or grounded*).[2]

In a not dissimilar way, in the context of religious instruction memorization is encouraged so that the individual is equipped for accessing key tenets at any time. The Catholic child, for instance, is presumably encouraged to recite the Catechism so that there is always an answer available to any question that could challenge his or her faith at a later date. For this and other reasons, it is of immense importance that deliberately memorized sequences are correctly remembered. There is little use in recalling *six sevens are forty-six*, and if you recite *Richard of York battled gallantly in vain* rather than *Richard of York gave battle in vain*, you will place blue and green the wrong way round in the colour spectrum. In the case of quotations, which are "socially-embalmed language ... placed on a pedestal" (Crystal 1995:184), there is a genuine deference for the validity of the original, correct version, tied to an esteem for the person who coined it. As a result, misquotations are frowned upon, and apocryphal ones, such as James Cagney's *you dirty rat* and Bogart's *play it again, Sam*, are consistently pointed out not to be real quotes, even though they are just as formulaic as genuine ones would be. Where there is variation in form, as with children's playground rhymes (see, for instance, Opie & Opie's 1969 list of 35 versions of the 'dipping' rhyme *Ibble obble black bobble*), it is not uncommon to hear arguments in defence of one version over another, purely on the grounds that "that's what I've always said".[3,4]

Do deliberately memorized strings save on processing? The answer is clearly that they do, and in two distinct ways. Those that carry information directly, such as lists, quotations, and religious texts, are memorized so that there is no need to expend undue attention on constructing them with the required accuracy. Mnemonics, meanwhile, are designed to favour easy processing over difficult processing. The string is made easy to recall, and some kind of simple analytic procedure is applied to it to extract the required information.

However, do memorized strings *only* save on processing? Here, the answer must be that they do not. Some perform an additional function, whether deliberately or incidentally, of signalling identity in some culturally significant way. In the case of quotations, it is the originator of the quoted string whose status is being elevated to that of 'worthy of quotation' (or, if the motives are less honorable, 'worthy of ridicule'). In other cases, something about the speaker's identity is signalled. For example, a teenaged boy might deliberately memorize all the names of the national soccer squad. Although it may certainly suit him to have easy access to the names, knowing them is also likely to be a mark of status amongst his peers. Entire speech communities can be marked out by culture-specific repertoires of memorized items. For instance, all American children memorize the Pledge of Allegiance but few British or Australian children would even recognize it. Meanwhile, a sizeable proportion of the British population could complete the rhyme *Remember, remember the fifth of November*, but few English-speakers from elsewhere would necessarily recognize the significance of the date, let alone the rhyme.

The Way We've Always Said It

At the opposite end of the formulaicity continuum, if continuum it be (see Chapter 3), are the sequences which characterize the idiomatic nature of native speaker language, and which, far from being deliberately memorized, are often hardly recognized as preferred forms until frequency counts indicate them to be so (see Chapter 2). Pawley and Syder (1983) point out that "Instead of saying *it's twenty to six* one might say *It's six less twenty; It's two thirds past five; It's forty past five; It exceeds five by forty; It's a third to six* [or] *It's ten minutes after half-past five.*" Similarly, "[O]ne may say that *John is five feet nine (inches)* but not, ordinarily, that *John is five and three quarter feet* or *John is six feet less a quarter (of a foot)*" (pp. 197–198).

But it is not just a question of *how* things are said. Pawley (1991), drawing on the views of George Grace, accounts for patterns like these in terms of "subject matter codes". These "refer to the conventions shared by a speech community that specify . . . what things may be said about a particular subject or topic, how these things are said, idiomatically, and when they are said, appropriately" (p. 339). In other words, there is more to formulaic sequences than *just* their agreed form, because that form is compulsorily associated with an agreed function and context. The corollary is that it is not just a question of excluding from output certain *ways* of expressing a message, but also of excluding many messages themselves, because they are culturally inappropriate. Such messages, of course, will not have a culturally agreed form. As pointed out in Chapter 1, the preference for one expression of an idea over another cannot easily be explained in the framework of any theoretical model that predicts all grammatical strings to be equally valid. Now we see that it also cannot be explained without reference to a theory of cultural interaction.

What is true of turns of phrase is also true of, and more problematic for, simple associations between lexical items, that is, collocations. In English you *reach* a decision, *carry* the responsibility and *reap* the benefits. It is less idiomatic, though still perfectly comprehensible, to speak of *alighting on* a decision, *holding* the responsibility and *collecting* the benefits.[5] This sort of collocational association can be very difficult for non-native speakers to master (see Biskup 1992), not least because the preferred pairings often vary from language to language. In English you *run* a business, but in German you *lead* it (*ein Geschäft führen*). In English you *smoke* a cigarette, but in Hindi you *drink* it (*sigaret piinaa*). In English you lie *in* the sun, but in Russian you lie *on* it (*na solntse*). Some types of collocation can be fairly readily identified by an alert native speaker, but others are beyond the scope of our intuition, which is, therefore, not a reliable source of judgements (see Chapter 2 and, for instance, Sinclair 1991:4). Stubbs (1995) nicely illustrates this with the words *small* and *little*. Intuitively we would tend to assume that *small* and *little* are synonymous. This would mean that they were interchangeable, and that a higher frequency of use for one over the other was consistent across comparable contexts. However, Stubbs found the following distributions in a corpus of 2.3 million words, combined with the *Oxford English Dictionary* on CD-ROM:

| *little girl* or *little girls*: 146 | *little boy* or *little boys*: 91 |
| *small girl or small girls*: 8 | *small boy* or *small boys*: 46 |

This distribution is statistically highly significant (p. 383) but, as Stubbs observes: "[r]eference and ostensive definition will not get us . . . very far. The words do not differ in their denotation and it is difficult for native speakers to make explicit the difference in meaning" (p. 384). He goes on to show that *small*, *little*, *big* and *large* are all subject to particular collocational restrictions and subtle semantic associations. For example, we say *big toe* and *little toe*, but *large intestine* and *small intestine*; *big boy* has the connotation of 'grown up'; *big* is often used metaphorically, as in *Big Apple* (New York), *Big Bang*, *Big Brother*, *big time*, and *big words*. Stubbs notes, in particular, that *little* often suggests 'cute and likeable' but can also be pejorative: "Of over 70 examples of *little man* in the corpus and the OED, none are obviously flattering, and some are definitely insulting (e.g., *a ridiculous-looking little man, a pumped up little man*)" (p. 385).

Lying somewhat between the idiomatic turn of phrase and the collocation are two types of sequence which involve the use of two or more words to express a simple idea. The first type is well exemplified by the class of compound nouns, such as *hand-stand, hand-rail, hand-cuff* and *hand-out*, discussed in Chapter 3. The interest in these lies less in what they do mean than in what they do not. What seems to happen is that the string becomes associated with one of its logically possible meanings, and from that point on, being stored as a single lexical item with that meaning, other meanings simply are not considered (unless deliberately, as noted earlier). The other type of multiword string expressing a simple idea might be termed 'circumlocutory', because, here, it is not a question of assigning a linguistic label to a new idea, but of the coexistence of a single-word label and a multiword one. Examples are *take/make a decision (decide), draw a conclusion (conclude), a sea-change (a change), at the end of the day (really)* and *up hill and down dale (everywhere)*. These are somewhat puzzling since even if the multiword strings, being formulaic, are stored as efficiently as the single words, they must take more energy to produce. So what do these, and the other types of idiomatic turn of phrase, tell us about the saving of processing effort?

Do multiword expressions save processing effect? Certainly, processing constraints could explain why we are inclined, overall, to use some expressions more than others.[6] If we anticipate pressures on processing (or if they are always present to some degree or other), it will encourage us to store certain frequently needed sequences whole. But how are we to explain an entire speech community possessing, to a large extent, the same set of idiomatic formulaic sequences? Other factors must be in play. An individual's inventory of holistically stored sequences is heavily influenced by the current patterns of usage in the speech community. We select, in our own usage, the sequences that we have stored whole. We have stored them because they 'sound right' to us, that in turn being because they have often been heard in the speech of others. And by using them we, in turn, contribute to what others hear most often and therefore store in their own inventories. The external motivation for this virtuous circle of cause and effect is the desire to sound like others in the speech community. This is not, directly at least, a consequence of processing constraints and although we shall, in the end, identify a connection between the two, the desire to sound like others needs to be viewed for now as an independent determinant.

Although, between them, processing constraints and the interaction of encounter and emulation can account for the predominance of some grammatical associations of words over others, one of our subtypes, the 'circumlocutions', is not easily accommodated by this scenario alone. It may be the practice of the speech community that determines that *take a decision* is idiomatic and *select a decision* is not, but why use three words for one in the first place? What possible processing advantage might there be in accessing five syllables instead of two? To answer this we have to reexamine our baseline assumptions about just what causes and what alleviates processing pressures. Up to now we have only considered the broadest contrast, that between constructing a sequence of words out of its smallest elements and retrieving it ready-made from store. But there are other aspects of processing too, including the struggle to retain fluency, and the sustaining of output while planning what to say next. One possible explanation of the preference for a longer over a shorter way of expressing an idea is that it buys time for planning and/or that it contributes to an even rhythm (the latter may also have some bearing on style – see later). If so, then the saving of processing effort is not simply about taking short cuts. It is about regulating production so that it is manageable, and this may mean, at times, taking the long way round, adding padding and/or establishing and maintaining a particular preferred rhythm and flow.[7]

Supporting a Difficult Job

Oral traditions. In a number of contexts the use of formulaic sequences can be associated with the particular demands of the genre or activity of which they form a part. One of these is oral storytelling and poetry. In the 1930s, Milman Parry and Albert Lord studied and recorded traditional South Slavic oral epic poets (Emeneau 1964:330; Kuiper 1996:5; Watkins 1992). In this art form "each epic singer constructed his narrative song by improvizing around a stock of fixed images, epithets, and conventional expressions, which he alone kept firmly in mind" (*Encyclopedia Britannica* 1999, "Folk Arts"). As such the activity involves a delicate balance between formulaicity and creativity. Kuiper (1996) summarizes Lord's conclusions about the oral poets of Serbo-Croatia as follows:

Because speech such as that of the oral poet is subject to the constraints of real-time performance, the poet does not compose from scratch but uses memorized bits of speech, *traditional elements*. These bits of memorized speech are also flexible. In other words, they permit a degree of novelty. (p. 5)

According to Watkins (1992), traditional texts of this kind play an important social and cultural role: "They are not remembered and repeated merely because they delight the ear, rather they are signals, in poetic elaboration and as verbal art, of the relations of things" (p. 393). He goes on to observe that "[t]he function of the Indo-European poet was to be custodian and transmitter of this tradition. The totality of themes as expressed in formulas was in a preliterate society entrusted precisely to the professionals of the word, the poets" (ibid.). In other words, the culturally sanctioned forms of words symbolize the identity of the society, and mastery of them is a mark of status and trust.

According to Kuiper (e.g., 1991, 1996; Hickey & Kuiper 2000; Kuiper & Austin 1990; Kuiper & Haggo 1984) and Pawley (e.g., 1991) there are strong similarities between the oral traditions described above and the structure of auctions and sports commentaries. The genres share five characteristics: they have a prescribed content and structure, they are highly formulaic, they adhere to particular grammatical patterns, they have a striking intonational and rhythmical shape, and they are delivered extremely fluently (Pawley 1991:340).

Sports commentaries. Kuiper (1996) likens the job of the sports commentator, particularly on the radio where there is no supporting image for the listener, to that of the simultaneous interpreter:

[t]he commentator must . . . not get behind. If he or she does, then there will be more and more of the game that has elapsed and must be remembered in order for it to be recounted. There will come a point, in that case, where omission is inevitable because people can only recall so much from memory. (p. 9)

According to Pawley (1991), "[t]he task is to instantly comprehend the action and with minimal delay to transform one's perceptions into an accurate, easily understood and entertaining description" (p. 365). A major way of speeding up the production of a commentary, and of remaining fluent, is to use formulaic sequences for commonly expressed ideas (Kuiper & Austin 1990:196). For instance, Kuiper (1996) reports the following, from horse-racing commentaries: *They're off and racing now; threading its way through; round the turn they come* (pp. 17–18). Pawley observes that it is the 'play-by-play' part of the commentary, that is, when the race is actually on or the cricket ball in play, that has the highest proportion of formulaic material, delivered extremely fluently in a droned intonation and with a "regular syllable-per-second delivery rate" (Kuiper 1996:19). The formulaic material creates the bedrock of the commentary,[8] and also fills potential hesitation places. For example, in Kuiper's data a horse-racing commentator says *They were followed through there now by as they make their way on to the top end of the course by Bahrein* (p. 18). Here, one formulaic sequence has been inserted into another, presumably because the commentator could not immediately access the name of the horse (ibid.).

Cricket is a slower game, and Kuiper reports that its commentaries feature fewer formulaic sequences overall than in horse racing, though there are still very many. Pawley's (1991) examples include: *[team] A won the toss and elected to bat* and *[batsman] A glides/chops/cuts (it) down to third man* (p. 359). As the second example illustrates, while in horse racing the formulaic sequences are relatively fixed – the major variability residing in the insertion of the names of the horses – in cricket there is a greater scope for novelty within partially fixed strings, so that "each formula is a schema for generating a family of expressions or word strings that are functionally equivalent" (Pawley 1991:359).

Auctions. Auctioneers have many demands on their attention, particularly spotting bidders and keeping track of the bidding sequence:

Like commentators, auctioneers are also under pressure to react instantly. The moment they see a bid they must react to drive the market on and signal accurately to all the potential buyers what is currently the highest bid. . . . It is up to the auctioneer to keep up the rhythm of bidding by the rhythm with which he calls the bids. . . . So, like the race caller, the auctioneer cannot break down. He has a rhythm that he must maintain even though that rhythm is often not matched by the rhythm of bidding. (Kuiper 1996:36–37)

Although in some other ways auctions are not like sports commentaries (Kuiper 1996:41), we shall focus here on the points of similarity. In a parallel to the comparison of horse racing and cricket, Kuiper contrasts different types of auctioneering style (1996:47ff). In slow-pace auctions, such as those of the international houses like Sotheby's, where the value of the commodities seems to instil a sense of dignity, only a few formulaic sequences are used, and Kuiper attributes this to the absence of processing pressure. In what he terms "medium rate" bidding, such as is found in local antiques and livestock auctions, the bidding is faster, but it is regulated by the presence of a large novice contingent in the bidders, which prevents the speed and jargon from approaching that of high-pace professional commodities auctions (see later). In these medium rate auctions, the inventory of formulaic sequences is similar in number and type to that of the sports commentaries (e.g., *oh what a beauty; I've got X dollars for them; Hold your hand up, that's the idea*, Kuiper 1996:61).

So far, there seems to be a close correlation between processing pressure, as determined by the quantity of information to be computed and expressed within a given time frame, and the proportion of formulaicity in the language. This would lead to the prediction that very fast rate auctions would be the most formulaic of all. However, Kuiper reports that at the World Tobacco Auctioning Championships, where the pressure is very high, with a sale every five seconds (p. 49), the quantity of different formulaic sequences is actually lower than that of medium rate auctions, not higher (p. 73). To appreciate why requires a look at the whole situation, and the way in which formulaic sequences are one, linguistic, solution to an essentially nonlinguistic problem. It is not as simple as saying that the greater the problem, the more formulaic sequences will be used, because it depends on what formulaic sequences have to offer in each circumstance.

In high-pressure auctions, the patterns of language are just one contributory solution to the problem of needing to work accurately at speed. Kuiper identifies a number of nonlinguistic solutions to this as well. For instance, at the tobacco auctions, the buyers stand in line, in the position preallocated to their company, so that the auctioneer can immediately identify who they represent. In wool auctions, where this practice is not adopted, the bidders shout out their bids rather than indicating them by gesture, so that the auctioneer does not have to scan the crowd to spot them (Kuiper 1996:53). It is significant that the buyers are an initiated group, so that "it is possible to have very rapid auctioning because everyone knows exactly what is going on" (p. 54). Because of the shared agenda and knowledge, descriptions can be pared to the bare minimum, and, as a result, there is very little for formulaic sequences to express.

In the context of the problems with identification noted in Chapter 2, it must be pointed out that Kuiper's lists are to a large extent based on intuition rather than anything more tangible. Kuiper's method is to immerse himself in the genre and slowly to develop a sense of what is formulaic and what is novel. Although sequences may occur more than once, this is not a formal criterion for identification, but one of several informal ones, including intonational shape, the position of hesitations, the role in the discourse structure, and the delivery context (Kuiper, personal communication). Although it would probably be an overreaction to doubt that these strings really are formulaic, there is, as a consequence of adopting the intuitive approach, no independent evidence of their being so: they are judged formulaic because they seem to be formulaic.

As Chapter 2 has indicated, it is for him or her who has a truly better method to cast the first stone, but it is beyond dispute that some way of measuring formulaicity more objectively would be a useful backup to intuition.

Are auctioneers and commentators (only) saving processing effort? One curiosity of the commentary and auction formulaic sequences is that there is more than one way of expressing the same message. Since the messages are simple, it might seem reasonable to argue that, under processing pressure, a speaker would stick to just one way of expressing them, rather than selecting different ones each time. As we shall see presently, the best way of explaining this oddity must be that other factors, unrelated to processing, need to be taken into account. One factor that will be found salient later, however, namely stylistic pressure, seems relatively implausible here, since neither commentators nor auctioneers would be expected to have time or inclination to engage in gratuitous variation. More likely is that our high-speed selection of holistic strings simply does not funnel us into a single choice for each message, but offers a range, all of which are effectively synonymous (see later).

Weather forecasts. Weather forecasts are an interesting case for research into formulaicity. As Crystal (1995) observes, the fluency of their delivery "is partly a matter of careful preparation, but is largely achieved through the broadcaster's ability to rely on formulaic phrasing (*with light winds and largely clear skies, blue skies and sunshine, widespread frost*) and on standard sequences of locations" (p. 385). As Crystal indicates here, the formulaicity is of two types: lexical and structural. Kuiper (1996) and Hickey and Kuiper (2000) analyze the structure of radio forecasts from the New Zealand Meteorological Office, and find both kinds of formulaicity. The districts are presented in a regular order, and the structure of the forecast is pointed up by standard introductory phrases, which occur with little variation (Figure 4.1). They note that these forecasts are scripted, so it makes little sense to explain the formulaicity in terms of saving the speaker's on-line processing effort. Rather, Kuiper proposes, forecasts are formulaic in order to help the hearer understand them.[9]

The relative importance of lexical and structural formulaicity becomes clear when one compares two styles of weather forecasting in Britain. The British Meteorological Office Shipping Forecast is scripted and is structurally highly formulaic. Figure 4.2 compares the first half of three such forecasts. Only two types of variation are seen. One is the important information: wind direction and speed, atmospheric pressure,

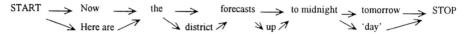

Figure 4.1. Formulaic structure of part of the New Zealand weather forecast. Reprinted from "'A depression covers the South Tasman Sea': New Zealand Meteorological Office weather forecasts" by F. Hickey and K. Kuiper, in *New Zealand English* (A. Bell & K. Kuiper, eds.), p. 287, copyright 2000, with permission from the authors.

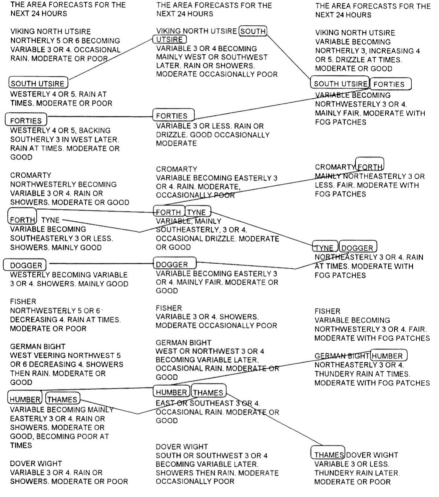

Figure 4.2. A comparison of the structure of the first half of three Shipping Forecasts from the British Meteorological Office (30 June at 17:25, 1 July at 17:25 and 3 July 2000 at 11:30).

precipitation and visibility. The other is the exact grouping of the districts, though they always appear in the same order (for a map of these areas, see Crystal 1995:385).

In contrast, the regular BBC Radio 4 weather forecasts, also from the Meteorological Office, do not have a structural formulaicity, though they still contain a great many lexical formulaic sequences. The principle of these presentations is that they are 'weather-led'. The forecaster homes in on the main 'action', which may, one day, be thunderstorms brewing in the southeast, and another day snow coming in from the north. The forecast then 'follows the weather', and districts are defined and combined according to how they will fare. One advantage of this approach is that it gives a much clearer picture of the nature of the weather patterns on that particular day, and so it makes more sense in scientific terms. However, it makes the order of presentation unpredictable, and requires the radio listener to apply the information to a mental map of the country, so that the local details can be extracted from it by inference. These weather-led forecasts have been the focus of considerable discussion and complaint, because listeners find them difficult to understand. This seems to be because they fall firmly into the trap which Kuiper (1996) describes as an undesirable hypothetical alternative to the New Zealand format:

weather forecasting would require high amounts of attention on the part of the hearer if each synoptic situation ordered the description of the weather in a different way. Hearers would also have to pay close attention if they could not rely on their region being mentioned in the same place in the sequence. (p. 91)

Listeners often argue that the BBC Radio 4 weather forecasts are subject to a clash of interests, since it is really only the forecasters themselves who want to know where the weather is coming from, or, indeed, what the weather is all over the country. What the individual listener wants to know is more mundane and local: Is it going to rain here this afternoon?; Will there be a frost tonight?; When I travel east tomorrow will I drive into a snowstorm?; and so on. If the forecasters were really taking account of the hearer, therefore, they would use a more formulaic format, since this is easier to decode and extract information from. Figure 4.3 illustrates the problem, by comparing forecasts from two consecutive days with different presenters (centre and left) and two bulletins an hour apart on the same day with the same presenter (centre and right). The boxes contain the names of areas of Britain. Areas appearing only in one forecast are dark-shaded, areas mentioned in the forecast in the central column plus one other are light-shaded, and areas mentioned in all three forecasts are unshaded. The lines are broken if the co-reference is only partial or is vague. The diagram clearly shows that mentions of

10th July 2000, 7am - Peter Gibbs

There is some dry and bright weather around across the south-east of England but it's not going to last very long because already we've got heavy rain across much of northern England down through Wales. It's edging in towards the Midlands and that'll arrive down in the London area and across East Anglia towards the end of the morning and certainly through into this afternoon.

The heaviest of the rain might well bypass the West Country so perhaps touching sixteen in Exeter although the wind's certainly picking up all the while.

But I think an average figure for the Midlands around about thirteen degrees through. In afternoon, and near those east coasts, the North Sea coasts, twelve degrees probably about the best, with gale force winds eventually coming in from the north during the latter part of the day.

Some brightness, though, coming through, perhaps for Cumbria into northern parts of Wales through the afternoon, but here too a pretty chilly northerly breeze.

For Northern Ireland, not faring too badly, one or two showers around, a cold wind, certainly, gusting up to about forty or fifty miles an hour but quite a bit of dry and bright weather in between the showers. Top temperature around fourteen or fifteen degrees.

And I think brightening up across most parts of Scotland eventually as well. We've got some rain at the moment though from Aberdeens and down through towards the Firth of Forth through the Borders, but that'll gradually ease away and there's brighter skies coming in. But again a cold wind, a strong wind, gales coming in towards the Aberdeenshire coast later on. So temperatures ranging between twelve and eighteen degrees.

Tonight the rain, the gales, hanging on all the way down those North Sea coasts, out particularly from the Humber down through into East Anglia, lingering here into tomorrow as well. But elsewhere a bit drier, a bit brighter but still very much on the cool side. Not very nice at all.

11th July 2000, 7am - Sarah Wilmshurst

Let's start across the far south-east of England through Kent and Essex through East Anglia, Lincolnshire and north-east England too.

It is quite a cloudy start, there's some rain around. That cloud and rain will slowly clear into the North Sea although it's going to linger longest across East Anglia

Elsewhere it should brighten up. There'll be a mix of sunshine and showers

with temperatures up to seventeen or eighteen degrees in the south around fifteen towards the east coast.

And it will still feel cold here in a strong north-west wind.

Now to the rest of southern England through the Midlands, north-west England and Wales.

There's quite a bit of rain around at the moment in the West Midlands, through Wales, Cheshire and Merseyside and some of that's heavy. And we'll see one or two showers cropping up elsewhere today, especially in the south.

Generally though it will brighten up and feel less cold than yesterday in a lighter wind and with more sunshine as temperatures reach seventeen or eighteen degrees.

Now to Northern Ireland and Scotland where in fact many places will be dry and bright today with some sunshine. But there will be a few showers around

with a temperature of twelve or thirteen degrees in the northern isles and around fifteen to seventeen elsewhere. Now there's still a strong northerly wind in the east. Elsewhere that wind will be lighter than yesterday.

And tomorrow, many places will be dry with sunny spells, but cloud and rain will move across the north-west later.

11th July 2000, 8am - Sarah Wilmshurst

Let's start today's forecast through south-east England, East Anglia, Lincolnshire and up into north-east England.

Any rain left in the far east will soon clear away and the cloud will break up.

And elsewhere there'll be a mix of sunny spells and scattered showers.

Temperatures will reach around fifteen degrees in Norwich, seventeen in Newcastle and Leeds and eighteen in London.

Now still with a gusty north-westerly wind near the east coast but with a lighter wind elsewhere.

Now to the rest of England and Wales.

There's some pretty wet weather around at the moment in parts of Wales, the West Midlands, Merseyside and north-west England and this will move southwards today,

and it's going to brighten up, and then there'll be a mix of sunny spells and just one or two showers later on. Top temperatures seventeen or eighteen degrees, and in generally lighter winds it should feel warmer than it did yesterday.

Now for Scotland and Northern Ireland and there's going to be a mix of sunny spells and just a scattering of showers. In many places a much brighter day than yesterday.

Top temperatures twelve or thirteen degrees in the northern isles, fifteen to seventeen elsewhere.

Then tonight it's going to be dry, clear and chilly in many spots

and then tomorrow many places will be dry again with spells of sunshine. Having said that, thicker cloud in the north-west is going to bring a little bit of rain.

Figure 4.3. Comparison of a BBC Radio 4 weather forecast (centre) with one 24 hours earlier (left) and another one hour later (right).

geographical locations do not occur in predictable places. Even when the content of the forecast is the same (centre and right), the mention of districts is still not consistent. This means that the listener has to pay careful attention and know well the map of the country in order to work out the weather for his or her own area.

In this section, we have seen that texts heavy in formulaic material may be so-constructed for the sake of the hearer rather than the speaker. As we shall see later, the use of formulaicity to aid the hearer has some very far-reaching consequences for an integrated model of how formulaicity figures in the overall shape of language.

Marking a Style

Formulaic sequences can contribute to the establishment and maintenance of an appropriate style for a particular genre. A writer can use structures and turns of phrase to suggest a relaxed or a formal style, and there are sets of formulaic sequences which belong together in achieving such effects. Drescher (1994), for instance, identifies the formulaic sequences associated with formal letters of rejection in German. It is a standard device of both written and oral text construction that a particular phrase be used again and again.[10] Just what is repeated varies from genre to genre and is part of what identifies a text for its purpose and context. According to Critchley (1970), selective repetition was a deliberate stylistic device employed by Field Marshall Montgomery: "We have been fighting the Germans a long time now. A very long time ... a good deal too long. It's time we finished things off. And we can do it. We can do it. No doubt about that. No doubt about that whatever" (p. 203). Research by Wharry (1996) shows that the sermons of African-American preachers characteristically feature a range of formulaic sequences performing different stylistic functions. One set of these is commonly perceived "as preachers' devices for elicitation of audience participation or as audiences' backchannel cues" (Wharry 1996:86); they include *Thank you Jesus; Hallelujah; Will you say Amen; Lord have mercy; Yeah Lord; Glory to God; We praise the Lamb for ever* (p. 125). Others might be viewed as 'textual fillers', such as *if there is one thing that I'm convinced of, in the church world today* (p. 187); *I want you all to know tonight* (p. 210); *I do wanna say* (p. 221). A third type supports a deliberate rhetorical structuring of the text; for example, *God wrote his first word to mankind in stone ... he didn't write it on paper, he didn't write it on [?], he didn't write it on anything that was transitory, that could fade away, that could be ... smudged over, but he wrote it on stone* (pp. 188–189); *the kingdom of God is not welfare, the kingdom of God is not rag[g]edy, the kingdom of God got streets of gold, the kingdom of God got gates of gold, the kingdom of God* (p. 217). In such sermons and also in, for example, the telling of jokes or stories, the structure provided by such elements can amount to a ritual, supporting a stylized activity in which the speaker and hearer collude to reach the expected conclusion.

Do stylistically-determined formulaic sequences save processing effort? The textual fillers support fluency, and rhetorical structures could support the speaker in constructing a point. But what of backchannel elicitations? It is impossible to view these, nor indeed the rhetorical repetitions, as independent of the hearer. We have already seen that some formulaic sequences seem principally aimed at aiding the hearer's decoding – could this be the case again here? It would seem so. One purpose, if not the only one, of starting sentence after sentence with the same words is to draw the attention of the hearer to what is new. And when listener responses are elicited by formulaic sequences, signalled not by their content but their form, they are presumably not intended to require much decoding by the hearer, just a reflex response. And returning to the formulaic sequences that feature in writing, it seems unlikely that they are primarily there to reduce the writer's processing effort, because it is possible to draft and redraft text, and there is not the same immediacy of time pressures that occur in spoken interaction. Yet, although they may be fewer in number than in speech (Butler 1997), there still are many. In this case, too, it seems reasonable to suppose that they are there to help the reader rather than the writer.

Getting into a Habit

We have already seen that sometimes word strings are used repeatedly in order to create a particular stylistic effect. A different pattern of repetition is observable when a text is recounted more than once. It is a well-known phenomenon that if you are called upon to tell the story of a recent incident several times in quick succession to different people, then the words you use will soon become relatively fixed. Peters (1983:109) attributes this to the process of 'fusion', whereby previously novel strings become stored whole for convenience (see Chapter 6). Bateson (1975) describes her (unwritten) year-on-year lectures as "a stream of new combinations [containing] great lumps that have been used before" (p. 61).

An experiment by Goldman-Eisler (1968) seems to indicate that this sort of repetition is beneficial to processing. She requested subjects to tell a story depicted in an uncaptioned cartoon and then to retell it several times. She specifically requested them not to change their wording unnecessarily, so that she could monitor the effect of repetition on the fluency of their delivery.[11] She found that the amount of pausing dropped sharply from the initial account to the first retelling, and continued gradually to decrease with subsequent retellings. She interprets this as indicating that "the difference between spontaneity and reiteration, between production and reproduction, is a qualitative one, reflecting the dual nature of psycholinguistic operations" (p. 59).[12]

These kinds of pattern are not restricted to 'retellings'. They can arise simply through a natural exposure to a particular interactional situation:

> Groups of people who share a great deal of knowledge and who interact regularly, such as groups of colleagues or intimate groups of friends, regularly negotiate new uses of language with which to talk about new ideas and/or events. At first such language may be laboriously constructive, but as both the constructions and the meanings become established, shortcuts are taken until conveniently brief new expressions have evolved. (Peters 1983:108)

Peters's observation links the processing advantage of formulaic sequences with another important role, that of representing interactional codes for members of a speech community. Clearly, these two functions are not mutually exclusive, but it is not at first obvious whether they are in a coincidental or causative partnership. We shall see at the end of the chapter that they are probably causative.

Marshalling Thought and Controlling Text

Moving the text on. As we saw earlier, direct repetition can be used to mark style. However, in conversation, direct repetition is highly marked, and it is more common to find a partial repetition, which builds on, rather than just copying, what has gone before. Repetition is a stylistic exception because

> [it] often suggests a non-increment to the topical progression of the discourse (increments are things which push the topic forward; a non-increment deliberately stalls it), and can be interpreted as staying with one's present position in the talk, of a refusal to converge or communicatively accommodate. (McCarthy 1998:114)

McCarthy illustrates how the augmented reiteration of messages is achieved via rephrasing and partial repetition, using a conversation which features the following: *... madly in love with ... very struck on ... Smitten ... Smitten with ... big house ... huge house ... awful lot ... tremendous amount* (p. 114). It follows that, if direct repetition is undesirable, then in order to continue benefiting from shortcuts in

Gerry

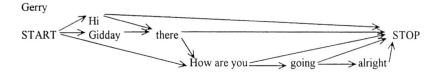

Allan

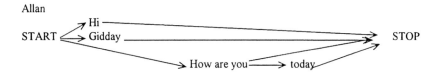

Dusty

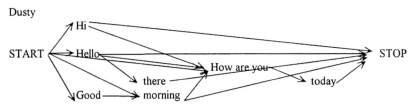

Figure 4.4. Kuiper and Flindall's "Greeting formulae of individual checkout operators". Reprinted from "Social rituals, formulaic speech and small talk at the supermarket checkout" by K. Kuiper and M. Flindall, in *Small talk* (J. Coupland, ed.), p. 199, copyright 2000, with permission from the authors.

processing, a speaker will need to have more than one formulaic means of expressing each message.

Evidence in support of the idea that we have several formulaic versions of a given message comes from Kuiper and Flindall's (2000) examination of formulaic language at the supermarket checkout. They provide schemata for the initial greeting and subsequent information elicitation (that is, versions of *hallo, how are you?*) for each of three checkout operators (Figure 4.4).[13] These operators were dealing with new customers each time, and not building on any pre-existing conversational text, so, in theory, they could have used the same form for their message over and over again. Yet, as the schemata clearly indicate, they had apparently free and random access to several versions of the message, all of which, we may reasonably assume, were formulaic.[14] Of course, we cannot rule out the possibility, as before, that these various versions of the message are not fully synonymous, and that, for instance, their selection was determined by the age, gender or some other feature of the addressee. However, it is at least as plausible that no such subtle level of selection is involved and that, in a job where some sort of linguistic exchange is expected, the operators simply trot out whichever of the several formulaic versions stored comes first to mind.[15] As for whether they save processing, we may assume that they certainly do: retrieving formulaic sequences is an easier option than having to think of something original to say.

Marking discourse. In Chapter 3, as part of our examination of function as a definer of formulaicity, we noted that some formulaic sequences perform discourse marking roles. Amongst other things, these sequences seem to signal the relationship between a piece of text and what precedes or follows it, and the speaker's attitude towards the surrounding text. Are these sequences formulaic because they support the speaker's processing? It seems reasonable to suppose that they are, on two counts. Firstly, they qualify as 'preferred' expressions, and, as we have seen, a preference for one way of expressing an idea over others is indicative of easier processing. For example, it is idiomatic to say *as a result of* and *as a consequence of*, but not the equally grammatical and comprehensible *as the aftermath of* or *as a repercussion of*. Secondly, the function of these 'discourse devices', to use Nattinger and DeCarrico's (1992) term, is to marshal the text, and this, presumably, is useful for the speaker. Language is being used to externalize relationships between ideas which are already in the mind of the speaker. It is useful for a speaker to say *There are three things* before embarking on talking about the first: it creates a projected textual structure, and by keeping in short-term memory a phonological trace of words like *firstly* and *secondly* or *a* and *b*, it will be easier to keep track of where on that mental map of the text the speaker has reached.

However, there is clearly more to it than this. For all the likely benefits that the speaker can obtain from using such discourse devices, it is undoubtedly the case that part of the reason for using them is to signal the discourse structure to the hearer. By so doing, the speaker can indicate when it will and will not be appropriate to interject, can acknowledge that a change of subject, or introduction of a tangential one, is deliberate (e.g., *by the way; talking of ____*), and can pacify an impatient hearer (e.g., *my point here is ____; so what I mean is ____*). If the speaker wants the hearer to decode these indicative expressions easily, then making them formulaic is one way to do that.

Manipulating the Situation

Finally we come to a very large set of formulaic sequences which seem to be geared towards manipulating the situation in which the speaker finds him- or herself. Some examples are listed under *conversational purpose* in Nattinger and DeCarrico's (1992) list of formulaic sequences for 'social interaction' (pp. 60ff), but they are more centrally the focus of research by such people as Aijmer (1996) as well as those with an interest in speech acts. Table 4.1 represents the main categories of formulaic sequence which may be considered to come under the heading of 'situation manipulators'. This list is not intended to be a formal classification so much as an exemplification of a particular priority which certain kinds of formulaic sequences appear to serve. Some categories have already figured in our earlier discussion, which would suggest that any given expression can have more than one function at the same time.

Getting people to do, think and feel things. What all of the types of formulaic sequence listed in Table 4.1 have in common is that they are used to influence the hearer in some way or another. Indeed, although we are terming them, in a fairly neutral way, 'situation manipulators' they are really all 'hearer manipulators'. Those in the first section of the table (*changing one's physical or perceptual environment*) involve the speaker using language to get the hearer to do something, feel something or think something, to the benefit of the speaker's physical, emotional or cognitive needs. Requests, demands, warnings, orders, and so on, are intended to get someone else to behave in a particular way, often acting as an agent in achieving something that we want for ourselves but cannot do personally. We are profoundly motivated actively to seek our own physical and emotional comfort (Maslow 1968), and from the earliest age are programmed to enlist the help of others in attaining it (see Chapter 6). Because this requires the acquiescence of the addressee, in the adult social context politeness formulas are an important component of the interactional event (Ferguson 1976; Laver 1981); see Aijmer (1996) for a thorough review of the formulaic sequences used for thanking, apologizing, requesting and offering, and Manes and Wolfson (1981) for an account of compliments. The subsequent categories in Table 4.1 also perform this function in a slightly less direct way. When the speaker asserts his or her separate identity this involves the hearer being led to perceive him or her as a significant individual. The speaker may draw attention to him- or herself by beginning to tell a story that will hold the floor, or may use an expression to take or hold the turn. A particular turn of phrase, whether used deliberately or not, can mark a speaker out as different from everyone else. The last section of the table illustrates how speakers may use a range of means to assert identity with a group:

Conventionalized forms . . . are group identifying. They separate those who belong from those who don't. They do this by serving as instruments for

Table 4.1. *Formulaic sequences as devices for situation manipulation*

Function	Effects	Types	Examples
Changing one's physical and perceptual environment	Satisfying physical, emotional and cognitive needs	• Commands, bargains, requests, etc. • Apologies • Politeness markers	• Keep off the grass; I'll give you ___ for it; pass that over, will you? • I really am sorry • I wonder if you'd mind ___
Asserting separate identity	a) Being taken seriously	• Storytelling • Turn claimers and holders, etc.	• You're never going to believe this, but . . . • Yes, but the thing is . . . ; Thank you very much (*in response to invitation to speak*); The first thing that you have to realize, of course, in addressing this issue is . . .
	b) Separating from the crowd	• Personal turns of phrase	• I wanna tell you a story (*Max Bygraves*); You know what I mean, Harry (*Frank Bruno*)
Asserting group identity	a) Overall membership	• 'In' phrases • Group chants • Institutionalized forms of words	• Praise the Lord!; as the actress said to the bishop • We are the champions • Happy birthday; dearly beloved, we are gathered here today . . .
	b) Place in hierarchy (affirming and adjusting)	• Threats • Quotation	• I wouldn't do that if I were you • "I wouldn't want to belong to any club that would have me as a member" (Groucho Marx)
	c) Ritual	• Forms of address • hedges, etc. • Performatives • Incantations • Prayers	• Your Highness • Well I'm not sure (as a polite denial or refusal) • I name this ship . . . ; I promise . . . • Touch wood; God willing • Our Father, which art in Heaven . . .

establishing rapport, reinforcing awareness of group membership, perpetuating goals, values, and norms of the group, indicating speakers' readiness to conform to group norms, and defining social relations and the relative status of the different communicators. (Yorio 1980:438)

We adopt linguistic forms used by group members (Le Page & Tabouret-Keller 1985:181) and engage in group rituals (e.g., saying *bless you* when someone sneezes). According to Ameka (1987), in Ewe (spoken in Ghana and Togo) if a person uses his or her left hand for a transaction, it is necessary ritually to mention this in order to indemnify the action, which is taboo. This can be achieved using the formula *Mia [ló]!* 'Left hand!', to which the addressee responds, by way of acceptance that the taboo action has been unavoidable, *Así-é!* 'It is a hand!' (p. 321).[16] In Turkish there is a ritual exchange when a person is leaving. The leaver says *Allah ismarladik* 'I commend you to God' and the addressee replies *Güle, güle* 'laughing, laughing' (Dogancay 1990:53). Tannen and Öztek (1981) note that obligatory formulaic sequences, of which Turkish has many, are extremely difficult for a speaker to resist saying, even in settings where it is inappropriate to speak (p. 38).

Many formulaic sequences simply signify initiation into the group (Coulmas 1979). For non-native speakers, the nontransferability of formulaic routines can be an indirect cause of group exclusivity. Ameka (1987) reflects on the nonmatch of English and Ewe formulas used in response to seeing someone have an accident. He notes that utterances like "*Hope you're not hurt* and *Are you alright?* ... not only sound cynical to me and many other Africans but also seem rude, unsympathetic and irritating when said to someone to whom something bad has happened" (p. 316).

Finally, speakers may indicate and negotiate their place in the group hierarchy by using linguistic signals of honour or disdain towards others, by issuing threats,[17] and so on. In addition, politeness formulas are a signal of appropriate acculturation and, as such, are prioritized by adults in respect of the behaviour of their children, whom they wish others to view as socialized (see Chapter 6).

Performatives. One subset of the situation manipulators, the performatives, are worthy of separate discussion. These are utterances that achieve, by being uttered, acts such as apologizing, naming, betting, and so on:

If a person makes an utterance of this sort we should say that he is *doing* something rather than merely *saying* something. ... In saying what I do, I actually perform that action. When I say 'I name this ship the *Queen Elizabeth*' I do not describe the christening ceremony, I actually perform the christening; and when

I say 'I do' (sc. take this woman to be my lawful wedded wife), I am not report-ing on a marriage, I am indulging in it. (Austin 1979/1996:121)

The forms of word strings acting as performatives are largely fixed, and "even minor changes in the way such performative acts are expressed makes them opaque or infelicitous" (Kuiper 1996:92). Performatives are a kind of ritual, and "the effectiveness of a charm depends on its liter-ally exact citation and . . . any departure from its precisely set mecha-nisms may render the magic wholly ineffective" (Sebeok 1964:356). Mr. Macey's anecdote in George Eliot's *Silas Marner* illustrates this:

Mr. Drumlow – poor old gentleman . . . when he come to put the questions, he put 'em by the rule o' contrairy, like, and he says, 'Wilt thou have this man to thy wedded wife?' says he, and then he says, 'Wilt thou have this woman to thy wedded husband?' . . . and they answered straight off 'yes' . . . and I said to myself, I says, 'Suppose they shouldn't be fast married. . . . Is't the meanin' or the words as makes folks fast i' wedlock?' For the parson meant right, and the bride and bridegroom meant right. . . . meanin' goes but a little way i' most things, for you may mean to stick things together and your glue may be bad, and then where are you? And so I says to mysen, 'It isn't the meanin', it's the glue'.[18]

Are performatives formulaic for the sake of the speaker's processing or the hearer's? As before, no doubt the speaker can reduce his or her processing by having performatives stored whole in memory, but the purpose of uttering them is to effect a change in the situation, and that depends on their being correctly recognized and fully accepted by hearers. Among the 'felicity conditions' identified by Austin (1979/1996:122ff) as necessary for a performative to be a successful act is the requirement that the hearer correctly understands what you have said and what you are referring to. Therefore, it is paramount in achieving the act that the speaker adopt a form of words which the hearer will recognize as appropriate for that act. This may, in certain circumstances, be different from the form which the speaker him- or her-self would normally use. When the Pope stands in St. Peter's Square and blesses the world in different languages, he is presumably obliged to read some of the messages phonetically off the page without much, if any, understanding of the meaning of the individual words. Nevertheless, for speakers of that language, he has performed a valid act of blessing. Moreover, in certain circumstances, the speaker may, in order to produce language forms easily decoded by the hearer, entirely abandon access to his or her own formulaic inventory and carefully create utter-ances on line that comply to that requirement. In this case, aiding the hearer would actually *increase* rather than decrease the speaker's processing effort.

Conclusion

In this chapter we have evaluated the likely roles of formulaicity in a range of text types, all relating to the language of adult native speakers. We observed that in all cases except, possibly, the last (manipulating the situation), the speaker could directly benefit from using prefabricated material as a means of reducing his or her processing load. In many cases, formulaic sequences enhanced the fluency of the speaker's output.

We also identified a number of other functions for formulaic sequences. Speakers seemed able to express their identity as an individual using deliberately memorized strings and stylistic markers, and their identity as a group member by adopting customary ritualistic utterances, idiomatic turns of phrase and collocations. Such groupwide sequences are cyclically harvested from and resown into the shared linguistic inventory of the community, as individuals both imitate the preferred forms of others and also contribute to the pool of idiomatic material from which others draw. This suggests that the formulaic material plays a central role in maintaining the identity of the community.

In the next chapter, we shall draw on the patterns identified here to develop a more sophisticated model of the role played by formulaic sequences in the adult native language. It will accommodate the saving of the speaker's processing effort with the range of other functions which seem, at present, independent, and show how they all work together in achieving a single overriding purpose.

5

The Function of Formulaic Sequences: A Model

The Many Functions of Formulaic Sequences

In the course of Chapter 4, we found that while most types of formulaic sequence appear to play a role in alleviating the speaker's processing effort, this is far from the whole story. Scripted weather forecasts indicate that formulaicity can be present where there are no pressures on the speaker's production, if there are particular pressures on the *hearer's comprehension*. It also seems likely that much stylistic repetition is dedicated to aiding the hearer's decoding, by directing attention and reinforcing particular aspects in the content. Formulaic discourse markers seem able to support both the speaker's and the hearer's processing simultaneously. By mapping out the structure of the text, they help the speaker to remain focussed, while making the content and the speaker's intentions easier for the hearer to follow. Another major role for formulaic sequences was found to be that they signalled the speaker's identity as an individual or as a member of a group. Finally, we identified a large set of formulaic sequences whose primary role is to manipulate the hearer into a desired action or perception. In total, then, the evidence in Chapter 4 presents a very mixed picture. There seem to be several roles for formulaic sequences, neither mutually exclusive nor obviously compatible. Many appear to relate to the speaker, but some are partly, or even exclusively, geared towards the interests of the hearer.

One way to interpret this is to suggest that formulaic sequences simply perform several unconnected functions, that is, that they constitute the solution to a range of different linguistic problems. However, there is another explanation. It entails taking a step back, to consider the motivation *behind* the desire to speak fluently, express identity, organize text and help the hearer to understand what you say. It ceases to view formulaic sequences as the solution to *linguistic* problems at all. Instead, it views them, in all of their uses, as linguistic solutions to a single, *non-linguistic*, problem.

In order to capture this wider perspective, let us revisit the final category discussed in the last chapter: the formulaic sequences which manipulate the situation. Why should the language that performs these manipulative functions characteristically be formulaic? Why does the army use agreed forms of words for commands, such as *By the right quick march* and *At ease*? Why do we say the formulaic *Excuse me* when we want quietly to absent ourselves from a conversation or meeting? Why, when making a polite request, do we say *I wonder if you'd mind VERB-ing*? What would be the effect of *not* using formulaic sequences in these situations?

Cornering the Hearer

Bernstein (1972) observes that "meanings which are discreet to the speaker must be offered so that they are intelligible to the listener" (p. 166).[1] The speaker, by virtue of deciding what is expressed and how, can exert control over the range of linguistic interpretations open to the hearer (Kuiper 1996:90) and corner the hearer into the maximum likelihood of getting, and reacting to, the message. The more novel our output is for the hearer, the more likely it is to be misunderstood. Relevance Theory tells us that the hearer will engage in the least processing effort that results in a plausible (relevant) interpretation (Sperber & Wilson 1987/1996:474). MacKay (1951), taking a broad-sweep look at the effective use of symbolic representation, states that "successful communication depends on symbols having significance for the receiver, and hence on their being already in some sense prefabricated for him" (p. 184).

If the army permitted commands to take any of the grammatical forms that the language predicts as possible, the potential for misunderstanding and for slow reactions would be greatly increased. In a life-or-death situation, simple commands, previously learned by everyone, and easily differentiated, are the most effective way of gaining a fast and uniform response from a large group. The goal of the commands is the accurate manipulation of many people at the same time, and this is achieved by the use of word strings which are formulaic for the hearer.

Depending on what it is that the speaker aims to achieve, the linguistic form of the message needs to attract a greater or lesser level of engagement from the hearer. If imparting important information, then the linguistic packaging which highlights the presence of that information can usefully be formulaic, so that the hearer has only to focus on the material of interest. A frame like *I wonder if you'd mind* . . . draws hearers' attention to the fact that you are about to request something, and gives them time to tune into your voice, so that they are ready for the novel message when it comes. It also serves its own manipulative function, by inviting the hearer to perceive you as polite. The aim of this is to increase the chances that the novel request, when it comes, will be responded to in the desired way.

In contrast, there are occasions when the speaker does not intend to engage in depth with the hearer, but only, say, to achieve a low-level, background reaction. In this case, the use of formulaic sequences can help to ensure that the hearer is not drawn further into the interaction than intended. When someone says *Excuse me* as they stand up or move away, the intention is an unobtrusive apology, which can be registered without any interruption to the main event. Using a novel utterance like *It's time for me to leave now* would require the hearer to pay more attention to the words, and so it would be more invasive. In the same way, it is less intrusive of strangers' conversation to use the formula *Mind your backs* as you pass behind them with a tray of drinks than to say *Please be careful. I am walking close to you with a tray*. The latter, being outside of the standard repertoire of things you say when you want to pass safely, requires more decoding, and would draw more attention to the situation than is necessary or desirable.

At first glance it may seem like altruism if a speaker selects a form that will be easily understood by the hearer. But this is far from the case. In all of these manipulative expressions, it is in the speaker's interests to ensure that the hearer understands, since the intended effect of the utterance is to create a situation beneficial to the speaker:

Whether we request information, goods, services, or merely recognition, we must accommodate the hearer's capacities, his constraints, our relation to him, and the conventions to which he adheres both in language and in the real world. The object of request is to get somebody to deliver the goods. (Bruner 1983:91)

Formulaic Sequences: The Common Property

On closer consideration, it becomes clear that *all* of the functions of formulaic sequences that have been identified in Chapter 4 actually serve a single goal: the promotion of the speaker's interests.[2] These interests include

- having easy access to information (via mnemonics, etc.);
- expressing information fluently;

- being listened to and taken seriously;
- having physical and emotional needs satisfactorily and promptly met;
- being provided with information when required;
- being perceived as important as an individual;
- being perceived as a full member of whichever groups are deemed desirable.

In pursuit of these interests, temporary problems can arise, for which formulaic sequences are a useful solution. Commands, requests, and so on, and a range of politeness features and hedges, are all ways of manipulating the hearer into a position where he or she is obliged to engage in a response that will leave the hearer materially better off, emotionally more secure or with greater knowledge than before. Where people feel unimportant as individuals, formulaic sequences offer several ways of raising their profile in the eyes of others, by drawing the hearer's attention to them as special or different. One important means of doing this is to use formulaic sequences to create a platform of organization and fluency for the delivery of a text which the speaker or writer considers significant. Where people feel excluded from a group, they can use formulaic sequences to signal membership. The use of formulaic sequences that are shared by a speech community offers speakers a powerful way of signalling to their hearers that they are to be identified as members of the group: "this is the reality of language: in order to survive in society we've got to know what to say, and we usually know it in advance by memorizing it" (Becker 1975:27).

Figure 5.1 represents the relationships just described, between the different subsidiary functions of formulaic sequences, as they contribute towards the primary function of protecting the interests of the speaker. In this model, the discourse functions are subsumed into the main functions of supporting speaker and hearer processing, both of which they do simultaneously.

Figure 5.2 takes a different perspective on the same processes: the speaker's choices in using novel and formulaic language to achieve a goal. In this schema, three primary aims are identified as the underlying motivations for speaker output. The majority of text is either referential or manipulative, with only mnemonics falling into the category 'access information', which leads directly to fully fixed formulaic sequences. Both reference and manipulation can draw on both formulaic and novel utterances, and the processes by which this can happen are an indication of why, in Chapters 2–4, the relationship between form and function seemed so complex. Each route through the schema represents a large

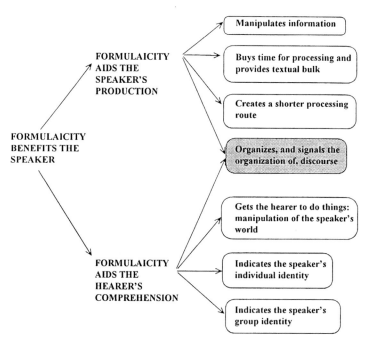

Figure 5.1. The functions of formulaic sequences. Reprinted from *Applied Linguistics*, vol. 21(4), A. Wray, "Formulaic sequences in second language teaching: principles and practice", p. 478, copyright 2001, with permission from Oxford University Press.

set of possible formulaic and nonformulaic strings, with the outcome determined by the speaker's priorities and ability to anticipate the hearer's knowledge. Where the speaker aims to be referential, there is most chance that novel constructions will be needed. However, there are opportunities for reducing the processing load by using preassembled polymorphemic words and fixed and semi-fixed formulaic word strings. When the speaker wishes to manipulate the speaker, be that by inciting an action or a perception, or by indicating the text structure so that the hearer can more easily map the shape of the discourse, the priority in selecting the form of words is the anticipation of the hearer's own formulaic inventory. Often this will coincide with sequences that are formulaic for the speaker too, but where it does not, the speaker will take the route of novel construction in an attempt to create a string that is easy for the hearer to decode, even though it is effortful to encode. In such instances, there is a direct conflict between the processing costs to the hearer and the speaker.

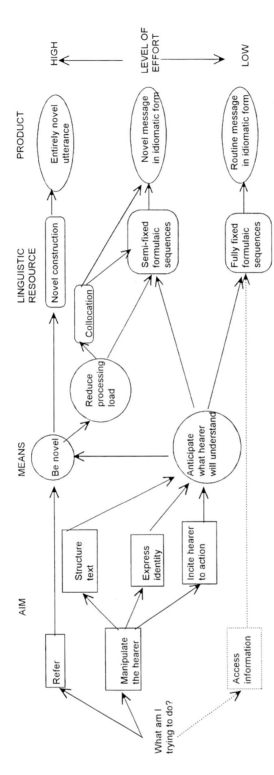

Figure 5.2. Schema for the use of formulaic sequences in serving the interests of the speaker.

The Alignment of Speaker to Hearer

This conflict comes about when the speaker and hearer possess non-identical inventories of formulaic sequences. This could be because they belong to different speech communities (say, one is British and one American, or they are members of different generations) or because one is a native speaker of the language and the other is not. Because it behoves the speaker to adjust his or her output to match what is anticipated to be the most easily decoded material for the hearer, the speaker will accommodate towards what he or she has observed to be the idiomatic patterns of the hearer. This has some obvious implications for sociolinguistic and historical linguistic theory, which we shall not pursue here, except to note that, in both cases, it helps explain why language change does not easily lead to progressive linguistic fragmentation within a speech community. However, in anticipation of our later detailed discussion (Chapters 8–11), a corollary for second language acquisition research should be mentioned here.

If the speaker's need to control his or her environment encourages the use of forms known to be in the hearer's repertoire, then a non-native speaker who engages in prolonged genuine interaction with native speakers will be highly motivated to pick up the idiomatic turns of phrase of the host speech community. Using word strings which the native speaker, as hearer, can decode easily (because they are formulaic) will greatly enhance the success of the messages' interactional purpose, not least because, if the speaker has non-nativelike phonology, the hearer will need to engage in extra processing for the phonological decoding. In addition, though, the use of nativelike formulaic sequences will signal to native speakers that this non-native speaker is able to cope with their idiomatic output. This is important because their own agenda in speaking will require that they, too, adjust their output to match the linguistic knowledge of their (non-native) hearer. If they believe their hearer *not* to know certain forms and, in particular, not to have certain idiomatic formulaic sequences stored, then they will need to edit them out, if their own messages are to be successfully received and acted upon. Thus, where the learner fails to convince native speakers that he or she can cope with idiomatic language, they will respond by supplying impoverished input, particularly in respect of nonliteral idioms (Irujo 1986:236), which, if not stored formulaically, require considerably *more* processing than a literal expression of the same idea. All of this throws light on the importance for second language learning of three conditions:

- engaging with native speakers in a genuinely interactive environment;

- the interaction being equal (that is, native speakers being equally motivated to ensure that the non-native speaker understands and reacts to their messages, as the reverse);
- the non-native speaker being sufficiently confident to pick up and use new forms, even without fully understanding them.

We shall see in Chapter 9 that the exemplary success of Nora, one of Wong Fillmore's (1976) subjects, in learning English as a second language, can be attributed to her meeting of these three conditions.

A Linguistic Solution to a Nonlinguistic Problem

The explanatory advantage of separating out the nonlinguistic motivation for selecting formulaic sequences from the linguistic forms that achieve it is that it enables us to see that this *linguistic* solution to the larger problem of how to get what you want is just one of several possible solutions. This, in turn, helps us make sense of the absence of a perfect correlation between the occurrence of formulaicity and the apparent need for it. For instance, we saw in Chapter 4 that in high-speed auctions formulaic sequences no longer serve a useful purpose, even though they play a major role in slower auctions. The specific demands of the fast auctions are better met by other solutions, such as lining up the bidders in a particular order or having them call out rather than gesture their bids. In other contexts, too, we can identify nonlinguistic solutions operating instead of, or alongside, linguistic ones. A final demand for a bill may contain formulaic sequences indicating the severity of the situation and the legal position, but the importance of the content may be further underscored by printing the letter in red or even delivering it by hand. In a quite different context, in order fully to convince a valued colleague that she will be missed on her retirement, or a friend that one is saddened by his bereavement, the customary formulaic expressions of good wishes or condolence may be supplemented by a card, a gift, or flowers. The problem of how to warn car drivers about road hazards is often solved entirely without language, but sometimes a formulaic warning accompanies the road sign. On motorway display boards the formulaic warning in words may be emphasized nonlinguistically, such as by making the words or their border flash on and off.

Conclusion

It is a central contention of this book that formulaic sequences are not rare, but extremely common. This claim is, in part, a natural consequence of taking a broad view of what counts as formulaic, but it is also a statement of commitment to a particular view of language processing, namely, that it is the accessing of large prefabricated chunks, and not the formulation and analysis of novel strings, that predominates in normal language processing. That is not to deny the important role that our creative linguistic capacity plays, however, for while "formulaic patterns . . . are indeed of very frequent occurrence in language use[,] and need to be accounted for[,] . . . they can hardly be said to represent the total language" (Widdowson 1990:81).

Taking a theoretical position that both places formulaic sequences at the centre of language description and also juxtaposes novelty and formulaicity as options for utterance construction requires a robust rationalization for the on-line selection procedure, able to account for the actual distribution of novel and formulaic (including idiomatic) strings in real text. To this end, a model has been proposed which collapses the various functions performed by formulaic sequences into three: the reduction of the speaker's processing effort, the manipulation of the hearer (including the hearer's perception of the speaker's identity), and the marking of discourse structure. These three functions have then been further reduced to one overriding priority, the speaker's promotion of self. It has been argued that while formulaic sequences appear diverse in form and function at the *linguistic* level, they are united in all being instances of a linguistic solution to this nonlinguistic problem. It has been demonstrated that, when seen in this light, the speaker is pursuing only two major, and one minor, aims in the formation of linguistic output. These are, respectively, to refer, to manipulate and to access information. These aims are fulfilled by means of creating novel text and/or selecting from the inventory of prefabricated strings, the level of fixedness being determined by the relative balance between the need for novel expression and the value of reducing either the speaker's own, or the hearer's, processing effort.

Seen in this light, formulaic sequences are a dynamic, not static, solution. What this means is that there is not simply a single stock of formulaic sequences which all speakers first learn, and then draw upon, but rather that the store is constantly changing, to meet the changing needs of the speaker. The three dimensions – processing, interaction and discourse marking – all operate largely independently, and so each person, in each unique situation, will apply slightly different selection criteria to a slightly different set of options, from those available to anyone else. Certainly there will be very many similarities between individuals, insofar as they share, within a given environment or speech community, an inventory of idiomatic forms and certain interactional expectations of, and towards, each other. But, just as it will be possible, through such similarities in formulaic speech patterns, to spot people who come from the same place, are the same age or share the same interests or beliefs, so it will rarely be possible fully to predict which formulaic sequences a given speaker will select, since the balance of priorities is constantly shifting, and with it, the relative usefulness of the stored sequences.

At the wider level, where distinct speaker groups such as children, learners and aphasics are compared, each will be found not only to select appropriately for their purposes from a set of preferred sequences, but also to create and edit sequences for the better management of their own agenda of needs. As a result, their formulaic language use cannot be characterized purely within the restricted terms of the adult native inventory, even though, as we noted in Chapter 4, adult native language is generally conceived of as the 'target' for learners and the pre-trauma norm of those who have suffered language loss. With this in mind, in the following chapters we shall ask, for each speaker or speaker group, what the role of the formulaic language is in alleviating the problems associated with meeting their need and desire to serve their own interests.

PART III

FORMULAIC SEQUENCES IN FIRST LANGUAGE ACQUISITION

6

Patterns of Formulaicity in Child Language

Introduction

In first language acquisition research, it has long been recognized that quite lengthy strings, which would correspond to several adult words, can be treated as a single unit by the young child (e.g., Bolinger 1975:100; Crystal 1997:244; Plunkett 1993:44). In this chapter and the next, an attempt will be made to reconcile a number of observations made over the last three decades or more about these strings, and to accommodate them within a model of the child's language use and linguistic development. Peters (1983) characterizes the child's encounter with spoken language as follows:

It is not a dictionary of morphemes that the child is exposed to, but rather an intermittent stream of speech sounds containing chunks, often longer than a single word, that recur with varying frequency. It is out of this stream of unknown meaning and structure that the child must attempt to capture some pieces in order to determine their meaning and to preserve them for future use. (p. 5)

It is that process of 'capturing pieces' that lies at the heart of understanding the role of formulaic sequences in first language acquisition. That children do store and use complex strings before mastering their internal makeup is generally agreed.[1] However, researchers have varied in their views about how significant they are. Brown (1973) acknowledges that strings like *What's that* in the very young child are not a product of a grammar, but, rather, "must be generated by some simpler mechanism either as fixed routines or as simple frames in which a set of words could rotate" (p. 181). In his view, "probably any form that is perceptually salient and highly frequent in the speech of a particular parent . . . can become 'lodged' in the speech of that parent's child though it will not be used in the full range of appropriate environments" (pp. 179–180).

He goes on to say, however, that while "[t]here is not, I think, any doubt that Stage 1 children control such forms", "they have little grammatical or semantic interest" (p. 180). On the other hand, Cruttenden (1981) sees formulaicity as central to the early stages of language acquisition. He proposes that the child's approach to all aspects of language – phonology, intonation, morphology, syntax and semantics – consists of two stages, first *item-learning* and then *system-learning*. Of the morphological and syntactic level, he observes that, in the item-learning stage,

> compound words and noun phrases involving several morphemes are commonly learned by children as unanalyzed wholes. *Cup of tea* may be learned as one unit and, when the plural morpheme has been learned, it may be pluralized as *cup of teas*. The child has learned the group of adult morphemes together with their reference, but has not learned that paradigmatic substitutions are applicable to each part. . . . He has not learned to segment the expressions, nor has he learned the possibilities of commutation for any part of the expressions. (p. 84)

In Cruttenden's model, "an utterance must be assumed to be item-learned if none of its parts is used in different combinations. Thus the child who said *here he comes* used neither *here*, *he*, nor *comes* in any other utterances. Nor were there any examples of similar structures" (p. 84). In fact, the young child seems to have very little notion of the word as a unit, nor of the morphemes and phonemes within it (Locke 1997:272).

The Forms of Formulaic Sequences in Child Language

Formulaic sequences are understood to fall into two types in child language. Either they have been borrowed from input (underanalyzed strings), or they have been created by the child and then stored whole (fused strings). Although they appear chronologically later, we shall consider first the fused strings, since the other category is more disparate and will require more exploration and discussion.

Fused Strings

Sometimes, sequences of words which the child has constructed using its grammatical rules and lexical entries are then stored whole and retrieved on subsequent occasions. They may or may not be grammatical in adult terms. Peters (1983) terms this process, which is a characteristic of adult as well as child language, *fusion*:

> children . . . fuse speech sequences, seemingly as shortcuts to avoid having to construct them anew each time. This strategy, of course, makes perfect sense in

view of the evidence that small children are, more than anyone, handicapped by short-term processing limitations. . . . Thus we find children adopting stereotyped expressions that are neither copied directly from nor even directly reduced from adult usage, giving evidence that some sort of construction process may have gone on before the expression became frozen. (p. 82)

It will not always be clear that a string has been fused, particularly if it conforms with a mature rule. Sometimes, however, the internal construction of the string will reflect an earlier stage in the child's progressing grammatical knowledge. Repeated use can also be an indication of fusedness, though a frequent string could also be being created afresh on each occasion.

Fused forms, because they are holistic in nature, require little processing attention, compared with novel constructions, and seem to be saving precious processing space. Clark's (1974) son Adam possessed a fused utterance *My shoes on a polish*, which he was able to correct to *Polish on my shoes* when prompted. However, he was unable to retain this new form when adding the word *brown*, and said *My shoes on a brown polish*. Clark says of this: "The utterance *Brown polish on my shoes* would not have been any longer than the one he actually produced. It seems that only well-practised sequences can be interrupted and that new, unfamiliar ones have to be practised as integral sequences before they can be modified in any way" (pp. 8–9).

Underanalyzed Strings

Cruttenden's (1981) example of *cup of tea* (discussed earlier) can be termed an 'underanalyzed string'.[2] Underanalyzed strings are sequences of words or morphemes which the adult understands to have a more complex structure than the child does. Characteristically, they display grammatical and/or lexical knowledge beyond the child's current generative capacities, and the meaning may have been misconstrued. For example, one child, Ellen, aged one year and nine months, used the string ['taipə'kɒpə'kɒpɪ] when she wanted a biscuit. Her mother often said *time for a cup of coffee* when she wanted to sit down for a few minutes peace and quiet. The children would each get a biscuit. Whatever Ellen actually thought *time for a cup of coffee* meant, saying it was a very effective way of requesting a biscuit, no doubt in part because it is less direct than *please may I have a biscuit*, and hence rather cute.

Not all underanalyzed strings are drawn from the child's lexicon. Some are simply immediate imitations of material just heard. Clark (1974:3–4) offers the following examples:

Mother: We're all very mucky.
Child: I all very mucky too.

Mother: That's upside down. (Child is putting on his coat the wrong way round.)
Child: No, I want to upside down.

In cases of imitation, unless the string is deemed useful enough to store subsequently, the usage is an isolated event with no linguistic consequences. For a discussion of the wider range of functions which imitation and repetition may play in child language, see Keenan (1977).

Some underanalyzed strings, on the other hand, are specifically memorized, as opposed to just picked up, and they play a particular role in the linguistic behaviour of the child and its carers. Two major types of such string are rhymes, songs and chants, and socializing institutionalized routines.

Memorized rhymes, songs and chants. When young children learn songs, rhymes, chants and prayers, they do not take an analytic approach. Rather than identifying the individual words of a song, say, and associating each with a note in the tune, they learn the sounds of the words along with the contours of the tune, relying on the strong beats of the music, just as they rely on the strong beats of speech (Gleitman, Gleitman, Landau & Wanner 1988:155–156; Wijnen, Krikhaar & Den Os 1994). Often, consonants and weak syllables are omitted, and words are distorted in a way that strongly suggests that the child has not actually identified them as being the same as words which they know perfectly well in speech. For example, Ellen,[3] at the age of three years and seven weeks, gave the following rendering of *Baa Baa Black Sheep*:

[ba̤ ṳa la ʃiːp̚ havəːɣ̊ ɛni jɛːl   *Baa baa black sheep have you any*
                                            wool?
jɛː ᶿsəː jɛː səː fɹiː ba fʌːl   *Yes sir yes sir three bags full.*
wʌm fɒdə maːstə wʌm fɒdə deː   *One for the master, one for the dame*
wɒm fɔːˈdɛ lɪtʊʰ‿bɔɪ lɛθs dɑːˈnɪ leː]   *One for the little boy (who) lives down*
                                            the lane.

According to her mother, Ellen did not know the words *dame* and *lane*, but she certainly did know *wool*, *bags*, and *lives*. Yet in the context of this song, they are not pronounced in a way that suggests she has realized what they are. However, Ellen did not always tolerate nonsense syllables in her songs, and would also use her immature linguistic and pragmatic knowledge for a post hoc analysis, making guesses about what the words ought to be. For instance, she had in her repertoire, at the same age, the Christmas hymn *Away in a Manger*. Here, too, Ellen's inaccuracies are at the ends of words and in unstressed syllables:

Away in a manger, no crisp for a bear.	*Away in a manger, no crib for a bed,*
The little Lord Jesus lay down on his hair.	*The little Lord Jesus lay down his sweet head.*

In memorizing texts as sequences of sounds, without, in the first instance at least, many words identified, it seems that children are deprioritizing analysis. They are, of course, routinely exposed to material that contains words and structures they could not possibly know (British children often learn *Frère Jacques* in nursery school), and they probably never really assume that they will understand it. As Locke (1993) points out, regarding input more generally:

Much of what the linguistically naive child hears each day must not make particular sense and cannot, given the lack of world knowledge enjoyed by three-year-olds. 'Does it make sense?' may not be among the questions that young children particularly concern themselves with. (p. 361)

In the case of songs and rhymes, having realized that the most important thing to do is reproduce the material as closely as possible to the original, the child may even fail to perceive it as message-carrying at all, or, at least, may consider the message incidental to the purpose of the learning. In this respect, the child is right, of course. Songs and nursery rhymes do not convey information that is either novel or situationally relevant, and you do not perform them in order to convey such information. All in all, the manner of the child's learning seems to reflect the purpose that the item is perceived to have. Of course, some rhymes and chants do convey information. Although not situationally or socially apposite, memorized strings such as counting, the alphabet, the days of the week, the months of the year and, later, times tables and rhymes like *Thirty days hath September*, play a useful role as mnemonics. Although first learnt like any other song or rhyme, they certainly do need to be available to internal scrutiny in the end, as they make available information that might otherwise be difficult to recall at will (see Chapter 4).

Institutionalized routines. Not unrelated to rhymes and songs is another kind of memorized string, the institutionalized routine. These are set phrases used in certain situations in order to perform rituals. There are many of these in the adult language, and those which children first encounter are often the ones that reflect good manners: *please, thank you, goodbye, goodnight, thank you for having me, please may I leave the table*, and so on. They are the 'magic words' used by the adult to demonstrate that they have a socialized child (Gleason 1980). They are an acknowledgement of the power relationship between adult and child and help the child to learn socially acceptable ways of operating in an adult environment. Children seem slow to acquire politeness forms spontaneously (Gleason 1980:26), so routines are often explicitly taught to the child. Thus, characteristically, the adult talks *about* the utterance: *don't forget to say X, did you say Y?* (Gleason & Weintraub 1976). Ely and Gleason (1995:252) quote the following example of this from Gleason's earlier work:

Child: Mommy, I want more milk.
Mother: Is that the way to ask?
Child: Please.
Mother: Please what?
Child: Please gimme milky.
Mother: No.
Child: Please gimme milk.
Mother: No.
Child: Please. . . .
Mother: Please, may I have more milk?
Child: Please, may I have more milk?

Such parental behaviour signals that there is a significance not just to *what* you say, but *how* you say it. This, in turn, alerts the child that, as with the rhymes and songs, some strings are not to be broken down, but simply remembered whole and produced at the right time, in order to achieve a speech act. Saying a routine incorrectly can be counted as a failure, even when the intention is clear, for only the permitted expressions are considered appropriate within the speaker culture.

Gestalt Language

Underanalyzed strings have formed the focus of a particular line of research into child language acquisition, where they are referred to as *gestalt* utterances. Peters's (1977) research led her to propose that certain stages of first language acquisition can be approached in either a holistic (gestalt) or an inferential (analytic) way, and that children vary in the balance they adopt between these two. She envisaged

a continuum of children, varying from those who are very Analytic right from the beginning, through those who use mixes of Analytic and Gestalt speech in varying proportions, to those who may start out with a completely Gestalt approach and have to convert slowly and painfully to a more Analytic approach to language. (Peters 1983:571)

Being underanalyzed, gestalt utterances contain material well in advance of the child's grammatical knowledge, and are delivered in a way that could easily be construed as precocious. They are "produced without pauses between words, with reduced phonemic articulation, and with the effect of slurred or mumbled speech but with a clear intonation pattern enabling the listener to construct the target utterance *in context*" (Nelson 1981:174).

Peters developed her insights while engaged in examining the acquisition process in a young boy called Minh. She expected to find him using individual words in one- and two-word utterances, much as Brown (1973) had in his subjects, Adam, Eve and Sarah. Although Minh did learn some isolated words, she soon encountered problems when analyzing his speech. His linguistic behaviour was different from what she had anticipated, to the extent that "notions such as 'word' and 'syntax' were called into serious question" (Peters 1983:ix):

I began to realize that perhaps I had missed so much of what Minh said because it was in an unexpected form. Perhaps I had expected approximations to *words*, but he had given me approximations to *sentences*. . . . In retrospect, I think that a large proportion of Minh's speech was aimed at the production of whole sentences rather than at the more classical one-word, two-word, or three-word targets. (Peters 1977:565–566)

Minh's language led Peters to question the standard paradigm in first language acquisition research, that children always perceive language as arrangements of discrete word-size units. The strategy Minh appears to have adopted, was to "approximate the general gestalt of his target sentence, aiming at such features as number of syllables, intonation (including contours of both pitch and amplitude), as well as certain key segments" (p. 566):

[n̥ hn̥ dʌ́nɪ mímɪ bíbm̥ dǽdi]   *There is ? mema baby daddy (?)* (16½ months)
– – – – – – – –

[bʌ wḷ wi dɛʰ]   *What will we do (?)* (19 months)
–   – – \
(Peters 1977:567)

As we saw earlier in Ellen's speech, the characteristic phonological imprecision of gestalt language is probably a reflection of the child's lack of knowledge about the internal structure of what he or she is saying. Minh's utterances contained

filler syllables which seemed to be used as place-holders to fill out not yet analysed parts of a phrase. . . . The fixed parts were reproduced faithfully; but the variable parts seemed to be less well analysed and were represented by place-holders. (p. 564)

Fillers are also noted by Tomasello (1992:233), and bear comparison with the 'dummy fillers' that feature in aphasia (see Chapter 12). Another explanation for the laxity in pronunciation could be that it is an effect of the desire for fluency (Clark 1974). As Plunkett (1993) points out, there is a tension between fluency and phonological accuracy: "under conditions which require precisely articulated speech, fluency tends to deteriorate, whilst articulation deteriorates when high fluency is demanded" (p. 46).

The 'unit' of acquisition. Peters (1983) accommodates the analytic and holistic strategies by suggesting that all children operate consistently with *units*, but that different children, and the same children at different stages, define the 'unit' differently in relation to the adult target.[4] Long strings that the child may produce as a single unit are, says Peters, compatible with the 'one-word stage' if one simply relabels it the 'one-unit stage'. "Since the child does not know the language, it is unreasonable to assume that the first units she or he extracts will coincide exactly with the words and morphemes of the system" (p. 5). Formulae are just a part of the lexicon, "for there is no evidence that what the linguist recognizes as unanalyzed routines are recognized and stored by the child any differently from items that we would call single words. . . . Reproducing a routine is in no way different from reproducing any other single item from the lexicon" (p. 15).

Children may overestimate the size of the units, homing in on multi-word strings, or underestimate it, choosing sublexical items (Plunkett 1993). This is not a problem if we assume that "young children come equipped to move in either direction – part to whole or whole to parts. . . . All children probably use both processes to some extent in different aspects of language acquisition" (Tomasello & Brooks 1999:166). Because the size of the unit can vary, some children will appear to be more advanced than others when, in actual fact, they are all subject to a "cognitive limitation constraining the child to processing (e.g., extracting and producing) what to the child is one unit at a time" (Peters 1983:5). It is important, then, to count the units, not the words, if one is to gauge the true developmental level of the child.

'Analytic' children, probably stimulated by a tendency in their carers to offer single-word prompts, and/or to exaggerate the prosodic contours of their utterances (Nelson 1981:80; Plunkett 1993:59; Poulin-Dubois, Graham & Sippola 1995), focus on word-sized chunks very quickly, using these as the building blocks for their grammar. Meanwhile, 'gestalt' children, perhaps encouraged by carer acceptance of, and comprehension of, their rough phonology (Peters 1977:570–571) and/or the carer's own "high . . . proportion of articulatorily imprecise expressions" (Plunkett 1993:58) favour longer sequences, which they will then have to break down. The production of lengthy strings with a whole-utterance meaning naturally corresponds with a comprehension strategy whereby the child derives a general meaning using pragmatics and context, without possessing the linguistic knowledge to discern the subtle precise meaning (Gelman & Shatz 1977:59; Golinkoff & Hirsh-Pasek 1995:430).

Isolation and segmentation. All children can be assumed ultimately to learn analytic techniques for language processing, and, for this to be possible, "a child must segment the speech he hears into morphemes because morphemes are the ultimate units of grammatical rules" (Brown 1973:390). A crucial insight for the child is that things have names (referentiality) (Bates, Bretherton & Snyder 1988:261–262; Kamhi 1986). The route by which the child arrives at an active lexicon of words and morphemes will depend on the size of the unit it has been working with. Analytic children *isolate* identifiable minimal units such as words and morphemes, usually beginning with nouns,[5] and then, using these as knowns, pinpointing verb meanings (Hirsh-Pasek & Golinkoff 1996:123ff). Gestalt children may reach the word or morpheme level only after identifying a series of shorter but still internally complex sequences, so that the approach can be characterized as one of *segmentation* (Peters 1983:35). Peters describes in some detail how the process of segmentation occurs, particularly with regard to the identification of possible boundaries between units. Segmentation will be supported if (a) there is a convergence of phonologically based cues including the salience of the last, first and stressed syllables, and rhythmic and intonational pointers; (b) the string has been encountered frequently; (c) "a clear meaning can be associated with a particular sub-unit resulting from a segmentation" (p. 41); (d) producing the segment does not result in being misunderstood, ignored or laughed at (p. 42). If a hypothesized segment fares badly in these evaluations, then it is likely to be discarded and the larger string reanalyzed. Peters illustrates the process with an anecdote in which a four-year-old is told to behave and later says "I'm /heyv/" several times. She is misunderstood as having said that she hates someone. After two exchanges of this type she reanalyzes and says "I am *behaving*" (Peters 1983:43). Despite the claims from research on gestalt language, however, there has been much dispute about whether multi-word chunks are actually analyzed at all. We shall review this debate presently.

Referentiality and Expressiveness

One explanation for the contrast between the analytic and gestalt approaches to acquisition is that they reflect different cognitive styles. In her longitudinal study of 18 children aged 12 to 36 months, Nelson (1973, 1975) identified two such styles: *referential* and *expressive*.[6] This referential-expressive distinction relates to the child's use of language either primarily to talk about things or else to achieve interactional functions, as Lieven (1978) nicely illustrates, comparing Kate, a 'referential' child, and Beth, an 'expressive' child:

> These two children appeared to be using language for different ends. Kate talked slowly and coherently about things happening around her and objects in her environment, while Beth devoted more time to using her speech to try and engage her mother's interest. (p. 178)

Referentiality requires individual word labels for objects (Nelson 1973, 1975; Lieven, Pine & Barnes 1992) and is thus supported by an analytic approach to language. Expressiveness, on the other hand, requires a command of longer strings with an associated function, and a means of successfully delivering them well before they could be constructed from scratch by the child's grammar. The expressive cognitive style, therefore, is best supported by the gestalt approach. As this would predict, while referential children possess a vocabulary of mostly nouns, and very little command of morphology, expressive children produce with equal ease, within formulaic sequences, nouns, verbs, adjectives and pronouns, as well as correct affixes. As a result, they can appear to have a more sophisticated knowledge of the language than they actually have. Bretherton, McNew, Snyder and Bates (1983), who studied 30 children aged 20 months, found that "early use of grammatical morphemes is linked to learning whole phrases" (p. 312), and does not signify real knowledge of the grammar.[7] These early differences in approach could have long-term effects. For example, Nelson (1981) suggests that they could lead to the establishment of "different rule systems" (p. 172) for the language. They could also manifest later in life in approaches to second language learning (Peters 1977) and/or in the natural level of context dependency applied in everyday speech.[8]

A child's preference for a referential and analytic, or else for an expressive and holistic, style might be determined by internal factors relating to personality, neural organization or early nonlinguistic experience:

> One child may have a well-developed faculty for memorizing strings with detailed phonology, whereas another child may make greater use of a faculty for

analyzing these same strings into their component parts. Differences in the patterns of development between these two children can then be seen as a reflection of differential use of these basic faculties. (Bates & MacWhinney 1987:159)

Nelson (1981) suggests that the difference may lie in "what the child prefer[s] to talk about. In turn, what the child talks *about* has implications for *how* he or she talks – that is, the forms used" (p. 177). Alternatively, the differences between children could be a result of linguistic input. According to Nelson (1973, 1975, 1981), the referential child may be responding to its carers' use of language as a tool for labelling the world, as manifested in pointing and naming games. In contrast, the expressive child, she suggests, has experienced language primarily as a means of social control:

Social-control language ... is likely to be heard in clumps that are not easily broken up; for example: 'D'ya wanna go out?', 'I dunno where it is', 'Stop it'. Segmentation of such sequences is difficult but the tune, as Peters (1977) would say, is easy to learn. (Nelson 1981:181)

Lieven (1978) concurs with Nelson's view, explaining the linguistic behaviour of Kate and Beth (discussed earlier) in terms of "features of the mother's own speech" (Lieven 1978:178). She notes that the referential child (Kate) received twice as many responses to her utterances, and these responses were often questions. The expressive child (Beth) received a response to fewer than half her utterances and these were often formulaic ones or comments that ignored what the child had said.

Lieven et al. (1992) reiterate the importance of understanding the function when examining the form of an utterance. They point out that a child may use nouns to manipulate people as well as to refer to things (p. 289) and that, in the early stages, "most language used by children ... is highly social", including the nouns used by referential children (p. 292). Lieven et al. attempt to tease out fundamental conflicts between the referential/expressive and the single-word/multiword oppositions and seek a means of demonstrating the true nature of their relationship. They conclude that "the proportion of frozen phrases acquired by the child in the first and second 50 words is a good candidate for a positive defining feature of non-referential style" (p. 304). This in turn forges a link between formulaic language and the preference for pronominal forms, because pronouns are associated with the expressive style (Bloom, Lightbown & Hood 1975:34; Bretherton et al. 1983). The use of pronouns in preference to nouns requires a different level of semantic analysis and categorization (Bloom et al. 1975; Nelson 1981:173), and, as it entails less learning of individual words, there tends to be a smaller overall vocabulary size relative to referential children with the same mean length of utterance (Nelson 1981). This association of formulaicity and pronominal reference reappears in the hypothesis that during human evolution, there may have been a prolonged stage of entirely formulaic, nonreferential protolanguage, with no individual words, and generalized reference-in-context at the equivalent of the pronoun level (Wray 1998, 2000a, in press).

Bias in the sample. The link between gestalt language and an expressive cognitive style, and between analytic language and a referential style, offers an explanation for why research has often failed to recognize a significant role for formulaic language in first language acquisition. Peters (1977) points out that, for circumstantial reasons, research has favoured the study of analytic children over gestalt ones. One key aspect of this is that it is often the first child in the family that has been studied – Adam, Eve and Sarah in Brown's (1973) study and Nigel in Halliday's (1975) were all first children – and the first child tends to adopt the analytic style in acquisition. This is because a first child is the most likely to receive predominantly referential input, as a great deal of carer attention is directed towards it in that vital early period. Children with older siblings are more likely to adopt an expressive style, because a sizeable proportion of the language that they witness is interaction between the mother and the other children, such as directives and requests (Nelson 1981:181). This sort of language (e.g., *take your shoes off; I told you not to X; I won't ask you again*, etc.) recurs often, is consistent in form and is highly contextualized, aiding understanding in the younger on-looker. As a result, children with older siblings will be more likely than first children to perceive language as a social tool that comes in large chunks (Nelson 1981:173, 180; but see also Bretherton et al. 1983, who failed to find a birth order effect in their study). Bates et al. (1995) suggest that gender may also be significant, the analytic style being associated with girls and the holistic with boys (pp. 122–123).

Peters and Nelson have also both pointed out that, for the same reasons of expediency, the children described in detailed case studies tend to belong to well-educated, middle-class families (see also Lieven et al. 1992), often being the child of the investigator him- or herself (Peters 1977:561). This fact is significant, as parental level of education appears to correlate with referentiality. Bates et al. (1994) studied the vocabulary development of 1,803 children, and found significant correlations between the percentage of common nouns (indicative of referentiality) and maternal and paternal education, paternal occupation and birth order (pp. 111–112). Although they are cautious about reading too much into these (pp. 112 fn.2), even a slight effect would be magnified by a substantial bias against the study of children from educationally impoverished backgrounds.

Finally, the tendency for gestalt children to speak in lengthy utterances that are phonologically indistinct has also made them less popular for study. Clear enunciation makes data analysis much easier. Brown (1973) states that one reason why Adam, Eve and Sarah were selected was "because they . . . had highly intelligible speech" (p. 51). According to Peters (1977), until her own study, researchers tended to assume that beneath the unclear speech of one child lay the same process of acquisition as beneath the clear speech of another, so that the former was not worth the extra effort needed in transcription. They had not realized that a lack of clarity was symptomatic of an entirely different approach to acquisition (p. 561).

Summary

We have seen that the early language of children features formulaic sequences of various kinds. Some are the child's own fused constructions, presumably helping reduce the demands of processing. Others appear to reflect the child's attempts to reproduce complex utterances heard from the mouths of carers, before there is the grammar or lexis to construct them as novel compositions. These gestalt utterances can be found in the output of most children, but in some it is limited to songs, rhymes, a few early simple greetings and the like, while in other children the gestalt style characterizes a great deal of what they say. It seems that the child's understanding of what language (in general, or in a specific instance) is for, can play a role in determining the approach that is taken to learning. A referential function (as in naming activities) seems more likely to encourage the isolation of individual words, whereas language that is used largely for expressive purposes, to effect interactional goals (e.g., directives, requests) or for social reasons, is more likely to be learned whole. Here, the child focusses on the strongly stressed syllables, the rhythm and intonational cadences, skimming over the other sounds or holding their place with phonologically indeterminate fillers. Where a string has actually been presented to the child as formulaic (e.g., rhymes, songs, institutionalized routines), something about its form or purpose indicates this formulaicity, so that isolation and segmentation are less likely to occur, even in those children who are normally analytic.

The Functions of Formulaic Sequences

In this section we shall review the functions of formulaic sequences in child language. In Chapter 5 it was proposed that all formulaic sequences are serving a single purpose, that of supporting the speaker in the promotion of self. We predicted that, in data from different speaker types, the distribution of the forms and functions associated with formulaic sequences would reflect contrasts in speaker priorities, and the availability of other linguistic and nonlinguistic options for meeting them. We shall test that prediction here. One major difference between the agenda of the child and the adult is the need to acquire the language. We shall look for evidence of how formulaic sequences support this process in ways consistent with our existing model.

Formulaic Sequences and Early Interaction

Children seem to be innately predisposed to communicate,[9] and as they are so physically dependent on their caretakers, the successful communication of their survival needs is imperative (Bruner 1983:26–27).[10] Even before the child can really talk, imitative formulaic sequences are produced as one of several solutions to the problem of communicating these needs; the others include reaching and other gestures, facial expressions and nonspecific vocal noises with a recognizable L1 intonation pattern (Foster 1990:15ff, 46ff; Locke 1997:269). As the child develops more phonological control, the storage and reproduction of material which cannot yet be grammatically analyzed is put to the dual purposes of physically manipulating others,[11] and supporting the process of social integration. According to Halliday (1975), from an early age the child "uses his voice to order people about, to get them to do things for him; he uses it to demand certain objects or services; he uses it to make contact with people, to feel close to them" (p. 11).

Rhymes and songs are learned, and joining in with these is a clear signal of identity with the carers who have taught them. It is a function which they continue to have for many years (Opie & Opie 1959:17). Similarly, the first institutionalized routines, such as *thank you* and *bye-bye*, set up significant social signals of the child's compliance with the expectations of the adult world. In contrast, at this time "the use of language in the sense of 'I've got something to tell you', which tends to obsess adults . . . is irrelevant to a small child; it has no direct social meaning" (Halliday 1975:64). As this observation would predict, Peters (1977) found that Minh's gestalt utterances tended to be used less for referential purposes than manipulative and social ones: "opening conversations/summonses (*What's that?; Uh-oh!; Mommy!*), playing with his brother (*Airplane go up*), requesting (rather than demanding) something (*I want milk*), and discussing objects sociably (rather than naming them) (*Silly, isn't it?*)" (Peters 1977:566).

We shall see in Chapter 12 that not all formulaic sequences are long and internally complex, and that it is a characteristic of the aphasic, whose range of output material is restricted, that a small word can be used to carry a large range of contrasting messages. The child, too, has more to say than there are always means of saying it, and, as in aphasia, an item which commonly takes on the role of *dummy filler* (see Chapter 12) is *no*, a word that is one of earliest learned by the child (Critchley 1970:372–373; Tager-Flusberg 1994:1921). The dialogue in Figure 6.1 illustrates how *no* can carry a huge range of intonation patterns and voice qualities,[12] while its use cannot be characterized in terms of a single specific meaning (Crystal 1997:245; McNeill & McNeill 1973).

Formulaic Sequences As a Processing Shortcut and Acquisitional Aid

The child will never be able to articulate all its needs, nor fully signal its identity, until it masters the linguistic system. Formulaic language appears to provide a means of supporting this process. In the earliest stages it "gives infants a set of 'starter' utterances that can be used appropriately in restricted contexts, and provides infants with the opportunity to participate in adultlike social interactions" (Locke 1997:273). Children can get the linguistic ball rolling, stepping onto the field and playing the adult language game, and presenting themselves as native speakers before they are vexed with lexical searches and rule applications. Formulaic sequences make available grammatical structures for which the rules are not yet formed, and "allow children to say more and more completely what they mean than they would if they had to construct an utterance from scratch" (Nelson 1981:181–182). As the child gets older, its developing grammar and lexicon opens up the possibility of novel expression. But the formulation of utterances is labour intensive. The child therefore finds it advantageous to fuse strings for use on subsequent occasions. The main function of drawing on fused sequences is the retention of fluency, since preassembled phrases or clauses can contribute to output for very little effort.

Because they anticipate the child's future grammatical capabilities, formulaic sequences are believed by some also to play a direct role in helping the child to learn the new forms. Proponents of this view see imitated strings as a valuable resource for raw material that feeds the

Conversation between Jane (mother) and
Hannah (age two years and two weeks).

J: Do you want those raisins yet?
H: No. No [nːɜːᵘ] \   [nːɔ] \
J: You don't.
H: No [nəʊɪ] \
J: Are you not hungry?
H: No. [nɪᵑⁿnːˀ] – ⁻ \   I want a cuddle
    [ɔŋːˈkʌdʊː] _ \
J: You want a cuddle?
H: Yes [jɛ̠] ∨
J: Come on then, I'll give you a cuddle. Do you
like big cuddles?
H: No [nɜː] \
J: Come here. Come on. A big cuddle. Ah. (Pats
her back). Better?
H: No [nəʊ] \
J: It's not. Do you need another one. Do you need
another cuddle
H: No [nᵘⁿnɔɜː] ↑∧ __
J: You don't. Do you love mummy
H: Um [ˈɑʊm] \
J: No? Do you love Harry
H: Ah [ɔˀ] \
J: Ah, poor Harry. He wouldn't like that, would he,
if he heard you saying that.
H: No [nɜːˀʊ] ⁻ \
J: I wonder where your brother is. He's been asleep
a long time hasn't he
H: No [nˆˀɜʊ] ∧
J: Poor Harry
H: No [nːɔ̠] \
J: Do you want your dolly?
H: No. De de [naːɪ] \ [dˢœ dˢœ] ⁻ –
J: Ah. Is she sad, your dolly.
H: No [nɪɪˀɔʊ] \
J: Is she going to cry
H: No [nːˀʊ̠ⁿ] \
J: You going to get her a ... (doll cries) hhhh. Oh
no. Shall I get her bottle?
H: No [ˈnːːɜ̠ː] ∧ __
J: Shall I get her bottle.
H: No [nːːˀɔ] \
J: Let's turn her off then. She makes far too much
noise. (Doll stops crying) She sounds like Harry,
doesn't she
H: No [nʲˀᵃʊ̠] \
J: All you've said is no. How about saying yes
H: No [nʌ̠] ⁻ \
J: (laughs) (***) Look stop it
H: No [nʊ̠ⁿ] ∨

J: What's what's in my.. mummy's hand. What's
that. Is that two pence?
H: No [nːɜʊ] ⁻ \
J: There's another one on the floor down there. Can
you see it. You going to get it
H: No [nˆɔ] \
J: Put it in your till. Harry'll get it. We don't want
Harry to get it do we
H: No [nɔːʊɪ] \
J: Well we'd better pick it up then and put it in
your till. Otherwise he'll put it in his mouth and
he's far too little
H: No [nʌʊɪ] ∨
J: Come on pick it up for Mummy. Shall mummy
do it. There we go
H: No No [nʌʊ] ↑\ [nɪɪˀɔʊɪ] ⁻ ↑ \
J: This is five pence.
H: No [nɜʊ] ∨
J: Do you want to buy some sweeties with that?
H: (Silence)
J: Do you
H: No [nɔʊu] \
J: You don't want any sweeties? I can't believe that
H: Uh Uh [ɜː] ⁻ [ɜːː] ↑ \
J: Shall we go to the shops. Yes
H: Yes [ᶦsˢ] ⁻
J: Would you like to go with Sally, and David?
H: Yes [jɛːs] ⁻
J: You would
H: Yes [jɛːs] ⁻
J: What about Harry
H: Yes [jɛʰˢ] ╱
J: Shall Harry come with us
H: Yes [jʌsʲ] ╱
J: What are we going to buy
H: No [nʌʊ] \
J: What would you like to buy at the shops
H: No [nʌʊu] ↑ \
J: You wouldn't like to go now
H: No [nʌʊˀ] ∧
J: You've changed your mind
H: No [nᵃʌːʉ] ⁻\

Transcribed from *Tuning in to Children* (BBC
Radio 4, 22.2.99) and printed here by permission
of Jane Soilleux.

H's utterances are followed by a phonetic
transcription in square brackets and then by an
indication of the intonation contour.

Figure 6.1. Uses of *no* in a two year old.

analytic process (e.g., Bloom, Hood & Lightbown 1978; Locke 1997:273; Snow 1981). They "may provide the child with templates, which, although initially unanalysed, have the potential for further subsequent analysis and conversion into lexically-based patterns" (Lieven et al. 1992:307). Because they are stored in memory, the child is able to access them at will, thereby gains the opportunity to hear the same material as often as necessary for analysis to take place, and is freed from a dependency on getting relevant, good quality input at just the right time (Clark 1974; Hickey 1993). The analysis of material beyond the current capabilities of the child is made possible because the meaning of the input is construed from context, at discourse level, and this provides a semantic lever by which the grammatical constituents can be identified (Clark 1974; Peters 1995). The processes of isolation and segmentation (described earlier) appear to be aided by prosodic cues (Gerken 1996; Tager-Flusberg 1994:1919) and by meaning (Peters 1995:463). "Even before infants understand the semantics of sentences – let alone their syntactic composition – they reveal an ability to locate the acoustic correlates of phrasal and clausal units" (Golinkoff & Hirsh-Pasek 1995:439). Christophe et al. (1997) propose that the child becomes accustomed to recognizing function words and uses them as a cue to phrase bound-aries.[13] They can then be stripped off, leaving the content word (p. 596). Locke (1997:274–275) makes a similar suggestion in his explanation of how the lexicon continues to grow after analysis has begun.

Whatever the precise mechanisms, prosody and semantics certainly seem to combine to support a process of pattern observation: "[The child] will begin to extract the system when he recognizes some part of the item being used in another utterance ... or the whole item being used in different situations or with different references" (Cruttenden 1981:87). In this way, "gradually, in the process of acquiring other chunks with similar syntactic patterning ... the child detaches the pattern from its connection in context, and analyzes and generalizes it into regular syntactic rules" (Nattinger & DeCarrico 1992:12). Burling's (1978) child subject, Stephen,[14] bears witness to this process:

In learning [a construction], he apparently always used the construction first in certain specific examples which he learned as a whole and by rote. After using several of these for a while, he would learn to generalize on the construction, and to substitute different morphemes or words in the same construction. (p. 67)

Weir (1962) provides some of the clearest evidence of formulaic sequences employed to an analytic end, and of the process by which this occurs. Over a period of two months, she recorded her son Anthony (age 2;4 to 2;6) when he was alone in his cot. While such output could be construed as simple play, Weir identifies a clear learning agenda: "the pleasure of play is structured so that it serves as a linguistic exercise . . . so that at times we have the feeling of listening in on a foreign language lesson with extensive pattern practice" (pp. 144–145). She recognizes specific analytic strategies too:

the exploration of combinatory possibilities . . . based on . . . grammatical parallelism. . . . The paradigmatic use of nouns as substitution items is more pronounced than that of any other form class. With verbs, grammatical markers are more frequently selected as the items to be changed in a pattern, be it the *-ing* form or the past alternating with the unmarked form. (p. 145)

However, Anthony clearly perceived language not as an abstract system to be learnt, but as a medium of interpersonal exchange: "he becomes his own interlocutor . . . he asks a question and provides the answer, he performs a linguistic task and commends himself on the accomplishment, he produces a linguistic event and explicitly corrects himself" (p. 146).

But not everyone agrees that formulaic sequences play a role in the actual acquisitional process. Bates et al. (1988) and Tager-Flusberg and Calkins (1990) view them as useful communicational fillers, but otherwise a linguistic 'dead end'. Once the child is capable of its own grammar, the communicational strategy is discarded in favour of the construction by rule of tailor-made utterances. Others, such as Plunkett (1993), identify them as the temporary product of erroneous segmentation. Once the word can be reliably isolated and combined, formulaic and sublexical units are no longer relevant, and they atrophy (p. 57). Brown and Hanlon (1970) and Bates et al. (1988) find support for the dead-end view in their observation that formulaic sequences often persist well after the mastering of the rules they have purportedly spawned. However, Lieven et al. (1992) challenge the position. They found that the use of frozen phrases correlated positively with general productivity. In general terms, the dead-end view makes more sense in the case of children whose style is to isolate small units and use them to build up simple, and then more complex, strings, than it is for gestalt children, who clearly make considerable use of lengthy, underanalyzed strings for some time. It is also more plausible in the context of imitated sequences (e.g., Tager-Flusberg & Calkins 1990) than some of the other types. However, as we shall see in Chapter 7, it may not be necessary to take either position in the extreme in any case. It will be proposed that prefabricated strings *can* be analyzed, but only are on a piecemeal basis, and often not at all. This position makes it possible to accommodate both Brown and Hanlon's and Lieven et al.'s findings.

Interpreting the Patterns

As with adult native speakers (Chapter 4), on the surface, the various explanations of the role of formulaic sequences appear to be contradictory, and the evidence seems incompatible. However, that is only the case if all formulaic sequences are expected to be of the same kind and to exist for the same reasons. In Chapter 5, it was proposed that formulaic sequences are a dynamic response to processing and interactional needs, and from this viewpoint we should not be surprised to find that some fulfil one function and some another, and that some appear only for a short time while others become a permanent feature in a speaker's vocabulary.

What Happens to Formulaic Sequences

Figure 6.2 sets out possible fates for the child's various types of sequence, both formulaic and nonformulaic, as described by the account so far. Analytic language derives from early (primitive) and late (adultlike) rules. Utterances created using the former will not be found in the language of the child in later life (represented by "Adult language" at the bottom of the diagram), while the adultlike rules will determine the adult patterns of novel language production. Of the holistic utterances created by the child, those which are the result of fusion will only persist into the adult language if they are a product of the adultlike (late) rules. Gestalt utterances, that is, strings which are reproduced whole, independently of

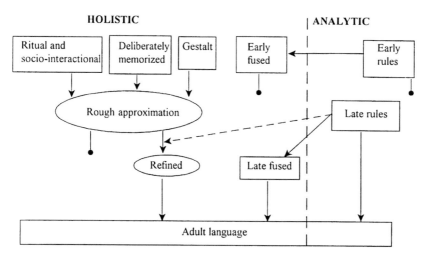

Figure 6.2. Predicted fate of different types of analytic and holistic language.

any knowledge of the internal composition, will not survive into adulthood unless they are refined from their initial 'rough' form, which contains phonological approximations and fillers where components are underspecified. The refining process can, but need not, involve the analytic rules in clarifying constituents. Other products of holistic processing will survive into the adult language, assuming they continue to have a function. More specifically, the underanalyzed strings that fail to undergo 'refinement' and are discarded rather than entering the adult inventory will be the ones which meet only a temporary need, such as compensating for the limitations of the early grammar, or expressing a need or desire which is subsequently met in other ways (such as by means of actions previously beyond the child's capability). Overall, the inventory will alter in a way that reflects the changing nature of needs as the child gets older, the changing expectations of others about how these needs are acceptably expressed, and the greater or lesser availability of alternative solutions.

In themselves, such predictions are of limited value, since the classification of a string is not fully independent of the theoretical perspective from which it is viewed. What is important, however, is that the different forms and functions of formulaic sequences do not all submit to a single fate. Some are a means to an end, others are the first of a large collection of adult formulae. This variation in what happens to formulaic sequences will be of central importance in the next chapter, when we consider how lexical development should be modelled.

The Child's Experience

Figure 6.3 represents an attempt to draw together the important features of the preceding discussion, by identifying the relationships between analytic and holistic processing, the range of functions which language must subserve in the young child (cf. Halliday 1975), and the types of utterance which we know feature strongly in the child's output. The figure focusses on the linguistic responses of the child to its most pressing agendas, but some nonlinguistic solutions are also included: crying, smiling, imitating, gesturing, and so on. Four basic agendas are identified, three of which correspond to aspects of communication and social interaction, and the fourth of which covers the acquisition of the grammar and lexicon.

Get things done relates to the child's need to manipulate people in order to achieve goals that cannot be achieved personally. These include being fed, emotionally and physically comforted, and amused. Many of

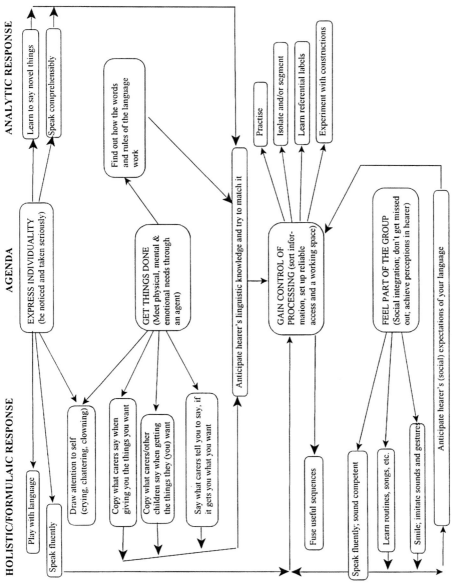

Figure 6.3. Agendas and responses of the young child.

125

the things which the child needs are part of a daily routine and have typical words or phrases attached to them. This agenda invites a variety of holistic responses. Children soon become aware that there is more to successful interaction than just being understood. They have to tune into the social context of linguistic expressions, creating a mental model of where they fit into a complex set of relationships and hierarchies (Ochs & Schiefflin 1995). Conforming with these external pressures is expedient for the child in achieving its goals.

However, as the child will be unable fully to express its needs until it can create novel utterances, there is also an impetus to learn the words and rules of the language, an analytic response. Because *Get things done* relies entirely on the correct interpretation of the message by the agent of the action, the child must prioritize anticipating what the hearer will understand (see Chapter 4). We are well accustomed to the idea of downwards accommodation, whereby carers adjust their output to help children understand what they are saying (Snow 1978, 1979),[15] but Figure 6.3 shows how the process of accommodation must also operate upwards, and depicts this as a significant stimulus for acquiring the language system. This is consistent with the child's earlier vocal accommodation at the prelexical stage (e.g., Locke 1995:290–291).

In this way, *Get things done* spawns a secondary response, *Anticipate the hearer's linguistic knowledge and try to match it*, and this, in turn, supports the agenda *Gain control of processing*. The latter arises from the need to convey novel messages to the agent, as just described, and, specifically, to master the mechanics of the language. This agenda also includes finding ways to minimize processing effort, via the proceduralization that comes with practice and the fusing of sequences into prefabricated units. The agenda *Express individuality* relates to ensuring that one is noticed and taken seriously, and indirectly supports the *Get things done* agenda. Achieving it requires fluent and comprehensible speech and the ability to express novel ideas. Another response to this agenda is a range of attention-gaining strategies, such as language play for its own sake, an aspect of 'clowning'. Finally, *Feel part of the group* encourages an assessment of how others expect one's language to be formulated and used.

Conclusion

The foregoing representation of how formulaic sequences are employed by young children draws together the linguistic behaviour observed in first language acquisition with that of adult native speakers, by identifying the same underlying agenda, realized appropriately for the two speaker types. However, there is more that we can learn from the patterns of formulaicity in child language. The process of acquisition offers some predictions of its own about the nature of the knowledge which the adult ultimately inherits. These predictions, and the models of language acquisition upon which they are based, are presented in the next chapter.

7

Formulaic Sequences in the First Language Acquisition Process: A Model

Introduction

In the previous chapter, we saw how formulaic sequences are able to support the process of first language acquisition in a variety of ways. They appear to

- establish a culture of interaction with carers;
- supplement gesture and other nonlinguistic behaviours in conveying the most important manipulative messages before the production of rule-governed language is possible;
- represent the entry of the child into the group of those who know this or that rhyme or song and expect certain linguistic behaviour;
- provide the child with material for analysis; and
- reduce the child's processing load once novel construction is possible.

It was also evident that for many commentators the default status of formulaic sequences (apart from the fused utterances) is that they are only temporarily holistic. They have been stored whole because that is the only thing the child can do with them, but once analysis is possible, they are routinely broken down in order to identify regular configurations and useful recombinable units. However, there is a major problem with this assumption.

The stream of language which the child hears can be divided into different types. There are novel constructions that may never be heard again: these can be analyzed, but there is only one opportunity to catch them. There are strings which are formulaic for a particular speaker, because he or she has fused and stored them: these are not necessarily a chunk in anyone else's lexicon. They will be good material for analysis as they are likely to be regular, and because they may be heard several times from the same speaker. Other strings are formulaic for many people in the speech community, normally because they have learned them from each other: such sequences are better *not* analyzed, because they may be irregular, and also because they are the mainstay of idiomaticity, so the child needs to store them whole. Finally, some formulaic material is more decisively formulaic. It is institutionalized and derives its power from the fixedness of its form, so, again, the child will gain little and could lose a lot by analyzing it. In short, not all formulaic sequences can, or should, be analyzed. So how is the child to know which are which? We must assume that the child accumulates its store of community-wide sequences on the basis of observation and pragmatic judgement. But avoiding the analysis of irregular strings takes more explaining than this.

The Other Degenerate Input Hypothesis

Part of Chomsky's argument for the existence of a Universal Grammar was that language as a product of performance is not always perfectly formed, and so would not constitute a fully reliable model for the child's development of rules. That assertion was challenged by evidence gathered by Snow (e.g., 1978). She found that adults modified their speech to children in a way that reduced the instances of incomplete or ungrammatical strings. As a result, she says, "children who are learning a language have available a sample of speech which is simpler, more redundant, and less confusing than normal adult speech" (p. 489).

But we have now encountered another sense in which the language of the adult to the child is 'degenerate', even though it is not in any way incorrect. It is the very formulaic sequences that are in most common use in a speech community that are most likely to be irregular in form and/or to lack transparency of meaning. The correlation probably exists because the more often a string is used and understood as it stands, the less likely it is to be subjected to alteration in order to make it more comprehensible. Adult native speakers appear able to use the literal and nonliteral and the grammatically canonical and noncanonical with a smooth integration that suggests that they either have no formal recognition of the differences, or at least do not need to activate that knowledge (Wray & Perkins 2000). Therefore, it is doubtful whether the modifications made by carers when talking to small children would include the entire elimination of word strings whose composition would be misleading if they were analyzed.

If, in order to work out the rules of the language, children are customarily breaking down word strings which they hear repeatedly, then they will undoubtedly encounter some that are formulaic for the speaker and irregular in some way. How could they avoid attempting to analyze sequences in which the compositionality is obscured or undermined by archaic vocabulary or grammar, or by metaphor? There would have to be some reliable means by which they could identify them and set them aside.

We saw in Chapters 2 and 3 that some of the identificational and definitional cues for formulaic sequences apply only to the irregular ones – but while these are useful for the linguist, they will be of no use to the young child. That is because spotting them relies on detecting a non-alignment between the form and/or meaning on the one hand, and the predictions of the rule system on the other. The child is still developing its rule base and its lexicon, so it will have no way of differentiating between strings which violate its current predictions because they are irregular and those which do so because they are useful material for revising the child's imperfect knowledge of the language. Even in referential language, where analyticity and creativity are best served by regularity and transparency, there are nevertheless collocational pairs and descriptive phrases which will not be useful in learning the grammar. For example, the child who hears that the slice of cake is *too big a piece* would be best to avoid seeking its grammatical construction. Even adults are stymied by it, as the problems with pluralizing it show: *Those slices are *too big pieces/*too big a pieces*.

Needs-Only Analysis

So how might the child ensure that only the correct information is accessed in assembling the lexicon and grammar? The key to answering this question may be that, in actual fact, irregular strings are not in danger of being analyzed in the first place. If the impetus to analyze were sufficiently sharp edged, the real issue would not be what is *excluded* from analysis, but rather what is *included*. In this view, the process of analysis which the child engages in would not be that of breaking down as much linguistic material as possible into its smallest components. Rather, nothing would be broken down unless there were a specific reason, and although rules were derived and words stored in the lexicon as the result of the analysis that did occur, few, if any, implicit generalizations would be made from one piece of linguistic data to another.

The exploration of this possibility can be built upon Bruner's (1983) contention that children have, at base, not a grammar-learning agenda but a socio-interactional one, in which language acquisition is achieved through a process of 'pattern detection' in a communicative context rather than by mapping input onto innate grammatical concepts. This means that the child would prioritize analysis only as a means of making the language communicatively pliable. Word strings whose distribution and meaning distanced them from any need for modification would be left aside. These would include rhymes, song, routines and so on, which expressly do not gain from modification, as well as strings which never displayed internal boundaries through paradigmatic variation. The child would be analyzing word strings *not* as a preprogrammed reflex but, rather, only as the need arose.[1] As a result, many word strings would remain unanalyzed for a very long time, even forever (Peters 1983:85–86, 91). In this way sequences which were at odds with the adult grammar and lexical system could survive into the adult language. These sequences would pass directly from the child's early experience into its adult system without ever being broken down. For example, the sequence *thank you for having me* has a strong performative function which would associate its specific form with its specific appropriate use. There would be no need to break it down, as there are no components that customarily change within its paradigm. As a result, the rather uncharacteristically lexical meaning which *have* has in this string would not be subjected to adjustment in the light of the productive lexicon, but rather would reach the adult system intact. Similarly, the now rather antiquated *if I were you* would exist unchallenged alongside regular products of the current grammar such as *if I was younger.*

The needs-only account of analysis enables us to avoid invoking the deeply mysterious procedure in first language acquisition described earlier, whereby the child somehow pre-empts its own lexical and grammatical knowledge so that it can separate out the regular and semantically transparent input material needed for developing the vocabulary and rules that it has just applied. Instead, the child's approach to its input and the analysis of it becomes an extension of the processes we have already seen in Chapter 5: they are a local linguistic response to a local nonlinguistic problem. The response is dynamic and specific, not governed by any general principle that all language must be pulled apart just because it is there. The separation of regular from irregular will not be dependent on the child's judgement at all. On the contrary, children will simply analyze whichever strings need analyzing, to the extent that they need to, and no further.

Needs-only analysis entirely turns the tables on the question of irregularity in formulaic sequences. The sequences that are irregular in the adult language are the ones whose usage is such that they do not invite analysis. Because they are unanalyzed, they are able to retain obsolete vocabulary and structures.[2] They are not an obstacle to the child's development of a set of regular grammatical rules, because the child is never tempted to analyze them (and neither is the adult, though the analytic mechanisms could indeed be turned on them at any point, if, for instance, the individual had an interest in etymology or the origins of idioms). The same applies to strings with a regular form but a nonliteral or otherwise opaque meaning: the ones that survive in the language will be the ones which do not invite principled variation and which are, therefore, never broken down. The word *large* in *by and large* is not associated with the regular word meaning 'big' because there is no demand on native speakers ever to analyze the phrase and assign a meaning to its component parts. Its meaning and function are stand-alone, so no analysis is necessary. In short, we are explaining irregularity as a product of the pattern of usage and of the resultant absence of any need to vary the form. The sequence is protected from the analysis that would threaten its irregularity. For further discussion see Chapters 11 and 14.

Needs-only analysis will naturally lead to the storage of simple and complex units with overlapping content. For example, while it might never have been necessary to break down the string *what time is it?*, and it is therefore stored in the lexicon as a unit, that does not mean that the individual words *what*, *time*, *is* and *it* might not have been analyzed out of other strings and separately stored. It is not a new idea that the lexicon contains both complete formulaic sequences and some or all of their component parts (see, for instance, Bolinger 1976:9; Nattinger & DeCarrico 1992:12; Peters 1983:89–90; Plunkett 1993:45). However, for most accounts it has been only a descriptive feature of a lexical model. Needs-only analysis offers an explanation of how variation in the size of lexical units comes about, and how it is sustained into adulthood.

A Model of Formulaicity in Language Acquisition

Up to now we have been focussing on the extent to which complex word strings encountered by the child in input are broken down or else are resistant to being broken down. It is important, however, that the idea of needs-only analysis does not blind us to the undoubtedly sophisticated and consistent grammatical insights which native speakers develop by the end of the acquisition process. In this section, therefore, we explore a model of how the development of the child's analytic knowledge of the language is able to coexist with the use of formulaic sequences.

The model described here derives from Wray and Perkins (2000), but has been slightly modified. The basic proposal is that during the child's longer term development towards adulthood, the relative proportions of holistic and analytic involvement in language processing alter, first in one

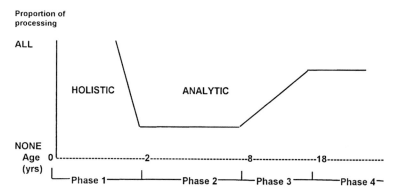

Figure 7.1. The balance of holistic and analytic processing from birth to adulthood.

direction and then the other. Wray and Perkins base their model on Locke's (1993, 1995, 1997) work. Locke reconciles the gestalt and analytic strategies in the child's language processing by viewing them as evidence for the existence of separate but complementary neural mechanisms which he calls 'specialization in social cognition' (SSC) and 'grammatical analysis module' (GAM). Wray and Perkins develop this theme into a four-phase model,[3] mapping the period of development from babyhood to adulthood. These phases are characterized by different distributions of the two types of processing (Figure 7.1).

Phase 1 lasts from birth until the child begins to combine units in a simple grammar at around 20 months. The child's communication is governed by the SSC (Locke 1995:295ff), which "supports an affectively oriented developmental growth path that channels infants in the direction of spoken language" (Locke 1997:269). The SSC, which operates initially in response to social stimulation, identifies features of the environment which are seen as socially important, and thus motivates the identification, selection and storage of units meaningful within the linguistic environment. Any internal structure that such units may possess is irrelevant to the SSC which in any case is presumably unable to process it. In consequence, during this phase, the approach to communication is holistic, beginning with the imitation, interpretation and employment of facial and body gestures (see Foster 1990; Locke 1993) and of intonation. It later features the production of approximations of utterances (gestalt utterances) that have been heard from carers and roughly interpreted using pragmatic cues. These count as single unanalyzed units. Some children continue to favour long strings during this single-unit phase, while others soon isolate word-length constituents which they reproduce in the classic 'one-word' stage.[4] The SSC is located by Locke in the right cerebral hemisphere (see Chapter 12 for discussion of the roles of the hemispheres of the brain).

Phase 2 begins when the child, aged approximately 20 to 30 months, has undergone the vocabulary spurt (Barrett 1994; Bates & Goodman 1997:510; Plunkett 1993; Poulin-Dubois et al. 1995) and grammatical development begins; that is, when the combinatory potential of the preferred units is recognized. In Locke's terms, the GAM is triggered and begins to operate.[5] The trigger is the success of the SSC in acquiring a requisite number and variety of linguistic items suitable for recombination (see Locke 1997 for discussion). If viewed within a generative grammar framework of analytic language processing, the GAM can be seen as responsible for identifying the constituent structure of the items acquired via the SSC. Locke associates the operation of the GAM with the left (dominant) hemisphere of the brain. Gestalt children, who need ultimately to identify word- and morpheme-sized units for aspects of their grammar to develop, may be delayed in fully entering phase 2 (Plunkett 1993), though their fluent and grammatically accurate holistic speech may be misinterpreted as precocity.[6] Individual differences in cognitive style that were apparent in Phase 1 and early in Phase 2 are eclipsed by the effects of subsequent general development (Bates et al. 1994:117). Even in the most analytic of children, formulaicity continues to play a major role in achieving routine interactional goals.

With the GAM in operation, the balance of formulaic to novel language (characterized by single referential words) changes to accommodate more of the latter, and we see evidence of the child's developing grammatical awareness. The principle of 'longest possible unit' continues to hold. But the GAM, as the agent of analysis, brings about an effective reduction in the mean length and complexity of those units, as part of the child's interest becomes focussed on the identification of words and morphemes, and as the drive to express more and more complex ideas creates the need to analyze input and work out how constituents combine. Although the involvement of the GAM can be seen as a natural consequence of maturation, motivated by the child's need to express ever more complex novel messages and interpret decontextualized linguistic input, the extent of the adoption of the analytic strategy may be affected by beginning literacy and the analytic method of formal education (see later).

The predominance of analyticity during this phase offers an explanation for the child's propensity to use language declaratively, simply to label things, rather more than the adult does (compare Tomasello & Brooks 1999). Aspects of this analyticity can even be disadvantageous.

For example, children in Phase 2 (that is, up to about the age of eight) are rather literal in their interpretation of input that would be better dealt with holistically. They struggle with pragmatics, including sarcasm (Pan & Gleason 1997:148) and irony (Chan & Cole 1986), and only gradually develop the ability to interpret noncompositional and nonliteral idioms (Anglin 1993:109f; Aphek & Tobin 1983; Gibbs 1987, 1991) unless the context is rich (Cacciari & Levorato 1989; Levorato & Cacciari 1992).[7] They also tend to struggle with metaphorical interpretations of text, particularly if they are abstract (Cicone, Gardner & Winner 1981; Wales & Coffey 1986), though there is no convincing evidence to suggest that they actually lack the cognitive means of creating and interpreting metaphor (Cameron & Low 1999:84). For reviews, see Clark (1995) and Perkins (1999).

In Phase 3, from about age 8 to 18, the analytic grammar is fully functioning, and formulaic language now begins to make up a greater proportion of the individual's output again. This occurs as it becomes increasingly inefficient to generate from scratch the now very wide range of utterances which are needed regularly. If the same, or similar, groups of elements are being continually encountered and/or produced, it will make good economical sense to store them as separate holistic items (Perkins 1999). The process of fusion releases the GAM from future involvement in the production of that item,[8] making it available for more complex operations, such as abstract thought and argument development (Wray 1992), which are seen to blossom during late childhood and teenage.

Finally, in late teenage, phase 4 is reached. Here the balance between holistic and analytic processing is settled, and corresponds to that described in Chapter 5. Evidence for this surprisingly late conclusion to the language acquisition process comes from studies of idiom comprehension by 14 to 17 year olds (Nippold & Martin 1989), aspects of intonation comprehension (see Crystal 1997:243), and a number of production phenomena in developmental language disorders (Locke 1994).

The Socio-interactional Bubble

This developmental account is strengthened by a significant observation regarding the nature of the child's microenvironment, as determined by its more general pattern of mental and physical development. At precisely the time when the GAM becomes most dominant (Phase 2 and the early part of Phase 3), the child is socially buffered. Having grappled, during Phase 1, with the business of harnessing interaction for the purpose of survival and comfort, the child's communicative needs become, and remain, essentially static:

much of early infant action takes place in constrained, familiar situations and shows a surprisingly high degree of order and 'systematicity'. Children spend most of their time doing a very limited number of things. (Bruner 1983:28)

This is precisely what the shift of dominance from the SSC to the GAM requires, but in the context of the wealth of worldly experiences which the child gains during this period, it is easy to overlook it. The fact is that, for a substantial period of time, the child is largely cushioned from the need to develop an additional interactional repertoire, because it has an extremely limited set of social roles (Gross 1996:525): it exists within a 'socio-interactional bubble'.

Parents are well aware that, in the early years, child-adult and adult-child routines do not greatly vary across situational contexts. The child is interested in satisfying its physical needs and does this through its relationship with its carers. The result is that the verbal interactions are largely constant in all settings: at home, in a restaurant, at the zoo or at a royal garden party. Certainly, referential utterances will differ, but a young child is both protected from, and largely impervious to, any need to interact with anyone other than its carers, let alone being party to any knowledge of how to do so appropriately. Although witness on many occasions to certain interactional situations (e.g., shopping, buying a bus ticket, asking directions), as a nonparticipant, the child may fail to notice the language used.[9] The result is that, when finally participatory, the language will not be readily available,[10] and carers may need to provide coaching in what to say. Thus, where new environments are encountered, and a new social role has to be adopted, such as the first days at nursery or school (Cook-Gumperz 1977) or the first time the child buys something in a shop, the effect can be traumatic, with the child literally lost for words. Aspects of this may last into adulthood: it is not uncommon for an adult to be similarly floored when first encountering a bereaved friend, a job interview panel or a visiting dignitary (Fillmore 1979:95). In essence, the child is afforded the luxury of developing the analytic grammar by being protected, during these vital years, from the need to accumulate the wide range of formulaic sequences that it will ultimately need in order to function as a normal social adult. These are learned later, in a piecemeal fashion, as the need arises (e.g., the routines of classroom discourse described by Griffin & Mehan 1981), and with increasing ease as the balance swings back in favour of formulaicity, during the latter part of phase 3 and in phase 4. In the meantime, it is the predictability of the situation that supports the analytic processes:

Language learning in context is essential; thoroughly routinized and familiar situations may provide the child with support for the next step. When children are removed from their familiar contexts, such as home or classroom . . . they may be unable to exhibit their most creative uses of language. (Lieven 1984: 22)

The Role of Literacy

It was mentioned earlier in this chapter that phase 2, the period of maximum analyticity, coincides with the development of literacy skills. Literacy is believed to affect linguistic processing profoundly (e.g., Carlisle 1995; Fowler & Lieberman 1995; Lecours, Mehler & Parente 1988, Lecours et al. 1987; Reis & Castro-Caldas 1997). It may be that the unnatural process of learning to read and, particularly, to write, effects a major transition from working with larger complex units to smaller ones (cf. Barton 1985). In order to write, various decisions have to be made which might otherwise not be made. As Garton and Pratt (1998:166ff) report in their review of the research, young children do not have a fully developed sense of the word as a linguistic unit, as distinct from its meaning (see also Locke 1997:272). As a result, they will identify phrases such as *the big man* as a word, and will not recognize function words as words, since they have no discrete referential meaning. It seems to be only in the context of reading and writing that the whole vocabulary is assigned word boundaries. Research on the written language of semi-literate adults indicates that one can speak a language without having fully analyzed it into its smallest components. For French, Guillaume (1927/1973) reports: *aidi* for *ai dit* ([I] have said), *cecerai* for *ce serait* (that would be), *semy* for *s'est mis* (placed himself), *a bitant* for *habitant* (inhabitant), *trou vais* for *trouvais* (found), *a ses* for *assez* (enough), *ja prends* for *j'apprends* (I am learning) and *dé colle* for *d'école* (of school). Tony Fairburn (personal communication), who has researched the formal letters written by barely literate nineteenth-century English parish petitioners, reports *take it into consideration* written as *taket into . . .* , and *I wish to inform you* written as *I wish to in form you*.

It is important to note that such errors do not simply indicate an alternative analysis, or superficial disagreements, such as could be argued for the writing of *middle class* as one word or *non-native, ladylike* and *lip-read* as two (Wray 1996). The grammar of English does not permit the structure *wish to + PP NP*, as appears to be represented in *wish to in form you*, and it would be bizarre to suggest that the writer's grammar does. What the spelling reveals is a lack of awareness about the internal construction of a formulaic sequence which there has never been any cause to analyze, seeing as, for that individual, it comes as a lump with no variation other than, perhaps, alternative object NPs. For most of the rest of us, the spelling of *by and large* might be similarly subject to guesswork were we not accustomed to its agreed written form, for that, too, appears to break the rules of English grammar.

The proposal that literacy is instrumental in creating a larger lexicon of word-sized units where there was previously greater reliance on longer strings, is significant in its *not* predicting that the literate child ends up with a lexicon of the *smallest possible* combinable units. Because the analysis directly linked with learning to write is focussed on the location of word boundaries, there will be no reason to break down words into morphemes (unless occasionally, to help with the spelling). Polymorphemic words will be stored whole, with the individual as oblivious to their internal makeup as he or she previously was to the composition of the formulaic sequences from which they have been extracted. In other words, alongside the original formulaic sequences, still stored in the lexicon, will be smaller units, but they will in many cases still be internally complex. While the mean amount of internal complexity may have reduced overall, there has not in any sense been a systematic overthrow of internal complexity under some general principle of maximum reductionism. We shall return to this theme in Chapter 11, when we compare the processing of first and second language learners.

Summary

In this chapter, it has been proposed that the key to understanding how grammatically irregular and semantically opaque sequences avoid interfering with the identification of regular patterns of form and meaning during first language acquisition is that the process of analysis is a highly restricted operation. The basic principle is to operate with the largest possible unit. This leads to the segmentation and isolation only of the specific subitems which signal their potential to be recombinable, while the remainder of a string, along with word strings in which no such subitems are identified, remain unanalyzed, even if they are grammatically regular and semantically transparent. This needs-only view of analysis explains many curiosities regarding the tolerance of children and adults for linguistic oddities.

A developmental account has also been presented, whereby the relative balance of holistic and analytic processing changes during the period from babyhood to early adulthood. In keeping with Locke's model, the natural impetus for the child to analyze language is attributed to a 'grammatical analysis module', which operates separately from the module which handles social interaction (the 'specialization in social cognition').

The establishment of analytic activity in Phase 2 coincides with a steady period of operation for the SSC brought about by the child's physical dependence, which creates a *socio-interactional bubble*. The bubble ensures that the learning of social language is staggered over several years, and does not compete strongly with the important task of working out the smallest constituents in the language and how they can be grammatically combined into novel sentences. The child's introduction to literacy skills may play a major role in identifying and separately storing individual words, though this is a supplement to, and not a replacement for, the store of formulaic sequences.

PART IV

FORMULAIC SEQUENCES IN
A SECOND LANGUAGE

8

Non-native Language: Overview

Introduction

To know a language you must know not only its individual words, but also how they fit together. Part of this knowledge entails developing suitable rules to generate all the possible grammatical utterances of the language, but another crucial aspect is coming to know which of the feasible grammatical utterances are idiomatic and nativelike. Pawley and Syder (1983) point out that one of the most difficult tasks for even the most proficient non-native speaker is learning to select that subset of utterances that are customarily used by native speakers, from out of the much greater inventory of those that *could* be. The choices that result in such 'customary' turns of phrase as *I'll be back in a tick/mo* in preference to *I'll return in a short while* and *let me have a go* rather than *I should like to try* are, because the choices lie entirely within the grammatically possible, subtle to the point of slipperiness, and a non-native can only learn to prefer those which are the usual forms in a given speech community by observation and imitation (see, for example, Willis 1990:63–64). For some idiomatic expressions, the whole is not even a literal reflection of the meanings of the constituent words, and the functional associations can be quite arbitrary. For example, in some varieties of English, *nice to meet you* is both a greeting and a closer, while *nice meeting you* is only a closer (Schmidt 1983:152). The conjunct *as I say* is a simple reiterater, while *as I said* conveys emphatic reiteration, even petulance (House 1993:171). Furthermore, they display complex restrictions on their appropriacy for use (Yorio 1980:437). Failing to use a nativelike expression can create an impression of brusqueness, disrespect or arrogance (e.g., Beneke 1981). Beneke recommends that non-native speakers learn a small set of formulaic sequences which bridge the gap between

native and non-native usage, such as *I don't quite know how to put it . . .*
(p. 92).

It was suggested in Chapter 5 that formulaic sequences are selected
as a response to specific needs in communication and processing. Precisely which formulaic sequences different second language learners use
should depend on their different priorities, and on the situations in which
they find themselves. Being most prevalent where the need is greatest,
the formulaic sequences produced by any individual should correlate
with an independent assessment of his or her socio-interactional and
processing priorities at that time.

Similarities and Differences in Learner Types

In order to assess these predictions, we need to compare the occurrences
of formulaic sequences in the output of different types of learner. This,
however, is more easily said than done. There have been relatively few
published data-based studies which specifically examine formulaic
sequences in L2. In those which do exist, there is such a diversity of aims,
methods and subject types that there are few opportunities for direct
comparison. The idea that every learner has his or her own profile of language use, priorities, strategies and outcomes, determined in part by characteristics shared with other learners and in part by personal traits and
preferences, is hardly new or contentious, yet, surprisingly, it has been
largely overlooked when it comes to the case of formulaic sequences.
Here, research has often tended to assume that the 'learner' label over-
rides all others, so that individuals who would easily be acknowledged
as different in aspects of their L1 behaviour and, indeed, different in all
other respects in their L2 learning, suddenly become a homogeneous
group when it comes to formulaicity. For example, Nattinger and
DeCarrico (1992) align adult and child data:

> there is no reason to think that adults would go about the [learning] task com-
> pletely differently [from children]. In important ways, the language learning sit-
> uation is the same for adults as for children, and makes it likely that an adult
> learner would also find prefabricated language an efficient way to begin to
> acquire a new language system. (p. 27)

Several other published commentaries on formulaic sequences in L2
(e.g., Granger 1998; Krashen & Scarcella 1978; Weinert 1995) follow this
trend, and amalgamate evidence from learners of different ages and
types. Weinert (1995), for example, juxtaposes data from child, teenage
and adult learners, and the latter in both naturalistic and classroom settings, in her discussions of the functions of formulaic language (pp. 186ff).

The effect, albeit unintentional, is to suggest that some tendencies in the data are stronger than they actually are, and to miss some striking differences in the patterns of form and function between different types of learner (Wray 1999).

However, it is not a simple matter to separate out learners into 'groups', since a learner can have a mixture of inputs and experiences, and variables may interact. Wong Fillmore's (1976) study, for instance, looks only at children under the age of eight learning naturalistically (that is, with no, or minimal, formal tuition). Yet even here there is a contrast in the level of achievement, which seems attributable to circumstantial and personal differences, the latter including possible age effects, even in this small age range (see Chapter 9). If there can be such variation in such a compatible subject group, how much more might there be between two learners of different ages and learning experiences?

Figure 6.3 related the holistic and analytic responses to basic agendas in the first language learner. If the position put forward in this book is right, then the agendas themselves, and their relative importance, will vary according to the age and type of learner, as will the range of responses available. For instance, whereas for the infant the primary way of getting fed has to be demanding food of a carer, an adult has other options too, including going to a shop and buying food. The availability of this option makes it less imperative, in most situations, for an adult learner to master the linguistic means of demanding or requesting food. But take away that shopping option, by, for instance, placing the adult learner in an L2-speaking household with little freedom to go out alone, and the imperative of meeting that, and other, needs through the agency of the L2 hosts is reinstated. Yet even with, essentially, the same agenda as that of an infant, the adult will, of course, select from a different range of possible responses, preferring, say, to suppress certain desires, or use a dictionary or phrase book to help frame a comprehensible request, rather than reaching towards the desired object and wailing or saying *that's mine*.

Our purpose in viewing the evidence from second language research, therefore, will be to explore the ways in which formulaic sequences seem to be used, or not used, to support the individual's promotion of self, by promoting fluency and ensuring hearer comprehension. The extent to which our evaluation can address this research directly varies according to the type of data. The work on children is on the whole thorough and inclusive of both detail and contextual information, so it is relatively easy to make judgements about the function of an utterance and how representative it is of the overall pattern of output. The reports on formulaic language in teenage and adult learners, however, are mostly much more limited. Either they provide snapshots, through one-time or sporadic testing, or they assemble a collection of anecdotes from observation. In both cases, one is much less able to guess what *else* the learner could do, than is the case with the child studies. These differences are taken into account in the survey, by not attempting to force all the reports into the same mould. As a result, Chapters 9 and 10 are differently structured.

A further problem arises with reading old data in new ways, as is being attempted here. Ideally, one would compare the data with the models in Chapters 6 and 7 by identifying contextual agendas for a given subject and then seeing how they are responded to. However, our starting place is the material reported by the original researcher, often for a different purpose. In most cases it has already been filtered, and examples, whether supportive or unsupportive to the current investigation, may have been omitted on entirely reasonable grounds. Every attempt has been made to guard against the problems inherent in post hoc interpretations, by taking into account the entirety of a research report, so as to assess as accurately as possible the prominence (or not) and role of the formulaic sequences that have been noted.

Since the factors of age and manner of acquisition are well established in the literature as likely to underlie broad similarities in style and success, the data will be examined under three general headings: children (Chapter 9); teenagers and adults acquiring naturally; and teenagers and adults in the classroom (both in Chapter 10). Two types of published study will *not* be considered here. One is the many which are concerned only with other features of language learning, such as pronunciation, morphology and vocabulary, and which make no reference to formulaic sequences at all. The other is the research on children exposed to two languages from birth (as reviewed by Vihman & McLaughlin 1982, for example), as opposed to those whose first language was well established when exposure to the second began. This is not to deny that such studies are significant; they could usefully be subjected to the same sort of analysis as the present one. They are excluded here in the interests of retaining a clear picture of the difference (if any) between first and second language acquisition, and must await consideration at some later date.

The Nature of L2 Data

A formulaic sequence produced by a learner may be nativelike or non-nativelike in form. Although nativelike output can reflect nativelike knowledge, it need not. It may be the result of simple imitation (e.g.,

Bygate, 1988), in which case the user may have control of all, part or none at all of the holistic or the componential meaning. It could be the result of *fusion* (Peters 1983), that is, a product of the learner's grammar, created by the application of a rule that may or may not be nativelike, and then stored whole and retrieved on subsequent occasions (e.g., Lennon 2000:39). In this case, the nativelike appearance and application could be no more than coincidence (Howarth 1998a:26). For advanced learners, the major problem can lie in the production of perfectly grammatical utterances that are simply not used by native speakers (Pawley & Syder 1983; Widdowson 1989:133–134). Where a formulaic sequence is not nativelike (e.g., Bahns et al. 1986:716ff), it could be because the right words are used in the wrong context (e.g., Moon 1992:16; Rehbein 1987:234, 241ff) or because the form itself reflects the learner's imperfect grammatical and lexical resources (e.g., Biskup 1992; Schmidt 1983). An additional problem is that a non-nativelike formulaic sequence cannot be identified as such unless it occurs several times (Howarth 1998a:40; Schmidt 1983:151), is used in a context that strongly suggests formulaicity (Schmidt 1983:152) or bears a strong resemblance to a native formula (Yorio 1989:61). Finally, the divide between native and non-native is not always a clean one. Kuiper and Tan Gek Lin (1989) demonstrate that the formulaic sequences typical of Singaporean English display many features derived from the Hokkien Chinese L1. Although to a native speaker of English from elsewhere these may seem like interlanguage features, they are part of the English model these learners are exposed to, and thus intrinsic to the local target (pp. 302–303). Other national varieties of English around the world, such as Zambian English (Chisanga 1987), could raise similar difficulties.

Overview of Findings

Since the surveys which follow in Chapters 9 and 10 are long and, particularly in the case of the children, rather detailed, the reader may find it helpful that a summary of the main patterns is presented here. This summary is not intended to be exhaustive but indicative, and many more patterns can be found in the body of the surveys. The points that follow relate to the overall agendas of the learner, as often, but not always, achieved with the help of formulaic sequences.

- While formulaic sequences are a great support in the early stages of L2 acquisition for most kinds of learner, their ability to offer a relatively painless way into communication is easily eclipsed by an even less effortful one, using the L1. Even in very young children, the L1 can hinder the process of L2 acquisition if it is perceived as being a legitimate medium of communication in the L2 setting. Thus, best L2 learning is obtained where the child is forced to engage with the L2 for meeting basic needs.

- Very young children seem naturally adept at employing formulaic sequences both to achieve manipulative speech acts, including the establishment of their identity in the eyes of others, and to access the internal workings of the language. They are charmingly guileless in trustingly imitating both the words and actions of others, with no apparent sense of limitations on appropriacy or "proper" behaviour. Such formulaic sequences are nativelike, with no evidence of interference from the L1 (Huang & Hatch 1978:124).

- In children of primary school age, the degree of success in L2 learning seems to depend in part on their social alliances with peers. Most helpful will be if their friends do not speak the learner's L1, are talkative, are committed to mutual social integration, and engage in patterns of play which naturally incorporate (second) language use. A successful learner will normally prioritize communication over language learning, while a less successful learner takes opportunities for avoidance (e.g., by using L1, walking away) when communication really matters.

- Naturalistic L2 learning in adulthood seems subject to considerable variation in the amount of formulaic language used. It also seems that formulaic sequences are not contributing to the mastery of grammatical forms. The drive to communicate may prompt the adoption of formulaic sequences, but avoidance may now take different forms from those in children. Besides using the L1 if this will work, L2 learners may cut their losses by fossilizing any useful string once it has been found to work, even if it is not nativelike, or may even specifically manipulate their behaviour to avoid certain situations which would be linguistically difficult.

- Classroom-taught teenagers and adults appear to be able to apply the analytic techniques of the classroom to holistically learned strings. There may be a pincer movement, by which items learned separately become identified in such strings, supporting a process of full or partial segmentation.

- In the early stages of classroom tuition, formulaic sequences may offer support and boost confidence. However, by later in the learning process, the knowledge of formulaic sequences tends to lag behind expectations (which may or may not be reasonable ones).

- Establishing and maintaining a balance between formulaicity and creativity seems to be essential for successful acquisition, but in taught adults, this is difficult to achieve, with the learner most often erring on the side of too much creativity.

In Chapter 11 we shall draw on these observations to consider whether late acquisition and/or taught input leads to a different type of lexical storage from that of the native speaker and early learner, and how the relative balance between the communicative and processing roles of formulaic sequences affects what is learned.

9

Patterns of Formulaicity in Children Using a Second Language

Introduction

Our basic and recurrent question in this chapter is whether the use of formulaic sequences by children learning an L2, as reported in the research literature, can be accounted for in terms of the agenda model presented in Figure 6.3. The full set of studies covered in this chapter is listed in Table 9.1, and the ages of the learners are represented in Figure 9.1. In all the cases of interest to us, the children had already established their L1 before they were exposed to the L2, and so are older than an equivalent L1 learner would be.

Very Young Children in L2 Daycare/Nursery

Because age is so tied into rapid physical, emotional and cognitive development in early childhood, we should expect the youngest learners to provide the closest match with the first language model, whether this be for neurological, cognitive or environmental reasons. We begin, then, with the youngest children. Virve and Karen were both under two years of age when their respective studies began, and were exposed to L2 in their daycare setting. Takahiro was two-and-a-half and attended an L2 medium nursery.[1]

How Did the Learners Get Things Done?

We saw in Chapters 6 and 7 that 'getting things done' is an agenda of great importance to the infant, who is relatively helpless in meeting its own needs. Virve, Karen and Takahiro[2] were not helpless infants: they could walk and feed themselves, and they already had a linguistic means

Table 9.1. *Studies of formulaic sequences in young children acquiring L2 in a naturalistic environment*

Study	Name of child	Age	L1	L2	Learning environment	Child of the data collector?
Vihman (1982a)	Virve (F)[a]	1;9–2;8	Estonian	English	Preschool daycare	Yes
Karniol (1990)	Karen (F)	1;10–3;0[b]	English	Hebrew	Preschool daycare	Yes
Itoh & Hatch (1978)	Takahiro (M)	2;6–3;1	Japanese	English	Nursery	No
Bahns et al. (1986); Bohn (1986)	Inga (F)	3;11–4;5	German	English	Everyday activities but L1 used at home	Yes
	Lars (M)	5;11–6;5				
	Birgit (F)	7;11–8;5				
	Heiko (M)	8;11–9;5				
Linnakylä (1980)	Antti (M)	4;11–5;8	Finnish	English	Kindergarten & daycare	Yes
Huang & Hatch (1978); Hatch et al. (1979)	Paul (M)	5;1–5;5	Chinese	English	Playgroup	Yes
Hakuta (1974)	Uguisu (F)	5;4–6;5[c]	Japanese	English	Kindergarten & local children	Yes
Rescorla & Okuda (1987)	Atsuko (F)	5;8–6;2	Japanese	English	Kindergarten & local children	Yes
Wong Fillmore (1976, 1979)	Nora (F)	5;7–6;4	Spanish	English	Kindergarten & friends	No
	Ana (F)	6;5–7;2				
	Alej (M)	6;9–7;6				
	Juan (M)	7;3–8;0				
	Jesus (M)	6;11–7;8[d]			School	
Wagner-Gough (1978)	Homer (M)	5;11–6;4	Assyrian/Persian	English	Nursery & friend	No
Willett (1995)	Yael (F)	c. 6;0–7;0	Hebrew	English	School	No
	Etham (F)	c. 6;0–7;0	Devehi	English	School	No
	Nahla (F)	c. 7;0–8;0	Palestinian Arabic	English	School	No
Kenyeres (1938)	Eva (F)	6;10–7;8	Hungarian	French	School	Yes

[a] Vihman has also researched the acquisition of English by her younger child Raivo but "he had bilingual input from the first" (1982b:143) and so falls outside of this survey.

[b] Previously exposed to Hebrew 4–7 hours a day, 6 days a week, from 0;5 to 1;3. No exposure to Hebrew from 2;4 to 2;6.

[c] First exposed to English at 4;11, but no significant output until 5;4.

[d] Put into second grade, where the others were in first grade or (in Nora's case) kindergarten.

151

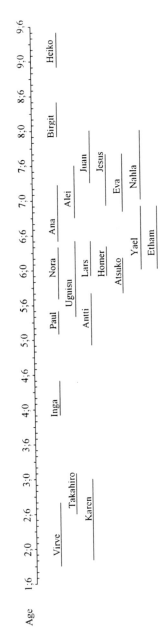

Figure 9.1. Distribution of child L2 studies in Table 9.1, by age.

of expressing their needs, their L1. On the other hand, they were still much less self-sufficient than an older child or adult. What strategies did they employ in trying to meet their needs through the agency of another? Is there evidence that their various responses were focussed on anticipating the hearer's linguistic knowledge and trying to match it?

The first step towards the successful manipulation of others is knowing whom you can successfully address in each language (Karniol 1990:152). Decisions about language choice are not required during monolingual L1 acquisition, and even the fact that more than one language exists is something with which the child first has to come to terms (ibid.: 153). The child has to find out by trial and error who speaks what, until enough of a pattern has developed for predictions to be made. Thus, Karniol reports that Karen initially tried to speak English to her Hebrew-speaking classmates, but soon learned that this was fruitless. For Takahiro, on the other hand, the L1 was very effective, because his mother (who stayed with him at school for the first two months, until it became evident that this was detrimental to his learning) and the researcher were both Japanese speakers. His strategy in meeting his needs was to avoid interacting with L2-only speakers and to rely on his mother and the researcher to provide for him (Itoh & Hatch 1978:78). As the researchers point out, "his strategy was successful. [The researcher] spoke more and more Japanese in his presence" (p. 79).

All three children were still of an age at which they gravitated towards interaction with a carer rather than other children (Itoh & Hatch 1978:77–78; Karniol 1990:154), though some of the girls' utterances were clearly aimed at the manipulation of children, and, in play, toys. Both Virve and Karen imitated phrases that they had heard others speak in the context of the outcome that they desired. These included strings seeking a physical response, such as *more juice*; *that's mine*; *stop it* (Virve) and *bo hena* 'come (MASC) here'; *lo liçok* 'don't shout'; *Assur lidxof* 'no pushing' (Karen). Karen also learned *Tishvi besheket ve-asaper lax sipur* 'Sit (FEM) quietly and I'll tell you (FEM) a story'. Other strings were for getting information, such as *What happened (there)* (Virve) and *Shel me ze?* 'Whose is this?'; *Eifo (ha) naalaim shelxa?* 'Where are your shoes?' (Karen). But Takahiro did not seem to imitate any multiword strings with this purpose, though he did copy *No* and *Don't*.

Virve learned some 'magic words' (e.g., *thank you*; *I want to get down please*), that is, phrases that she understood hearers to require, if she was to get what she wanted. Virve and Takahiro created their own, fused, sequences, such as *I wanna X* (Virve) and *you do X*; *I/I'll get X* (meaning 'I want X') (Takahiro). Because fusion involves the construction of an expression, it bears the hallmark of an active grammar and thus indicates that attempts are being made to 'gain control of process-ing' (see later).

How Did They Demonstrate Their Group Membership?

While Virve and Karen took quickly to group activities, Takahiro seemed to avoid joining in with the class, either physically or linguistically (Itoh & Hatch 1978:78). After his mother ceased to attend, Takahiro became more integrated into the class group. The transition of identity was, it appears, at least in part facilitated by a bridging stage of 'repetition' (p. 80), using a game which seemed to give him entry to the world of English. Besides the actual choice of language, the major way in which the chil-dren signalled their group membership was by learning the words asso-ciated with group (or pair) activities, including extracts from songs, and the announcements *lunch time!* and *happy birthday to you* (Virve) and *Good morning* (Takahiro).[3]

How Did They Demonstrate Individual Identity?

The two girls used memorized sequences to promote themselves: *I'll get it; I will be back* (Virve); *Ani avi lexa* 'I'll bring it to you'; *Ani aazor lexa* 'I'll help you' (Karen), while Takahiro used the partly fused construc-tions *I wanna* X and *I get (a)* X 'I want (a) X', to give *I wanna cake; I get a shovel car; I get high*, and so on. In the pursuit of self-protection and defiance Virve had the sequence *I don't want* X and Karen had *Ze koev li* 'It hurts me'; *Lo axshav* 'not now'; *Od lo gamarti* 'I haven't finished yet' and *Ze lo yafe* 'This is not nice'. Finally, Virve had a partic-ular strategy for 'performance':

> With a devilish air, early one morning, she reached for a journal on her mother's bed, saying [aː gadit hɔ̃n pëːk] ('I've got it (one?) book'). Repeating this two or three times, she proceeded to turn pages and 'read' aloud in English-sounding gibberish, making heavy use of the sequence [hɔ̃n]. (Vihman 1982a:276)

This illustrates another aspect of formulaicity, the repetition of gibber-ish for a particular effect. Although such sound strings are, presumably, not stored in the lexicon, they can be compared with some of the 'auto-matic' output of aphasics (see Chapter 12).

Of course, identity is somewhat malleable, and the strategies for pro-tecting the sense of self may be different in different environments (this is much clearer in adult learners, as we shall see later). Itoh and Hatch (1978) observe that Takahiro was a different person at home and school (p. 79). In the former environment he was "affectionate, outgoing and noisy", whereas in school he was shy and reserved (ibid.). The account of his early reaction to the L2 environment suggests that his sense of identity was severely threatened. Not only was he unable to communicate with the strangers around him, but his own mother and her friend (the researcher) were also trying to speak the L2 to him: "Each time [the researcher] spoke English to him, he ignored her, turned away, or ran out of the room" (p. 79).

How Did They Gain Control of the Language?

This part of the learner's agenda is the one which requires most engagement with analytic processing (see Figure 6.3). Driven by the other agendas, so that learning the language becomes a necessary part of attempting to accommodate towards the linguistic system of the hearer, it requires the learning of words and structures. We have seen that in first language acquisition, some children rely on formulaic sequences for this process more than others do.

The three children employed various strategies which drew on formulaic sequences to support acquisition. One very direct use was in requesting linguistic information. Karen used *Ma ze?* 'What's this?' as a request for naming (Karniol 1990:157), and the sequence *Ex omrim X* 'How do you say X' (where X is an L1 word or phrase) (p. 169). For Virve this strategy was part of a linguistic game, where she would supply the answer (Vihman 1982a:275), resulting in lexical rehearsal. Takahiro, having been given much practice in the *What is this?* game, produced a great many *This is a X* utterances (Itoh & Hatch 1978:84).

A second strategy, used particularly by Takahiro when he did not understand input, was simple repetition. He had possibly been particularly encouraged into this by adults, who instigated repetition games with him, until he took "an active interest in all English spoken to him" (p. 83). Itoh and Hatch note that "as he became proficient in repetition, he was no longer satisfied with repeating just what was said to him" (ibid.). He introduced a new strategy, also formulaically based: "He began to expand on his own spontaneous repetitions by recalling other possible similar patterns: *This is my fork. Fork. This is my fork. The sun. Sun. This. This sun. This is a sun. Don't know. I don't know. I don't know, dummy*" (p. 83).

This practice strategy was used by all three children in their play. In Karen's play "dolls and teddy bears . . . were given the names of children at daycare (with the name being assigned consistently over time), and were reprimanded, changed, sung and 'read' to, danced with, fed and generally conversed with" (p. 159).[4] Virve, in her play, would interject L2 sequences into her chatter (Vihman 1982a:276).

All three children appear to have progressively segmented formulaic sequences. Karen's strategy for coping with linguistic expression appeared to be "when in doubt, extract from known formulas and juxtapose all the relevant semantic elements" (Karniol 1990:162). Both Vihman (1982a) and Itoh and Hatch (1978) chronicle the progress of *wanna*, with Virve ultimately differentiating between *want* + NP and *wanna* + verb (Vihman 1982a:277–278). Takahiro also progressively segmented *This is a X*. Initially, he used it for all values of X (e.g., *This is a four; This is a racing cars; This is a my spoon*). Then he appeared to realize that the article was not appropriate unless X was a noun, and he deleted it with adjectives (*This is broken; This is upside down*), though he sometimes deleted BE as well (*This broken; This my house*) (p. 84).

As in first language acquisition, the segmentation of formulaic sequences could lead to a form being hypercorrected. Karen, having used correct inflections in the memorized *Tishvi besheket ve asaper lax sipur* 'Sit quietly and I'll tell you a story', used, once she had begun segmentation processes, incorrect (infinitive) inflections in *lo laçet haxuça ima, ani lesaper sipur* 'Don't go out Mummy, I'll tell you/I'm telling a story'. Similarly, she correctly inflected *Tiftax at hape* 'open the mouth' and later, incorrectly inflected *Abba, liftoax hadelet* 'Daddy, open the door'. According to Karniol:

> These examples suggest that the original and correct forms were learned as unanalyzed chunks. When enough grammatical analysis had been conducted for the child to know that verbs have to be inflected but these inflected forms are unavailable to her, she resorts to a simplification strategy. (1990:161)

Karniol observes that Karen's priority was "meaning is more important than syntactic well-formedness" (p. 162). This is highly compatible with the model in Figure 6.3, in which the pursuit of the rules of the language is not an aim in itself, but a way of delivering meaning more successfully.

Discussion

Although there are similarities between Virve, Karen and Takahiro, it is also noticeable that Takahiro adopted many strategies different from those of the girls and that, on the whole, he engaged less with the language learning task. Various factors may have contributed to this, including gender. Karen and Virve both created make-believe interactional situations in their play, whereas Takahiro's games seemed to be mostly naming games initiated by adults. A similar female-male difference will be seen in the next section. Another possible cause of the differences could be that Virve and Karen were both learning a language of which the researching parent was a native speaker, after a specific decision on the parents' part not to use it at home with the child. Both had the opportunity to hear the language in action long before they came to learn it, and may have had a stronger sense of its potential as a communicative tool. In contrast, Takahiro's home environment appears to have been monolingual Japanese, except when his Japanese mother and the Japanese researcher deliberately addressed him in English (Itoh & Hatch 1978:79). Not only would he have had little experience of English as a successful medium of communication, but he may also have been confused about why it was necessary to interact in L2 with people whom he knew shared his L1.

Most striking of all, however, is that Takahiro was not obliged to use the L2 to service his needs, at least not for as long as his mother and the researcher were complicit with his L1 use. While Virve and Karen had to sink or swim in their L2 milieu, Takahiro was able to enlist the help of his agents, who buffered him from the need to use L2 to achieve his highest priority goals. Because young children rely so much on others to meet their most important needs, it is inevitable that they will use the L1 (or gesture) if it can be made to work. This will relegate L2 to only the tasks of less immediate importance to the child.

Virve and Karen integrated more into their daycare environment than Takahiro, and this enriched and shaped their learning experience. They were surrounded by other children able to understand and produce language of a more advanced level, and with whom they had to compete for attention. In this respect, their experience in the second language was probably substantially different from that in the acquisition of their first, since neither had older siblings. As we saw in Chapter 6, characteristically, only (or eldest) children are often more analytic in their acquisitional style, while those in the company of other children tend to use more formulaic sequences. Vihman (1982a), indeed, notes of Virve that she used more formulaic sequences in her L2 than her L1 acquisition (p. 272). Vihman's own explanation is that either there is something in the nature of Estonian and English that makes them differently suited for a formulaic treatment, or that Virve, being older when she learnt her L2, was better equipped than before for memorizing lengthy strings. It is at least as plausible to point to the difference in the two learning environments, which offered her quite different types of input and set up different socio-interactional priorities.

Children Aged Five to Ten

We turn now to the other children listed in Table 9.1 and Figure 9.1. With the exception of Inga, who was the youngest of a family group,[5] they were all at least five years old at the start of their respective studies. To what extent might the dynamics of their various agendas in communication be different from those of the very young children just discussed, and how might that affect their learning? As before, we shall examine their use of formulaic sequences according to the four agendas represented in Figure 6.3.

Again, it is important to realize that comparisons of this kind, across studies, rely on extrapolating from reports with very different emphases. For instance, Linnakylä (1980) makes considerable mention of the ways that formulaic sequences achieve interactional functions, and Wong Fillmore (1976, 1979)[6] focusses heavily on the entire range of roles that formulaic sequences have in acquisition. In contrast, Bohn (1986) claims that most of what might pass for formulaic sequences, both in his data and in Wong Fillmore's, are actually not formulaic at all (though Bahns et al. 1986, drawing on the same data from the Wode family, take a different view). Lest the contrast of views be construed as clearly a function of the interpretative stance of the writer, however, it should be mentioned that Wong Fillmore (1976) found no formulaic sequences at all in the first month and a half of output of Alej: "He did not even attempt any English greetings, politeness formulas, or useful expressions such as *I dunno* which the other children learned in self-defense within the first few weeks of exposure to English" (p. 368). We shall see, in due course, that *not* using formulaic sequences is also an expression of strategy choice.

Also as with the younger children, many of the accounts are not very explicit about the circumstances in which an utterance has been produced, and it has been necessary to guess the details in some cases. Bahns et al. (1986) fail, in many cases, to state which of the four Wode children uttered a particular expression, thus undermining any opportunity to differentiate between the learning styles and success of, say, the girls versus boys, or older versus younger children. In the following analysis, it has not made sense to take into account, most of the time, at precisely what age or stage of learning a sequence was used, since it would be misleading to imply that such comparisons can be made. Intensive input over a few weeks for one child could easily lead to greater levels of acquisition than less intensive input over a longer period for another child.

In almost all cases, the observations reviewed here were largely or exclusively made in the nursery/kindergarten/school environment. The exceptions are Eva, Atsuko, and the Wode children, where the accounts are primarily from the home and, in the case of Atsuko, also hour-long sessions with one of the researchers. Our model predicts that formulaic sequences will be employed to meet the communication shortfall where the priorities are highest. In the case of first language acquisition, the highest single priority was getting things done and we saw this also reflected in the young children acquiring L2 above. But what are the priorities of older children? Within the educational context, there are structures and rules in place which preclude the need for certain kinds of manipulation of teachers or carers. For instance, there are times for eating and times for listening to a story, so it is not as appropriate to request these events as it would be at home. In care and educational settings, the individual child exists as one of many, expected to be self-sufficient in meeting his or her own basic needs, in a way that a younger child would not have to. The existence of the class as a group gives the learner a moment-by-moment agenda of activities, but it also sets up types of interaction which would not occur in a simple one child-one carer situation. A higher priority than manipulating adults may be manipulating other children. The desire to be part of the group is probably stronger in the children in this age-range than younger ones, and may promote certain types of linguistic behaviour. And the competition for the attention of adults and friends may promote attention-getting devices. In what follows, then, we shall be looking for evidence of formulaic sequences shifting towards the support of the interactional priorities of the young school-age learner, as compared with the toddler learners we considered in the last section.

One of the children under discussion, Nora in Wong Fillmore's (1976, 1979) study, turned out to be a particularly successful learner, and her strategies for learning will be used as a reference point. To this end, it is useful briefly to examine her case before we begin the comparisons.

Nora

Nora was one of five Spanish-speaking Mexican immigrant children studied by Wong Fillmore as they acquired English in a naturalistic setting (kindergarten and school) over a nine-month period. In the course of her account, which focusses on the role of formulaic sequences in the acquisitional process, Wong Fillmore identifies a number of factors which appear to have contributed to Nora's "spectacular success as a language learner" (1979:221). Some relate to Nora's own personality and approach; others, to her environment. None appear to have been consciously manipulated by her, though her conscious actions undoubtedly supported their beneficial effects. The factors include the following:

- No inhibitions about using a form from the moment it was learnt, and a willingness to advance on all linguistic fronts at once.
- A preference for play that used a large quantity and range of language, including role play.
- A personal interactional style that was uninhibited: she was "constantly embroiled in one controversy after another, all of which required a great deal of verbal activity" (1976:223).
- A preference for the company of children over adults. Hatch et al. (1979) point out that children's activities offer more contextualized input (p. 277).
- A disinclination or inability to postpone the need to communicate until L1 speakers were available.
- An ability to play with language at a syntactic (as opposed to just a phonological) level.
- A generally analytic mind, an ability to see patterns, and a willingness to adapt to new knowledge.

However, the pivotal factor was that her principal goal was not to learn the language, but rather to establish social relationships with a group of children who happened to speak it (Wong Fillmore 1979:208). Indeed, "she not only wanted to be around English speakers, she wanted to be *like* them, and, therefore, she adopted their way of talking" (Wong Fillmore 1976:227). This is significant in a number of ways. First, and most obviously, it increased the quantity and quality of the input, and maximized her opportunity to engage in meaningful interaction. Second, it motivated her to seek the company of English rather than Spanish speakers within and outside the school environment (in contrast with the other children in the study), and meant that whenever she fell out with her best friend, it would be another English speaker that she chose as a replacement. But third, and perhaps most importantly, it meant that the task in which she was engaged was one which she shared with her friends. Had Nora's primary agenda been to learn the language, there would have been a fundamental misalignment of her purposes in interaction and those of her interlocutors. As it was, they all shared the same priority, to operate as a social group, and Nora's linguistic disadvantage was everyone's problem in equal measure. Every effort that Nora made was matched by the efforts of her friends, all in the interests of their social aims, not linguistic ones. The upshot was a commitment to understand on Nora's part, and a commitment to facilitate understanding on the part of her friends.

As this account suggests, Nora's success was not a product only of who *she* was, but also of a supportive environment. Several factors came together for her in a way that they did not for the other children in Wong Fillmore's study. For example, Nora was not the only child motivated to play with English-speaking children out of school hours, but she was the one who was fortunate enough to have her best friend living nearby. She was also fortunate that the children she made friends with chose to welcome her into their group, and that her friends were talkative. One of the other subjects, Ana, had only one English-speaking friend, who was neither particularly talkative nor sympathetic. Nora's friends also combined a sensitivity that led them to make their input comprehensible, with a working assumption that Nora could, or would, understood what they said (1976:209, 220). "Because they believed that the learners could learn, the friends talked and interacted with them in ways that guaranteed that they would" (p. 219).

How Did the Learners Get Things Done?

As we saw earlier, understanding how formulaic sequences contribute to acquisition entails recognizing what alternative solutions the learner has access to. One of these is use of the L1. The children with greatest opportunity to take this option were the Wode children, and those in Wong Fillmore's study, though Wong Fillmore attempted to pair her subjects with friends who did not speak the L1. In any case, the L1 strategy did not always work:

[Ana] had many wants and needs; these she tried to communicate in Spanish. However, when she failed to persuade her interlocutors to give her what she wanted, or to do what she was asking, she assumed that she had failed to communicate, and tried to say the same thing in English. (Wong Fillmore 1976:437)

After a period of considerable frustration, Ana broke through into the use of English to meet her needs. Alej, on the other hand, persisted for a while with using his L1, even in conversations with his English-speaking partner (ibid.:369).

Given the limitations of their L2 knowledge, the children were more or less obliged to adopt formulaically learned strings to express manipulative messages. Examples addressed to adults include: *De l'eau, s'il vous plaît, Maman* 'Some water, please, mother' (Eva); *OK, sit down over here. Sit down Judy* (Homer); *Milk, please* (Antti) and *Hold my hand; I want to open the window* (Paul). Ana used *more, more, more* formulaically to mean *I want more*, and had the fused sequence *Can I play for dese* meaning *Can I play with this?* (Wong Fillmore 1976:432). Overall, there seem to be fewer manipulative formulaic sequences addressed to adults in these data sets (e.g., none for Uguisu, only one for Nora's first

20 weeks of learning, and few if any for the Wode children) than there were in those of the younger children. This may be because they were more rarely in one-to-one situations with an adult, something which could affect both their learning of this category of formulaic sequence and their opportunity to demonstrate their knowledge in the data. However, just as likely, the effect is no more than an artefact of the reporting, examples simply not having been recorded in the published accounts.

The story is different, though, when it comes to formulaic sequences used to manipulate the behaviour of other children, often in a fairly aggressive way. Antti's included: *C'mon*; *Get out of my way*; *Let's go* and Paul's *Get out of here*; *Don't do that* and *You shut up*. Huang and Hatch (1978) confirm that when Paul used the first of these to another child who was pestering him, he did not know its real meaning, "yet he understood its meaning in a global sense, stored it in memory, and recalled it for use in the appropriate situation" (p. 121). The Wode children accumulated a sizeable repertoire of formulaic sequences for use between each other and with other children (occasionally addressing them to their parents too), including *shut up*; *you're crazy*; *stupid idiot*; *come on*; *wait a minute*; and *knock it off* (Bahns et al. 1986:701). Juan's and Jesus' repertoires were similar to this, including: *shaddup you*; *come here* and *wait a minute* (Juan) and *Be quiet you*; *Wait a minute*; *hurry up hurry up* and *don't cry* (Jesus). Alej, when he finally began to speak English, relied entirely on formulaic sequences, including *Shut the door* which meant 'Stop it'. Most of his utterances were preceded by *stupid* or *silly* (Wong Fillmore 1976:372) and so, presumably, were addressed to other children. Nora had just one directive formulaic sequence in her repertoire[7] at 20 weeks: *Get out of here*. However, by the end of her nine months of exposure, her range of output was so varied and nativelike that problems comparable with those for native speaker data arise, in identifying what is formulaic and what is simply fluently constructed by rule (see Chapter 2).

'Magic words' are more a feature of child-to-adult manipulative speech and so, not surprisingly in the light of the learning situation, they are sporadic in the data. Antti had several politeness routines, including *Thank you*; *thank you very much*; *please* and *Have a nice day*. Paul had *excuse me* and *may I be excused?* (Huang & Hatch 1978:127). Wong Fillmore's subjects also knew some (e.g., *thank you* (Ana, Jesus), *please* (Nora), *'Scuse me* (Juan, Jesus)), and the Wode children used *I'm sorry* and *thank you* (Bahns et al. 1986:701). Eva used *s'il vous plaît*, as illustrated earlier. None are reported for Nahla, Etham and Yael, nor for Uguisu or Homer.

Whereas the younger children made relatively little use of manipulative formulaic sequences to gain information, they are common in these older children (except Homer). Examples include: *What are you doing?* (Yael, Nahla); *Where are you?* (Etham); *Quelle heure est-il?* 'What time is it?' (Eva); *How do you do this?*; *What's happening? Hey, what's going on here?* (Nora); *How much? Wha' happen?*, meaning 'What are you doing?', 'What are you making?' and 'What do you want?' (Alej) (Wong Fillmore 1976:372); *Do you know? How do you do it? Where did you get that?* (Uguisu); *What time is it? How come? What happened?* (Wode children). When Antti wanted to know if his friend wanted some orange juice, he used the expression he had heard adults use to a whole group: *Orange juice? Raise your hands.* Also in evidence are formulaic frames, such as Eva's *Où sont les N* 'where are the(PL) N?' which she used with both singular and plural nouns. Paul had *Where's the N?*

As a few of these examples indicate, for all three of these manipulative functions, formulaic sequences were also created and fused, presumably to express messages for which the child had not encountered, or could not remember, a suitable sequence. Antti invented *What you V?*, Homer *What is this X?* and Nora *How do you do dese X?* (e.g., *how do you do dese flower power? How do you do dese in English?*) (Wong Fillmore 1979:214). The Wode children created a variable but clearly still formulaic sequence *This/That window is (for X) safe* and another *I got that/the/one window*, both used to establish claims to window seats in the car (Bahns et al. 1986:704f).

How Did They Demonstrate Group Membership?

Social integration seems to have been extremely important. We have already seen how Nora's language learning was closely linked to her status in her peer group, and this applied to most of the children to some extent. "Jesus' use of formulas was intended less for communicating information than for establishing and maintaining phatic contact with his peers" (Wong Fillmore 1976:346). Irrespective of the relevance of what he said, "he was talking, and that kept him in social contact with people from whom he could learn the new language better" (ibid.). As Willett (1995) observes of Nahla, Yael and Etham, "Although their language consists almost entirely of prefabricated language chunks . . . the children use these chunks to enact a socially significant event in order to construct identities as competent students . . . and construct collaborative relations with one another" (p. 490). In keeping with the desire to be perceived as a member of the L2 speaker group, Yael "studied the behavior of her classmates carefully for clues and mirrored their actions and expressions. She began using English much earlier than Nahla and Etham" (Willett 1995:484). Eva was greatly distressed at her inability to integrate linguistically:

Ne pas être admise dans la société des enfants, voilà le coup le plus dur qui puisse frapper notre fille. Elle en comprend la raison et prend le parti de cacher autant que possible son ignorance de la langue.[8] (Kenyeres 1938:324)

As we saw earlier, the desire to sound like an L2 speaker is one of the most powerful catalysts for the adoption of formulaic sequences, so a strong pro-L2 identity is significant to understanding the patterns of language use. Antti, by six months into his exposure to English, "avoided speaking Finnish outside the home if English-speaking friends were listening", which increasingly meant that he had to speak English to his parents in mixed company (Linnakylä 1980:388). Nora, too, soon began "to reject the use of Spanish, even when she could have expressed herself more easily in it" (Wong Fillmore 1976:575). Juan was less taken with his English-speaking peers and chose not to communicate much with them (Wong Fillmore 1979:217). This disadvantaged his learning considerably, since "he avoided those who might have provided him with input" (Wong Fillmore 1976:341).[9]

As with the toddlers, an important way of insinuating oneself into a group was to imitate the linguistic patterns used in group activities. For some, including Paul, Antti, Nora and Eva, this included the learning of songs, and for all the children, routines associated with group games such as *catch me, catch me*; *one, two, three, go!* (Antti) *ready, get set, go*; *my turn* (Antti and Juan), *time in*; *I got you*; *I got it* (Lars). A related strategy was the adoption of formulaic routines that indicated conformity with the group culture, particularly relative to adults. We have already seen the 'magic words' aspect of this conformity. Other manifestations were *Good bye. See you tomorrow*; *I'll see you* (Paul), *Hi teacher* (Nora), *Bye-bye*; *How are you?*; *Good morning*; *Have a nice day* (Antti) and *Bonjour maman* (Eva). Other formulaic sequences played the role of ingratiation, relative to the hearer (e.g., *I like you, honey* (Antti) and *I'm sorry* (Nora)).

How Did They Demonstrate Individuality?

Differences in personality and confidence seem able to have a substantial effect on the approach to interaction and to learning achievements. Self-expression is probably best achieved in most circumstances by using formulaic sequences without too much analytic engagement. Wong Fillmore (1976:367) contrasts Juan, who did not like to say anything until he knew he was getting it right, with Jesus, who "was filled with confidence and was even slightly reckless since he assumed he knew what he was doing, and that what he was doing was correct". Yet, while Juan suffered from his overcaution, Jesus was also disadvantaged by his intransigence in the face of evidence that he had learned something wrong (ibid.). As Juan and Jesus jointly illustrate, it is necessary to protect oneself in the context of major compromise to one's sense of linguistic and social capability, but yet be sufficiently confident to continue to engage.

Overprotection of the self often led to avoidance, as we saw with Takahiro, who ran away when he was addressed in the L2. In a similar vein, Eva refused to enter a classroom because she believed the cook's son to be in there, and she was frightened that he would ask her a question she could not answer (Kenyeres 1938:324). Formulaic linguistic realizations of this avoidance strategy include various versions of *I don't know* (Paul, the Wode children, Juan, Jesus), *nothing* (Jesus), *I don' speak English* (Alej), *I can't* (Juan and Ana), and *I can't do it*; *I'm not playn* (Ana), which "permitted her to get out of doing things she felt she could not do or did not want to do; during this period, many of the things she felt she could not do involved language use" (Wong Fillmore 1976:436). Self-protection took other forms too, including defiance (e.g., Nora's fused *I don't wanna do dese*, Nahla's *don't be silly*, Jesus' *Nuts to you* and *Shaddup*), and self-deprecation, such as Jesus' *I goof* and *Oh stupid*, which Wong Fillmore identifies as "expressions that would help him to interact with his friends in idiomatically approved ways" (1976:353).

The best attested way of protecting the sense of self, however, was self-promotion (e.g., *I'm so lucky* (Nora)). The children would draw attention to themselves with expressions like *I know dis*; *I can do this*; *I did this* (Nahla, Etham, Yael); *Hey look*; *Hey Teacher*; *Hey you guys* (Antti); *Oh Teacher*; *Look Teacher* (Juan); *Hey look* (Jesus); *This is mine* (Paul); *I know how to X* (Uguisu); *I can say it NP*; *Lemme see it (NP)* (Ana). In addition, almost all had the fused sequence *lookit* and other fused expressions, such as *gimme see*; *looky see* (Alej). Paul, Nora, Antti and Uguisu were all prepared to take initiatives, both social and linguistic, to start up or prolong interaction. The Wode children provide a wealth of examples of formulaic sequences for self-promotion, which probably reflects the apparently endemic sibling rivalry between them.

Part of Nora's flair for language learning was the ability to pick useful, even comical, formulaic sequences which could be used to good effect on many occasions. When she had got some playdough stuck to her paper, the observer asked her *What happened?* She replied *I don' know.*

I think I oughta know, "said with exaggerated intonation, and comic gesture: hands up-turned, head cocked to one side, and with a shrug" (Wong Fillmore 1976:492). On the surface, this sequence is effective because "it can be spoken whenever anyone asks a question that is not easily answered" (ibid.), but quite clearly it also served the function of defining Nora's personality as engaging and cute, which no doubt was part of what made her popular and worth communicating with.

How Did They Gain Control of the Language?

The acquisitional pattern reported in these studies is, almost invariably, that some sort of silent period, longer for some learners than others, was followed by a period of imitation without full comprehension.[10] Next was a period of apparent competence, characterized by fluent and accurate output made up of formulaic sequences used in pragmatically appropriate ways. At this time there would be little attempt to dissect sequences, particularly if they were exclamations or purely referential:

Paul's imitated sentences were grammatical (he sounded like a native-speaker of English), and he was not aware of the smaller units within such utterances. He made no attempt to break up these sentences and recombine words into new sentences during the first month. While he said, "It's time to eat and drink" along with other children as juice and crackers were put on the table, he didn't say "It's time to" anything else. (Huang & Hatch 1978:123)

Subsequently, the children increasingly attempted to express novel ideas, with the output being rather less fluent and nativelike. Atsuko used "a small number of patterns or modules rather than . . . composing a host of varied sentences from a large stock of single words. [These] served as frames which she could vary by lexical substitution" (Rescorla & Okuda 1987:293). One obvious tactic for gaining access to the linguistic system is to use translation. But, as we have already seen, none of the children was particularly disposed, after the first few weeks, to use the L1 much.

As with the younger children, one important use of formulaic sequences for gaining control of the language was in asking for linguistic information. The sequences were both nativelike ones and fused ones: *What's this name? What's that? What name?* (Antti); *What is it?* (Wode children); *What? What you say? Huh?* (Jesus); *I don't understand; How do you dese in English?* (Nora). Homer had two fused formulas *What X* and *What is this X*, where X was the material he did not understand. For instance, asked to draw a tree, he said *What draw a tree?* 'What does *Draw a tree* mean?'(Wagner-Gough 1978:170). When Homer's friend said, of the tower they were building, *Quit making it so tall!*, Homer did not understand 'so tall' and replied *What is this sulta!* (ibid.:156).

In first language acquisition, referential naming has been identified as a sign of the analytic style, in which fewer formulaic sequences are used (see Chapter 6). Probably as a function of age, there is less direct evidence of naming games for their own sake in these studies than there was with the two year olds, though Antti did get some vocabulary tuition (Linnakylä 1980:381–382). However, there are other indications of personal acquisitional styles. Atsuko favoured referential utterances overall (Rescorla & Okuda 1987:293). Juan "interpreted all questions about the [elicitation task] pictures as requests for object identification, naming all the things he could in each picture. These activities brought out the fact that what he was learning in English was mostly vocabulary items" (Wong Fillmore 1976:317). Juan appears, then, to have perceived language learning as more of an activity in its own right than did, for instance, Nora. As Wong Fillmore (1979) observes, he was quite motivated to learn English for its own sake, but, unlike the other four children in the study, had no interest in socializing with English speakers "and hence, he had little reason to use what he was learning" (p. 208).

In contrast, Nora tended to use a word or phrase first, and worry about what it meant later (Wong Fillmore 1979:215). Her strategy was to identify a sequence and then use it on every possible occasion; the result was that "she never seemed to be at a loss for words, or for idiomatic ways to phrase them" (Wong Fillmore 1976:525). One sequence, *in the high school*, "was just a nice phrase which she sometimes appended to her sentences. It sometimes meant 'in class'; at other times, it meant nothing in particular" (1976:494). A similar example from Ana was *when I come home*, which she added to her utterances for no apparent purpose (1976:446). As with Nora, this had the effect of creating extra fluency. Ana extended this to her pretend reading, using *One day* to begin the story and link the sentences in a way that mimicked the story format (p. 445).

For Nora, fantasy and role-play were a major means by which she gained her wide-ranging linguistic experience (Wong Fillmore 1979:223), as she tried out different situations and found language to handle them, drawing on imitated utterances that she had heard native speakers use. Antti, too, was prepared to practise prefabricated strings; he sat in the car saying, over and over again, *What do you say?* (Linnakylä 1980:385). In situ too, utterances could be imitated effectively. Nora copied not only her English-speaking friend's words, but also her actions (e.g., Wong Fillmore 1976:745ff). Homer also copied utterances wholesale. When, in his second week, he copied a complete sentence from his friend, the friend said *Don't copy* and Homer repeated that too.[11] In the early stages of learning, Alej was 'helped' during elicitation questioning by his

English speaking playmate, Kevin, who would whisper the answer to
him. Alej understood that he only needed to imitate what Kevin said.
However, this occasionally led to difficulties:

(The observer is asking Alej about some pictures in a book.)

Observer:	What are they doing here? (Classroom scene with children at work).
Alej:	A la escuela.
Kevin:	(Whispers into Alej's ear) Talking!
Alej:	Talking!
Observer:	What are they talking about?
Kevin:	(To Alej) Gettin' a book.
Alej:	Getna book.
Observer:	Where is the book, Alej?
Kevin:	(He takes over the questioning) Where's the book? Touch the book, Alej.
Alej:	Touch the book.
Kevin:	Touch the book, the book! Here's the book; touch the book.
Alej:	Touch the book.
Kevin:	TOUCH it!
Alej:	TOUCH it!
Kevin:	Don't SAY touch it – TOUCH it!
Alej:	Touch it!

(Wong Fillmore 1976:370–371)

Repeated material could also take on its own linguistic function. Paul
repeated just the segment that he did not understand, using a rising intonation (e.g., Jim: *Take the pencil.* Paul: *Pencil?*; Jim: *No, Paul, this way,
please, this way.* Paul: *This way?*) (Huang & Hatch 1978:129). Homer
used repetition to meet a shortfall in his ability to restructure questions
as answers. When asked *Is Mark at school today?* he replied using exactly
the same words, but with a falling intonation, indicating that he meant
'Yes, Mark is at school today' (Wagner-Gough 1978:164). A more sophisticated version of imitation involved using input as a basis for an
expanded response. This strategy was used by several of the children,
including Nora, Uguisu, Homer and Nahla. Nahla "answer[ed] the aide's
questions by appropriating the textbook language and the ends of the
aide's phrases" (Willett 1995:488). This seems to have been part of a more
general feature of her social interaction and play: "Early in their development . . . one of the girls would produce a rhythmic monologue (reg-
ularized pattern of accented syllables) of nonsense sounds and words
from the work-book. The other two would echo and develop these
sounds with additional nonsense flourishes" (ibid.:491). Homer also
incorporated input into an expanded response. For example, he replied
to the question *Where are you going?* with *Where are you going is house*
('I'm going home'). Nora would repeat her own utterances, with modifi-

cations, as she sought a better result: Observer: *And was it raining by her house?* Nora: *No, no, no – no! She said to me that it wa' not too raining by she house. She said it wa' not too raining by she house. She said she not raining by she house* (Wong Fillmore 1976:806).

As control of the language increased, the formulaic sequences which formed the basic currency of interaction were used more creatively. They were added together, or embedded into novel structures, to make new or better utterances. This building strategy is well illustrated by Antti, whose leave-taking utterances developed in the following way: *Bye!; Bye-bye; Bye-bye teacher!; Bye-bye teacher, see you!; Bye-bye teacher, see you soon!; Bye-bye teacher, see you another week!* (Linnakylä 1980:370). Homer also juxtaposed formulaic sequences, and then deleted common material, to create his own brand of syntax (see Wagner-Gough 1978:166–167 for a description of this process). Nora, too, added formulaic sequences together, such as *put it* and *right here*, to create a new, single sequence (Wong Fillmore 1976:506).

Finally, formulaic sequences were segmented into smaller strings (see Robinson 1986 for one treatment of this process using examples from Nora and Homer). Wong Fillmore offers many illustrations of this, from Juan (Wong Fillmore 1976:329), Alej (p. 380), Ana (p. 439) and Nora (p. 495). Only Jesus "tended to preserve his formulas rigidly in the form he learned them" (p. 493). For instance, Ana segmented *I wanna play for dese*, her own fused formula based on input she had heard, and separated out a section *I wanna X* (e.g., *I wanna over here*; *I wanna make café*). Nora segmented *I wanna play wi' dese* to identify *play wi'*. Nora was quick to segment, but, importantly, she did not discard the original formulaic sequence once she had extracted parts of it, but used both types of unit (p. 493). In stark contrast, little segmentation is evident in the language of the Wode children, though this could be an artefact of the accounts.

Discussion

When a five-year-old boy enters a new country, he may find circumstances quite different from those he is used to. However, his basic needs are all the same. He looks for security, he desires friends, and he wants to explore the surrounding world and his own imagination. In order to satisfy these basic needs in the new milieu, the child often has to acquire a new functional language. (Linnakylä 1980:367)

The common theme in all of the accounts above has been the children's use of their L2 to express their own needs, and their own personalities. Willett (1995) notes that it is not a question of which formulaic sequences aid language acquisition, but rather how formulaic sequences "enable learners to construct positive identities and relations and manage competing agendas" (p. 499).[12] Linnakylä, following Wong Fillmore (1976), outlines strategies for successful integration into an L2 environment, a side effect of which will be acquiring the language. The framework has much in common with the models developed in this book, particularly in recognizing that formulaic sequences are the key to being perceived as belonging, and making yourself understood. As with the younger children reviewed earlier, the extent to which they are forced to meet their social and physical needs through the L2, and are able and willing to do so, seems to make a difference to the success they achieve. At one extreme there is Nora, who threw herself whole-heartedly into being a member of the English-speaking community. In contrast, the Wode children, who were operating as a German family unit in an English-speaking environment for a finite time, seem to have learned in a much more piecemeal way, and to have relied on formulaic sequences rather less:

[they] learned their second language in an environment that was, at least in part, bilingual. Because they were free to use English or German at home, it could well be that they did not have to rely on formulaic stereotypes as much as other L2 learners in monolingual environments. (Bohn 1986:199)

Juan, who was in a similar environment to Nora, though he did not have an exclusively English-speaking circle of friends, seemed to be much more conscious of English being a language to learn, rather than the language that happened to be used by those he wanted to identify with. Perhaps he fell foul of the danger which Hakuta (1976) recognizes: "if learners always have to wait until they acquire the constructional rules for forming an utterance before using it, then they may run into serious motivational difficulties in learning the language, for the functions that can be expressed . . . would be severely limited" (p. 333).

Children have many advantages over adults in language learning, even leaving aside any possible biological ones. They mix with other children, who seem very tolerant of incomprehension. And they engage in many kinds of ritualized play, which provide a wealth of oft-repeated, highly predictable and contextualized language (Hatch et al. 1979:275, 277). Also of benefit to their learning, though not to their sense of well-being, is their inability to take the kinds of steps that an adult might to avoid the trauma of their situation as a nonspeaker of the new language (e.g., Kenyeres 1938:324). We shall see that, in adult learners, the option *not* to communicate becomes ever more viable, and can replace language use as a major strategy for protecting and expressing identity. There may already be glimpses of a limited version of this in some of the children. Wong Fillmore (1979) notes that while Nora appeared to be unable to suppress her desire to communicate, the other children in her study could, and did, postpone communication until they were linguistically better equipped (p. 224).

The art of using formulaic sequences effectively for language learning is not so simple as it might seem. Alej overextended his use of them, so they were hard to understand (Wong Fillmore 1976:386), and Jesus was too wedded to his (Wong Fillmore 1979:225). Nora's success as a learner seems associated with a flexible range of functions for them. She used them to sound native and idiomatic, and the more nativelike she appeared to be, the more like a native speaker she was treated, and the greater the quantity and variety of input she received. Being perceived as competent has social and academic benefits, as Willett (1995:497) illustrates in a comparison of the teachers' perceptions of the three girls Nahla, Etham and Yael on the one hand, and the socially less integrated boy Xavier.

Although Bohn (1986) questions Wong Fillmore's claim that formulaic sequences are a major point of access for identifying component forms, her enormous body of evidence is hard to gainsay. All of the children in her study engaged in segmentation, and none so successfully and actively as Nora. Nora was able to acquire formulaic sequences, and then segment them almost immediately (Wong Fillmore 1976:549). It is worth noting, since it will form the basis of discussion later (Chapter 11), that even though she was quick to spot component parts of formulaic sequences, Nora's strategy did *not* become one of entirely bypassing the formulaic stage, and homing straight in on the smaller units, as adult learners seem more inclined to do (Chapter 10). She was still operating from the large and integrated unit *downwards*, not cutting straight in at the bottom level. As a result, she did not end up knowing components without also knowing idiomatic contexts in which they occurred. She may have had to guess and experiment about how *else* they could be used, but she always had, as a reference point, her knowledge of an item within the formulaic sequence from which she had first isolated it. Local appropriacy of use is something that is much more haphazard if a learner focusses on the individual word or morpheme, without first engaging with the larger multiword unit.

10

Patterns of Formulaicity in Adults and Teenagers Using a Second Language

Introduction

In the last chapter, it was possible to engage in some depth with the detail of formulaic language output from individual learners. This was because the research on children tends to be in the form of case studies, recording either all of their L2 utterances, or else regular samples. Research on adult learners is generally not like this. Within the case study approach, which predominates in the work on naturalistic acquisition in the L2 environment, accounts of formulaic language tend to be anecdotal rather than reflecting a full record or disciplined periodic collection. Meanwhile, formulaic language research on classroom-taught learners focusses on groups rather than individuals, so that it is rarely possible to gain more than a glimpse of a particular learner's profile over time. As a result, the data from adults and teenagers in published sources does not lend itself to a direct consideration of the interactional and processing functions of formulaic sequences, since the necessary context of utterances is not always given, and individual examples cannot be judged for their representativeness. In this chapter, then, we shall engage first of all with the data on its own terms, identifying the common patterns that are relevant to our current discussion. Only after that will it be possible to raise our main questions, regarding the roles which formulaic sequences may be playing in adult and teenage second language learners.

Adults Acquiring the L2 'Naturally'

There have been several studies, some quite sizeable, of adult learners acquiring the L2 largely or entirely without formal tuition, including three examinations of Gastarbeiter (immigrant workers in Germany):

the Heidelberg Research Project (see Dittmar 1984, for example), the ZISA project (e.g., Clahsen 1984; Meisel, Clahsen & Pienemann 1981) and a European Science Foundation study (e.g., Klein & Perdue 1992; Perdue 1984, 1993). Strikingly, however, these accounts find little of importance to say about formulaic language. The lack of discussion is undoubtedly due, in part, to a theoretical bias towards looking at lexis and grammar separately and assuming that language learning primarily entails the building up of larger units from smaller ones. Such an approach may fail to see formulaic patterns or may view them as being of so little significance to the learning process that they are unworthy of mention. However, as will become clear presently, there may also be another reason for the absence of descriptions of formulaic sequences in such research reports.

Only a handful of studies, mostly of one subject each, really engage with even describing, let alone accounting for, formulaic sequences (Table 10.1), and, for the reasons outlined at the start of this chapter, care needs to be taken not to place too much weight upon them individually. One study which has been much cited in the literature as indicative of high levels of formulaicity in the naturalistic adult learner is that of Hanania and Gradman (1977). They certainly report the existence of "memorized utterances", but, on closer examination, doing so turns out to be supplementary to the main focus of their research, which is the subject's ability to create novel utterances by rule. As a result, it is unclear how representative the examples of formulaic sequences are, and what their role was. They report only seven actual sequences, and one strategy: *come on* and *come in*, which were phonologically indistinguishable; *This is + N*, which was learned in a language class; *Thank you*; *I can't* . . . ; and *Do you like* . . . , which were "perceived as single units" and not segmented; *See you*, which she used for saying goodbye, but could not combine with *I can* to make *I can see you*;[1] and the repetition of selected items from utterances she heard (pp. 78–79). All of these occurred during the earliest stage of her learning. It is, of course, possible that she used other formulaic sequences not reported, or that some of the strings treated in the analysis as novel constructions were in fact formulaic, but we cannot tell this from the report. Overall, Hanania and Gradman offer little evidence of formulaicity as a strategy, and, in fact, they view its role in their subject's language as minor and facilitatory only.

Despite Ellis's (1994) claim that, in the early stages at least, formulaic language "figures frequently in the speech of all learners, irrespective of their age" (p. 85), it turns out that there are vast differences in the extent to which formulaic sequences are reported for different learners. Like Hanania and Gradman, Schumann (1978a, 1978b) and Shapira (1978)

Table 10.1. *Studies examining formulaic sequences in adults acquiring L2 'naturally'*

Study	No. of subjects	L1	L2	Location of study (L1 or L2 environment)	Data type
Hanania & Gradman (1977)	1	Arabic	English	L2	Recordings of conversations
Huebner (1983)	1	Hmong/Lao	English	L2	Recordings of conversations
Rehbein (1987)	3	Turkish	German	L2	Recordings of conversations
Schmidt (1983)	1	Japanese	English	L2	Monologue recordings made during returns to L1 environment
Schumann (1978a, 1978b)	1	Spanish	English	L2	Recordings of conversation and elicited speech
Shapira (1978)	1	Spanish	English	L2	Recordings of planned and unplanned conversations
Yorio (1989)	1	Korean	English	L2	Written compositions

found that their subjects made little use of formulaic language. On the other hand, Schmidt's (1983) subject Wes, a 33-year-old Japanese immigrant to Hawaii who developed a high level of fluency, seemed to call on formulaic sequences as a "major linguistic strategy" (p. 150). Similarly, Yorio (1989) reports that K., an 18 year old Korean whose written English he examined, had a high level of facility with idioms and set phrases (p. 60). There is too little evidence either way for us to be certain whether this really reflects variation between individuals in the use of formulaic sequences, or just different identificational criteria in the research, but if it does, then the many studies which hardly refer to formulaic sequences at all, including the Heidelberg, ZISA and ESF projects mentioned earlier, may have been forced to that position by an absence of any to report, rather than a failure to notice them.

If there are individual differences in the use of formulaic sequences, it should be possible to link these to variation in the processing and interactional pressures encountered by different learners. Salient factors to consider would be the interactional and other purposes for which the L2 was being used, the amount of internal or external pressure on the learner to achieve certain goals, and the level of the learner's desire to interact with the L2 native speakers. Overall, sparse though it is, the evidence is consistent with our model: there seems to be a link between the use of formulaic sequences and a need and desire to interact, these two together contributing to the overall achievement of communicative competence. K., Yorio's (1989) subject, had taken grades 8 to 12 in an English-speaking environment, with only minimal preparatory teaching, and had since worked as assistant manager in a store. Thus, he had considerable experience of using English for the moment-by-moment communication of ideas. In his writing, 98% of what he said was "perfectly comprehensible" even if not correct. Schmidt's (1983) Wes was also communicatively competent, was very focussed on real interaction, and would persevere with an utterance until he was understood. In contrast, Schumann's (1978b) subject, who achieved much less success in learning, kept a social and psychological distance from the target language speakers (p. 259), and Shapira's (1978) Guatemalan subject "socialize[d] with Spanish-speaking people, watche[d] Spanish TV, read [. . .] Spanish and listen[ed] to Latin-American music" (p. 247). Rehbein (1987) found that Turkish Gastarbeiter applied a "self-imposed reduction of their own system of needs" (p. 245), that is, they simply avoided situations in which they might need utterances which they could not produce. In a similar vein, Hinnenkamp (1980) suggests that the Gastarbeiter population tended to resist the L2 because they associated it with disadvantageous encounters: "to communicate with Germans, who are primarily socially above them or function as superiors or officials, means communicating against themselves" (p. 180). If social integration plays a key role in the success of language acquisition, then it may be no accident that the learners who find themselves most isolated from other speakers of their L1 generally achieve more success in the L2. Where there exists an L1-speaking community, into which assimilation is a social priority, there will be fewer incentives, and indeed even some disincentives, for acquiring the L2.

What of the role of formulaic sequences in promoting the acquisition of the grammar and lexicon? Shapira's (1978), Schumann's (1978a, 1978b) and Huebner's (1983) subjects, whose use of formulaic sequences was minimal, also achieved only low levels of learning overall, while Schmidt's (1983) subject Wes, who used them much more, also learned more. Yet Schmidt (1983) reports that despite his fluency, Wes did not attain accuracy of form, which suggests that he was not using his formulaic language as input for analysis (p. 150). Similarly, Yorio (1989) found only 32% of T-units (main clause plus associated subordinate clauses) to be error-free in K.'s writing (p. 60). Overall, there is little evidence, in adult naturalistic learners, of a progression of the kind identified for first language acquisition, from using formulaic sequences as an aid to initial communication, through a process of segmentation, to nativelike abilities. In short, the developmental aspect of the model outlined in Chapters 6 and 7 with respect to first language acquisition is not matched in this context, somewhat belying Nattinger and DeCarrico's (1992) claim, quoted earlier, that adults and children approach language learning in the same way (p. 27).

Adults Learning L2 in the Classroom

The most common way for people in the industrialized world to learn another language is in a classroom, whether this be in the L1 or L2 environment. Clearly, in the latter case, it can be particularly difficult for researchers to separate out the influences of formal tuition from those surrounding the learner outside of class time, but even in the case of foreign language classes conducted in the learner's home country it is not always possible to ascertain the extent of alternative types of input, whether access to TV and other media, holidays, parental knowledge of the L2, L2-speaking friends, or whatever. Such factors simply compound an already complex set of interacting influences on learning approach and style.

Stevick (1989) offers some indication that successful learners recognize a role for formulaic strategies in learning. These include deliberate mimicry of the teacher's utterances (p. 97), mechanical practice (p. 148), structured rehearsal of formulaic frames with different open class items in them (p. 147), memorizing entire texts (p. 29) and 'stockpiling' sentences (p. 60). But research offers little insight into why such an approach might appeal, or what the spontaneous appearance of formulaic sequences in interlanguage might signify. What it does reveal, however, is that, as Pawley and Syder (1983) suggest, the formulaic sequences used by native speakers are not easy for learners to identify and master, and that their absence greatly contributes to learners not sounding idiomatic.

Studies specifically aiming to examine formulaicity in taught L2 learners are listed in Table 10.2. The discussion which follows will be arranged according to five themes, which relate to the use of formulaic sequences in the early and later stages of learning, how their use is balanced with creativity, how they aid acquisition, and how they can be taught.

The Use of Formulaic Sequences in the Very Early Stages of Learning

We should not be surprised to find that one of the first ways in which classroom learners succeed in stringing two or more words together is by repeating sequences that they have learned whole. It is, after all, a standard component of first-level textbooks to 'get the ball rolling' by introducing some basic greetings, questions which can be asked around the class (*what is your name? where do you live? what job do you do?*), useful classroom management material (*please would you repeat that; I don't know; I don't understand*), and the like (Jaworski 1990:397–398). The rate and success with which such sequences are learned and used seems to depend on a number of factors, however, besides the extent to which they are targeted in the input, and, as we shall see, not all of them necessarily support the intention to approximate aspects of nativelike language use. In addition to memorizing externally proffered models, a learner may store the solution worked out on one occasion and reproduce it from memory subsequently, so that what was, at first, a creative construction becomes a fused one (e.g., Schmidt & Frota 1986:310). It may or may not be correctly formulated in target language terms.

Dufon (1995) followed the progress of 18 beginner learners of Indonesian over five consecutive days' classes a few weeks into their period of study. Her focus was their take-up of the 'gambits' which they heard from the teacher or read in their textbook. Of the 98 gambits which the students encountered, they used, between them, 24. The functions of the ten most frequent were to mark hesitation, appeal for a response, indicate the start of a turn, conjoin ideas, give neutral response or exclamation, mark focus, and request repetition (p. 42). In her definition, gambits are

formulaic expressions whose primary role is strategic rather than propositional in nature; they serve to guide the hearer through the discourse by semantically framing propositional information (e.g., *The main point is*), by facilitating turn exchanges (e.g., *May I interrupt for a moment?*), and by marking discourse boundaries (e.g., *That's all I have to say about that*). (p. 43)

Although the examples in this extract fall well within the customary definitions of formulaic expressions, the inventory of gambits that she actually observed includes not only phrases (e.g., *Saya rasa* 'I feel'; *Saya tidak tahu*, 'I don't know') but also single words (e.g., *jadi*, 'so/therefore'; *serkarang*, 'now' as an opener), and nonlexical expressions (e.g., *uh*, a hesitation filler). Not all definitions of formulaicity are geared for handling the latter two types, though the evident homogeneity of the set as

Table 10.2. *Studies examining formulaic sequences in adults and teenagers acquiring L2 in the classroom*

Study	No. of subjects	L1	L2	Location of study (L1 or L2 environment)	Data type	Summary
Biskup (1992)	34 28	Polish German	English English	L1 L1	Translations of collocations from L1 to L2	Comparison of collocational knowledge when L2 is closely or only distantly related to the L1
Bolander (1989)	20 20 20	Finnish Polish Spanish	Swedish Swedish Swedish	L2	Recordings of free speech and a picture description task	Role of 'chunk learning' in acquisition of inversion and negatives
Bygate (1988)	20	Spanish	English	not stated	Self-recorded communication activities	Discourse management devices, including repetition
DeCock et al. (1998)	25 (+25 natives)	French	English	L1	Informal interviews	Collection of repeated word sequences, to compare quantity and nature in natives and non-natives
Dufon (1995)	18	English (17) + French (1)	Indonesian	L1 (i.e., English)	Recordings of 5 consecutive classes of 50 minutes, incl. 1 student in pairwork	Take-up and spontaneous use of 'gambits'
Ellis & Schmidt (1997, study 2)	20	English	Artificial language	L1	Tests administered by computer	Role of phonological memory in learning utterances and extracting grammatical patterns
R. Ellis (1984)	1 (11 yrs, male) 1 (11 yrs, male) 1 (13 yrs, female)	Portuguese Punjabi Punjabi	English English English	L2	Notes and recordings of language in classroom (1–3 visits per year, over 1 year)	Role of formulaic sequences during first year of acquisition

Study	N				Data	Focus
Farghal & Obiedat (1995)	(a) 34 + (b) 23	Arabic	English	L1	Questionnaires: (a) in English, fill in the blanks (b) in Arabic, provide the English equivalents of the Arabic collocations	Comparison of knowledge of collocations in (a) students of English and (b) experienced teachers of English (all non-native speakers)
Foster (2001)	32 (+32 native speakers)	Various	English	L2	Recordings of spoken dialogue in three tasks	Effect of preplanning on use of formulaic sequences.
Granger (1998)	n/a	French (+ native speaker comparison)	English	L1	Corpus of written work (from International Corpus of Learner English); native corpus from three sources	Comparison of quantity of formulaic sequences in non-native and native writing, to illustrate preference for 'open choice' vs. 'idiom' principle
Howarth (1998a)	10	Various (compared with large native corpus)	English	L2	Written essays (10 each)	Comparison of native and non-native collocations with most common verb lemmas
Irujo (1993)	12	Spanish	English	L2	Translation from L1 to L2, including cognate and noncognate idioms	Knowledge of L2 idioms in highly proficient non-natives
Jaworski (1990)	30 (+31 native speakers)	English	Polish	L1	Written dialogue	Comparison of native and non-native use of formulaic sequences in dialogue between two friends
Lennon (1990)	4	German	English	L2	Recordings of spoken monologue task	Comparison of fluency at start and end of 6-month stay in L2 environment
Myles et al. (1998, 1999)	8 (11–14, female) 8 (11–14, male)	English	French	L1	Recordings of pair- and group-work and subject-adult pairs, in bespoke activities	Observation of learning progression over six terms, including breaking down of formulaic sequences

(continued)

Table 10.2 (continued)

Study	No. of subjects	L1	L2	Location of study (L1 or L2 environment)	Data type	Summary
Raupach (1984)	2	German	French	L1	Recorded responses to written questions	Comparison of length and phonological nature of word sequences before and after one term's residency in L2 environment
Scarcella (1979)	30	Spanish	English	L2	Filled in blanks on cartoon captions	Knowledge of common idiomatic phrases
Schmidt & Frota (1986)	1	English	Portuguese	L2	Diary and recorded conversations with native speaker	Detailed account of progress before, during and after instruction, supplemented by interaction beyond classroom
Towell et al. (1996)	12	English	French	L1	Recording of spoken retelling of film plot	Comparison of fluency before and after 12 month's residency abroad (6 months in L2 environment)
Yorio (1989)	(a) 25 (+15 native speakers)	Unspecified, but including some Spanish natives	English	L2	Written compositions	Accuracy of formulaic sequences and non-native vs. native use of two-word verbs
	(b) Unspecified	Spanish Spanish	English English	L2 L1	Written compositions	Relative accuracy and amount of use of formulaic sequences by non-natives living in L2 environment vs. studying L2 as FL in L1 environment

nativelike measures for handling interactional functions suggests that they should be included.

Dufon's interest in expressions which manage the discourse reflects the view that language learning is about achieving functional communication. In one of the few studies to focus on the use of formulaic sequences by secondary-school-age children learning a second language in the classroom, Rod Ellis (1984) concludes that "formulaic speech did not have to be taught to be acquired. Its communicative value together with frequency of use were sufficient for acquisition to take place" (p. 64). His account reports on the first stages of acquisition of English by a male aged 11 and a female aged 13 with Punjabi as their first language, and a male aged 11 whose first language was Portuguese. Ellis found that all three initially relied almost entirely on formulaic sequences, especially a limited range of "ceremonial" ones such as *good morning* and *thank you* (p. 63), and these supported their participation in the life of the classroom, though not necessarily acquisition (see later). The Portuguese subject made friends of several nationalities, so that he needed to use English as a lingua franca in his social interaction, while the other two mostly interacted with other L1 Punjabi speakers. If the major role of formulaic sequences in these early stages is interactional, we should expect to find that such differences play a role in the extent of their use, just as Wong Fillmore (1976, 1979) found with her younger, naturalistic learners. Unfortunately, Ellis's study is too small-scale to reveal any differences between the three in the range or quantity of formulaic sequences used.

Myles, Hooper and Mitchell (1998), whose study we shall consider in more detail later, also associate the early use of formulaic sequences with communicative needs, but suggest that this period is short-lived, as the communicative ambitions of the learners soon outstrip the limitations of the fixed forms. As we shall see, they provide evidence for the sequences then feeding into the grammar acquisition process, but their strong role in meeting basic interactional needs is underscored by the fact that, in the more successful learners, the original sequences continued to operate alongside the modified, more custom-made variants (p. 359).

The drive to achieve a basic level of communication may not always support authentic learning. Jaworski (1990) reports that an American learner of Polish overused formulaic expressions (greetings and so on), leading to exchanges that were inauthentic not because the Polish was wrong, but because the pattern of usage was non-nativelike. House (1996:227–228) makes a similar observation about German speakers of English. Jaworski attributes the effect to L1 interference at the level of interactional need and/or expectation – the learner, in collusion with the teacher (Jaworski himself), had "transfer[red] . . . his native habits of formulaic language use into Polish" (p. 399). Jaworski's observations suggest that viewing the learner's interactional agenda only from the L2 perspective may be misleading. The formulaic sequences which are learned may be those that the individual most needs *as an individual, not a learner,* with, perhaps, little respect for the L2 as a communication system at all. If so, then although the achievement of nativelike form and usage will clearly be dependent on the nature of the input, it will not be because the learner is tuned into the language, but because he or she grabs whatever is closest to hand that appears able to do the job. The influence of the L1 on the choice and use of formulaic sequences is also noted by Granger (1998), Irujo (1993) and Biskup (1992), as we shall see later.

Subsequent Poor Knowledge of Routines

Despite the apparent ease with which formulaic sequences seem to be picked up in the early stages of learning, by the time the learner has achieved a reasonable command of the L2 lexicon and grammar, the formulaic sequences appear to be lagging behind. This could just be an impression. Native speakers can tend to take for granted that certain expressions are so common as to be elementary, whereas, in fact, because they often have idiosyncratic grammar or vocabulary, learners cannot know them unless they have actually encountered them before, and that at a point in their learning when they have a chance of making sense of them. Irujo (1986) suggests that there may even be a tendency for learners to be somewhat protected from certain kinds of idiomatic expression. She notes that "idioms are frequently omitted in the speech addressed to second-language learners" (p. 236) and adds that although they are common in television and film dialogue, "input without interaction is not sufficient for language acquisition" (p. 237).

In a simple pseudo-experiment, Scarcella (1979) tested two groups of "advanced" adult ESL learners on their knowledge of common 'routines' such as *shut up, look out* and *who's there,* by getting them to complete captions for single-frame drawings. She found the test scores "surprisingly" low (p. 81), with 38% correct responses for one group and 30% for the other. Irujo (1993) examined the ability of highly proficient ("bilingual") adult learners of English to translate paragraphs containing an idiom from the L1 (Spanish) into English. Although she views their 59% hit rate as indicative of "a high degree of knowledge of English idioms" (p. 208), there is still a clear shortfall, relative to their general proficiency, which featured "very few grammatical or lexical errors" (p. 207). Where they failed to produce the correct idiom, they made a guess, usually either using their productive knowledge of the L2 to create a plausible version of a half-remembered one, or based on a direct translation of the L1 equivalent.

What has been found for idioms seems to extend also to collocations. Biskup (1992) asked Polish and German students of English to translate L1 lexical collocations such as (in the target language) *run a bookshop, take someone's pulse, wind a watch, domestic trade.* The Germans seemed much more willing to take risks with their knowledge of English to create a plausible construction, while the Polish learners were more likely to rely on word-for-word translation from the L1. Biskup attributes this to a difference in the perceived closeness of the L1 to the L2: the Polish learners tended not to assume that knowledge of the L1 gave them an intuition for what was correct in the L2. The Germans, in contrast, tended to make assumptions about the form of English on the basis of German (pp. 89ff). This suggests that interference from the L1 is at least partially under the control of the learner, not just unavoidable 'leakage' caused by psycholinguistic processes. Farghal and Obiedat (1995) tested the ability of English majors and language teachers (L1 Arabic) to supply the missing words in common collocations relating to topics such as food, colour and the weather, and also to translate them from the L1. They also found that the subjects were poor in their knowledge of collocations, and employed strategies of synonymy, avoidance, L1 transfer and paraphrasing to make up the shortfall.

As with idioms and routines, collocations can only be learned if they are encountered, and it may be that our expectations of learners are too high, relative to their experience of language input. On the other hand, it would be difficult to argue with regard to collocation, as Irujo does for idioms (see earlier), that the language directed to learners contains fewer than are found in normal language. A more plausible explanation is that, for some reason, learners do not pay attention to collocational relationships (see Chapter 11).

Difficulties in Balancing Formulaicity and Creativity

It was suggested in Chapter 1 that human language is "an uneasy compromise between a rule-based and a holistic system" (Wray 1998:64). Neither can account, alone, for the structure of our output:

Without the rule-based system, language would be limited in repertoire, clichéd, and, whilst suitable for certain types of interaction, lacking imagination and novelty. In contrast, with *only* a rule-based system, language would sound pedantic, unidiomatic and pedestrian. (ibid.: 64–65)

In the L2 context, problems seem to arise with the balance between the two systems, for we find both overuse and underuse of formulaic sequences (Granger 1988:155), as well as too much creativity within them. Evidence of overuse comes from Bolander (1989), for instance, who looked at the free speech and spoken responses to a guided task in high- and low-proficiency learners of Swedish. The data featured memorized chunks which the subjects had reproduced whole, both where it was correct to do so and where it was not (e.g., in subordinate clauses where inversion was required). There was also evidence that they had created their own chunks, based on early incorrect assumptions about the grammar. These had then fossilized, and produced perseverant errors.

Foster (2001), on the other hand, offers evidence of underuse. She examined a corpus of 20,000 words of spoken data collected from native and non-native speakers during a classroom task. Native speaker judges were asked to identify in the transcripts any language that appeared to have been produced as a 'fixed chunk' rather than word by word (p. 83). More chunks were identified in the native than non-native language. Native speakers produced fewer, but of greater variety, in preplanned than in unplanned tasks, but planning did not affect the overall quantity for non-natives, and appeared to reduce, rather than increase, the variety of chunks. This suggests that native and non-native speakers are using formulaic sequences for different purposes. However, as with so many studies in this field, we must exercise caution in reading too much into the apparent effects. Foster does not subject her figures to statistical testing, so we can't tell if the differences are significant. Also, as she points out, non-nativelike chunks will not be as easy for judges to spot as nativelike ones are, and there is a great deal of intersubject variation. Furthermore, planning can produce temporary chunks out of novel material (via rehearsal, for example, or even just temporarily heightened familiarity). Such material would be indistinguishable from novel language unless it appeared several times.

DeCock et al. (1998) report a mixed picture. They extracted two- to five-word combinations over a certain frequency in a computer corpus derived from spoken informal interviews with native and non-native speakers of English. They found that the non-native speakers used a smaller range of 'formulae' (such as *you know, sort of*, and *I mean*) and in particular used far fewer vagueness tags (e.g., *and everything, and stuff like that, sort of thing*). They summarize their findings as follows:

> advanced learners use prefabs, and in some cases even more prefabs than [native speakers]. Consequently, they can be said to apply the idiom principle, but the

chunks they use (1) are not necessarily the same as those used by [native speakers], (2) are not used with the same frequency, (3) have different syntactic uses, and (4) fulfil different pragmatic functions. (p. 78)

Granger (1998) suggests that a small number of familiar and safe sequences become, in Dechert's (1983) terminology, "islands of reliability":[2] "learners' repertoires for introducing arguments and points of view are very restricted and they therefore 'cling on' to certain fixed phrases and expressions which they feel confident in using" (p. 156). She compared native and non-native (L1 French) written English using computer corpus techniques. Amongst her findings for the non-native material was an underuse of collocational amplifiers such as *perfectly natural, closely linked, deeply in love* (p. 147). While *highly* was underused, *completely* and *totally* were overused. Her explanation is that the latter two are treated by French learners as 'safe bets' for a nativelike outcome (p. 148) because they have direct cognates in French with a similar collocational distribution. *Highly* is less frequently used because the French equivalent, *hautement*, is collocationally much more restricted than the English word (p. 148). In the case of 'boosters' (amplifiers expressing high, but not the highest, degree), native speakers used stereotypical pairings (e.g., *acutely aware, vitally important*) and also creative ones (e.g., *monotonously uneventful, ruthlessly callous*). In contrast, the non-natives' creative collocations were sometimes non-nativelike, and their stereotyped ones, again, closely matched a French equivalent (pp. 150–151). In another of her studies, non-native and native subjects had to circle the adjectives, from a list of 15, which collocated with 11 amplifiers. The non-natives marked far fewer and their choices were more disparate, indicating a "weak sense of salience" (p. 152).

Other research findings support Granger's suggestion that non-native speakers are failing to recognize when words 'belong together'. Yorio (1989) examines the use of idioms, formulas and collocations in the writing of students of English as a Second Language who had failed the University's Writing Assessment Test. He found that although they attempted to use formulaic sequences, "they had little formal control over them" (p. 62), displaying a range of grammatical errors, incorrect lexical choices, incorrect usage, and mixing of different sequences. These findings indicate that they had failed to identify the restrictions on form of the sequences they had encountered. This failure may mean that they had never been identified as formulaic in the first place, that they had not been memorized as a single unit, or that they had not been remembered with sufficient accuracy, the shortfall being made up by contributions from the interlanguage grammar. It seems plausible that learners who have lived in an L2 environment would be more sensitive to idiomaticity than classroom-taught foreign language learners. However, when Yorio compared ESL learners who had informal as well as formal exposure to English, with EFL learners studying outside the English-speaking environment, he found that the EFL group not only had greater grammatical accuracy but also used more idioms and "their written English, despite errors, is more authentic than that of the subjects in the immigrant group" (p. 65). Although this seems to contradict the other findings, there are many uncontrolled variables, not least the quality and quantity of the language to which the two groups had been exposed, which would inevitably influence their knowledge.

Howarth (1998a) focussed on the use of 'restricted lexical colloca-tions' (transparent lexical associations, such as *under attack*), in corpora of academic writing by native and non-native speakers. He found that non-natives tended to make assumptions about the transferability of a collocation from one item to another with a similar meaning. Of the sequence *perform a project* he says: "aware of the acceptability of *perform a task*, [the writer] believed that *task* and *project* share identical collocability with verbs" (p. 37). Howarth's view is that there is a con-tinuum of collocational restrictions, and that "the problem facing the non-native writer or speaker is knowing which of a range of collocational options are restricted and which are free" (p. 36). He proposes that the less restricted ones, such as *perform a task*, may not be prefabricated for native speakers at all: they "are probably not all learned as inflexible wholes" (p. 38). There are some problems with this view, which we shall revisit in Chapter 11.

The Acquisitional Role of a Balance Between Formulaicity and Creativity

Learning a language involves the development of many skills. Somehow the brain has to be provided with a comprehensive store of linguistic information, and must learn how to access it quickly and with the correct outcome. Formulaicity may be best seen as a strategy that can be employed at various times to enable a particular stage to be reached. It may then need to be discarded, before, perhaps, being re-enlisted to help with a subsequent stage. This plan enables us to make sense of the appar-ently major role which formulaic sequences play in the very first stages of learning; their retention, in the most successful learners, alongside the burgeoning ability to create novel strings (Myles, Mitchell & Hooper 1999:75–76); their patchy presence in intermediate and advanced learners (e.g., DeCock et al. 1998; Howarth 1998a, 1998b; Pawley & Syder

1983; Scarcella 1979; Yorio 1989); and yet their full presence by the time a learner achieves native or near-native competence.

Formulaic sequences as a resource. Myles et al. (1998, 1999) observed English learners of French in British secondary schools, by tracking them over two years (from ages 11 and 12 to ages 13 and 14) via fortnightly class observations, termly interviews and paired activities. (For a full description of the study design, see Mitchell & Martin 1997.) One focus was the use across time of *j'habite, j'adore* and *j'aime*. They monitored the appearance of *je* in other contexts, and of the three verbs with other subjects than *je*. The results divided the subjects into three groups: those who clearly segmented the subject and verb components, those showing no evidence of separation, and those presenting a mixed picture (1998:347). They conclude that

Clearly, for most of these learners, initially unanalysed utterances did break down. Moreover, this breakdown was linked with the emergence of the pronoun system, and seemed to be triggered by the need to establish reference. (p. 358)

They think that the segmentation both contributed to and was supported by the development of insights into the language grammar (ibid.). In the early stages, the formulaic sequences helped with communication, but later their communicative needs overtook what the formulaic sequences could offer (e.g., needing to talk about third persons when the formulaic sequences were second or first person). In response, they "gradually 'unpacked' their early chunks, [and] also used parts of them productively in the generation of new utterances" (p. 323). The formulaic sequences weren't dropped but retained and modified. At first, they simply tagged the new referent onto the unchanged formula, but then gradually broke them down (e.g., *Richard est j'adore le ping-pong (. . .) Ah oui il adore la musée* 'Richard is I love table-tennis [. . .] Ah yes he loves museums' (p. 358)). Other chunks were also initially overextended (e.g., *mon petit garçon euh où habites-tu?* 'my little boy umm where live-you' for 'where does your little boy live?'; *comment t'appelles-tu la fille?* 'How yourself-call-you the girl' for 'what's the girl's name?' (Myles et al. 1999:51)). These, too, transformed over time into more appropriate variants, and, again, the pattern which emerges is that those learners who were most able to use, and who continued to use, formulaic sequences were also the most creative in the later stages (Myles et al. 1999:76). Those who could not remember the early-learned chunks were also not creative. Of course, this need not mean that it was the chunks that were facilitating the learning, as a learner who was poor for other reasons might manifest this in both the formulaic and creative spheres. Myles et al. (1998,

1999) are clear, though, that L2 learning entails the attempt "to resolve the tension between structurally complex but communicatively rich formulas on the one hand, and structurally simple but communicatively inadequate 'creative' structures on the other hand" (1999:49).

Although theirs is a significant study, it needs to be interpreted with caution. Many of the subject groups, subsets of the original 60 subjects, are quite small and, by the end of the two years, the overall progress of the learners does not seem to be all that great. Indeed, the teachers interviewed in the study did not expect most of their pupils to have any grasp of grammar, or even of basic morphological concepts such as noun gender, after two years of tuition (Mitchell & Martin 1997:14–15). Furthermore, the researchers obviously could not control for the effects of explicit teaching, so it is impossible to say for sure whether a learner's isolation of, say, the verb *appeller* in *comment t'appelles-tu?* was due to segmentation of the formulaic sequence, encounters with *appeller* in class, or, most likely, both. As we shall see in the next chapter, it may be of some significance that while the researchers believe that the motivation for segmentation was an increasing communicative need, the teachers attributed it to their explicit teaching of words and grammar (Mitchell & Martin 1997:24–25).

Despite such reservations, it remains highly plausible that formulaic sequences are supporting the acquisition process, whether this be simply by maintaining in the learner a sense of being able to say something, even when there is only a small database to draw on, or by providing a wealth of stored nativelike data for later analysis.

Formulaicity and memory. Bolander (1989) believes that analysis occurs naturally, as a response to crossing a threshold in memory, after which "syntactic rules are derived as help for the memory to economize and rationalize processing" (p. 85). This idea notwithstanding, Nick Ellis (1996) proposes that success in language learning actually depends on the individual's having a well-developed ability to perceive and remember sequences. If stored in long-term memory, chunks of regular material will support subsequent learning by aiding the identification of input. He argues that these chunks are available for analysis, thus promoting the acquisition of the language grammar. Learners vary in their ability to remember word strings, something which, he suggests, directly impinges on the degree of their success in gaining proficiency in the language as a whole. This hypothesis was tested in an experiment using an artificial language with no reference (Ellis & Schmidt 1997, study two). A subject's ability to remember a sequence in short-term memory (STM), that is, immediately after seeing it, correlated with the ability to remember it later. Ellis and Schmidt believe that the significant determiner was that the strings were new to the learner, since previous experiments show that the repetition of known elements in STM does not affect long-term memory (LTM) performance.

Fluency. Nick Ellis's work makes a clear link between formulaicity and the operations of memory. Towell et al. (1996) also address this, though from the perspective of *declarative* versus *proceduralized* knowledge:

Declarative knowledge requires the attention of the speaker. Knowledge of this kind takes up much more 'space' than knowledge which does not require the attention of the speaker. Therefore, less of it can be handled at one time. Procedural knowledge, on the other hand, does not require the attention of the speaker and can be processed by working memory in larger units without exhausting the working memory capacity. (p. 88)

Proceduralized knowledge "is recalled as a single unit and cannot be modified by the learner" (p. 89) and thus appears very similar in definition to formulaic language. However, it does not consist of prefabricated chunks of material stored whole in the lexicon, but is generated: "[it has] units known as *productions* and takes the form of condition/action pairs of the IF/THEN kind" (p. 88). That is, while formulaic sequences are chunks that started big and may or may not ever have been broken down, proceduralized chunks are assembled from small units at the time of use, but in a fully predictable way. This is not the same as fusion (see Chapter 6) since fused sequences, once initially constructed out of their parts, become entirely formulaic. However, the difference is dependent on one's model of linguistic processing, and theories which dispose of a static lexicon in favour of networked construction processes will find little to distinguish formulaic sequences from proceduralized strings.

That the difference may be more apparent than real can be seen by the fact that, like formulaic sequences (see Chapters 2, 4 and 5), proceduralized strings are also attributed with promoting fluency. Without proceduralization,

The fact that single sentences and even phrase structures are split up by sometimes quite lengthy pauses suggests that the subject has great difficulty formulating even very simple sentences in one production unit. . . . The structure and lexis may be known but combining them is a laborious process and requires constant pausing within the structures. (Towell et al. 1996:108)

Towell et al. found that after living in the L2 community, the mean speaking rate of a learner had increased, as a function of an increase in the mean length of uninterrupted utterance:

even if there is a pause in the execution, structures with introducers must be formulated as a whole. . . . [T]he learner has assimilated the conventions of sentence
building in French and . . . she has now sufficiently proceduralized the relevant
syntactic knowledge to be able to formulate larger units of syntactic structure.
(pp. 108–109)

Since a means of differentiating empirically between proceduralized and
formulaic strings does not yet exist (Norman Segalowitz, personal communication),[3] we shall treat them, for the present, as identical, and review
the other research without distinguishing between them.

   Lennon (1990) reports something similar to Towell et al.: increased
fluency was characterized by fewer and shorter pauses rather than by
faster speech. The position of the pauses also changed, with fewer found
within T-units (sentences including any dependent clauses), as opposed
to at the borders. Bygate (1988) offers evidence that memorized chunks
may not only be symptomatic of fluency but also the cause of it. His subjects were Peruvian teachers of English engaged in communication
games. He describes how the oral medium was exploited for accessing
and retaining linguistic material, presumably as a means of avoiding
memory overload (p. 75). Strategies included picking up words and
phrases that had just been uttered by someone else, repeating the previous utterance as turn holder while planning a response, and uttering a
short version and then expanding it (e.g., *in front of the boy, the little boy;
what about the clock, the clock on top of the door*, p. 71).

   A different twist to the fluency story is provided by Pawley and Syder
(1983), who consider the 'puzzle' that "the human capacities for encoding
novel speech in advance or while speaking appear to be severely limited,
yet speakers commonly produce fluent multi-clause utterances which
exceed these limits" (p. 191). Like Towell et al., they identify the preplan-
ning of the shape of the discourse as central to fluency (p. 201), but they
show that even a confident speaker will fail to be fluent if the structure of
the discourse is too complicated, that is, if he is "committing himself to
constructions which require him to take account of the structure of an
earlier or later clause when formulating a current one" (p. 202). The
reason for this, they claim, is that we have very limited memory space for
planning and it is easily overloaded. Maximum fluency is achieved by
'clause-chaining', that is, "string[ing] together a sequence of relatively
independent clauses, clauses which show little structural integration with
earlier or later constructions" (p. 202). Yet they observe that despite this
'one clause at a time constraint', we are able to produce many integrated
multiclause sequences fluently. That is possible, they argue, because we
use prefabricated word strings and frames, which reduce to a minimum
the strain on memory, leaving scope for clause-level complexity.

The Role of Formulaic Sequences in Acquisition and Teaching

Teaching for idiomaticity. Given that advanced learners struggle to sound idiomatic, even when they sound grammatical, one obvious solution is to raise awareness of useful formulaic sequences and sanction their holistic use (e.g., House 1996). Welsh language materials furnish us with an interesting example of how to support the learner. Welsh is a thriving minority language heavily overshadowed by English. Competence in Welsh is required for many posts in the civil service in Wales, and employees, whether native or non-native speakers, may find themselves unable to operate in the official registers of the language. This has created a niche for books like Hughes's (1998) *Canllawiau ysgrifennu Cymraeg,*[4] which provides forms of words for use in, amongst other things, business letters, advertisements and formal documents. Besides short phrases that might be more generally found in practically oriented language books, such as the Welsh equivalents of *the successful candidate* (p. 21.5) and *please submit . . .* (p. 21.7), there are much longer strings like *The company is in the midst of an investment and expansion programme in anticipation of the continued success of its existing and future product range* (p. 21.3).[5]

Such books can be viewed as phrasebooks even though they are not intended to plug a gap in the overall ability to communicate an idea, but rather to ensure that the expression is idiomatic and 'correct'. Both this kind of advanced user's phrasebook and the more common variety used by travellers, which demands comprehension and production skills only at the broadest functional level, share a significant feature: they are not concerned with an analysis of the language they present. The BBC's *Spanish Phrasebook* (Stanley & Goodrich 1991) gives the traveller the following advice: "whenever possible, work out in advance what you want to say" and "practise saying things aloud" (p. 4). Although 10 of the 287 pages are devoted to describing the grammar of Spanish, there is no attempt to engage with a grammatical or lexical analysis of the phrases.

Teaching for communication. The phrasebook approach, when aimed at beginners, offers, as do many regular L2 textbooks, word-strings which are to be memorized and reproduced whole, as formulaic sequences, enabling learners to communicate at a level beyond their grammatical and lexical knowledge (Jeremias 1982).[6] Hakuta (1976) considers this function important, for "if learners always have to wait until they acquire the constructional rules for forming an utterance before using it, then they may run into serious motivational difficulties" (p. 333).

One good example of the specific targeting of formulaic sequences for communication is Gatbonton's teaching method (e.g., Gatbonton & Segalowitz 1988).[7] Her view is that formulaic sequences can be classroom-taught with considerable success, provided that five criteria are applied to the design of the materials. First, the activity must be genuinely communicative. This means that the participants must care about the result. For instance, not only must they be exchanging information which they do not possess, but also it must matter to them that they obtain that information. The second criterion is psychological authenticity, "allow[ing] learners to experience some of the normal psychological pressures felt by people engaged in real communication" (Gatbonton & Segalowitz 1988:486). Thirdly, the focus should be on everyday activities that the students are likely to need, such as directing, apologizing and describing. Fourthly, the utterances must be formulaic. In other words, this task-design is really only suitable for practising utterances which genuinely are the same time after time, and which are "multi-situational; that is, . . . useable in many situations with little or no modification" (p. 488). Finally, the task must be inherently repetitive, since this provides the opportunity for multiple rehearsal.[8]

Teaching for linguistic knowledge. The memorization of phrases for their own sake has been somewhat unfashionable for the last few years, but Ellis and Sinclair (1996) view it as central to successful learning:

> much of language learning is the acquisition of memorized sequences of language (for vocabulary, the phonological units of language and their phonotactic sequences; for discourse, the lexical units of language and their sequences in clauses and collocations). . . . Short-term representation and rehearsal allows the eventual establishment of long-term sequence information for language. (pp. 246–247)

As mentioned earlier, Ellis (1996) proposes that success in a second language is heavily dependent on the ability to learn sequences, so that differences in success are determined by "individual differences in learners' ability to remember simple verbal strings in order" (p. 91). In the light of the rather low level of success in foreign language learning in the United Kingdom, it is perhaps ironic, then, that, according to Mitchell and Martin (1997), British secondary school practice has not been heavily swayed by the general falling out of favour of the audiolingual method, drilling and parrot learning, and "it is clear that prefabricated phrases have maintained a place in contemporary classroom practice", not least because "national GCSE examinations at 16+ positively reward such memorized material" (p. 6).

Approaches to teaching often focus on the role that formulaic sequences might play in learning the individual words and grammar of the L2. Krashen and Scarcella (1978), Schmidt (1983), Ellis (1984), Yorio (1989) and Granger (1998) are amongst those who believe that "there does not seem to be a direct line from prefabs to creative language" (Granger 1998:157), so that teaching formulaic sequences for this purpose will have no point. It can be noted, in this regard, that Gatbonton's task-based approach (see earlier) does not aim to encourage the learner to examine the internal workings of the formulaic sequences used in the activities (personal communication).

In contrast, Nattinger and DeCarrico (1992) work very much on the basis that adult learners do use formulaic sequences as input for their analysis of the language, out of which they will derive grammatical and morphological rules (pp. 27ff):

> The goal would not be to have students analyze just those chunks introduced in the lessons, of course, but to have them learn to segment and construct new patterns of their own on analogy with the kind of analysis they do in the classroom. (p. 117)

The syllabuses of Willis (1990) and Lewis (1993) are both based upon the belief that "grammar will, to some extent at least, be acquired through generalizing, and learning the restrictions on the generalization from these sentences" (Lewis 1993:100). Willis (1999) states that "we need to encourage learners to analyse the language they have experienced in such a way as to facilitate development and to inculcate productive approaches to learning" (pp. 117–118). For a full discussion of the legitimacy of these assumptions, and of the status of formulaic sequences within the approaches of Nattinger and DeCarrico, Lewis, and Willis, see Wray (2000b).

If learners *do* customarily analyze the sequences that they have memorized, they must encounter the same procedural problem as young children in first language acquisition (Chapter 6). How are they to tell which strings can and cannot be usefully analyzed?

> Unless the irregular sequences are excluded, or at least formally flagged up, by what means is the learner to know that it is possible to use *large amounts* and *largely speaking* as input for analysis and rule-building, but that *at large* and *by and large* will not succumb to that treatment and should not be analysed? (Wray 2000b:482–483).

This difficulty must be exacerbated if special attention is paid to idioms (e.g., Milton & Evans 1998), since, as we saw in Chapter 3, these are particularly likely to be grammatically irregular or semantically opaque, making their analysis valueless. The usefulness of an idiom in terms of expressive power or interactional function does not correspond with its transparency or comprehensibility, and the sequences which the learner may need most are not necessarily those with the easiest vocabulary or grammar. The syllabus-writer's job entails making fine judgements about the extent to which introducing a particular turn of phrase may lead to this kind of overanalysis, as well as to the overextension reported earlier in this chapter. For one such writer, there is no simple answer to this problem, and it is a question of the lesser of two evils:

frames like 'idea/possibility/chance/danger + OF + -ing' ... carry with them the seeds of language development. ... [Teaching them] leaves open the possibility of, perhaps even encourages, a sequence like 'the wish of + -ing' by analogy with idea/hope/intention etc. This doesn't worry me at all. It's a 'mistake' along the lines of 'She suggested me to . . .' or 'Can you explain me the problem?' – a very useful and productive overgeneralization. It leaves us with the mystery of how learners gradually eliminate these overgeneralizations, but as a pedagogic principle we have no alternative but to encourage creativity. (Dave Willis, personal communication).

Discussion

Horses for Courses

We turn now to consider how all these findings reported relate to the models proposed in this book. It follows from the basic model of function presented in Chapter 5 that, insofar as the learner's communicational agenda and processing priorities differ from those of a native speaker, this will create a different set of formulaic sequences, and lead to a different use of them. Furthermore, different populations of learners will also have different inventories of, and uses for, formulaic sequences, according to the nature of their experiences of learning and language use. This prediction is, however, virtually impossible to evaluate empirically, since it would require the comparison of matched subjects in different learning situations, while fully controlling for other variables.

However, it has been possible to observe certain patterns in the existing research, which can be interpreted in terms of the model. Firstly, the integration of the communicational and processing functions of formulaic sequences seems to be poorer in adults than in young children, which is what we should expect, given the focus on words which comes from attaining literacy skills (see Chapter 7). Within the adult learner population, naturalistic learners seem to use formulaic sequences for effective communication without accuracy, and classroom learners appear able to analyze them more readily than they can apply them idiomatically. This would be a natural consequence of having to choose either to analyze or to communicate, which could be a feature of phase four in the first language acquisition model (Chapter 7).

Each individual has a range of linguistic and nonlinguistic strategies available for meeting the urgent demands of self-promotion (Chapter 5) but this range is different for children and adults. As predicted, overall, adults seem to have a wider selection of nonlinguistic alternatives to the formulaic strategy, including reducing their needs to match their language rather than increasing their language knowledge to meet their needs. Powerful social and psychological forces may undercut the desire to achieve the social integration which seems to characterize successful learning, and there may be positive reasons for a learner to maintain signals of non-native status, by *not* learning the preferred sequences of native speakers.

Thus, understanding how, and when, the second language learner uses formulaic sequences requires a recognition of the complex interactional agenda of the individual in his or her particular environment, which may, from time to time, even undermine targetlike learning. We have already seen this in the fossilization process described by Rehbein (1987). Further evidence comes from Rampton's (1987) account of teenaged ESL classroom learners. When embarrassed at having said something that might be construed as rude or boastful, they adopted the formulaic beginner's form *me no + Verb* in place of *I don't + Verb* as a face-saving strategy. Rampton's interpretation of this is that they were deliberately signalling themselves as linguistically weak, so that the hearer would react more leniently towards them (pp. 52–53.). This has much in common with the adoption by a native speaker of a babyish voice quality. Importantly, only a learner is in the position to signal linguistic ineptitude in quite this manner, and this is a timely reminder that learners are not to be viewed as just weak imitations of native speakers. Rather, they are powerful individuals, able to use all of their linguistic resources in positive and creative ways to handle the range of interactional situations in which they find themselves.

A Critical Period for Language Learning?

Up to now we have focussed on how the patterns of usage for formulaic sequences can be attributed to differences, some age-related, in learners' sense of identity, options for coping with their physical and emotional needs, and range of strategies for handling interactionally stressful situations. However, there are no grounds for dismissing the other aspects of the maturational process which may affect language learning. The different learning patterns of adults and children undoubtedly reflect an inextricable combination of biological, emotional and intellectual factors, and we shall probably never get to the bottom of just how they interact. However, the case of secondary school foreign language teaching does invite particular scrutiny, since preteenage learners appear to be on the cusp of the child and adult styles of learning (see, for instance, McLaughlin 1978:55–56). In theory this could be a help to their achievements, but in practice it may be a considerable hindrance.

It is a striking feature of the reports from the teachers in the British study reported earlier (Mitchell & Martin 1997; Myles et al. 1998, 1999) that 11 and 12 year olds are assumed to be unable to tap their implicit L1 grammatical knowledge when learning French in the classroom. Rather, the teachers consistently state that the major problem with teaching this age group is that *they are not sufficiently mature to engage with grammatical analysis* (Mitchell & Martin 1997:12). In other words, understanding grammar requires greater intellectual capacity than they currently have, such that engaging with it at that age will only serve to undermine their confidence and demotivate them (ibid.). In lieu of teaching grammar, the first and second years of tuition are focussed on amassing a corpus of memorized formulaic sequences that can be used in certain communicative situations. This activity is perceived as easier and more rewarding for them, "enabling children who don't understand grammar to use language" (p. 15). That formulaic sequences are valuable is not in dispute, but it is notable that they seem to be perceived as a tolerated alternative to 'real' learning, which involves analysis.

It seems, indeed, from this study that success in secondary school language learning is entirely viewed in terms of the ability to engage with grammatical analysis. Poor learners may never get beyond using their memorized sequences, while those of greater ability will be able to substitute items within sequences, or even use words and grammar creatively (pp. 12, 15). Although one teacher observes that the "obsession" of the high ability pupils to break down sequences can undermine their ability also to continue using them as sequences, something which is detrimental to their overall success (p. 15), there is no other recognition that the learning of chunks might actually be the key to success for some learners, as opposed to a stop-gap.

Mitchell and Martin's account reveals that there are two dynamics at work in the teacher's mapping of the learning process. One is the difference between able and less able children, whereby it is believed that the weaker ones will simply never understand grammar (p. 21). The other is the process of maturation, by which all children will be more able to engage in analysis the older they get. The interaction of these two dynamics requires our attention, since teachers are unlikely to be able fully or consistently to differentiate between intrinsically weak learners and those who are intelligent but intellectually immature.

Ironically, if the immature learner's perceived *failure* in the secondary school classroom is the perseverance of the childlike skills which lead to *successful* language learning in children aged five to eight, such as those in Wong Fillmore's (1976) study, then that child is being poorly served.[9] The teachers' association of successful learning with analytic skills (which is undoubtedly a legitimate one, given the learning environment and the requisite outcomes) means that they have to *wait* for their pupils to be ready to learn in this adult way. Their resources (three hours a week in an L1 environment) entirely preclude capitalizing on any residual ability in the immature learners naturally to pick up another language through genuine social interaction (as Nora did).

Meanwhile, since it seems that 11 is too young an age for the intellectual engagement required to learn like an adult, the pupils, and teachers, are suspended in a barren no-man's-land, in which existing skills that may be independent of intelligence have to be lost, so that new ones, which are dependent on it, can develop. The less intelligent children plus, importantly, those not showing their intelligence *early enough* are likely to be alienated and demotivated as well as de-skilled, for by the time the latter are capable of the adult-style task, they may be well behind their more mature classmates. Not surprisingly, as Mitchell and Martin's account makes clear, the biggest difficulty for language teachers of this age group is keeping the children motivated.

If this interpretation of the Myles et al. study is even halfway right – and it certainly deserves some careful further investigation – then it would be more profitable to start language teaching either a few years *earlier*, when none of the children have replaced their inferential abilities by analytic ones, or else *later*, when those without the intellectual capabilities can be excluded from faster-track teaching and the slower to mature are ready to compete on an equal footing. Conversely, if language teaching is to start at 11, perhaps more account should be taken of the effects on language learning that differences in intellectual maturity could be having. Entirely different kinds of teaching methods might need to be targeted at the 'children' and the young 'adults'. This would surely be preferable to requiring teachers to ignore the advantages that childhood offers for language learning, and mark time while they wait for their charges to be ready to learn like adults.[10]

Conclusion

It seems clear that there are some fundamental differences between different types of learner, and that, in particular, part of the well-recognized contrast between the success of adults and young children in second language learning may reside in the maintenance of two crucial balances. One is the balance between the two central functions of formulaic sequences, namely, the achieving of successful interactional events and the saving of processing effort. A very important aspect of the latter is the processing entailed in actually identifying features to be learned. The second balance, which we have seen is also linked to acquisition, is that between formulaicity and creativity. These patterns will be of central importance to our exploration, in the next chapter, of possible differences in the nature of the first and second language lexicons.

Finally, we have seen that the differences between adult and child uses of formulaic sequences, insofar as they reflect fundamental differences in the approach to learning, may create difficulties for young secondary school learners, who find themselves in transition from childlike to adultlike learning. I have suggested that recognition of this transition could make the teaching of preteens a very fertile ground for the development of teaching methods sensitive to the changing intellectual approach of the maturing learner.

11

Formulaic Sequences in the Second Language Acquisition Process: A Model

Introduction

Chapters 9 and 10 have revealed that the roles of formulaic sequences in second language production, comprehension and learning are various and complex. This chapter seeks to capture this complexity by developing a second language version of the first language model proposed in Chapter 7. Central to this will be the differences in use and extent of use of formulaic sequences in younger and older learners, and in naturalistic and taught learners. But first, we shall consider some puzzles which the model needs to be able to solve.

The Control and Use of Formulaic Sequences

The first puzzle is the one raised by Yorio's (1989) data. He found that the written English of a group of advanced ESL students in the United States contained a great many *attempts* at formulaic sequences, but that they were riddled with errors. For example, he found *take advantages of; are to blamed for; those mention above; being taking care of; a friend of her; make a great job; on the meantime; with my own experience; put more attention to* (pp. 62–63). Yorio's interpretation is that "these expressions are not simply memorized or taken in as wholes, but ... are subject to whatever interlanguage rules the learner is operating under" (p. 62). The question, then, is: are they formulaic or aren't they? The examples seem close enough to their target not to be straightforward inventions. That means that the correct version has been encountered by the student, and that it has been recognized as formulaic. So why has it come out wrong? Why did the student engage the grammar at all, rather than just reproduce the sequence in its original form?

199

Part of the answer to this could simply be that the formulaic sequences were encountered at an inappropriate stage in the student's learning. If useful phrases are taught, or even just met, before the learner is equipped to analyze them, then, unless they are to be ignored entirely, there is no choice but to memorize them whole. Holistically learned strings are, by definition, subject to loss of detail, because they rely on the memory of the visual and/or phonological shape of the entire unit. Unless they continue to be encountered, and are regularly used, the memory of them will fade, and, because they were not analyzed, there will be no way to reconstruct any details that have become difficult to recall. The learner will be obliged to engage in an analysis of the incomplete sequence, and attempt to patch it, using the current interlanguage grammar to do so.

This explanation could reasonably account for errors in formulaic sequences encountered very early in the learning process, such as simple greetings, classroom talk, and so on, but it is less convincing in the case of strings learned for the management of written discourse or for expressing abstract ideas, such as those which Yorio lists. It seems unlikely that such strings, when first introduced to the learner, would be so impenetrable that they *had to be* memorized whole. In that case, two explanations are possible. The strings could have been memorized, but incorrectly, because the interlanguage grammar edited the forms to something consistent with its expectations. Alternatively, they could have been correctly memorized but edited as part of the production process. This is an empirical question, because, in the former case, the errors would be consistent with the grammar at the time of learning and, in the latter, with the grammar at the time of use. The basic question, however, remains: why interfere with formulaic sequences at all, since the advantage of them is that they do not need to be internally scrutinized?

As we saw in the last chapter, one current view is that formulaic sequences are not analyzed, so that "[i]t would . . . be a foolhardy gamble to believe that it is enough to expose L2 learners to prefabs and the grammar will take care of itself" (Granger 1998:157–158). But if they are not, how can errors occur in them at a later date? One possibility is that formulaic sequences actually are analyzed, but not in order to extract the grammatical information, only the lexical material. The result would be that the learner had a store of the *words* which had occurred in the formulaic sequence, but none of the detailed grammatical (particularly morphological) information about how they combined. In reconstructing them, the correct words would, therefore, be conjoined according to the current interlanguage rules. In the model developed later in this chapter, it will be a central principle that formulaic sequences are broken down primarily for the sake of their words.

Should Teaching Emulate First Language Acquisition?

Our second puzzle relates to a question which extends over the whole of second language teaching. Should the teaching of adults aim to emulate as closely as possible the childhood pattern, or should syllabus designers cut their losses, so to speak, and break right away from the child model to focus on what adults are best at? In the case of formulaic sequences, since they appear to be useful to children learning a first or second language, should they form a targeted part of the teenage and adult classroom syllabus? We saw in the last chapter that Nattinger and DeCarrico (1992) consider it entirely logical that they should: "If lexical phrases characterize language acquisition and language performance to such an extent, they would seem to be an ideal unit for language teaching" (p. 32). Even Peters (1983), who doubts that any real learning results from memorizing formulaic sequences, believes that they have a place because they promote fluency and provide opportunities for practising phrases which can be used later for real interaction (p. 110). But Dave Willis (personal communication) has observed that even the phrases which are introduced to meet clear and regularly encountered communicational needs, such as *please would you repeat that*, will be dispreferred by many students in favour of creations influenced by the L1, like *please repeating*.

Overall, the previous chapters have shown that there is very mixed evidence regarding the effectiveness of teaching formulaic sequences. Why should this be so? A highly plausible explanation is that the adult approach is, simply, different from that of the child, so that a different route may be required in order to reach the same target.

> The network of associations between words in a native speaker's brain may be set as a goal for second language learners, but this does not mean that directly teaching these associations is the best way to achieve this goal. In fact there is clear evidence that it can make learning more difficult. (Nation 1990:190)

The model developed in this chapter will propose a formalization of the difference in lexical storage between child and adult learners, which can be used to explain why formulaic sequences will not be used in the same way by the two groups.

The Tricky Case of Collocations

The third puzzling issue is the status of collocations. As we saw in the last chapter, adult L2 learners apply too great a level of creativity to word pairs, making overliberal assumptions about the collocational equivalence of semantically similar items. According to Howarth (1998a), the learners' problem arises because there are arbitrary gaps in what is, otherwise, a combinatorial system serving flexibility in expression and creativity (p. 42). Learners are confounded, he argues, by "the way in which specific collocations might be predicted by analogy, but are arbitrarily blocked by usage" (p. 37). His solution is to suggest that the less restricted collocational strings (e.g., *perform a task*) are not formulaic *for anyone*. But Granger (1998) prefers a different explanation. She proposes that while native speakers treat collocational pairs *as pairs*, non-native speakers perceive them as two separate units, "more as building bricks than as parts of prefabricated sections" (p. 151). This concurs with Foster's (2001) view, that "the non-native speakers were constructing a great proportion of their language from rules rather than from lexicalized routines" (p. 90). As we shall see in the next section, the model in Chapter 7 provides the basis for explaining how this difference might come about.

Modelling the Second Language Lexicon

According to the *needs-only* approach to input analysis in first language acquisition (Chapter 7), word strings are treated holistically unless there is a specific reason to break them down, and even then, they are only analyzed to the minimal extent necessary. The lexicon of the native speaker is depicted as a collection of items of different sizes and internal complexity, including morphemes, polymorphemic words, collocating word pairs, phrases, clauses and even whole texts. Some of these units are to be seen as fully fixed forms, while others are lexical frames containing spaces for items to be inserted, either by entirely free choice, or from a limited set. This, it has been argued, makes it possible to explain how adult native speakers appear able to work with both large and small units of language, and how the internal composition of the large units is often inconsistent with what would be produced if the grammatical rules of the language were applied to smaller units.

The four-phase model of acquisition (depicted in Figure 7.1) shows how the period of maximum analytic activity, through which the child attains full flexibility for novel expression, coincides with a relatively stable period of social interaction, and also with the mastering of literacy skills. It has been suggested that, as literacy requires the definitive pinning down of language into word-sized units, learning to read and write might play a major role in the final balance of large to small units in the adult lexicon. Since word strings could continue to be stored whole, even after they have been broken down, the effect would not be that the store of sequences reduced, but rather that the store of words increased. The result would be a great deal of multiple representation. It would still be advantageous to retrieve strings whole from store whenever possible, for all the reasons identified in Chapter 5, but there would be flexibility for handling novel ideas and unexpected input by shifting to smaller units when necessary (compare Wray 1992:10).

This model of lexical development rests on the timing of certain events in the individual's linguistic life, relative to the passing of milestones in physical and intellectual maturity. As a result, some interesting effects would result from the introduction of a further language at an early, versus a late, stage. Furthermore, since formulaic sequences play a role in both processing and interaction, the way in which the language was learned, and what it was used for, should make a profound difference to how the linguistic material is stored. We shall explore these predictions here, with reference to the findings of Chapters 9 and 10.

Very Young Learners

Babies and young children have a very good chance of becoming fully nativelike in a second language, and Chapter 9 revealed that they use formulaic sequences in particular ways which seem linked to this success. Our model of first language acquisition offers some insights into the reasons for this. At this early age, the child is still in phase one or the early part of phase two of his or her first language acquisition: language is primarily employed for socio-interactional functions (in the widest sense), word strings are being broken down only as necessary for pliability in expression and comprehension, and the child is still preliterate. The physical limitations and emotional needs of baby- and young childhood ensure that children are highly motivated to acquire linguistic expressions which will get them what they want, however many languages they have to use in the process.

The child may have limited awareness that it is actually different languages that are being used in different circumstances, but it will certainly know that different strings are effective with different hearers: the simple principle of accommodating one's output to the anticipated comprehension capabilities of the addressee (Chapter 5)[1] will ensure that the child learns to use the linguistic material appropriate to each hearer, whether that be two different languages or different registers of the same one. The child's objective is simply to achieve a current desire through the agency of whoever is there to deliver it, with no need to speculate as to how that desire might be met by someone else who is not present at the relevant time. The child will not attempt to import messages from one language into another, and will naturally adhere to the cultural norms appropriate to the different languages.

The socio-interactional bubble, which protects the child from an onslaught of new socially motivated exchanges (Chapter 7), will allow the consolidation of the necessary analytic knowledge (grammatical rules and words) but, as with first language learners, not at the expense of the continued holistic storage of formulaic sequences which are useful. Those sequences that are not useful will, however, fall away, including any strings memorized to help with analysis.

Because of all this, the experience of the very young second language learner will be virtually identical to that of the first language learner, because the interactional conditions which promote the use of formulaic sequences and curb their unnecessary analysis are so similar. The cases described in Chapter 9 are a good test of this. Takahiro had most difficulty in making initial progress in his L2, and it was he for whom the rubicon between the first and second language contexts of use was least clear. He was also the child who was most encouraged into the learning of isolated referential words. Once he was forced to use the L2 consistently in his day care context and he adopted some formulaic strategies (particularly repetition) to support his communicative acts, his acquisition progressed considerably better than before. The other two children discussed in that section, Virve and Karen, proceeded to learn their L2 efficiently and effectively, using the expected range of interactional strategies.

Older Children

Our model predicts that children well into Phase 2 and already acquiring literacy skills will break down word strings more than younger children. The effect of this in first language acquisition, where the child is already fluent and confident, is that the analysis supports the development of the more flexible system for creating novel utterances. However, if one is not yet capable in the language, the intellectual drive to analyze will have a quite different effect. The older children described in Chapter 9 seemed to fall into two groups, characterized by the relative balance in their language use of analyticity and social interaction. Nora, the paragon of a successful learner, had a very strong sense of what she wanted, and did not see her initial lack of linguistic skills as a barrier to getting it. Her interest in the second language was entirely focussed on its ability to meet her needs and desires, and her analysis of it appeared to be a natural extension of this motivation, rather than any kind of intellectual pursuit detached from usage. Her success was probably partly a product of her personality and her good fortune in making the particular friends that she did. However, she was also only 5; 7 at the start of the study, and was in a kindergarten class rather than main school. Probably she was effectively preliterate, and was not being encouraged to analyze language at the word level.

In contrast, Juan, who was a little older, was more tentative in his expression and more focussed on learning words than on using the language to communicate. The further a child is into the school system, the more he or she will be encouraged, through reading and writing, to examine language as a succession of words, rather than just trusting the socio-interactional effect of whole memorized sequences. It may be that the very focus on language at this level makes the process of learning it seem daunting. Certainly, a reluctance to use the L2 to interact until the workings of the language have been mastered appears to be much more prevalent with increasing age. The older the child, the more the attitude to the new language seems to approach that of an adult foreign language learner.

Teenage and Adult Learners

Teenage and adult language learners are in Phases 3 and 4 of their first language acquisition, which means that they are increasingly relying on formulaic language in their L1 (see Figure 7.1). However, the same will not hold for the new language. Formulaic sequences are adopted as a dynamic response to the specific needs of the moment. In the first language, it can be taken for granted that a comprehensible message will be produced, and it is only a question of which strategy is used to do this. In the second language, both the linguistic resources and the needs which they meet are different, particularly in the classroom. Firstly, classroom learners are rarely aiming to communicate a genuine message with a beneficial outcome to their physical, intellectual or emotional state, so there is no drive to use formulaic sequences for manipulative purposes. Indeed, the desire to signal group membership may even encourage the use of non-native sequences or the avoidance of nativelike ones, since the strongest group pressures are not from the community of L2 speakers but from peers in the class. Secondly, focus on form will feel natural, and will be encouraged by the teacher. Short formulaic components may be employed to help alleviate the processing load (as found in the Myles et al. study), but the overall effect will be an analytic approach, bolstered by the deliberate introduction of new words and rules as the currency of progress.

For adult learners in a naturalistic setting, socio-interactional pressures will encourage the adoption of some formulaic sequences, but the awareness of the word as a possible unit of linguistic processing (a natural product of having passed through Phase 2 and of being literate) will tend to make the learner feel uncomfortable with not knowing how a memorized string breaks down or is written. Any tuition, including self-study, that relies on the written medium, will, again, underline the importance of small units over large ones. All in all, after literacy, the second language learner is increasingly likely to deliberately aim to acquire a lexicon of word-sized units. The relative balance of words to formulaic word strings will be quite different from those of a native speaker.

L2 Learners Have Too Much Choice

Pawley and Syder (1983) observe that non-native speakers, specifically those who learn the L2 after childhood, often give themselves away, even when they are highly proficient in terms of vocabulary and grammar knowledge, by not knowing which of the grammatically possible ways of expressing a message is most idiomatic for native speakers. We can now see how this might come about. Where the first language learner starts with large and complex strings, and never breaks them down any more than necessary, the post-childhood second language learner is starting with small units and trying to build them up. Phrases and clauses may be what learners encounter in their input material, but what they notice and deal with are words and how they can be glued together. The result is that the classroom learner homes in on the individual words, and throws away all the really important information, namely, what they occurred with. These two approaches are represented in Figures 11.1 and 11.2 respectively.[2] The diagrams clearly illustrate that the lexicons of the native and taught non-native speaker contain different balances of the various units,[3] and the arrows show how this difference is created.

Given these different compositions of the lexicon, and the different emphases regarding which units are to be most focussed on, it is not surprising that non-native speakers are at a disadvantage when trying to express ideas idiomatically. Where a native speaker would draw an expression whole from the store of formulaic sequences, the non-native has to compose it out of individual words, and this offers too much choice: there are plenty of comprehensible and grammatical ways of expressing an idea, but only those combinations which are stored formulaically by native speakers will be received as idiomatic (compare Sinclair & Renouf 1988:156). The following example illustrates this.

When a native speaker of English first came across the string *major catastrophe* in input, it would be noticed and remembered as a sequence, so long as context and pragmatics furnished it with a sufficiently clear

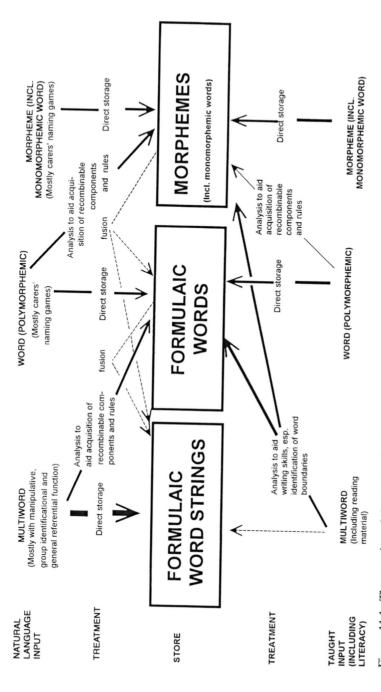

Figure 11.1. The creation of the lexicon in first language acquisition (including the effect of literacy).

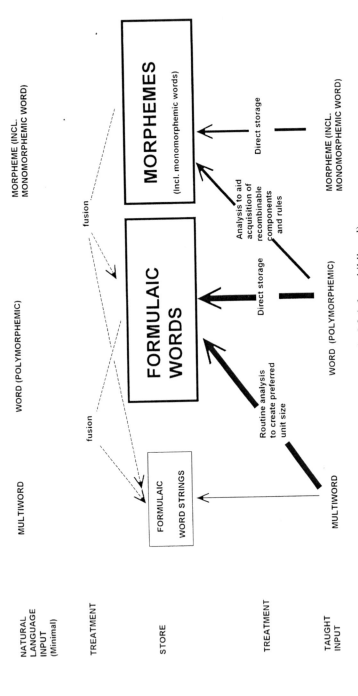

Figure 11.2. The creation of the lexicon in classroom-taught L2 (after childhood).

meaning for it not to need breaking down. It would remain unanalyzed by default, that is, for as long as, when heard subsequently, the stored meaning was found satisfactory for a relevant and sufficient interpretation. As a result, the native speaker would simply know that the idiomatic way to talk about a big disaster (in a particular context) was to call it a *major catastrophe*. There would be no automatic assumptions about what else may be referred to as 'major', since *major* would not have been singled out as a separate component of this string. There would not have been any cross-reference with any other strings containing *major*, nor with the separate entry for *major* as a lexical item (which, we shall assume, had arrived there at some point, either through the analysis of another string or because the word had been subject to other analytic operations, such as learning in school the opposition between *major* and *minor*). As a result of this absence of 'joined up knowledge', native speakers would never dream of calling their large intestine their *major intestine* or their big toe their *major toe*, since they would have no experience of *major* in these lexical contexts and, furthermore, they *would* have experience of *large* and *big*, respectively, in those places. Nor would they try to impose other adjectives on *catastrophe*, such as *large catastrophe* and *big catastrophe*, though if they encountered these pairs in use they would be added, as recurrent strings in their own right, to the list of idiomatic possibilities for expressing the idea.

In contrast, the adult language learner, on encountering *major catastrophe*, would break it down into a word meaning 'big' and a word meaning 'disaster' and store the words separately, without any information about the fact that they went together. When the need arose in the future to express the idea again, they would have no memory of *major catastrophe* as the pairing originally encountered, and any pairing of words with the right meaning would seem equally possible: *major, big, large, important, considerable*, and so on, with *catastrophe, disaster, calamity, mishap, tragedy*, and the like. Some of these sound nativelike, others do not, and the learner would have no way of knowing which were which (Cowie & Howarth 1996:91).

An interesting implication of this account is that a language learner who was able to ride the difficulties of not having a nativelike command of formulaic sequences and who continued to study the language to a high level of grammatical and lexical proficiency could, in principle, end up with a *larger* lexicon of individual words than a native speaker, since the process of breaking down text into word-sized units would have been more systematic and extensive. This lexical knowledge might manifest itself in a striking ability on the part of the non-native speaker to appreciate poetry and to use the language with imaginative creativity.

However, unless there were some means of building up the store of nativelike formulaic sequences post hoc,[4] probably by residing and fully interacting for some time in the L2 environment, the non-native speaker, however accurate in grammar and knowledgeable at the level of words, would always be a potential victim of that lesser store of formulaic sequences. There would be situations in which a native speaker would call on an idiomatic prefabricated expression, while the non-native had to create one, an activity both more labour intensive and more risky. As a result, language production and comprehension might always feel more effortful than in the native language. Of course, as we saw in Chapter 8, L2 learners can also alleviate processing effort by creating their own formulaic sequences.[5] However, non-nativelike sequences would get a mixed response (they would not support the decoding processes of an uninitiated hearer), making them appear rather less reliable than those at the command of a native speaker.

Evaluating the Model

The puzzles. At the start of this chapter, three puzzles were identified. How can these be handled by the model described here? The first regarded the apparent failure of adult language learners to extract grammatical information from formulaic sequences. This could not be because the sequences were being learned and treated holistically, as that would not explain why errors are so common in them. The presence of errors indicated that some kind of analysis was going on, yet it seemed to be ignoring the grammatical information. According to the model that we have just explored, the characteristic way for formulaic sequences to be handled by post-childhood language learners is that they are broken down in order to access the lexical constituents, which are then stored separately. The information about which words were found together within a sequence, and how they were linked, is not retained. This means that, as indicated in the research literature, formulaic sequences will make no direct contribution to the learning of grammatical rules (which is, on balance, a good thing, since so many such sequences are irregular in some way). It also means that when the learner wishes to reconstruct the formulaic sequence it will be necessary to apply the interlanguage grammar, and this will often introduce errors.

The second puzzle regarded the appropriacy of emulating first language acquisition processes in classroom language teaching. According to the model, even though there is no intrinsic reason why formulaic sequences could not be learned and used by the adult in the same way as by the child, the conditions of learning and the different intellectual experiences of the adult, particularly the perception of the word as the base unit of language, will make this highly unlikely to occur. As Nation (1990) suggests, it is probably necessary for adults and children to take different routes to their goal. For instance, the process of proceduralization described by Lennon (1990), Towell et al. (1996) and others involves automatizing the planning and assembly of utterances. Although the effect is a pattern of fluency which resembles nativelike output, this does not mean that natives have gone through a process of proceduralization in order to attain their fluency. Their ability for linear planning may have developed at an earlier stage in acquisition, and be triggered by lexical rather than grammatical operations.

The final puzzle concerned the status of collocations as formulaic, or nonformulaic. It was suggested that native speakers may have the former arrangement, and non-native speakers the latter, and this is intrinsic to the model. Howarth's discussions assume a continuum of formulaicity, from fully fixed to entirely free, whereby it is the looseness of the connection between collocated items that raises the question of their status. It was argued in Chapter 3 that the image of a continuum may be more attractive than it is useful, since it is not always clear what, precisely, is subject to gradation. Nevertheless, Howarth's point, that collocation is slippery and difficult to explain in terms of the firm relationships associated with formulaic sequences, is entirely valid, and cannot be overlooked. In the context of this model, it is now possible to separate out the problematic looseness experienced by the learner from the apparently *un*problematic looseness of the native speaker's associations. Because native speakers start with big units and analyze them only as necessary, their treatment of collocations can be framed not so much in terms of loose associations per se, but fully formulaic pairings which have *become loosened*. That is, they are pairs which can become separated under certain circumstances. In contrast, the adult learner's collocations are to be seen as separate items which *become paired*. It is this pairing, and, particularly, the establishment of the strength of the association, which causes the characteristic difficulties described by Howarth (1998a, 1998b), Pawley and Syder (1983) and others.

Reading the evidence. The predictions made by this model are highly testable. However, it will require a different perspective on the validity of data from L2 learners than has been customary up to now. Because the models in this book depict formulaic sequences as just one of many legitimate solutions to the problems which arise for an individual on a particular occasion in the course of protecting his or her interests, the language, and general behaviour, of the learner need to be viewed as a fully legitimate application of the available resources to the alleviation of those problems. It follows that learner output cannot be examined solely from the narrow perspective of its proximity in form and usage to a native 'target', and the profiling of error types will be only one of a much wider range of aspects to be examined. At present, L2 performance is all too often largely used to show us evidence of incomplete learning – it represents deficit. In order to gain full insight into what determines the linguistic performance of the language learner, we need to view that data as a map of the learner's wider agenda, one in which, on some occasions, a perfectly nativelike performance may be of relatively little importance.

Conclusion

In this chapter it has been proposed that the lexical stores of the native speaker and the post-childhood language learner are fundamentally different, because there is a different expectation about the size of unit that is most salient. That comes about because neither type of learner is focussed on setting up the storage that might be most useful one day, but rather on solving the immediate problems of dealing with the kind of input to which they are exposed, and achieving their own current goals as effectively and efficiently as possible. For young children these goals relate to controlling their environment and establishing a place of importance within it, and full language acquisition is a natural consequence. The goals of adult learners are more variable and may conflict, even to the extent of undermining the learning process entirely. In the absence of immediate gains from dealing with large and internally complex units, L2 learners will fall into the process of analysis which provides a more manageable outcome and offers a stronger sense of control over the language material. Teaching characteristically reinforces this approach, even when it incorporates formulaic sequences as input and/or introduces task-based activities, and the reliance on written materials amplifies the perceived value of focussing on word-sized units. The consequence is a failure to value the one property of nativelike input which is most characteristic of the idiomaticity to which the learner ultimately aspires: words do not *go* together, having first been apart, but, rather, *belong* together, and do not necessarily need separating.

Insofar as young children learning an L2 are subject to the same needs in, and expectations of, communication as first language learners are, many of the characteristic differences between adult and child L2 learners are naturally accounted for by this model. Rather than attributing them to some magical 'critical age' whereby specific biological mechanisms cut in or out to make nativelike acquisition difficult or impossible, the age-related differences can be explained as circumstantial. In other words, there is no inherent reason why individuals should not, as adults, learn a language to fully nativelike competence (which is a useful prediction, since people occasionally do exactly that), but there are a great many obstacles which their social and intellectual experience and their learning situation will set up to prevent it. The critical age, seen from this view, is a conglomeration of factors which affect the individual's approach to learning. The learning itself is subservient to the real agenda, which is to accommodate the immediate needs – all of them – of the individual, not only as a learner but as a functional entity in his or her own complex world.

PART V

FORMULAIC SEQUENCES IN LANGUAGE LOSS

12

Patterns of Formulaicity in Aphasic Language

Introduction

Aphasia is a term used to describe a number of different kinds of disruption to language following damage or surgery to the language-dominant hemisphere of the brain (usually the left). People with aphasia offer some insights into the nature of formulaic sequences which it would be difficult to obtain from those whose language-processing faculties are functioning normally. Formulaic, or automatic, language has long been recognized as a key feature of aphasia, and indeed it was being described in the medical literature long before it was identified by linguists as a significant component of normal language (see Benton & Joynt 1960, Critchley 1970 and Espir & Rose 1970:24ff for historical overviews). Case studies of aphasic patients date back several centuries, and in the twentieth much detailed work was made possible by the localized brain injuries of otherwise healthy young men returning from war (e.g., Goldstein 1948; Head 1926; Russell & Espir 1961). Accounts characteristically highlight as a curiosity the survival of some lengthy sequences even when very little other language remains. In one of the earliest published reports, from 1683, Peter Rommel wrote of an aphasic woman:

she lost all speech with the exception of the words 'yes' and 'and': She could say no other word, not even a syllable, with these exceptions: the Lord's Prayer, the Apostle's Creed, some Biblical verses and other prayers, which she could recite verbatim and without hesitation, but somewhat precipitously. But it is to be noted that they were said in the order in which she was accustomed to saying them for many years, and, if this regular sequence were interrupted and she were asked to recite a prayer or Biblical verse not in its accustomed place, she could not do it at all, or only after a long interval and with great difficulty. . . . Then we tried to determine whether she could repeat very short sentences consisting of the

same words found in her prayers. However she was also unsuccessful in this.
(Benton & Joynt 1960:113–4, 209–210)

It is of considerable significance to understanding their nature that
formulaic sequences have been attested in the spontaneous output of
individuals with most, if not all, the major types of aphasia, including
Broca's, Wernicke's, global, dynamic, conduction, anomic, transcortical
motor, transcortical sensory and transcortical mixed aphasias (Code
1982a, 1987; Goodglass 1993:ch. 12; Nespoulous, Code, Virbel & Lecours
1998; Van Lancker 1987:70–86). Code's (1982a, 1982b) survey of 75
patients suggests that formulaic sequences are more common in the nonfluent than the fluent aphasias.[1] However, consistency of identification is
something of a problem in this field, and it is possible that formulaic
sequences are difficult to recognize in some kinds of data, and are easily
overlooked. In order to measure formulaicity more consistently, Perkins
(1994) has proposed calculating the *stem variability quotient*. This calculation captures, more sensitively than is possible with the standard type-
token ratio calculation, the way in which new and previously used words
appear in a text.

Several overviews of the types of formulaic language in aphasia
already exist (e.g., Caplan 1987; Code 1994; Van Lancker 1987). Rather
than simply provide another, it will be more useful here to examine the
range of realizations of the phenomenon from the perspective of two
questions which can illuminate our understanding of formulaicity. The
first question derives from one of the basic assumptions about formulaic
sequences, that they are stored and retrieved from the lexicon like single
words.[2] Do they, as this would predict, succumb to wordlike rather than
phrase- or sentence-like symptoms? The second question offers a means
of testing the claims made in Chapter 5 about the functions of formulaic
processing: what role can formulaic sequences be seen to play in supporting the interests of the aphasic speaker, given the extreme processing pressures and basic communication difficulties which are associated
with the condition?

There are inevitably problems with interpreting data collected by
other people, and for that reason, all the observations made here should
be viewed as indicative only, and as an invitation for further research.
Most research on aphasia does not consider the wider role of formulaic
sequences *at all*, and particularly not the role of those which are grammatically regular and semantically transparent. Yet this material is
pivotal. If it is possible for a speaker to access in prefabricated form
linguistic material that looks identical to a novel construction – and this
book has provided ample evidence that it is – then recognizing when an

aphasic person has done so will make an enormous difference to how his or her ability to create novel language is judged.

For the sake of clarity, a frame of reference for reviewing the manifestions of the most common kinds of sequences in aphasia will be useful. Five categories can usefully be distinguished:

- previously memorized material, including prayers, songs, poems and mnemonic chants.
- short conventional phrases such as *take care* and *that's a lie*.
- sequences considered idiosyncratic to the particular individual, possibly reflecting pre-trauma discourse mannerisms.
- words or phrases, which may or may not resemble something meaningful, repeated involuntarily.
- pause fillers and single words, most commonly *yes* and/or *no*.

The last category may seem somewhat odd. Some justification for including it will be given later.

Do Formulaic Sequences Succumb to Wordlike or Phrase- and Sentence-like Symptoms?

Length of Utterances

In nonfluent aphasia, formulaic sequences stand out, being long and fluent strings of words within output that is generally only single words, or, if longer, produced haltingly. If formulaic sequences had the psycholinguistic status of phrases or clauses, then they would be dysfluent and disjointed in the same way as other structured output. The fact that they are not supports the hypothesis that they are being treated like single words. In fluent aphasia, of course, the speaker is able to produce utterances approaching normal length and fluency, so in data from such patients we cannot so easily use utterance size as an indicator of the status of formulaic sequences.

Internal Resilience

Fully fixed strings. In both fluent and nonfluent aphasia, a novel phrase or clause, if it can be produced at all, is likely to succumb to internal errors. There may be phonological or morphological omissions or substitutions (e.g., Goodglass & Mayer 1958), and even entire words may be unavailable or replaced (see later). Yet, at least some types of word string appear to be internally immune from these symptoms. The clearest evidence of this is the ability of patients to recall lengthy passages of prose, verse and song perfectly (Benton & Joynt 1960). Singing sometimes survives when even memorized speech does not (Van Lancker 1987:92), a phenomenon which Goldstein (1948) attributes to "the close relationship of singing to expressive movements and to emotional language" (p. 147). Also often retained intact are serial lists such as the days of the week (Goldstein 1948:247; Russell & Espir 1961:99), though there are some grounds for categorizing these separately, as Espir and Rose (1970:27) do, because serial lists seem more vulnerable to error than other memorized material. Denès (1914/1983), for example, describes a nonfluent aphasic person trying to count from one to ten: "she starts, but skips a number. When made aware of this, she puts the number in its proper place. When a second number is skipped and the patient is informed of it, she mumbles as if to relocate the missing number but instead, she says A B C" (p. 110). Two- or three-word-long casual interjections and idiosyncratically repeated phrases such as *take care*; *that's a lie*; *I told you*; *wait a minute*; *the other day* and *that's mine* (exemplified by Code's 1982a survey, and discussed at some length by Critchley 1970:206ff) also appear to be resistant to the symptoms of aphasia (see also Nespoulous et al. 1998 on 'modalizing' as opposed to 'referential' language). Marshall (2000) speaks of a nonfluent aphasic man who, on seeing him each day, "always said 'hi, how are you doing? Fine. Thank you'. This entire greeting sequence was uttered fluently but [he] offered it regardless of whether or not I greeted him, asked how he was, or responded appropriately" (p. 82).

The ability to produce such formulaic sequences without error turns out to be of limited worth to the aphasic person, however. With the occasional exception (e.g., Goldstein 1948:342; Luria & Tsvetkova 1970:191), the internal components cannot be extracted and used for creative purposes (Critchley 1970:191; Goldstein 1948:280). Van Lancker (1987) notes that "[it is a] common observation in non-fluent aphasia that the patient can say a phrase, such as 'son of a bitch', and does so quite fluently, but cannot say the word 'son' to refer to his male offspring" (p. 80). As we have seen from Rommel's account (earlier), the rigidity of the memorized pattern can extend to the ritual order in which different pieces are customarily recited, such that the entire set is itself a formulaic sequence, from which the complete pieces (in this case prayers) which make up the whole are inextricable.

Semi-fixed strings. If formulaic sequences can be internally resilient, what of those which are only semi-fixed? They require morphological tuning (e.g., tense or person marking), or the insertion of one or more open class items. Are such sequences produced in aphasia, and if so, are they appropriately completed, are they produced with fixed values in the variable slots, or are the novel parts actually subject to the limitations of the aphasia, even when the fixed parts remain immune? Answering this question is important for understanding the way in which formulaicity and novelty combine in the production of language. Most reports of formulaic sequences in aphasia relate to fully fixed interactional expressions such as *take care* and *I don't know*. However, looking at data with an eye to semi-fixed sequences can reveal some interesting indications. The following example of speech in Wernicke's aphasia comes from Gardner (1985:185).

"What kind of work have you done, Mr. Johnson?" I asked.

"We, the kids, all of us, and I, we were working for a long time in the . . . you know . . . it's the kind of space, I mean place rear to the spedwan . . ."

At this point I interjected, "Excuse me, but I wanted to know what work you have been doing."

"If you had said that, we had said that, poomer, near the fortunate, forpunate, tamppoo, all around the fourth of martz. Oh, I get all confused". (p. 185)

Possible fixed and semi-fixed sequences in this passage are:

- *NP be-*TENSE *working for a long time in the N (*LOCATION*)*. Here, the *NP* is realized by a range of options, of which *all of us*, and possibly *the kids*, also appear to be formulaic. Alternatively, the frame could be identified as *NP be-*TENSE *V-ing for NP (*TIME PERIOD*) in the N (*LOCATION*)*, with the verb and *NP (*TIME PERIOD*)* correctly selected from the lexicon. A third possibility is that the string is actually several smaller formulaic sequences (e.g., *NP be-*TENSE *working + for NP (*TIME PERIOD*) + in the N (*LOCATION*)*).
- *you know* is a fully fixed sequence.
- *it's the kind of N*. The target for *N* is *place*, but *space* is erroneously selected first and then corrected. If *the* was an error for *a* (i.e., the target was *it's a kind of N*), then this would be evidence of internal disruption to a formulaic sequence (see earlier).
- *near to the N*. Here, *near* has been mispronounced as *rear* and a nonword has been produced for *N*. In his next turn, he uses a similar sequence, *near the N*, in which *near* is correctly pronounced, and he has a series of attempts to fill the *N* slot.
- *(If) NP had said that*. Here, *NP* is first realized as *you* and then as *we*.
- *all around the N*. Here, *N* is filled with a formulaic sequence.
- ORDINAL *of* MONTH. *March* has been mispronounced.
- *Oh, I get all confused* is a fully fixed sequence.

The detail in this analysis is, of course, open to debate. For example, grammatical subjects have been represented by *NP* slots, whereas grammatical objects have been depicted as *N* slots, with the article already in place. One could just as easily use *NP* throughout, coupled with an assumption that the speaker has no difficulty in accessing the determiner. The distribution of *NP* and *N* used here reflects the predominance of subject pronouns and object nouns in the extract, and may be a regular feature of this sort of discourse.

It is striking that, in the extract from Gardner just examined, it is the formulaic sequences (if they *are* formulaic sequences) that provide a great deal of the apparent sense. The problems of clarity seem to derive from the speaker's difficulty in selecting novel items to fill the gaps in the formulaic frames. We have seen that normal language can be highly formulaic, and that such frames are a major feature of that formulaicity. So fluent aphasic speakers such as this one are not inventing a new way of speaking, just adopting one of the strategies that they have always used in certain types of discourse. Using formulaic sequences always imposes restrictions on novelty, and this is usually compensated for by inserting the appropriate open class items into the slots. For people with aphasia, however, word-finding difficulties make this problematic.

The observations made here are consistent with those of Nespoulous et al. (1998), who suggest "a dissociation in speech production: some words or word strings are massively distorted or absent, whereas others seem to be unaltered" (p. 313). If some of the fluency achieved by people with Wernicke's aphasia is the result of using formulaic sequences, then assessing the extent of an individual's linguistic disability will be much more complicated than just assessing the level of fluency and the linguistic structure of the output.

Customarily, in fluent aphasia, the coherence of output has been used as a means of judging the severity of the disruption to the speaker's grammar and/or comprehension abilities. Now, however, we see that the speaker's success in appearing coherent might reflect *not* the intactness of these faculties, but rather his or her ability to access formulaic sequences. In other words, the grammatical faculties could appear far more spared than they actually were, if most of what seemed to be on-line grammatical activity was actually just fixed and semi-fixed formulaic sequences. Furthermore, if, as has been proposed in this book, formulaic sequences are drawn upon as a solution to problems with getting one's message across, then the *greater* the speaker's difficulty in commanding language in the normal way, the greater his or her reliance on formulaic sequences is likely to be. If so, then the speech that had fewest grammatical errors could belong to the individuals with *most* damage to their novel linguistic processing abilities, while those less severely damaged, by making more of an attempt to construct bespoke sentences, would produce more errors. We might predict that a speaker of the latter kind, having more control over the discourse structure, would use formulaic sequences more at the lexical than the phrasal and clausal levels. The result would be more hesitations, and short, coherent formulaic sequences chained together inappropriately, besides, of course, an absence of target referential vocabulary.

Butterworth (1979) provides the following transcription of an interview with a person with jargonaphasia, which may illustrate this pattern. It was elicited in reply to the question *did you have lunch today?*[3]

Ooh, I didn't late before, no, yesterday I simply went with my # breakfast with my # er # [znɪks] thing (claps right palm on back of left hand several times) # one, # then again at twenty, # [zplən] # an a [ti·k] (tea?) thing. # Nothing to [i·k]. # But I would work tomorrow, tomorrow, I would [ntərm] # league er # barrack stuff then, # but not # not the [rowi] thing because I'm [wtrɛd] waiting (taps belly). # I've been very much [wtiŋ] # what to do. # For years I've been second to just be # keen whether or not I got it, # but I've been necking to # get # quite well. # (Cough) and my [mtræks] is better # the last # two years better #. (p. 158)

The following may be formulaic:

* *I didn't X.* Here, *X* should be a verb but is not. This suggests inappropriate chaining of material.
* *yesterday I simply V + PAST.*
* *with my N.* Three attempts are made to fill the gap, including, finally, the proform *thing* (see later). This sequence does not easily follow from the previous one, again suggesting that the strings have been independently selected.
* *then again.*
* *at twenty.* Once more, the relationship between this and the previous string is not clear.
* *and a N.*
* *nothing to V.*
* *but I would V.* Several attempts are made to fill the *V* gap, including, apparently, two nouns.
* *but not the N.* Again, *thing* is selected to stand for the unavailable target.
* *because I'm V-ing.*
* *I've been (very much) V-ing what to do.* In normal language, the verb would be restricted to *worry, wonder,* and the like. The former may well be the target here. The insertion of *very much* would be associated in normal language with a following adjective, rather than a

participle (e.g., *I've been very much concerned*), whereas without *very much*, a participle form is appropriate (e.g., *I've been wondering, I've been worrying*). Formulaic variations found here are *For years I've been X*, where an adjective is placed at *X*, and *I've been V-ing to VP*.

- *to just be ADJ.*
- *whether or not I VP.*
- *to get ADJ.*
- *quite well.* The string *I've been V-ing to get quite well* appears at first to be odd because of the nonword in the *V* slot, but in actual fact there is another anomaly. If we insert a plausible verb (e.g., *I've been hoping to get quite well*), the result is still not fully idiomatic (compare *I've been hoping to get well/get better*). Again, this suggests that the sequence *quite well* has been selected independently of any wider frame of the kind which might create the idiomatic versions in normal language.
- *my N is better.*
- *the last CARDINAL years.*

In this extract[4] there are, overall, more appropriately selected content words, as well as a number of inappropriate ones, than in the previous extract. The speaker also seems able to embed one formulaic sequence into another (e.g., *quite well*). This evidence supports the hypothesis that this individual is taking a greater command of the text than the speaker in the previous extract. Although not always successfully, an attempt is being made to fashion the text at the lexical level, rather than setting up a clausal level formulaicity which will feature correct words if they are part of the sequence but still leave the open class gaps difficult to fill. Yet a hearer might not find this speaker's output any easier to understand than that in the previous example: the greater reliance of the first speaker on formulaic sequences gives a superficial impression of grammatical competence which the more competent second speaker forgoes.

The only way to establish whether these observations are valid or not would be to find some reliable way of identifying the formulaic output of a given individual. We have already seen in Chapter 2 that there are immense problems with the process of identification. At the very least, it would entail collecting a great deal of data from that individual, so that a large enough corpus could be constructed for patterns to begin to appear. It might also be possible to compare the speaker's natural conversational output with his or her abilities on formal linguistic tests that drew on the analytic processes underlying novel linguistic construction. Provided that the patient did not find it appropriate to solve the communication problems in the test context by using formulaic language (and Wray 1992 suggests that tests probably do not encourage the abrogation of the analytic mechanisms), then a contrast should be found between the amount of grammatical material in the two kinds of output. Specifically, an individual whose conversational output was fairly fluent and grammatical but containing hardly any appropriate content words (that is, a person hypothesized to be drawing heavily on formulaic material) would have severely limited expression when prevented from relying so heavily on formulaic language. In contrast, a person whose conversational output was less obviously formulaic (that is, one who appeared to be attempting to control the novel content rather more) should display less of a contrast between conversational and test-elicited output, since the strategies for the two activities would be more similar.

The purpose of this exploration of semi-fixed formulaic sequences was to establish, firstly, whether they occurred at all in aphasic output. The analyses conducted here suggest that they do, at least in fluent aphasias. The second question was whether they were appropriately completed. The answer seems to be that they are not, even to the extent that a noun can be placed in a verb slot, and so on. The slots appear to be genuinely open, not able to be filled by a fixed item. Finally, we asked whether the novel items in the slots were subject to the symptoms of the aphasia, even when the fixed parts remained immune. The answer to this appears to be 'yes'.

One puzzle remains. If, as has been assumed up to now, formulaic word strings and single words are both stored in the lexicon, why should there be, as it seems, a greater success in accessing the former than the latter? We shall return to this question later.

Word-Finding Difficulties

A common feature of aphasia is *anomia*, that is, difficulty in retrieving words (Code 1991; Goodglass & Wingfield 1997:3ff). If formulaic word strings are stored and retrieved like words, then similar accessing problems should be expected. There is some evidence to support this. One feature of anomia is that a phonological cue may help to access an otherwise unavailable word, something that seems to be true of memorized sequences too. For instance, eighteenth-century writer Olof Dalin described a man with no creative language, who was able to sing hymns and recite prayers, but only if someone started them off (Benton & Joynt 1960:115/211; see Goldstein 1948:8, 209 for other examples). However, it must be said that normal speakers also often need the first few words of a rhyme or song in order to recall the remainder, and indeed church liturgies formally build in such prompts, by allocating to a clergyman the first two or three words of a prayer, before the congregation joins in with the rest. So perhaps we should not read too much into the need for such prompts in aphasia.

Another characteristic of anomia is that some words are easier to recall than others (see, for example, Blumstein 1988:220; Goldstein 1948:60). Are formulaic word strings affected in the same way? This is difficult to judge. While descriptions of word-finding difficulties focus on how many items are *not* available, descriptions of formulaic sequences tend to focus on how many *are* available. Too little attention has been paid to date to the question of what is missing in the formulaic repertoire. But if the deficiency model is applied to both, then similarities are likely to appear: just as with words, we need to explain why so many of the formulaic word strings common in normal language are *not* produced by aphasic speakers. Van Lancker (1987) reports a person with fluent aphasia who, in a repetition task, could say *how are you*, *I'm fine*, and *good morning*, but could not say *thanks very much* (p. 92). There do not appear to be any conditions in which disruptions to repetition occur without more general word-finding difficulties. Therefore, we can be reasonably confident that Van Lancker's example illustrates selective difficulties in accessing formulaic word strings.

Ideally, we would want to find patterns in this selectivity. In the case of words, differences in accessibility can relate to a variety of criteria. One is word class. Zingeser and Berndt (1990) found people with Broca's aphasia significantly less proficient in producing verbs than nouns, while anomic patients showed a superiority for verbs over nouns in some types of task, and no difference in others. There can also be specific impairment in certain semantic categories, such as words for living versus nonliving things (Tippett, Glosser & Farah 1996), for colours, animals, fruit, vegetables and tools (see Goldfarb & Halpern 1991; Goodglass & Wingfield 1997:22–23). Selective impairment can also relate to the familiarity of a word and/or when it was acquired (Hirsh & Funnell 1995) or its frequency in normal language (Goodglass & Mayer 1958:103). As always, there is far less evidence when it comes to formulaic word strings. Frequency may be a factor (Code 1982a), but even here it would be premature to make a firm judgement. We are only just accumulating information about the frequency of various word combinations in normal language, and we need this as a baseline for assessing what appears in aphasic speech. As for the animate/inanimate distinction, careful examination may provide an answer to whether a sequence like *my brother-in-law* is more accessible than an inanimate one like *the in-store café* or an abstract one like *the wrong side of the blanket.*[5] However, the most frequent, and most easily identified, formulaic word strings are probably those with an interactional function rather than an ideational one (Butler 1997), and, as such, they are nonanimate and abstract. If so, then the animacy and frequency effects which both contribute to the accessibility of single words may work in opposite directions in case of formulaic word strings, making it difficult to identify consistent patterns.

The most direct test would be confrontational naming. However, it would be necessary to create matched elicitation tasks for words and formulaic word strings, and, once more, this would be difficult, since the easiest words to elicit are frequent referential nouns, but the most frequent formulaic word strings are not referential. Frequent interactional formulaic word strings could be elicited by asking such questions as *what would you say when you met someone for the first time?* or *what would you say if someone sneezed?* However, this requires a considerable capacity for linguistic comprehension – much greater than is needed for word elicitation, where the subject can be shown an object or picture.

Neologism

In some forms of aphasia, particularly Wernicke's and jargonaphasia, nonwords are uttered (Christman & Buckingham 1991; Goodglass 1993:ch. 12). These are often, but perhaps not always, associated with a target word which has been incorrectly accessed at the phonological level or incorrectly constructed out of its component morphemes, or which has suffered mispronunciation at the articulatory stage. To some extent, neologism is in the ear of the beholder, since an item will be termed a neologism if the target is not recognized and, conversely, a genuine neologism may be interpreted as a word if it happens to coincide with some recognizable form. Recognition may be particularly difficult if the distortion co-occurs with paraphasia (see later), where the incorrect word is selected in the first place. Despite all this, Butterworth (1979) believes some neologisms to be genuine inventions. Buckingham (1981) proposes the existence of a 'random syllable generator' (p. 43, note 2), and Blanken and Marini (1997), too, argue for a separate origin for what they term 'nonlexical automisms'.

Does neologism extend to formulaic word strings? Again, it is not easy to establish this. Firstly, while production errors may render a single word sufficiently unintelligible for it to be termed a 'nonword', a formulaic word string is more likely to remain recognizable – there is more of it, and any inaccuracies may be at its edges since, as we have seen, formulaic word strings can be somewhat resilient to internal disruption. Secondly, if a lengthy sound sequence is judged to be nonsense, on what basis is it to be viewed as a *sequence* of words rather than a single word? The categorization entirely depends on whether it is transcribed with spaces or without. Even if there is a phraselike intonation and/or stress contour to it, this does not necessarily mean that it is not a single word, as our exploration of dummy fillers later in this chapter will show. It is, in fact, a corollary of the lexical models developed in this book that formulaic word strings and words are indistinguishable without reference to the conventions of writing, and knowledge of the lexicon and grammar of a language (see Chapter 14).

An alternative approach would be to associate formulaicity, in the case of neologism, with repetitive use, because a nonsense string that is produced on many occasions has probably been stored whole, rather than being spontaneously created in the same way many times. For this to occur, the sequence would have to have been created by the damaged mechanisms, and, for some reason, stored for later retrieval (compare Code's 1994 model described later). According to this view, if a nonword occurs once only, it counts as a spontaneous neologism, but if it occurs many times, then it counts as formulaic. Repetition is common with nonwords in aphasia. Examples in the literature include nonsense sequences repeated sporadically (e.g., *pittimy, monomentif, to do*) or immediately (e.g., *tan-tan, cousisi-cousisi*) (Van Lancker 1987:88; for examples from German patients see Blanken, Wallesch & Papagno 1990 and Blanken & Marini 1997). However, while this approach offers a way of formally differentiating the spontaneous creation from the stored one, it does not get us any closer to differentiating between single nonwords and 'nonsequences'. The bottom line is that both words and formulaic word strings are defined in terms of their *presence* in the lexicon. Nonwords and nonsequences are by definition absent from the normal lexicon. There is therefore no point of reference for formally differentiating them.

Semantic Paraphasia

In paraphasia the target word is replaced by another nonword or real word, often one sharing semantic or phonological characteristics with the target. Semantic paraphasia is a symptom of Wernicke's aphasia and transcortical sensory aphasia (Goodglass 1993:ch. 12). If formulaic word strings are just lexical items like any other (they are both types of formulaic sequence), then we should expect that in paraphasia a word could be replaced by a string, and a string by a word. There does not appear to be any evidence on this question to date. However, experiments reported by Hittmair-Delazer et al. (1994), with German aphasic speakers, and Semanza et al. (1997) with Italian ones, indicate that paraphasia is sensitive to features of the target, possibly length or internal complexity. They found that when the target word was a compound (e.g., *apribottiglie* 'bottle opener', literally 'open-bottles', *colapasta* 'pasta strainer', literally 'strain-pasta', *portabagagli*, 'trunk', literally 'carry-luggages' (Semanza et al. 1997:43); *Gießkanne* 'watering can', literally 'pour jug', *Eichkatzl* 'squirrel', literally 'oak kitten' (Hittmair-Delazer et al. 1994:32)), the paraphasic substitution was likely to be another compound word, and a simple word was almost never replaced by a compound one. While sensitivity to length (or other phonological features) is entirely compatible with a single storage and access mechanism for words and formulaic word strings, sensitivity to internal complexity is not. It is the latter, however, which Semanza et al. (1997) identify as critical. Among their subjects were six people with Broca's aphasia, who had selective difficulty with retrieving verbs. When required to produce compound nouns which were composed of a verb and a noun component (such as the three examples given earlier), they often omitted the verb part and produced just the noun part.

If these findings and the interpretation are reliable, they suggest that common compound nouns are not stored whole but are assembled online when required. This would be a major difficulty for the model proposed in this book, because if it is true of compound nouns, it should also be true of formulaic word strings. However, it would also be a problem for many other models of the lexicon. Suggesting that an Italian speaker does not have a separate lexical representation for *pianoforte* (piano, literally 'softly-loudly') or *girasole* (sunflower, literally 'turn-sun') is equivalent to suggesting that an English speaker constructs words like *handbag* and *teacup* out of their morphemes, rather than retrieving them whole. In short, their findings somewhat shift the boundary between morphology and etymology, and are, as a result, counterintuitive. This encourages closer scrutiny of their methods and results. Firstly, of the 49 compound items used in the test, 37 were verb-noun, and only 7 noun-noun, 3 adjective-noun, 1 noun-adjective and 1 adverb-adverb. Thus, if there was a general tendency for the first part of long words to be omitted, it would look, predominantly, like a tendency to omit the verb. Secondly, the subgroup with particular verb-retrieval problems actually performed quite well in their retrieval of verb-first compounds. They correctly retrieved 113 of the 294 compound targets (38%), and failed on the first element in only 35 trials (less than 12%), of which some, as we have seen, may not have been verb-first. In a further 11 cases (4%), the second, not the first, component was omitted, something which could not be due to omission of the verb, as there were no verb-final compounds.

An alternative explanation of Semanza et al.'s results is that while common compound words are stored whole, their component parts are also stored separately, and that the subjects were unable consistently to access the holistic forms, whether by virtue of their linguistic dysfunction or the design of the test. Multiple storage of this kind is a central feature of the lexical models presented so far in this book, and in Chapter 13 we shall model selective access.

Vagueness, Proforms and Dummy Fillers

In some forms of aphasia, particularly Broca's (Edwards & Garman 1991), words can lose their precise meaning, becoming referentially vague. In addition, anomia is typified by vague general words termed 'proforms', such as *someone, suchlike, thing*, which seem to relieve problems in retrieving items with a more exact meaning (Code 1991:10; Goodglass 1993:214). One German patient used *Stückle* ('little piece') and *Ding* ('thing') for objects and *überfahren* (dialect word for 'achieve/perform/do') for verbs, saying, in response to being shown a knife and asked to name it, *Stückle zum überfahren, wenn ich's nur hätt*, 'A thing for doing, if I only had one' (Goldstein 1948:248). Even if the patient cannot control which words are retrieved, it may be possible to treat as a proform whatever is uttered. By acting as a phonological 'filler', any word can convey messages "by dint of varying the tones with which the words are spoken, and by resort to facial mimicry" (Critchley 1970:374). The words most commonly performing this filler function are *yes* and *no*[6] (see discussion by Critchley 1970:373ff and the cases cited by Head 1926 (II):295, 395; Russell & Espir 1961:80, 98, 101, 117; Salomon 1914/1983:119; Scoresby-Jackson 1867:697–698). Exclamations such as *oh*, and swearwords, are also commonly retained and used in this way (see later). Goldstein (1948) considers dummy fillers important in rehabilitation. He emphasizes the priority of reaching "as soon as possible a condition which renders communication possible", in pursuance of which a patient "should learn to use words as sentences" (p. 331).

Like words, formulaic word strings can also act as dummy fillers,[7] and the longer the string, the more suprasegmental information it can carry. Characteristically, though, the strings employed for this purpose seem to be relatively short. The poet Baudelaire spent the last days of his life able to say only *(Sa)cré nom*: "With these two words, he who had loved and practised the art of conversation was obliged to express the whole gamut of his feelings and thoughts – joy, sorrow, anger and impatience" (Starkie

1958:512). As we shall see later, recovery in aphasia is often characterized by the use of one or more repeated phrases to express a range of
needs and feelings according to the different tones of voice and intonation patterns with which they are uttered (Alajouanine 1956:10).

Dummy fillers seem particularly useful for expressing emotional
reactions, and indeed Van Lancker (1987) associates them with *only* this
function (p. 89). However, she adds that "the observation that nonpropositional speech occurs in emotional outbursts may well be attributable to the fact that only a strong impulse will motivate the person to
speak using the only phrases still available" (p. 88). Critchley (1970), on
the other hand, believes that, given a liberal application of pragmatics
by the hearer, content messages can also be conveyed (pp. 26 and 192).
Exactly as in normal language, the success of the utterance in achieving
the desired behaviour in the hearer will depend on the hearer's ability
easily and accurately to decode it (ibid.: 192). The utterance need only
match these interpretative abilities in the addressee, and may remain
incomprehensible to a third party.

Verbal Stereotypy

Dummy fillers, discussed earlier, are examples of words or sequences
which have relinquished not only their normal meaning, but any consistency of meaning at all, in order to take on another function. However,
both words and formulaic word strings can also be uttered with no
meaning or function at all, but as a simple reflex of the attempt to communicate, without specific intention. This is the phenomenon known as
'verbal stereotypy' (Alajouanine 1956). Code (1994) notes that such
"speech automatisms" have "no apparent referential or contextual connection with the patient's world . . . [and] . . . appear . . . to be phonologically, syntactically and semantically identical each time [they are]
produced" (p. 137). A patient described by Nespoulous et al. (1998) pep-
pered his speech with the automatism *reams assessor* (pp. 313–314). Code
(1982a) reports both single-word and multiword recurrent utterances,
the former including *away, because, milk, money, factory* and *Wednesday*
(p. 143) and the latter *I can talk, fucking hell, funny thing, washing
machine, I did not hear, I told you, I'm a stone, I bin to town* and *I want
to* (p. 149). Sometimes a word is repeated immediately, as in *yes-yes,
come-come, school-school* (Van Lancker 1987:88).[8]

One suggestion has been that such words or phrases are an imprint
of the last thing said or thought before the trauma occurred: "The patient
who kept saying *list complete* was an accountant who lost consciousness
just after making up his books for the half-year. Another patient

sustained a head injury in a street fight; his recurring utterance was *I want protection*" (Critchley 1970:207). Although this is unlikely to account for the majority of stereotypies, it seems sensible, at the very least, to keep in mind the likelihood of a speaker displaying, in his or her post-trauma inventory of words and formulaic word strings, features of the pre-trauma inventory. Lecours et al. (1981) mention "a jargonaphasic nun who remained quite good at praying and related verbal activities" (p. 37).

Comprehension

So far, we have considered the effect of aphasia on the *production* of formulaic word strings. But in some forms of aphasia comprehension is affected too. Therefore we need to establish whether, in individuals who experience problems with comprehension, formulaic word strings display wordlike or phrase- and sentence-like patterns of deficit. Comprehension is inherently less easy to investigate than production and, in particular, it would be difficult to tell whether a breakdown in comprehension had occurred within, or at the boundaries of, a sequence. However, Van Lancker (1987) does observe that "aphasic patients seem to comprehend more in conversational interaction than they do in formal tests of language comprehension; much of this may be attributable to . . . comprehension of speech formulas" (p. 72). If, as Wray (1992, 1998; Wray & Perkins 2000) and Bybee (1998) suggest, formulaic sequences can become subjected to analytic processing under certain circumstances, then measures need to be taken to ensure that the test conditions do not drive the patient into such analysis when, because of the aphasia, holistic processing could achieve a better outcome (Wray 1992:119ff).

One way of gaining insight into how formulaic word strings are processed for comprehension is to select, as test items, strings which have a different meaning when processed as a whole from that which they have when processed as the sum of their parts. In one experiment of this design, Van Lancker and Kempler (1987) tested 28 patients, with an array of aphasias resulting from left hemisphere damage, on their comprehension of common idioms, such as *he's turning over a new leaf* and *she has him eating out of her hand*. Subjects had to select from four pictures the one which best represented the meaning. The results showed that the aphasic people were better at interpreting the metaphorical sequences than matched sentences with a literal meaning, which suggested that they were processing them holistically (formulaically), not componentially (analytically). This indicates that "the preservation of abilities for formulaic speech production in aphasia extends to comprehension" (p. 271). Interestingly, in contrast, subjects who had right hemisphere damage performed better on the literal interpretations than the idioms. We shall return later to a consideration of what role the right hemisphere might play in the storage and access of formulaic word strings.

The Functions of Formulaic Sequences in Aphasia

Little research has directly addressed the question of what people with aphasia use formulaic sequences for. Exceptions are the writings on dummy fillers, described earlier, and occasional isolated studies such as McElduff and Drummond (1991) and Oelschlaeger and Damico (1998), described later. It might seem relatively easy to establish the function of at least some formulaic sequences found in the output of an aphasic speaker. One would only need to identify the function which the sequence has in normal language and ascertain whether that function is still evident. However, there are both practical and theoretical difficulties with this. At the practical level, to be sure that a certain formulaic sequence has retained all or part of its previous function, we should need evidence of its range of usage in the output of that individual, something that would require a great deal of data. Most accounts of formulaic language in aphasia to date are in essence anecdotal. Nor have they been subjected to the scrutiny of discourse analysis. Furthermore, the identification of the function of a unit may be undermined by other aspects of the disability. For example, formulaic sequences will not be used to mark discourse structure unless there is structured discourse to mark. In fluent aphasia, it is hard to be sure when there is even an intention to structure, and so it will be difficult to establish whether a sequence normally associated with that role really has it in that instance.

The more fundamental problem arises in respect of the underlying reasons for selecting a formulaic sequence in given circumstances. This book has proposed that formulaic sequences facilitate the processing of the speaker, hearer or both, and are selected in response to immediate difficulties with the promotion of the speaker's interests. Since the specific problems that will arise in this regard are so different for normal and aphasic speakers, no assumptions can be made about a transfer of function from normal to abnormal language. Rather, an utterance can only be said to have a particular function if there is evidence that it is used for that purpose. This calls for a different approach. If we see the selection of formulaic sequences as a dynamic operation, brought about by the immediate need to reduce production effort and/or to deliver a comprehensible message, we need to look for evidence of that dynamism in the aphasic speaker's use of them. Rather than assuming that the formulaic sequences found in aphasic speech will be a subset of those in the individual's inventory before the trauma, we need to ask what the aphasic person's processing and interactional needs are, and how surviving, and newly created, formulaic sequences might be contributing to meeting them.

Code's Adaptive Model of Output Processing

Code (1994) proposes a model of speech automatism production in aphasia (Figure 12.1) which captures the flexibility which such a dynamism would require. According to his model, the individual formulates speech acts (e.g., questions, commands, statements) under two different conditions. One is when there is the intention to communicate a specific idea. The other is when there is a noncommunicative impulse to express his or her state. In the former case, the speech act takes the linguistic form of a formulaic sequence selected whole from the "holistic speech lexicon" in the right hemisphere (the role of the right hemisphere is discussed later). In the latter case, a nonlexical utterance is formulated

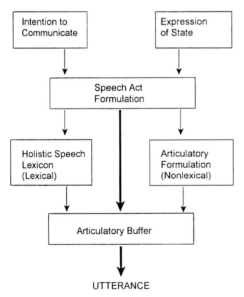

Figure 12.1. Code's "Preliminary model of initial and subsequent production of aphasic lexical and nonlexical speech automatisms". Reprinted from *Journal of Neurolinguistics*, vol. 8, C. Code, "Speech automatism production in aphasia", p. 144, copyright 1994, with permission from Elsevier Science.

in the damaged left hemisphere. Crucially, once it has been so accessed or created, an item may be stored and recycled. This means that a sequence first produced as an expression of state (e.g., a nonword used to register disgust) could subsequently be employed for the intention to communicate (p. 145), that is, as a dummy filler (see earlier). According to Code's model, then, there is a mechanism for the patient to act strategically by using the available language effectively, even if somewhat idiosyncratically.

The Primacy of Need

Code's model supports the hypothesis that the need to express certain emotions or communicate ideas may create new ways of harnessing language to use. Furthermore, if he is correct in invoking the right hemisphere, it may facilitate access to linguistic resources that are otherwise subject to inhibitory mechanisms (see later). An aphasic individual, like anyone else, needs to convey important information, minimize the effects of the acquired processing problems, feel integrated in a community, and retain a sense of genuine identity in a context where many people's eyes will not see beyond the disability. The extent to which a person is able to apply dynamic mechanisms to find ways of meeting these needs may contribute to the level of recovery, and certainly must affect the sense of success in making the best of the situation. Goldstein (1948) notes "the different capacity of the patients to cover up their defect" (p. 63), and Van Lancker (1987) describes one patient who was able to disguise her problem through the clever use of conversational formulaic sequences. She reports that her novel speech was "halting and hesitant", but that she used the formulaic sequences with considerable interactional appropriacy, encouraging the continuation of dialogue:

[she] got on by conversation openings, then continued with 'I think . . .', she responded to queries with 'I don't know and that's about all', 'sure', 'I guess so', and followed up with 'I was . . . just . . . that was all . . . Well, I'm glad'. On pursuing the dialogue it could be ascertained that these expressions occurred over and over, with normal intonation, appropriate pragmatic gesturing and eye contact, and an air of sincerity each time. (Van Lancker 1987:91)

Indications that aphasic speakers rely on formulaic sequences more than normal speakers do, and that they use them differently, come from studies by McElduff and Drummond (1991) and Oelschlaeger and Damico (1998). The former analyzed the speech of four acute nonfluent aphasic people and four normal controls according to 12 speech act categories. The aphasic speakers used considerably more formulaic language for communicative purposes (44.75%) than the controls did (19.56%), and used it primarily for commenting and answering, whereas the normal speakers used it for questioning and expressing personal beliefs, attitudes, feelings and emotions. Oelschlaeger and Damico (1998) analyzed eight naturally occurring conversations between an aphasic person and his wife. They showed that the former used repetition of fragments of his wife's preceding utterances to express uncertainty, agreement, alignment and acknowledgement (p. 985).

As pointed out in Chapter 5, once we view formulaic sequences as one linguistic solution to a nonlinguistic problem, this invites us to see their use in the context of other, nonlinguistic, solutions. In aphasia, a whole gamut of communicational strategies are equally valid in the quest to cope (Goldstein 1948:248, 254), and, just as we have seen in second language learners (Chapters 9 and 10), different individuals may make different choices. One may simply duck out of much of what constitutes normal interaction (Goldstein 1948:102), with little offered and little demanded, while another uses every opportunity to speak, even if what he can say is severely limited (Critchley 1970:200).

Insofar as effective communication is the goal, an aphasic individual will do well to find his or her own way towards that end, whatever combination of strategies this entails. In that case researchers must take an open view, evaluating the purpose of every utterance and every gesture as a means of coping with the shortfall of ability over need to communicate. New approaches to data gathering may also be needed, since many of the interactional abilities most associated with formulaicity will not show up in standard tests. Edwards and Knott (1994) describe the case of a man who substantially improved his abilities in conversation over two years, but whose test results did not improve, because the tests could not measure performance in conversational speech (pp. 93–94). For similar reasons, general linguistic comprehension also often seems more impaired than it actually is (Edwards & Knott 1994; Goldstein 1948:248, 280; Lecours, L'Hermitte & Bryans 1983:88; Wray 1992:119–120). If, as has been suggested in this book, function lies at the heart of understanding the nature of formulaic sequences, then we must take the evidence available so far as a spur for developing measures sensitive enough to observe holistic processing in action.

Insights into Storage and Access

So far in this chapter we seen that there is considerable evidence that formulaic word strings behave like words rather than phrases and sentences. However, the picture has turned out to be complicated in an unexpected way. There is some difficulty in characterizing the behaviour of formulaic word strings in the lexicon, because they appear to fragment into different classes of item:

- Some formulaic word strings are less internally resilient than others.
- The size of formulaic word string selected appears to vary from person to person, perhaps as a function of the severity of the condition.
- In paraphasia, selection appears to be sensitive to formal features.

These features raise the possibility that it is too simplistic just to see formulaic word strings as part of the lexicon, on an equal footing with words. Code's (1994) model separates out a left hemisphere lexicon of single words from a right hemisphere lexicon of formulaic word strings, and in the next chapter we shall explore a model of the lexicon which accommodates the impression of such a distribution. In order to set the scene for this model, we need, here, to consider the particular challenges which aphasia in general, and formulaic language in aphasia in particular, present to our current assumption, that words and formulaic word strings are all part of a single lexical store. One crucial aspect of this is the association of different aspects of linguistic processing and storage in different locations in the brain (see Nespoulous et al. 1998:327–328 for one discussion of this).

Language and the Right Hemisphere

Since Hughlings Jackson first suggested it in the mid-nineteenth century, many have explored the idea that language functions may not be entirely located in the left hemisphere, but rather divided, in some way or other, between left and right (e.g., Beeman & Chiarello 1998; Code 1987, 1997; Joanette et al. 1990; Nespoulous et al. 1998; Wray 1992). Most are careful to acknowledge that it is difficult to be sure of the real *cause* of a given effect in language disability, and that while a language function may, by virtue of its disruption or survival, *appear* to be located in a given anatomical area, that does not mean that it necessarily is (Larsen, Skinhøj & Lassen 1978:193). Furthermore, Gazzaniga (1977), one of the originators of the modern paradigm of hemispheric differences, reminds us to be cautious of a too simplistic view.

[The] popular psychological interpretations of 'mind left' and 'mind right' are not only erroneous: they are also inhibitory and blinding to the new students of behavior who believe classic styles of mental activity break down along simple hemispheric lines. (p. 416)

With that proviso retained, we shall pursue the notion that the language faculty may be divisible into parts *broadly associated with* the left and right hemispheres, leaving aside the difficult issue of whether that association is direct or indirect. Our purpose will be, primarily, the identification of the patterns, not a firm commitment to anatomical locations.

Propositionality and mediacy. John Hughlings Jackson (e.g., 1866, 1874) was the first person to pay close attention to the patterns of language loss and retention in aphasia. His interest was focussed on what he termed *nonpropositional* language, that is, phatic utterances with no intrinsic referential meaning, but a significant interactional function. He contrasted such utterances with *propositional* language and noted that it is the propositional language that is severely impaired in aphasia, while the nonpropositional is less affected. This observation led him to suggest that the latter was managed by the undamaged right hemisphere of the brain, an idea which clinical evidence continues to support. He identified four levels of linguistic activity in normal speakers, according to increasing propositionality and decreasing automaticity:

(1) Receiving a proposition. (2) Simple and compound interjections as 'oh' and 'God bless my life'. (3) Well-organized conventional phrases as 'goodbye', 'Not at all', 'very well'. (4) Statements requiring careful, and, metaphorically speaking, personal supervision of the relation each word of a proposition bears to the rest. (Hughlings Jackson 1874:133)

He saw language loss as entailing the absence of one or more of these, with (4) the most vulnerable and (1) the least. As he was certainly aware that some aphasias entail a loss of comprehension, the scale is perhaps better understood in terms of volitional linguistic activity (that is, automaticity not as a function of processing route but of conscious desire to process meaningful language), because (1) on the scale derives from his belief that comprehension is always automatic: when someone speaks "I am, so to speak, his victim ... there is no effort on my part; the revival occurs in spite of me if my ears be healthy" (1874:132). Of particular interest to us here are his categories (2) and (3). (3) consists of sequences which we use with their literal meaning, but which are prefabricated, whereas those in (2) either have no meaning or are not meant literally:

The communist orator did not really make a blunder when he began his oration, 'Thank God, I am an Atheist', for the expression 'Thank God' is used by careless, vulgar people simply as an interjection, there being no thought at all about its primitive meaning. (ibid. 135)

Although the current view of how language is processed is somewhat more sophisticated than Hughlings Jackson's was, the propositional-nonpropositional distinction continues to be a useful one. However, it does not map directly onto novel versus formulaic language. Hughlings Jackson does not recognize a category of 'well-organized, conventional phrases' that perform an informational, as opposed to a phatic, function. So he cannot accommodate sequences such as *a baker's dozen, fair to middling,* BE *in the same boat as* and *by a long chalk.* These are both formulaic and also propositional in his sense,[9] as we can tell from their ability to be directly glossed with another referential word or expression: *a group of thirteen, reasonable, experience the same unpleasant circumstances as, by a considerable measure.*

Jakobson (1980/1990) separates the lexicon into what he terms *mediate* forms (those mediating between meaning and expression) in the left hemisphere, and *immediate* forms (direct signals of emotion) in the right. Almost all linguistic material counts as *mediate*, because it conveys ideas or other messages by means of the language code. In contrast, expletives, spontaneous expressions of endearment, and exclamations such as *oh*, are, like a sob, a laugh, or cough to gain attention, a *direct* expression of the message. He considers immediate expressions to be controlled from the right hemisphere, along with the phonological modifications that are made to mediate expressions in order to convey emotion, such as an elongated initial consonant, or a tremor in the voice (p. 504).

The mediacy-immediacy distinction is different from Hughlings Jackson's propositional-nonpropositional one since, as Code (1987:69) implies in his discussion of 'real word recurrent utterances', not all non-propositional utterances are emotionally charged (see also Code 1982a, 1982b). There is also no direct correspondence between the notion of mediacy and our definition of the formulaic sequence, because although immediate forms can be viewed as formulaic, so can many mediate forms. As a result, neither Hughlings Jackson's nor Jakobson's proposals about the scope of the right hemisphere for processing automatic language would accommodate the entire range of what seems to be formulaic. To what extent, then, might it be possible to stretch the putative role of the right hemisphere to cover all formulaic sequences? In order to establish this, we need to consider what the linguistic capacities the right hemisphere are believed to be.

The linguistic role of the right hemisphere. There have long been suggestions that the right hemisphere may be involved not just in automatic but also in high-level language processing, despite the customary absence of aphasic symptoms after localized right hemisphere damage (e.g., Eisenson 1962). Beeman and Chiarello (1998) offer a range of evidence for language comprehension by this 'nondominant' hemisphere. They conclude that the right hemisphere's linguistic abilities in comprehension have tended to be underestimated because the left hemisphere is superior at the standard language tasks and "special techniques may be required to reveal subtle [right hemisphere] contributions to language processing" (p. 378). These contributions should not be seen as a weak imitation of what the left hemisphere does: they are qualitatively different (p. 382).

Information about the role of the right hemisphere in language processing comes from looking at individuals with a range of conditions. Some subjects have undergone hemispherectomy, where one of the two halves of the brain has been removed, and so cannot be the source of any remaining abilities, or commissurotomy, where the connections between the two hemispheres have been severed, and each can be tested separately on its linguistic abilities.[10] Finally, methods exist for observing the capabilities of one hemisphere in normal subjects, by anaesthetizing one hemisphere, or by measuring electrical activity or tracking blood flow, and hence cell activity, in different parts of the brain during various tasks. For reviews of this research see, for example, Code (1987), Eysenck and Keane (1995:21ff), Joanette et al. (1990), and Wray (1992).

Bloodflow experiments indicate the involvement of the right hemisphere in at least one type of nonpropositional formulaic sequence that is not 'immediate' (see earlier discussion), the serial lists. Lassen et al. (1973) found no increase from rest in left hemisphere activity, but between 2% and 24% increase in right hemisphere activity during counting or recitation of the days of the week. Studies of brain-damaged patients have shown, in addition, that the right hemisphere has some abilities in comprehension, exceeding its production abilities (Galloway & Krashen 1980; Joanette et al. 1990), and that it possesses a lexicon, albeit limited. Apart from formulaic phrases, this lexicon seems to contain only highly imageable or concrete words (e.g., Code 1987:50ff; Joanette et al. 1990:54ff), and perhaps to favour nouns over verbs (Gazzaniga 1977; Joanette et al. 1990:45).

If a subset of words and sequences is indeed stored and/or accessed using the right hemisphere, it raises a considerable number of questions. Has it always been so, or is this arrangement set up as a reaction to left hemisphere damage (e.g., Gazzaniga et al. 1996)? In other words, should right hemisphere processing feature in models of normal language processing as well? If so, how should we accommodate the wide-ranging variation in right hemisphere ability across individuals (Beeman &

Chiarello 1998:380)?[11] Do the words and/or processes of the right hemisphere belong *only* there, are they a copy of part of what is stored in the left, or have they been acquired independently, so that individual items may or may not duplicate entries in the left hemisphere store? If there is systematic or incidental duplication, under what circumstances, in normals, might an item be drawn from one store or the other? If the right hemisphere store is for backup purposes, is its activation inhibited in normal circumstances? If so, then what, precisely, disinhibits it in aphasia, and under what circumstances might the disinhibition fail to occur (see, for example, discussion in Brown 1975; Joanette et al. 1990:ch. 4)? What would be the evolutionary advantage of a backup vocabulary, albeit of imageable and/or concrete words, given that the chances of a person surviving after a major intrusive brain injury were minimal until recent developments in medical science, and that strokes are most common at an age that was rarely attained until the modern era? See Wray (1992:105ff) for a review of these various proposals and their problems, and Code (1987:140ff) for discussion of the possibility that, after left hemisphere damage, the right hemisphere takes over language processing, so that some features of aphasia reflect the abilities not of the dysfunctional left but of the fully functioning but limited right.

Paralinguistic abilities of the right hemisphere. Although its role in the comprehension or production of sentences is contentious, the right hemisphere has long been recognized as handling prosodic features (e.g., Buchanan et al. 1999; Wildgruber et al. 1999)[12] and pragmatics (e.g., Brownell & Martino 1998); see Code (1987:ch. 5) and Joanette (1990:ch. 6 & 7) for reviews. Where the right hemisphere is damaged, subtle linguistic deficits are often found. These include failing to see the import of a pragmatically loaded phrase (Gardner, Brownell, Wapner & Michelow 1983) or to spot inference (Brownell, Potter, Bihrle & Gardner 1986), and being unable to infer discourse structure from an explicit prompt (Chernigovskaya 1994:61; Schneiderman, Murasugi & Saddy 1992). Although Leonard, Waters and Caplan (1997a, 1997b) found that the right hemisphere was able to disambiguate pronouns using inference based on the immediate surrounding context, Caramazza, Gordon, Zurif and DeLuca (1976) found that right hemisphere damaged patients could not solve inferencing problems involving antonyms, such as 'John is taller than Bill. Who is shorter?'; see also Brownell and Martino (1998). Right hemisphere damaged individuals have also been found unable to recognize the emotional force behind an utterance (Gardner et al. 1983:178–179; Geschwind 1979:192), unable to understand metaphor (Joanette et al. 1990:183–184; Winner & Gardner 1977), puzzled by bizarre elements in narratives, which they tend to rationalize to more logical ones (Gardner et al. 1983:179–180), and likely to miss the point of humour (Gardner, Ling, Flamm & Silverman 1975; Joanette et al. 1990:177ff). See Code (1987:88ff) and Joanette et al. (1990:181–183 and chap. 7) for general discussion. In addition, right hemisphere-damaged subjects repeat word for word parts of a story when asked to recount it, whereas normals tend to paraphrase (Gardner et al. 1983:178).

All of these findings are considered consistent with the right hemisphere's association with holistic impressions, and the expression of feelings (e.g., Chernigovskaya 1994; Joanette et al. 1990; Moscovitch 1983). For a more detailed account of the roles of the right hemisphere in paralinguistic processing, see Caplan (1987), Chernigovskaya (1994), Code (1987), Gazzaniga 1977, Joanette et al. (1990), Moscovitch 1983, Van Lancker (1987, 1997) and Wray (1992).

Subcortical involvement in language. There is considerable evidence that damage to subcortical structures in the dominant hemisphere can lead to aphasia (Murdoch 1996). However, a further curiosity relates to the suggestion that "the right hemisphere has a special relationship with affective subsystems of the limbic system which the left hemisphere does not enjoy" (Code 1987:71). On the basis of what is understood about the causes of Gilles de la Tourette syndrome, which is characterized by coprolalia (the involuntary expression of obscenities), it has been suggested that, in aphasia, formulaic sequences associated with swearing and exclamations may be the result of hyperstimulation (or reduced inhibition) of some part of this evolutionarily and functionally more 'primitive' part of the brain (Brown 1975; Code 1987:72; 1994:139), probably the basal ganglia or corpus striatum (Jay 1999:ch. 5; Van Lancker 1987:74, 77–78; Van Lancker & Cummings 1999). The basal ganglia appears to recode patterns of activity originating in the cortex, chunking them into automatic sequences of behaviour (Graybiel 1998). The effect is that slowly learned behaviours, such as sequences of motor activity, can become automatic after practice. If, as research suggests, this reactive automaticity extends to word strings, it could account for the automatic, uncontrolled production of emotionally stimulated expressions. This might give us grounds for separating off these highly emotive expressions from the rest of the lexicon. However, research by Speedie, Wertman, Ta'ir and Heilman (1993) suggests that at least some formulaic sequences, such as counting, reciting prayers and singing songs, may also be controlled from the basal ganglia. They found that, in a patient with damage to the right basal ganglia, the production of such sequences, and of swearwords and exclamations, was disrupted, while idioms and social greetings were unaffected, as were the rest of his linguistic skills, and his declarative (but not procedural) memory (he could remember words and objects that he was asked to memorize, but could not learn new ways of dressing) (p. 1768). Electrically stimulating subcortical areas of the brain has even been found to induce interactional sequences such as *thank you* and *let's go home* (Van Lancker 1987:76). Nespoulous et al. (1998) speak of one individual with no Broca's area, Wernicke's area or arcuate fasciculus in either hemisphere, but who was still able to "produce messages such as 'I don't know whether you have understood what I said'" (p. 328).

Discussion. What the evidence reviewed so far does not sufficiently indicate is that information on the capabilities of the right hemisphere is currently somewhat unbalanced. Most of what is known about its *paralinguistic* activity derives from observing what is lost when it is damaged, whereas virtually none of the research on its *linguistic* abilities is based on such observations. Rather, the linguistic abilities of the right hemisphere are judged by observing what is still possible after *left* hemisphere damage, on the basis that, if the left hemisphere is inactive, any success in language tasks must be due to right hemisphere capabilities. The reason why so little has been recorded about language deficit after right hemisphere damage is that, at first glance, there is nothing *to* record. However, it is now widely recognized that right hemisphere damage probably does affect language processing, but in ways that are difficult to detect, since the left hemisphere is likely to engage in heavy compensatory strategies. Only careful examination of how tasks are being carried out will reveal any subtle oddities in the processing style that result from a conscious, analytic, approach replacing the normal automatic one.

In the case of expletives, a further problem arises in interpreting the available data. Since research into language disability tends to focus on comparisons with what is considered 'normal' in terms of both communication and social behaviour, a *reduction* in the ability to swear is, on the whole, less likely to be noticed and recorded than is the marked *increase* which is associated with the loss of inhibitory mechanisms as a result of *left* hemisphere damage.

Patterns of Recovery

If different parts of the brain are involved in different types of language processing, then we might expect to gain insights into its operations by observing patterns of recovery after a trauma. Of course, in any given case it is difficult, if not impossible, to tell whether the recovery of a previously absent ability indicates the reactivation of damaged areas, or new activity in undamaged ones (and, if the latter, whether this reflects normal, but previously untapped, or newly adopted, abilities). However, if the right hemisphere is involved in some aspects of language processing, then we might reasonably expect to find that those aspects either survive the trauma entirely or recover first, and do so irrespective of the location of the left hemisphere damage.

Reviews of clinical research offer an insight into the relative resilience of different types of lexical material, and the order of their re-establishment during recovery (e.g., Van Lancker 1987:89–90). Goldstein's (1948) account of a 22-year-old university-educated man, wounded by shrapnel during the First World War, is representative of many cases which he reports: "at first . . . [he was] completely speechless except for *yes* and *no* which he could use in their proper sense, or if he made a mistake, he corrected it. He could not repeat these when asked to do so" (p. 191). A few weeks later he was able to say a number of single words and phrases including *I don't know, just so, good night, to tell you the truth* and *I want something* (ibid.). Smith (1966) reports that a left hemispherectomy patient had, five months after his operation, "sudden recall of whole old familiar songs (e.g., *My Country 'tis of Thee, Home on the Range*, church hymns)" (p. 469). The following general observations are particularly noteworthy in our present context:

- Some patients retain only the words *yes* and *no*, while others have "a diversity of expressions" (Van Lancker 1987:88).
- Expletives are common residual utterances, but less common than *yes/no* (ibid.).
- Recovery occurs in stages[13] (Alajounine 1956:9ff):
  - Sequences previously uttered in exactly the same way every time begin to vary in manner of delivery and intonation, taking on the role of dummy fillers (see earlier).
  - It begins to be possible to control when the sequences are uttered, though not perfectly at first.
  - Additional sequences become available, in place of, or in addition to, the previous ones. There are even some more tailor-made utterances.
  - The stereotypy is no longer a problem. In place of fluent but not always meaningful utterances, there are now meaningful ones, but they are dysfluent because of the agrammatism. However, there are still occasional bursts of fluent speech, which Alajouanine identifies as "a new aspect of automatic expression different from the first" because it is apposite and controlled (Alajouanine 1956:12).

Reinterpreting Aphasic Language

In Caplan's (1987) detailed discussion of how the deficits in aphasia can be best characterized, he is forced to dismiss a suggestion of Goodglass that phrase length might be a useful measure of agrammatism, because

[p]hrase length has no status in either linguistic theory or models of language processing. . . . Phrase length is simply something one can measure that is defined over linguistic elements. . . . Unless phrase length can be related to some part of a model of language processing, which has yet to be done, knowing that a patient has short or long phrase length tells us nothing about which parts of the sentence production system are working properly and which are not. (Caplan 1987:155)

Caplan is right, within the context of models of language processing in which all utterances are defined, in some way or other, as novel constructions. However, formulaic sequences, which are not novel, undermine the consistent primacy of constituent structure, and equate – as potential single lexical items – morphemes, words, phrases, clauses and entire texts. In this context, phrase length might well be a useful measure of agrammaticism, though not for the reasons that Goodglass presumably has in mind, since it will not be an indication of grammatical competence.

In models that recognize only on-line analytic processing, there is a tremendous significance – and no little mystery – associated with an otherwise agrammatic individual suddenly producing a grammatical string (e.g., Goodglass 1993:213), because it must mean that the incapacitated mechanisms for sentence construction and word retrieval have become temporarily reactivated. But a model which attributes to formulaic sequences a major role in normal and abnormal language processing offers a different interpretation. Much, if not all, of what appears to be unusual grammatical activity may be no more than simple lexical retrieval. As we saw in our brief examination of data from Gardner and Butterworth earlier, access to semi-fixed formulaic word strings, which create frames around open class items, easily creates the impression of grammatical competence. In such cases, the use of formulaic sequences may at least obscure, if not entirely distort, the genuine analytic competence of the individual for the creation of novel utterances.

For a model of processing which recognizes formulaicity as central, the major question is, therefore, not why some types of aphasia feature a greater capacity for grammatical processing than others (though this may still be a valid focus of investigation) but why fluent aphasia offers access to one or more subtypes of formulaic sequence denied in nonfluent aphasia.

The same practical problem then arises as in previous chapters. In order to assess the role that formulaic sequences play in aphasic language, there needs to be some independent means of identifying them. Although some strings will be easily recognized as formulaic, by intuition and experience or by virtue of their repeated occurrence, there is no string, however unusual or irregular, that we can definitely assert is *not* formulaic. Any string, once created on-line, can become fused and stored, including ungrammatical and nonsense strings assembled after the onset of aphasic symptoms.

The evidence reviewed in this chapter is complex and difficult to tease apart. Formulaic sequences do not appear to be a homogeneous set, since some types are more easily accessed than others. Memorized sequences and simple expressions seem to be equally available in most types of aphasia. But semi-fixed strings, a plausible means of accounting for the fluent, grammatical and morphologically accurate output characteristic of fluent aphasia, are absent in the language of nonfluent aphasic speakers. If the semi-fixed strings *are* what characterizes all or part of the difference between fluency and nonfluency in aphasia, then their role in creating the impression of grammatical competence needs to be calculated and subtracted before the actual grammatical capabilities associated with these conditions can be assessed.

Two questions emerge from this chapter. The first is whether we need to divide formulaic sequences into subgroups that are differently processed and stored. The second is where such dividing lines might be drawn. We address these questions in the next chapter.

13

Formulaic Sequences in Aphasia: A Model

Introduction

In this chapter we shall explore the consequences of incorporating the formulaic features of aphasic language into a lexical model. In the models developed so far in this book, it has been possible to speak of a single lexicon containing units of different sizes, namely, morphemes, formulaic words and formulaic word strings.[1] Now, however, it seems that it will be necessary to make finer distinctions, both because of what all aphasias have in common and because of the ways they differ.

As we have seen, formulaic word strings are strikingly resilient to most types of aphasia, but, as with single words (mono- and polymorphemic), not all types are equally spared, either within an individual's repertoire or from one patient to another. This seems to suggest that the lexicon needs to be divided in some way other than by unit complexity, so that subsets of words and longer strings can be lost, or spared, together. These different parts of the lexicon would need to be managed from different locations in the brain. Physical distance between operational centres does not necessarily need to be represented in terms of separate components in an abstract processing model. However, if such physical separation influences the pattern of deficits after localized brain damage, then it certainly does need to be modelled in some way.

The Challenges to Modelling

In order to keep a clear sense of just what needs to be accommodated in a model of lexical access in aphasia, it is useful to itemize the major findings of the research, as explored in the last chapter:

- Expletives, including swearwords and expressions like *ouch* and *oh*, are available to most aphasic speakers. They seem to be retrieved reflexively to express subjective emotional reactions, and some researchers have suggested that they are a product of subcortical processing.
- Serial lists, rhymes, prayers, songs and quotations constitute the only fluent and grammatical output for many aphasic speakers, but their components cannot be used to create novel utterances. Right hemisphere storage and/or control have been proposed as a way of explaining their survival.
- Single words such as *yes* and *no*, short phrases and memorized material such as songs can sometimes be harnessed to the function of dummy filler, using intonation and pragmatic context to help carry messages otherwise inexpressible.
- Formulaic word strings with a manipulative function are more commonly observed than ones with a referential function, though this could be a reflection of the aphasic speaker's priorities in test and nontest situations.
- The residual abilities for analytic grammatical activity in fluent aphasia may be substantially obscured by an ability to retrieve prefabricated frames with gaps that take open class items.

Modelling the Aphasic Lexicon

The Distribution of Lexical Units in Normal Language

We explain abnormal language with reference to normal language, so our model in Figure 13.1 represents the way the lexicon would have to be divided in normal speakers in order to account for the pattern of deficits found in aphasia (working on the assumption that aphasia does not entail a reorganization of the lexicon). The figure divides the lexicon according to the five functions which it serves (referred to below as Columns I to V), and indicates, in each case, the processing which items undergo (prior to phonological generation), the outcome of that processing and the effect of language so produced. The lexical resources in the top layer of the diagram feed into processes which, in turn, create linguistic outcomes of the kind that we have encountered throughout this book: novel sentences, referential words and expressions, utterances with a socio-interactional (including manipulative) function, performance and mention, and spontaneous exclamations.

Column I concerns the lexical store which supplies the grammatical construction of novel utterances. The predominant lexical forms used for

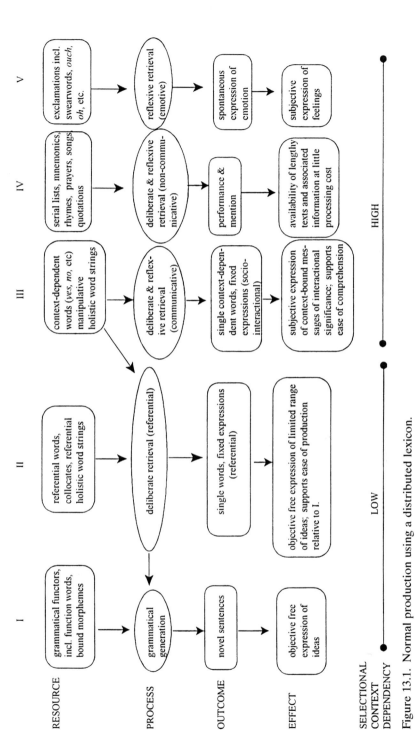

Figure 13.1. Normal production using a distributed lexicon.

249

this are single bound morphemes (e.g., *-ed*; *'s*) and monomorphemic words (e.g., *the*; *and*; the infinitive marker *to*; *over*), though there are some word strings too, such as *in order to* and *on account of*. These are the units of the lexicon which have the least autonomous meaning. Lexical units used in this function are low in context dependency (see bottom of diagram) because they are selected freely as part of the *creation* of context, rather than being constrained to appear in *response* to context, as some of the other unit types are.[2]

Column II deals with referential expression. Pure reference draws to a large extent on mono- and polymorphemic words (e.g., *dog*; *fearful*; *magically*), but word strings, including customary collocations, also play a role (e.g., *date for your diary*; *major bone of contention*; *face the problem*; *take medicine*). Novel utterances with interactional functions also derive from here, as they are unpredictable in form (e.g., *step through the gap*).

Column III subserves routine interactional functions. Its lexicon contains units which are a response to context and which are, overall, subject to less creativity than utterances deriving from the columns to the left. As we have seen throughout this book, manipulative and socio-interactional functions are characteristically accomplished using fully fixed and semi-fixed word strings (e.g., *get out of my way!*; *pass the N please*; group chants). There are also some stand-alone words (e.g., *Careful!*; *Ready?*).

Column IV covers memorized texts. The lexical items supporting this are even less creative, in the sense that both the appropriacy of their selection and also their form are externally determined and they do not contribute directly to referential expression (though they often contribute indirectly by providing access to relevant information). They are almost all word strings, though single-word mnemonics are also possible.

Finally, Column V relates to fully reflexive expression. The lexical units that it draws on are not retrieved consciously but as an automatic response to external or psychological stimuli. Because of this, they are subject to the greatest selectional context dependency. Pure emotional responses are, for many people, most effectively expressed using swear-words, though habitual usage can as easily establish word strings and single words with less of a social taboo (e.g., *my goodness!*; *What the . . . !*; *golly! What?*).[3] In Van Lancker's continuum model (Figure 3.2) reflexive expression lies *beyond* automatic language, and is depicted as as different from it as novel language is. Later in this chapter we shall reconsider its status relative to the other four functions.

A number of features of this model need to be highlighted. Firstly, utterance types range from the unfettered expression of new ideas at high processing cost on the left of the diagram, through increasingly constrained freedom of expression, which is the trade-off for reduced processing, as one moves to the right. Secondly, units of different sizes can, in principle, be found in any column, though they are not equally distributed (see earlier). Thirdly, any unit in a column can be independently manipulated but only holistically; that is, it is stored and accessed complete, irrespective of its internal complexity. However, one or more of its components may also be separately stored. For instance, the phrase *good morning* is located in column III but the words *good* and *morning* as separate manipulable items are located in column II.[4] Fourthly, items from different columns can contribute to the same utterance. For example, if a speaker creates the novel sentence *could we just consider your bookshelf for a moment*, this might be constructed from the formulaic word string *could we just consider DET N for a moment* (Column III), a word-sized unit[5] *bookshelf* (Column II) and the function word *your* (Column I).

Exploring the Model

Locating the Distributed Lexicon

As we saw in Chapter 12, various researchers have proposed that some, if not all, formulaic words strings, are stored in the right hemisphere and/or subcortex. This is one way to explain how they can survive damage to the language centres of the left hemisphere. The model presented here accommodates this idea, but only indirectly: the lexicon is not distributed according to form, but function. In principle, any size of unit – morpheme, polymorphemic word or word string – can subserve any function. However, some units are more suited to some functions than others. Novel reference and creative expression tend to require the flexibility of smaller units assembled using the grammar, while routine interactional expression is well-suited to large units with agreed meanings, and culturally significant texts (such as oral poetry, national anthems and 'in-phrases') specifically need to adhere to a prespecified form. As a result, if part of the suite of lexical stores (or access to them)[6] is damaged, while the rest remains, the effect will be different for units of different sizes. Damage to Columns I and II, as in aphasia, will give the appearance that the smaller units have been selectively removed while the word strings remain, though, in actual fact, this is just an artefact of the different balances of unit sizes in the lexical stores. (The converse, after damage to the functions on the right, will be less obvious, since smaller items can be built up into larger ones through a compensatory strategy – see later.)

Assuming that the lexical units represented in the leftmost columns in the diagram are to be associated with left hemisphere processing, and the rightmost with right hemisphere processing (compare the discussion in Nespoulous et al. 1998:328–329 to this effect), where should the line be drawn? The units associated with Column III are like those to their right in that they are relatively context dependent, and tend to be spared in left hemisphere damaged speakers. Furthermore, the right hemisphere's paralinguistic abilities are highly complementary to the manipulative and socio-interactional functions of the Column III units. This tends to suggest that the Column III units are located in the right hemisphere. On the other hand, Column III shares with the unit types to its left the feature of being deliberately retrieved to meet immediate communicative needs. In addition, the near-normal linguistic capabilities of the right-damaged patient suggest that the Column III material is not affected. This would be consistent with its operating from the left hemisphere. However, its apparent survival could easily be an effect of left hemisphere compensation.

An additional complication is evidence for parts of the Column II unit inventory also being associated with the right hemisphere. As we saw in Chapter 12, some research indicates that the right hemisphere has access to a referential lexicon of highly imageable or frequent words. If so, there must be some sort of duplication, since an isolated left hemisphere can also access these words. For the moment, we shall draw a notional line between Columns II and III, to represent the division of the hemispheres, but we shall also take a closer look at the whole question of multiple representation.

Multiple Representation

It is a problem for most models to accommodate a duplication of storage or function, because multiple representation epitomizes inefficiency in a streamlined system. However, our model is full of multiple copies. For instance, the string *watch your bag* contains three words, the first and third of which we would expect to be stored separately in the referential lexicon (Column II), with the second in the lexicon of functional units (Column I). If a speaker wanted to indicate to a hearer that there was something usual about the bag (e.g., there was an animal moving about inside it), then this string might be created by rule as a novel utterance using the individual words. However, if the speaker wanted to warn the hearer that they were in an area renowned for pickpockets, the word string *watch your bag*, a standard idiomatic string used for this purpose, would be drawn whole out of the Column III lexicon, or, possibly, constructed out of a Column III frame *watch your N*, with the referential item *bag* retrieved from Column II. Finally, if the speaker had just remembered that someone should be warned about pickpockets in a short while, some effort might be made to memorize the string, perhaps by means of rehearsal. In this case it would be stored holistically in the Column IV lexicon, since it had a mnemonic rather than an interactional purpose.

We are dealing, then, not just with a minimal level of duplication, but with widespread multiple representation. The same unit can be stored in different lexicons for different functions, and one or more of the components of a unit may be stored in the same, or a different, lexicon, according to the purpose of their storage.

Tests would not necessarily detect with accuracy the patterns created by damage to the distributed lexicon. Those tests which aimed to elicit single word responses would be trying to tap the single word entries (mono- and polymorphemic) in the leftmost columns. If the patient could not respond, it would be quite reasonably concluded that these lexical stores had been destroyed, or that access to them was blocked. Meanwhile the other lexicons (to the right of the figure) would still be accessible, but would not be activated in an elicitation test, as this is too analytic.[7] They would only be triggered by the desire to express an important interactional message rather than complete a referential task (Wray 1992). When a formulaic word string was produced, it could disguise the nature of the damage to other lexicons. For instance, the expression *how are you?* might be retrievable from Column III, while the word *how* was not available as a separate unit (Column I). The phenomenon of words being accessible in a formulaic word string but not in isolation has long been recognized (compare Van Lancker's example of *son-of-a-bitch*, but not *son*, in Chapter 12). However, these accounts have dealt only with material that is very obviously formulaic, such as memorized texts or common idiomatic phrases. Our model extends the effect of formulaic retrieval well beyond this, to unexceptional referential strings that are grammatically regular and semantically transparent. If this type of output is not recognized as formulaic, the patient's ability to produce this or that word will appear to indicate that a whole new linguistic resource has suddenly opened up, only to close down again under formal test.

Compensatory Strategies

Assuming a fundamental drive for self-promotion, with language one of its primary agents, we should expect that when part of the lexicon is unable to provide the material for linguistic expression, the remainder will be drawn on to compensate as best it can. If the resources and their associated processes are as depicted in Figure 13.1, then the patterns of compensation should be consistent with this profile. Specifically, after right hemisphere damage we should see a rightward shift of resources and processes, as the left hemisphere lexicons are harnessed to help achieve the outcomes usually within the realm of the right. After left hemisphere damage we should see a leftward shift of resources and processes, to meet the shortfall in outcomes created by the unavailability of the left-hand column resources and processes.

Right hemisphere damage characteristically leaves intact the ability to encode and decode linguistic material, but can affect the interpretation of suprasegmental detail such as intonation, and comprehension at the pragmatic level (e.g., Beeman & Chiarello 1998). These features seem to be beyond the capacity of the left hemisphere to compensate, but, if our model of distribution in Figure 13.1 is right, there should also be subtle differences in the way that certain kinds of lexical unit are handled. Specifically, input normally matched to units stored holistically in the rightmost columns should be handled analytically, that is, treated as a string of smaller units, each with its own lexical entry in Columns I and II. The result will be that any meaning associated with the whole, rather than the sum of the parts, will not be recognized. A context-dependent meaning will be interpreted as context independent. A figurative expression will be interpreted literally. Such tendencies are indeed observed (see Chapter 12). We should also expect that an attempt to produce a memorized string such as a serial list would be pedantic and laborious, as the parts were assembled as if for the first time. The effect overall of the compensation would be one of increased processing effort, as messages were constructed out of, and unpacked into, smaller units than was necessary formerly. The greater work involved in processing language might affect other activities that were previously achieved with ease during speech production and comprehension, as if the individual now suffers from reduced powers of concentration.

Compensation in the other direction – when the left hemisphere was damaged – would look rather different. The left-hand side of the diagram in Figure 13.1 relates to the processes of grammatical generation and the deliberate retrieval of referential material. If the lexical units that achieve these functions were unavailable, compensation would entail the appropriation to referential functions of lexical units that normally had a more context-dependent meaning. We saw in Chapter 12 that this occurs: lines from songs, short phrases, words like *yes* and *no* and pro-forms can act as dummy fillers. The units are overlaid with a new meaning in order to make some progress towards the expression of messages that cannot be created or retrieved in the normal way.

The impetus behind compensation is the agenda of the speaker to promote self. The aphasic individual has urgent needs and desires and has to take measures to meet them. Encountering problems with expression, strategies will be adopted in pursuit of alternative means to the desired end. Since language is just one of the resources used to meet these needs, it is likely to be supplemented by gesture and, if things just seem too difficult, avoidance strategies, even a total withdrawal from communication. In this last case, the individual is raising the threshold of 'urgent needs', better to match the reduced ability to express them. This is the same strategy which we saw used by certain types of second language learner, particularly immigrant workers, to avoid confronting their limitations in the L2 (Chapter 10).

Another Look at Exclamations

The class of exclamations (Column V) behaves in ways consistent with its allotted position in the model. Exclamations have been associated with the right hemisphere (indeed, with the right subcortex), and are entirely context dependent, are resilient to the symptoms of aphasia (Van Lancker & Cummings 1999:96), and can be adopted as dummy fillers to compensate for gaps in expression. There is evidence that a loss of access to Columns IV and V can co-occur, as, for instance, in a case reported by Speedie et al. (1993), where the speaker had suffered a stroke to the right basal ganglia. Yet they break a clear pattern found in the progression from Column I to Column IV. We noted earlier that the farther a column is to the right in Figure 13.1, the more its functions will tend to be subserved by formulaic word strings as opposed to morphemes or words. According to its position, Column V should be largely realized by long word strings, yet, as Crystal (1997) points out, "the most common utterances [of swearing] consist of single words or short phrases (though lengthy sequences may occur in 'accomplished' swearers)" (p. 61).

This anomaly is not a problem for the account overall, since the ultimate determiner of unit size is expediency. We need only propose, as seems entirely reasonable, that an emotional exclamation gains expressive power from its brevity[8] and that will account for the unit size difference. However, it does raise the question of whether this category of lexical material is the same as those to its left. The indication that it is not comes from looking to the heart of what drives the selection of all linguistic units, that is, the interactional purpose of the utterance.

Formulaic sequences (lexical units) of all sizes have been associated with the speaker's desire to promote self. They support this end by reducing the speaker's own processing, and/or that of the hearer, to the speaker's benefit. However, in the case of reflexive exclamations, there is no such underlying motivation. The speaker is not pursuing self-promotion, and there is no interactional component to the utterance (even though it may have an effect on a bystander). Of course, swearwords *can* be used for referential and manipulative effects, but they are separately stored for that purpose and so count as independent items – see earlier discussion of multiple representation, and note 3.[9]

It seems, then, that reflexive exclamations, although they are served by their own lexicon, are fundamentally different from the utterances which we have been dealing with in this book. That they are not involved in self-promotion may be directly related to their association with the subcortex rather than the cortex. The cortex is substantially more developed in man than other animals and, as far as we can tell, man also possesses a much stronger sense of self. On this basis, we can draw a notional line between Columns IV and V in Figure 13.1, and, on the grounds of their function, set the Column V lexicon apart from the rest of the units that have been discussed in this book.

Polyglot Aphasia

If the model developed in this chapter is juxtaposed with the one presented in Chapter 11, a number of questions can be raised about the way that aphasia might affect the second language learner. In most cases, no attempt can be made to answer these questions here, because the existing data are largely inappropriate to the task. All of the difficulties with understanding what is going on in the language processing of an aphasic individual are compounded when one must also track a second language learning history. The pattern of loss in a second language could be affected by learning style, quality and quantity of input, intellectual and other aptitude, motivation in learning and use, and so on. In addition, it is rarely possible to find out sufficient detail about the pre-trauma linguistic capabilities of a polyglot.[10] All this being said, research methods which provided sufficient clarity on these variables, and a depth and breadth of data coverage to pick up the necessary subtleties, might shed light on the kinds of questions which our model of the lexicon raises.

One such question is how the projected differences in the balance of unit sizes in the L1 and L2 lexicons might manifest in the symptoms of polyglot aphasia. In Chapter 11, it was proposed that an L2 learned after early childhood is likely to operate with a lexicon of smaller units, customarily put together by rule, relative to the L1. If this means that the L2 is biassed towards having more units in Columns I and II,[11] then, assuming the mechanisms of both languages were equally and equivalently damaged, the L1 could appear more fluent, and more spared, than the L2, because there was a greater resource of prefabricated grammatical material to draw on. It could even result in the same individual being diagnosed with fluent aphasia in the L1 and nonfluent aphasia in the L2.[12] According to Obler, Centeno and Eng (1995), there are some 200 reported cases of differential symptoms across the languages of polyglot patients (p. 134),[13] though they point out that many actually reflect a pre-existing difference in competence or fundamental differences in the structure of the two languages which make the same symptom appear more severe in one than the other (ibid.). For caveats about interpreting this evidence, see various discussions in Paradis (1995, which he summarizes on p. 217).

Conclusion

The distributed lexicon model presented in this chapter aims both to describe and to explain the patterns of aphasic symptoms which relate to formulaicity. The lexicon is notionally divided into five components which engage with different functional processes and produce different linguistic outcomes and communicative effects. These five components all contain, in principle, units of any size (morpheme, word, word string), holistically stored. They are ordered in a way that reflects fixedness of form, creative flexibility and context dependency, and also maps relative accessibility after left and right hemisphere damage. Two of these lexicons can be associated with the left hemisphere, and two, with the right. As the functions that they support favour units of different sizes, this can explain why left hemisphere damage appears to affect single words more than formulaic word strings. The fifth lexicon, which serves reflexive exclamation, has been associated with a subcortical rather than cortical location. The units in this lexicon fall within the definition of the *formulaic sequence* in Chapter 1, but are different in their basic function from all the others that have been identified in this book.

A balanced assessment of this model as a plausible explication of lexical organization cannot be achieved until data suitable for the task have been collected. This is because both the predictions themselves and the linguistic behaviour which they project, are subtle, to the extent that the existing data fail to present the level of detail needed to identify relevant features. In addition, most existing reports focus on the patterns of deficit, whereas this model seeks evidence for, amongst other things, the strategies for coping with deficit, particularly in the context of the self-promotion agenda identified in Chapter 5.

It is fitting that the chapter has concluded with an attempt to juxtapose the distributed lexicon model with the second language acquisition model introduced earlier in the book. In Chapter 14, the wider implications of this reconciliation will be addressed, along with a range of other issues arising from the development and extension of all the models.

PART VI

AN INTEGRATED MODEL

14

The Heteromorphic Distributed Lexicon

Introduction

If there is a standard view of what formulaic language is (and the range of descriptions reviewed in this book must cast severe doubt on that), at its heart will be something about word strings which 'break the rules'. They can break phonological rules, by displaying fewer stresses than expected and by being articulated faster and less clearly. They can break syntactic rules, by resisting pluralization, passivization and so on, and by containing constituents which do not take on their normal grammatical function. They can break lexical rules, by containing items which are archaic or have no independent existence. And they can break semantic rules, by combining to mean something other than they ought to, and by being more idiomatic than an equivalent nonformulaic combination.

Because of the focus on these various kinds of irregularity, formulaic language has customarily been viewed as exceptional, and has been relegated to a minor part of the lexicon. Although individual lines of research have noted its role in processing economy, interaction, language learning, and expression and recovery in aphasia, it has seemed sufficient to place formulaic word strings awkwardly at the edge of lexical models and, often, entirely outside of grammatical ones. In contrast, this book has drawn formulaic language from the edges of an account of linguistic processing to its very centre, by recognizing its many roles and by aligning the irregular minority with a regular majority of formulaic strings which are normally either overlooked entirely or treated with puzzlement.

Our final task is to draw together the various models that have been presented in this book as representations of how formulaicity appears to operate for different speaker types. This is not the same as collapsing all the models into one, since this would be neither informative nor helpful. In other words, there is no sense in which the models relating to first language acquisition in Chapters 6 and 7, for instance, are impoverished by not featuring aspects of the model of aphasia in Chapter 13. Each model aims to depict the processes from the perspective of the relevant data. The aim of the 'macro' model is to accommodate the mechanisms of those processes within a single framework.

The Heteromorphic Distributed Lexicon

The models presented in the course of the book have focussed on different aspects of formulaicity and the lexicon. Figures 5.1, 5.2 and 6.3 dealt with the interactional priorities of the speaker and how formulaic sequences support them. Figures 6.2, 7.1, 11.1 and 11.2 depicted different developmental aspects: Figures 6.2, 11.1 and 11.2 related to the means by which formulaic sequences enter the lexicon, while Figure 7.1 represented the process by which the balance between novel and formulaic language is established. In addition, Figures 11.1 and 11.2, along with 13.1, dealt with the internal organization of the lexicon, from the perspective of unit size and function.

Of these various aspects of formulaicity, the most fundamental is the underlying functional drive, and this aspect lies at the heart of our combined model, the Heteromorphic Distributed Lexicon (Figure 14.1). There are five lexicons, as in Figure 13.1, and each features three types of holistic unit: the morpheme, the formulaic word and the formulaic word string, as in Figures 11.1 and 11.2. The functions associated with the five lexicons are those identified in Figure 5.1, plus the two extremes of novelty and reflexivity (compare Van Lancker's continuum model in Figure 3.2). The detail of this model, as we shall explore it in the rest of this chapter, offers a number of useful insights into the nature of lexical items and their fluid status within a language over time.

The Relationship Between the Lexicons

Even if a string is segmented and one or more of its component parts are separately stored, it may also continue to be stored holistically. The result is multiple representation. For instance, *take it slowly!* might be stored holistically in Lexicon III, *take* and both *slowly* and *slow* in Lexicon II and *it* and *-ly* in Lexicon I. Since Lexicons I and II contain the necessary components, a string *take it slowly* could also be created by rule. However, it would have a different meaning. The holistic unit *take it slowly!* means 'perform your action with care' – it is idiomatic, and

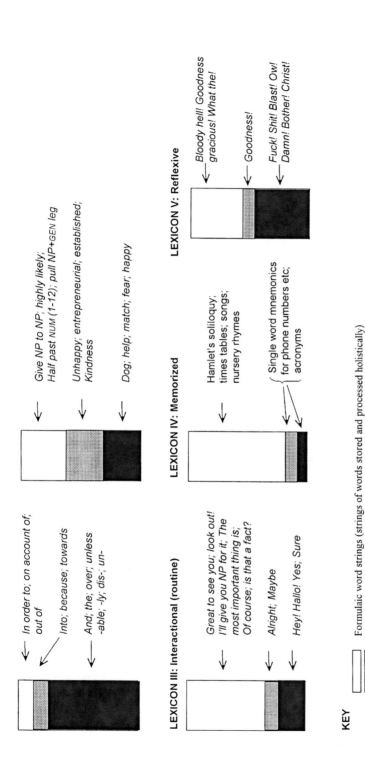

Figure 14.1. Notional balance of three types of lexical unit (formulaic sequence) in distribution: The Heteromorphic Distributed Lexicon model.

LEXICON I: Grammatical

→ In order to; on account of; out of

→ Into; because; towards

→ And; the; over; unless -able; -ly; dis-; un-

LEXICON II: Referential

→ Give NP to NP; highly likely; Half past NUM (1-12); pull NP+GEN leg

→ Unhappy; entrepreneurial; established; Kindness

→ Dog; help; match; fear; happy

LEXICON III: Interactional (routine)

→ Great to see you; look out! I'll give you NP for it; The most important thing is; Of course; is that a fact?

→ Alright; Maybe

→ Hey! Hallo! Yes; Sure

LEXICON IV: Memorized

→ Hamlet's soliloquy; times tables; songs; nursery rhymes

→ { Single word mnemonics for phone numbers etc; acronyms

LEXICON V: Reflexive

→ Bloody hell! Goodness gracious! What the!

→ Goodness!

→ Fuck! Shit! Blast! Ow! Damn! Bother! Christ!

KEY

☐ Formulaic word strings (strings of words stored and processed holistically)
▨ Formulaic words (polymorphemic words stored and processed holistically)
■ Morphemes (bound or free, including monomorphemic words)

this meaning is encoded for it as a whole. The componential *take it slowly* would mean 'grasp the object at a slow speed'. This comes about because the meanings of *take* and *slow* in isolation reflect only part of their full range of meanings in longer strings (see the discussion of the status of intuition later in this chapter).

The Relationship Between Units of Different Sizes in One Lexicon

The division of the units in a lexicon into three sizes is a useful way to relate this model to other lexical and grammatical models, and to other accounts of formulaicity. No model of language which includes a notional lexicon can avoid storing in it morphemes on the one hand and irregular words and word strings on the other. In this respect, the basic design of each lexicon in Figure 14.1 is unexceptional: it is the repository of all linguistic units which are not subject to further segmentation, and which are therefore handled as holistic units. The difference between this and other models is in what qualifies as 'not subject to further segmentation'. In this model, a polymorphemic word or a word string can qualify simply by virtue of its not *needing* to be segmented in normal use, rather than its being *unable* to undergo segmentation.

Unit size is just an explanatory device for the linguist who is trying to make sense of lexical storage in terms of standard language descriptions. In Figure 14.1 the three unit types are represented as layers, but this is for presentational convenience only: *the unit types are not intrinsically discrete*. Any internal structure, including word breaks, is externally and secondarily imposed (see later).

This is well illustrated by some difficulties that are encountered in trying to allocate examples to the layers. In Lexicon I, it is far from clear whether *into*, *because* and *towards* really can count as polymorphemic words. They all derive from word strings which have lost their spaces, and the transition could be argued to have bypassed the polymorphemic word level and to have progressed the items directly to single morpheme status. In Lexicon II, transparently polymorphemic words like *motorway* and *mistaken* could also be construed as monomorphemic, and, in Lexicon III, so could *careful!*, *furthermore* and *really*, along with the two nominated examples *alright* and *maybe*. Part of the difficulty lies in the one-way relationship between the components and the whole: they are transparent enough to render their meaning, but not regular enough to be reliably constructed by rule.[1] However, the crux of the issue is that all units in the lexicon are effectively monomorphemic, so differentiating them according to how many morphemes they contain cannot be expected to render a clear answer on every occasion.[2] Units can, in effect, hover between the levels, as neither fully one thing nor the other. Because the units are not segmented, active morphology can drift slowly into etymology over time, as a function of language change, without us being able to, or needing to, track that transition in relation to the morphological rules which operate outside, and independently of, the holistic system.[3]

A further collapsing of unit types occurs in Lexicon IV, where it is, once again, difficult to differentiate between formulaic words and morphemes. Where mnemonics even retain their own intrinsic meaning, it is only so that the desired material can be more easily accessed. For instance, the mnemonic *Trafalgar* as a way of remembering the PIN number 1805 retains only the aspect of its meaning that makes possible the link to the date of the Battle. Many mnemonics relinquish all their meaning, their status as a word being the sole source of their memorability (e.g., *added* to remember the number 14454, using the alphabetic position of the letters). Because of this, it makes little sense to force a distinction between poly- and monomorphemic units in this category.

Matters Arising

Morpheme Equivalence, Atomaticity and the Accommodation of Irregularity

It is not contentious to define the lexical unit (formulaic sequence) as morpheme-equivalent.[4] As we saw in Chapter 1, in Chomskian-style models, "the lexicon lists the syntactically atomic elements" (Webelhuth 1995b:32).[5] In that context 'atomic' means that they cannot be broken down any further, so the typical lexical unit is a single morpheme, while words or strings which are in any way 'regular' are excluded. The idioms have to be admitted to the lexicon, because their meaning (and occasionally their form) cannot be generated from their components, but the aim is to marginalize the irregular and capture as much as possible within the scope of regularity. Unfortunately, language systems show a striking resistance to this (Weinreich 1969:47). As Chomsky (1965) acknowledges, there are awkward half-regularities, consistent with "quasiproductive" rules: patterns are no sooner generated than they are subject to arbitrary blocking. Examples at the lexical level include sets like *horror, horrid, horrify; terror (*terrid), terrify; candor, candid (*candify)* (Chomsky 1965:186). At the multiword level, the same problem occurs with selective collocation, which cannot be predicted using a model of base units and general combinatory rules. In short, a Chomskian approach struggles with lexical patterns that are too restricted for plausible rules, but whose "meaning is clearly to some extent predictable ... by the inherent semantic properties of the morphemes that they contain" (ibid.). Chomsky admits that "[t]his dilemma is typical of a wide class of examples with varying degrees of productivity" and that "it is not at all clear how it is to be resolved, or, in fact, whether there is any non–*ad hoc* solution that can be achieved at all" (p. 187). In the event, he is forced to the "very unfortunate conclusion" that "these items must be entered in the lexicon directly" (p. 186).[6]

In other words, even the most streamlined of lexicons is obliged to accommodate holistic strings as well as base morphemes, in order to cope with not just full-blown irregularity but also fuzzy half-regularity. This is, as Chomsky admits, an ad hoc solution, and this should alert us to the inherent inadequacy of that approach to modelling.[7] In contrast, the Heteromorphic Distributed Lexicon model can handle the various degrees and types of irregularity integrally.

In the standard accounts, 'atomaticity', as a prerequisite for admission to the lexicon, means that the item "does not have the form or interpretation specified by the recursive definitions of the objects of the language ... [so that it] and its properties must be 'memorized'" (DiSciullo & Williams 1987:3). To put it another way, "[t]he lexicon is like a prison – it contains only the lawless" (ibid.). Being defined as 'lawless' is a requirement for separate listing in the lexicon, and so this definition demands that a clear line be drawn between regularity and irregularity.

In contrast, this book proposes that units of different sizes and internal complexity can be stored in the lexicon as morpheme equivalents, and, in so doing, it provides a much more useful explanation of irregularity. When first encountering a new word string or polymorphemic word, the individual has to decide whether to deal with it holistically or to segment it. The decision will depend on whether the unit has a discernible holistic meaning and/or whether it needs breaking down to make it either comprehensible or useful. Of the units which are identified as suitable for holistic storage without segmentation, some are already irregular. For instance, *by and large*, which takes a disjunctive adverbial function despite its apparent coordinate form, will strongly resist segmentation, since its form does not fall into paradigm with any other strings with similar meaning or function. The result is that an irregular form, once stored in the lexicon, is unlikely ever to be subjected to any 'correction', since it will never be analyzed (unless by the linguist or pedant). It is irregular units like this that give the impression that the lexicon is a prison for the 'lawless'.

However, it has been argued here that it is not only irregular strings which can be stored whole. If a regular string is not segmented or, having been segmented, is still retained as a unit in the lexicon, then, by being holistically stored, it side-steps an analytic processing that it could have successfully undergone. Over a period of time, not being analyzed will tend to lead to the form being stranded from the productive rules and combinatory units of the language (that is, *fossilized*). Such a string may end up being the last stronghold of a word or morphological form that has otherwise disappeared from the language. On the way to that state, it may have passed through stages in which it came across as, say, marked for style or register, archaic, nonstandard or even 'incorrect'. The more irregular it becomes, relative to the active rules and morphemes of the language, the more distance there will be between it and any other strings which might have fallen into paradigm with it. This distance, in turn, will reduce even further the likelihood of segmentation, and protect the increasingly idiom-like status of the unit.

Irregularity, then, can be the result of a gradual distancing of a regular form from the active rules and morphemes which created it and which would, in other circumstances, keep it in step with their change over time (compare Lamb 1998:165). The lawlessness of which DiSciullo and Williams (1987) speak is, therefore, not the *cause* of a unit's incarceration in the lexicon, but the *effect* of it. Rather than defining the lexicon as a 'prison' which admits and contains complex items that are *already* lawless, it makes more sense to define it as a 'house of ill repute' which takes them, regular or not, and is liable to *corrupt* them to lawlessness over time.

An Alternative Economy

As we saw earlier, in Chomskian models the economy of the system rests upon the storage of the set of most basic lexical units, and their combination by rule in the most efficient way possible. An ideal system permits the generation of all and only the grammatical sentences of the language. What the economy does not extend to is any way of excluding the potential to generate sentences that are grammatical but not meaningful or communicatively useful (Chomsky 1957:15).

This book, on the other hand, has proposed that a unit gains entry to the lexicon not by virtue of some fundamental drive to have a complete set of linguistic building blocks, but as a result of pure expediency. We store the things we have a use for, whether morphemes, words, phrases or whole texts. What ends up in the lexicon is a direct reflection of the way the language is operating for the individual in his or her speech community or communities. The nature of the lexicon is determined not by structural principles which decide whether an item is simple enough to be stored, but by the individual's priorities in handling real language input. The result is a direct link between the speakers' knowledge and the shape of the language in use around them, rather than only an indirect one, via a filtering system of innate or acquired abstract rules.

Although this model depicts, in one respect, a wasteful scenario, with a great many entries and a large amount of multiple representation (see Chapter 1), it is, in another way, more streamlined than a standard Chomskian 'streamlined' model. The reason is that the lexicon lists only those units – large or small – which direct experience has identified as communicatively useful. Since we are armed with a capacity for analysis which can make up any shortfall, should it arise, no great disadvantage ensues in practice. The effect is simply to prioritize the likelihood of the expected over the potential for the unexpected (Wray 1992:19).[8] Since the 'expected' is, by definition, that which the individual has observed to occur most of the time, we have a shortcut for handling the linguistic material that is normally encountered and produced.

No two lexicons are the same. They contain what has revealed itself, so far, to be useful for that individual. Highly literate people with a love of words may have a large and active store of morphemes alongside their stores of words, phrases and texts, affording them the luxury of constructing and understanding novel words and sentences that may be beyond the easy competence of someone whose lexicon has a smaller store of such units. The makeup of the lexicon is determined by the individual's needs. The flexibility of the analytic system ensures that, as these needs change, the language knowledge of the individual will be able to keep up; but needs are not anticipated, for they may never arise. That is the economy of expediency.

Objections to Complex Units as Morpheme-Equivalents

It has been argued in some quarters that the holistic storage of complex units is hard to justify when certain language types are taken into account. Nickels (1997) contends that agglutinative languages like Finnish and Turkish are too morphologically productive for polymorphemic word storage to be possible: "a single Turkish noun can have more than four million different forms" (p. 8). It is implausible, Nickels argues, that all of these forms are separately stored, and "more likely that the Turkish speaker has stored representations of all items and affixes and a set of procedures or rules to produce new words" (ibid.). However, this position is an overreaction, since it is not necessary to argue that just because *some* polymorphemic units are stored whole, *all possible* ones are. As Nickels indeed points out, most of those 4 million forms are never going to be used by a given speaker. So what would be the value of storing them? Nickels's problem disappears if, instead of looking at the *principle* of holistic storage, one looks at the *pragmatism* of it. The polymorphemic words that a speaker of Turkish is likely to have stored formulaically are those which are heard and used often, and which have a serviceable holistic meaning. Many may never have been segmented, though overall, segmentation will have created a store of the separate morphemic units that are found useful for new formulations to be constructed and decoded. Seen in the light of the current model, there is nothing about a Turkish word like *indirilemiyebilecekler* '[they] will be able to resist being brought down' (the example that Nickels cites) that is not equally applicable to the structure of its English translation: if the juxtaposition of the morphemes is novel to the speaker or hearer, it must be created or understood using the individual morpheme entries in the lexicon, and rules for their combination. However, if it is a commonly occurring configuration, there may be a shortcut in processing, by accessing it (or part of it) ready-made from the store of larger, complex units. Indeed, if anything, the agglutinative languages serve to underline the arbitrariness of distinguishing between different unit sizes in the lexicon.

A second objection to the morpheme-equivalence argument comes from looking at languages in which the internal organization of common phrases changes according to some grammatical or semantic variable. In German, for instance, the position of the verb in a formulaic verb phrase would need to vary, depending on the structure into which it was embedded. Again, the sticking point here is allowing formulaicity to outstay its welcome, so that it is seen as an obstacle to our use of language, rather than as a facilitator. It is not necessary to argue that just because the German verb needs to be movable, sequences can't, in principle, have a fixed form. Rather, the extent of a form's fixedness is determined by what the speaker needs to be able to do with it. If it works for a complex string to be kept fully fixed, then it can be so. If not, then it will be loosened, to accommodate the variation required. While an English phrase might be fully fixed except for, say, the verb morphology, its German equivalent might need to contain two slots for the verb, with one or other being filled according to the syntactic environment. In the case of the most common expressions, it might even be that both versions – verb second and verb final – are individually stored. The decider will not be some principle that demands a neat and symmetrical pattern across the language. It will be what the individual finds most expedient for expressing and understanding language efficiently and effectively.

Other Models of the Lexicon and Grammar

How does the Heteromorphic Distributed Lexicon model compare with other models of the lexicon and grammar? We shall briefly consider a range of accounts which support or contradict it. First, however, we need to establish which are open to direct comparison. Models of lexical and grammatical knowledge operate at many different levels and aim to explain different things. For instance, Murphy (2000) and Lamb (1998) address the question of what, if any, semantic information is stored within, as opposed to outside, the lexicon. Many models focus on the relationship between the semantic and phonological aspects of lexical knowledge and retrieval (e.g., Butterworth 1989; Dell 1986; Harley 1993; Levelt 1989; McClelland and Elman 1986; Marslen-Wilson & Tyler 1980; Morton 1969). The question of whether comprehension and production make use of different lexical stores is also a major topic of discussion. The present model has nothing to say on any of these issues, though it offers some grounds for challenging the methodology behind some of the investigations which support the claims about them (see below).

The Heteromorphic Distributed Lexicon model is neutral on all features of the entire 'lexicon' package, except two. The first is the nature of the lexical unit, and the second is where in the brain different types of lexical material might be stored or brokered from. Of these, the latter need not concern us in this discussion, since it is rarely addressed in other models, despite the evidence from clinical studies (see, for instance, discussion by Butterworth 1983:chap. 7). The former issue, however, bears some measure of cross-model comparison. As first discussed in Chapter 1, the central issue is whether the lexicon can contain nonatomic units, that is, units that are internally complex in a predictable way.

Evidence for an Atomic Lexicon

Despite plenty of evidence indicative of a full listing of lexical base units and their compounds (see, for instance, Butterworth 1983:chap. 7), models based on certain kinds of experimental results consistently speak against it. Marslen-Wilson, Tyler, Waksler and Older (1994), for instance, in a direct mirroring of the Chomskian position, maintain that all polymorphemic words and phrases which possibly *can* be broken down *are* broken down, and the components, not the wholes, are stored in the lexicon. The basic unit of the lexicon is the morpheme (p. 31), and they consider it "strongly counter-intuitive to represent semantically transparent forms like *happily*, *happiness* or *unhappy* as unanalyzed individual entries such that the semantics of *happy* are duplicated for each separate derivational variant" (ibid.).

There is a fundamental difficulty with this position, even without invoking a competing model. Corpus linguistics shows us that we may not rashly assume that morphologically related words like *happy*, *happily*, *happiness* and *unhappy* really would 'duplicate' their semantics if separately listed, since "meanings are conveyed not only by individual words and grammatical forms, but also by the frequency of collocations and by the distribution of forms across texts" (Stubbs 1996:89). Stubbs (ibid.:85ff) shows that *happy* and *happiness* collocate differently, and it follows that, to this extent at least, they have different meanings.[9]

This objection aside, what are we to make of Marslen-Wilson et al.'s experimental evidence in support of the atomic lexicon? The answer is much less difficult than it might seem, and relates to the methodology of investigation. Swinney and Cutler (1979) point out that different investigative techniques tend to support different models of how the lexicon is organized (see also Chialant & Caramazza 1995), and the Heteromorphic Distributed Lexicon model enables us to see why this might be: units of different sizes, and different processing strategies, will be useful in different situations. Wray (1992) points out that much of the experimental methodology employed in psycholinguistic testing is biased towards a metalinguistic focus. A good example is the lexical decision test, as used by Marslen-Wilson et al. This test requires the subject to respond as quickly as possible by pressing one of two keys, according to whether the stimulus is judged to be a word or not. The time taken, in milliseconds, is the unit of performance assessment in the task. This activity, quite patently, has nothing to do with language processing in the real world, and it would hardly be surprising to find that it employs different processing strategies. The counterargument is that it should not matter: if the lexicon only stores its items in one way, then however you choose to access them, the patterns will be the same. But if the lexicon contains more than one representation of an item and more than one way of processing, as proposed here, then this conclusion no longer follows.

Specifically, while large units will be preferred when one is recounting an anecdote in the bar with friends, because they support fluency and are easily decoded, in many language testing situations small units will give a greater level of control. In tests where only single words are offered as stimuli, and where those stimuli clearly fall into patterns based on morphological variation, operation at the morpheme level is likely to be preferred. In other words, lexical decision tests, along with many other experimental tasks, will tend to block out access to the larger lexical units in Lexicons I and II, and probably to all units in Lexicons III and IV.[10] The result will be that a small part of our lexical knowledge, effected using only one of the two processing strategies, will be taken as representative of the much more intricate balance that is engaged outside the laboratory.

Models Supporting Complex Lexical Units

Connectionism and other approaches to modelling which take their inspiration from, and aspire to represent directly or indirectly (including metaphorically), the physical relationships between neurons, have no quarrel with the existence of complex lexical units. According to Schmidt's (1993) *Hierarchical Chunking Theory*, speakers possess networks of conceptual knowledge, with which lexical units, including multiword strings, are associated. Oppenheim tested this model by getting (non-native) speakers to extemporize twice on the same subject. She found between 48% and 80% similarity between the two renderings, which she explains in terms of Schmidt's model: "when speakers need . . . to express the same message, the same neural networks [are] excited, causing speakers to repeat many same-word sequences" (Oppenheim 2000:229).

Dyer (1989) proposes a "dynamic phrasal lexicon, constructed from language-use episodes, and multi-indexed by (pattern, meaning, use) triples" (p. 198). It "supplies an active context during natural language comprehension, generation and learning and forms a unified foundation upon which to study the acquisition and use of figurative phrases and other formulaic expressions" (ibid.). Dyer's model requires no independent grammar component, the relationships between lexical units naturally resulting from processes of pattern recognition.

Lamb (1998), also within the framework of a type of connectionism, similarly accepts that phrases (both continuous and discontinuous) and polymorphemic words can be 'lexicalized forms' (pp. 163–164, 169). Since the component parts of such forms are also in the lexicon, it follows naturally in his model that there is an equivalent of the dual systems processing proposed in Chapter 1 (pp. 167, 171–172). In his view, the reductionist arguments of the "analytical" linguists stem from a desire to describe language as an independent entity rather than as a system in use (p. 164). He maintains that "[their] revulsion for redundancy must make way for cognitive realism" (ibid.). In some respects, however, Lamb's model differs from the Heteromorphic Distributed Lexicon model. For him, *complex lexemes* (p. 164) are created as a response to repeated activation of their components, since "whenever something is experienced many times it becomes learned as a unit" (ibid.). Specifically, "it is repeated use rather than degree of idiomaticity that determines presence or absence of a [complex lexeme]" (p. 165). This is the equivalent of fusion which is, of course, not impossible in our model, but is not the sole, or indeed even the primary, way in which complex units enter the lexicon.

Lamb's fusion principle has some unnecessary consequences which would be avoided if segmentation were also permitted. He proposes (pp. 72ff) that the units *lap-dog*, *under-dog*, *hot-dog* and *puppy-dog* are all complexes of which *dog* is one element. This is not particularly plausible, since the *dog* element in *under-dog* and *hot-dog* is probably not related, for most people, to the *dog* in the remainder. In the Heteromorphic Distributed Lexicon model, *hot-dog* and *under-dog* would be unlikely to have undergone segmentation, while the genuinely 'dog-related' compounds of *dog* (e.g., *lap-dog* and *puppy-dog* along with *hound-dog*, *hunting dog* and *show dog*) would. Since the semantics of a component entry is informed only by those usages from which it has been segmented, this principle correctly predicts that we will not call up images of sausages or losers when we consider the meaning of *dog*. Our understanding of what *dog* means is not influenced by *hot-dog*, any more than our understanding of *bird* is influenced by *ladybird* (see later).

Cognitive Grammar

Langacker's (1987, 1991) Cognitive Grammar[11] fundamentally disputes the assumption that the lexicon is a list of idiosyncratic items which supplements the grammar, and that "the regular aspects of language structure can be segregated in any meaningful way from the irregular ones" (1987:26). In Langacker's view, "[f]ocusing our attention solely on constructions that pass the litmus test of generality and regularity does not promise to leave us with a coherent body of phenomena constituting a natural grouping on any other grounds" (ibid.). In Cognitive Grammar, language production and comprehension are not rule-governed in the narrow sense of a Chomskian model, and, indeed, the entire structure of the language is portrayed as driven by the messages it carries, not by an external system of rules and restrictions. Cognitive Grammar makes no formal distinction between the phonology, morphology, lexis and syntax of language (p. 35; Langacker 1986:2). All consist of conventionalized *units*.

A unit is a structure that a speaker has mastered quite thoroughly, to the extent that he can employ it in largely automatic fashion, without having to focus his attention specifically on its individual parts or their arrangement. Despite its internal complexity, a unit constitutes for the speaker a 'pre-packaged' assembly; because he has no need to reflect on how to put it together, he can manipulate it with ease as a unitary entity. It is effectively simple, since it does not demand the constructive effort required for the creation of novel structures. (Langacker 1987:57)

Cognitive Grammar accommodates the flexibility of linguistic process-ing that we need for explaining patterns of real language within and between individuals. Tuggy (personal communication) identifies a set of maxims arising from Cognitive Grammar which are directly compatible with the Heteromorphic Distributed Lexicon model.[12] They juxtapose two parallel processing options: computation and (access from) storage, which are equivalent to the dual systems proposed in Chapter 1 (i.e., analytic and holistic):

1. "Computation or storage of some members of a category does not guarantee computation or storage of all its members".
2. "Computation or storage of a form by some speakers does not guarantee its computation or storage by all speakers".
3. "A form which has been exclusively calculated or accessed from storage may begin to be processed in the other way as well".
4. "Computation or access from storage of a form by a speaker on one occasion does not guarantee computation or access from storage of that form by the same speaker on another occasion".
5. "A single speaker can both calculate a form and access it from storage, or calculate it in more than one way, sequentially or perhaps even simultaneously on the same occasion".

Maxim 1 resonates strongly with the idea of needs-only analysis and the absence of a general principle of cross-referencing in the lexicon (see later). Maxim 2 reflects the natural consequence of segmentation and analysis being based on the actual input experienced and on the need to express variations of it, rather than an underlying quest to master all the manipulable forms of the language. Insofar as different individuals get different input or have different messages to convey, they will have dif-ferent lexical arrangements. Maxims 3, 4 and 5 correspond to the flexi-bility in handling linguistic material that comes from the availability of different processing strategies. It is clear, then, that Cognitive Grammar has a great deal in common with the Heteromorphic Distributed Lexicon model.

Some However, as with Lamb's model described earlier, there is one way in which Cognitive Grammar differs from the account in this book. In Cog-nitive Grammar, units *become* formulaic through a process of automati-zation (proceduralization), having first been composed of smaller, more flexible units (see also Givón 1989:260). This process has a great deal in common with what has been proposed in Chapter 11 for the acquisition of formulaic material in second language learning (so it is not formally precluded as a mechanism) but is not consistent with the identified operations of native language learning.[13]

Pattern Grammar

Pattern Grammar (Hunston & Francis 2000) is fully grounded in corpus-driven research. Corpus linguistics is not directly concerned with formulaicity as we have characterized it in this book, and the work on corpora which underlies Pattern Grammar developed out of the COBUILD project for the creation of dictionaries that defined words according to their use in context, rather than their meaning in isolation. As a result, the impetus for the Grammar is how a word derives aspects of its meaning from "the company it keeps" (Firth 1957/1968:179).[14] It attempts to resolve the inherent fuzziness regarding which aspects of linguistic patterning should be attributed to lexical properties and which to grammatical ones, by making a direct link between individual lexical items and the patterns which characterize their typical behaviour in text. The power of this approach lies not in the range of patterns which can be identified overall, but in its direct engagement with the distributional restrictions on that range, as defined not by some abstract principle about what should be 'grammatical' but rather by direct evidence from corpus research about what we typically say and write. These restrictions can often be characterized in semantic terms. Take one example:

The pattern **V n** *into -ing* is exemplified by utterances such as *He talked her into going out with him*. Some of the verbs associated with this pattern are concerned with making someone feel something, usually fear. These verbs are: *frighten, intimidate, panic, scare, terrify*, and, extending the range of emotions, *embarrass, shock* and *shame*. (Hunston & Francis 2000:102)

This approach makes it possible "to group together words which share pattern features, but which may differ in other respects in their phraseologies" (p. 248). Pattern Grammar has no difficulty with accommodating creativity, which, simply, is the use of an unaccustomed word with an established pattern, though, significantly, usually one which it is fairly easy to link semantically or pragmatically (e.g., metaphorically) with the customary lexical associates of that pattern, since the effect of the new association relies on the resonances it creates with what *might* have been said.

In this respect, Pattern Grammar nicely codifies the semi-fixed frames which are a major feature of formulaicity in language, and accommodates with ease the relationship between routine and creativity. It also copes readily with fully fixed strings, since patterns can be associated with any part of speech, and there is no restriction on the internal complexity of items and their patterns. It also prioritizes the function of the utterance over its structure (p. 253), and favours the *idiom principle* (Sinclair 1991:110), by which large units are preferred to small ones whenever possible (Hunston & Francis 2000:21). Finally, it fully captures the normally problematic concept of idiomaticity, at least insofar as this is reflected by frequency (see Chapter 2 for a discussion of possible limitations of this association).

Explaining Why Intuition Is Unreliable

Despite many points of alignment between Pattern Grammar and the observations and proposals in this book, there are important differences too. One of these offers an insight into a persistent problem for all theories, namely, the status of intuition relative to evidence from linguistic data (see discussion in Aarts 1991 and Sampson 1996, for example). We saw in Chapter 2 that there are some curious nonalignments between what native speakers believe they do, and what corpus research reveals as actual practice. As Francis (1993) observes, "[i]ntuition may be useful to linguists in a number of ways, but for the purposes of saying exactly how language is used, it is notoriously unreliable" (p. 139).

There is something rather bizarre about this, since it is a basic assumption of most, if not all, grammatical models, that speakers draw on a knowledge of rules or patterns to guide their linguistic production and comprehension and *also* draw on a knowledge of rules or patterns to make judgements about grammaticality, acceptability and idiomaticity. In Pattern Grammar, it is implicit that the native speaker somehow internalizes patterns, so that the forms which the Grammar identifies are both descriptions of real text and also of some kind of knowledge on the part of speakers. This makes it difficult to explain why intuition should not be an accurate reflection of knowledge. The only way to resolve the problem is to impose a threshold on insight, so that aspects of our procedural knowledge are not available to intuition (e.g., Chomsky 1965:8). This is an ad hoc solution, since it is not clear why we should be so restricted, nor how our intuition could be prevented from gradually catching up with our practice, if only by virtue of observing the relative frequencies with which structures occur.

The solution offered by the observations and models in this book is that there is no direct correspondence between patterns of knowledge and patterns of use. If speakers process language in the largest units possible, and do not break them down unnecessarily, then there is no guarantee that all of the patterns revealed by an examination of their linguistic behaviour are represented in their rule system. You no more have to know whether *ago* is a postposition or an adverb in order to use the string *10 years ago*, than you have to understand French grammar in order to sing *Frère Jacques*. What the speaker knows about the forms in the language will be a direct reflection of the amount and nature of the *analytic* activity which he or she has engaged in, and analysis operates on only a subset of the language that the individual uses.

In Chapter 5, it was suggested that analysis in Phases 2 and 3 of language acquisition will culminate in sufficient knowledge to make the standard judgements about grammaticality which we associate with intuition. That means that we will not make gross errors about what is and is not possible in the language. However, more subtle aspects of the way that language falls into patterns could consistently evade analysis, and thus not form part of our intuition. We saw in Chapter 2, for instance, that Stubbs found the distributions of *small* and *little* relative to *girl* and *boy* to be very unequal, even though we might intuitively judge *small* and *little* to be pretty well synonymous.

When we tap our intuition to find out about a word like *small*, we presumably have access to our entire lexicon. However, since formulaic word strings are holistically stored, finding a single word within them would require each one to be separately searched, which is costly in processing. Much easier is to look up the word as a single unit entry. However, the information stored with the single unit entry will not be an accurate reflection of all the uses of the word, because it will be based on the word's use in the subset of contexts which underwent segmentation.[15] Segmentation is most useful where the word occurs in a context of actual or potential paradigmatic variation, and so it will tend to favour isolated referential meaning, rather than, say, delexicalized or metaphorical meaning, and will not tend to separate the word from a strong collocate. As a result, the intuitive meaning of a word is likely to be concrete and discrete. Native speakers asked to define *small* and *little* will find them synonymous, because they do not have access to the patterns of their distribution within formulaic word strings. Similarly, an intuitive definition of *take* will home in on its concrete meaning of 'grasp' or 'capture', because it is in this meaning that it is most segmentable. Its common occurrences as an abstract carrier verb in, for example, *take part, take on, take down* (see, for instance, Allan 1998; Stubbs 1995:381) are much less visible to our intuition, because there will have been little if any drive to segment *take* out of these strings.

Single Systems and Dual Systems

In this book we have accepted the existence of a separate set of grammatical rules, but held at bay the profound implications of a rule-based system for how language is processed, by introducing a rival, holistic means of processing which is less flexible but more efficient, and which is therefore preferred in routine interactional situations (see Chapter 1, and Sinclair 1991:114; Wray 1992:chap. 1). Many otherwise plausible models of lexical and/or grammatical knowledge and processing share with the standard Chomskian models a reliance on a single system of processing to handle all linguistic material,[16] and it places a severe restriction on them all. In the case of a Chomskian model, the problem, as we saw earlier, is that the regularities in language are much more easily explained than the irregularities. Pattern Grammar is much more able to cope with the irregularities, but can only look to the precedent of practice for an explanation of the often quite convoluted sense of grammaticality and declarative knowledge about language that Chomsky's models focus on. All in all, it is difficult to see how any single system account, whereby all linguistic forms have to be a product of the same processing procedures, can be adequate. The evidence is better accounted for in terms of two different types of process, of which one adheres to well-defined rules and the other does not.

Within a dual systems model, where language is processed both holistically and analytically, it is possible to attribute different types of linguistic knowledge independently to, on the one hand, how grammar works and, on the other, how language use determines patterns of distribution and frequency. Much of what is objectionable about the narrow Chomskian perspective when it is seen as the *only* agent of processing language, falls away on the introduction of a second, holistic, system that can handle not only irregular strings like idioms but also entirely regular ones. Instead of placing the onus on the grammatical model to explain the novel and the routine as two aspects of one operation, the power of determinacy is placed with the *speaker*, who controls the balance between ease of processing and depth of analytic engagement, a balance that can be adjusted from moment to moment towards the consistent single goal of achieving the best interactional outcome. As such, a dual systems account is a viable alternative to any grammatical model which simply replaces the Chomskian single system with another single system. For while such a model may capture more satisfactorily aspects of function, interaction, performance, pragmatics and/or variation, it may equally tend to sacrifice features of the Chomskian approach, whose validity and usefulness are responsible for much of its long-term resilience to criticism and counterevidence.

Conclusion

Getting the Measure of Formulaic Sequences

The models presented in this book place formulaicity at the centre of language, and extend it to include words and strings of regular as well as irregular construction. Large units are most useful for routine interaction, where the utterance achieves a standard function by means of a preagreed form. The smaller the unit, the greater the processing required to create fluent output, but the more that output can be tailor-made. Particularly useful are semi-fixed frames in which only the morphological details or the novel referential items need to be separately selected. The organization of the lexicons reflects the whole impetus of language production: the promotion of the speaker's interests. It is this agenda which motivates the child to attend to, copy and store useful utterances and to break them down for better control and flexibility. It leads speakers to adopt strategies which reduce their own processing, and to match their lexical store to that of their hearers, so that *their* processing is also reduced, making the messages more readily understood. The changing priorities of the speaker over time alter the strategies, favouring in later childhood the analytic approach which formal education, and particularly literacy, support, and leading to an accumulation of the smaller, more flexible units needed for the expression of decontextualized and creative messages. By adulthood, the prevailing strategy has swung back to holistic processing in the native language, but the desire to control a second language as an object of study, coupled with the absence of opportunities for interaction and the encouragement of classroom and textbook teaching, will haul the management of that linguistic knowledge firmly towards the analytic, and disfavour the holistic storage of long strings, with its implicit rather than explicit command of constituents. In aphasia, one or more lexicons may be damaged, or access to them disrupted, sparing the ability to retrieve words and phrases with interactional and mnemonic functions, relative to those used for reference and the construction of novel utterances. The patient is left with the desire to achieve the function but no means of doing so, unless by adopting new linguistic and nonlinguistic strategies.

It should be clear from the discussion in this book that the models proposed appear to be generally consistent with research findings to date. However, that research was not setting out to test them, and the true resilience of the models will not be established until their inherent predictions are more directly examined empirically. The tests, however, will need to take account of the sensitivity of the relationship between analytic and formulaic processing, and measures will need to be taken to avoid forcing experimental subjects or clinical patients into a situation which deprives them of their full range of strategies (Wray 1992:26ff, 119). Since the relationship between processing and the speaker's agenda is subtle and intricate, ways must be found to avoid any distortion of that agenda. In particular, the quest to measure and monitor language processing must not compromise the subject's focus on genuine interaction. We are quite able to 'perform' linguistic tasks, but that typically invokes a more analytic approach to processing than we employ in unmonitored language production and comprehension.

If the account in this book is at all accurate, then there are far-reaching implications for the way in which we construe language as a phenomenon and seek to explain its manifestations in performance:

- Models of linguistic processing which view the encoding and decoding of text as the manipulation of minimal components with precise grammatical roles and meanings, are missing half the story. Equally important is the strategic management of large units with complex meanings that are often independent of their constituent parts, and into which small, manipulable units may be inserted in order to tailor-make the message for the occasion.
- Models of linguistic knowledge which attribute patterns of adulthood processing to innate or early environmental factors may be overlooking the effects of formal education, particularly literacy.
- Experimental and clinical procedures which naturally encourage the operation of an analytic strategy will entirely fail to measure the effects of holistic processing. Models based on the results of such tests will represent only one of the two strategies, and will tend to contradict the findings of research based on more naturally elicited language.
- Approaches to second and foreign language teaching which promote the formulaic sequence as a unit worth learning may easily overlook the complex factors which determine the acquisitional and processing strategies of any given learner. In particular, learners may use formulaic language not only to support learning, but also in ways detrimental to it. Teaching needs to create situations conducive to genuine language use, or else discard the expectation of the holistic strategy and focus directly on analytic learning.
- The validity of native speaker intuition can be reinstated, as an accurate reflection of a significant subset of our linguistic knowledge. Its

nonalignment with the patterns revealed in corpus research needs proper consideration as a legitimate indicator of lexical organization.

- Linguistic behaviour must be examined as one manifestation of more fundamental, and more ancient, socio-interactional priorities such as the promotion of self. This may give better clues to its nature and provenance than are gained by perceiving it as an independent faculty of sudden origin (Wray 1998, 2000a, in press).

In all types of speaker, formulaicity bridges the gap between novelty and routine, and makes it possible for us to protect our own interests by producing language that is fluent and easily understood. The central role which this book has identified for formulaic sequences in interaction provides an important insight into the nature of linguistic knowledge: it is not only a question of knowing the words that go together into strings, but also of knowing the strings of words that go together.

Notes

1. The Whole and the Parts

1. The adverts were scripted and performed by actors, but based on consumer research (J. Walter Thompson Co Ltd, personal communication).
2. Coates (2000) explores in some detail the loss of sense when a designation becomes a proper name.
3. Mel'čuk (1998), who estimates that "in any language . . . phrasemes [i.e., formulaic sequences] outnumber words roughly ten to one" (p. 24), sees collocation as "mak[ing] up the lion's share of the phraseme inventory" (ibid.).
4. For instance, Haggo and Kuiper (1983) define *idioms* as having noncompositional meanings, while *formulae* "have perfectly normal semantic interpretations" (p. 544). Pawley (1985) defines a 'formula' as "a conventional pairing of a particular *formal construction* with a particular *conventional idea* or *idea class*" (p. 88).
5. It is impossible to find a term that has absolutely no previous history or affiliation. No significance should be read in the fact that it has occasionally reached print before (e.g., in Watkins 1992).
6. In earlier accounts (Wray 1998, 1999, 2000a, 2000b; Wray & Perkins 2000) the wording is 'a sequence . . . of words or other meaning elements . . .', but this excludes some items of child and aphasic language which are customarily considered to be formulaic, but are not decomposable into meaning elements (see Chapters 6 and 12). In the new wording, a sequence of sounds, making up a single morpheme or a meaningless utterance, can still also count as formulaic. Compare Langacker's (1987:57) *units* and see Chapter 14.
7. It is also patently a psycholinguistically oriented definition, in contrast to, for instance, that of Erman and Warren (2000): "A prefab is a combination of at least two words favored by native speakers in preference to an alternative combination which could have been equivalent had there been no conventionalization" (p. 31).
8. A significant feature is that they effectively define language as a "linear process" rather than a "hierarchically organized product" (Altenberg

1990:133). See Ellis (1997) for one account of how the Chomskian tenets are undermined in new models.

9. From, respectively: Wilfred Owen, "Anthem for Doomed Youth", *Wilfred Owen: War Poems and Others*, ed. D. Hibberd (London: Catto & Windus, 1973), p. 76; e.e. cummings, "suppose", *Selected Poems*, 1923–1958 (London: Faber & Faber, 1960), p. 6; William Shakespeare, *Sonnet no. 63*; Roger McGough, "Six Shooters", *Waving at Trains* (London: Jonathan Cape, 1982), p. 15.

10. Ironically, however, poetry is a prime candidate for memorization, transforming it from the highly novel to the highly formulaic.

11. e.e. cummings, "anyone lived in a pretty how town", *Selected Poems, 1923–1958*, pp. 44–45.

12. Chris Baxter, "Dreaming of you" (unpublished).

13. Actually spoken by a Dutch airline stewardess.

14. That is, if the grammar is based on generation from atomic lexical units.

15. In actual fact, there are phrasally based models of language knowledge which are able to account for how we handle novel material, without placing any kind of discrete syntactic knowledge at the centre (e.g., Dyer 1989). See Chapter 14.

16. Furthermore, the assumption that the brain can be modelled as a kind of computer, in which storage space is limited and operations are optimized for serial simplicity, is an error of our times (Crick 1979:132).

17. It may seem odd that we should have evolved a grammatical capability that is insufficiently supported by our processing capacities. However, it is only puzzling if we assume that human language grammar evolved as a specific response to linguistic need, rather than either for some other reason, or as a package determined by nonlinguistic parameters (Wray 1998, 2000a).

18. Biassou, Uftring, Chu and Towle (1999) have demonstrated, using fMRI, that working memory during lexical processing is associated with the left inferior frontal cortex, which is "recruited for the selective organization of attentional resources in the context of increased cognitive load" (p. S1052). This finding is consistent with the proposal that attention to language requires left hemisphere activity, while attention to other things enables language processing to shift in part to the right hemisphere (Wray 1992). See Chapters 12 to 14.

19. "A working definition of fluency might be *the rapid, smooth, accurate, lucid, and efficient translation of thought or communicative intention into language under the temporal constraints of language processing*" (Lennon 2000:26). For an assessment of the psychological characteristics of fluency, see Segalowitz (2000).

2. Detecting Formulaicity

1. In practice, both processes are iterative and support each other. The initial identification of some prototypical examples will facilitate the development of definitional criteria, which can then be applied to less prototypical examples (my thanks to Chris Butler for pointing this out).

2. Pawley (1986) lists 27 such criteria, categorized under the headings of: institutionalized status in a culture, resemblance to simple lexemes, syntactic restrictions, ellipsis, writing conventions, and arbitrariness.

3. For the difference between *idiomaticity* in the sense intended here and in the sense of 'being an idiom', see Chapter 3, note 9.

4. The arguments about whether such informants are representative of the normal population of native speakers, or whether it matters, will run and run. What is important here is that all the judges were compatible in background and experience, so the judgements should be consistent and meaningful.

5. Stubbs provides further examples of the deliberate use of formulaic sequences, in German (1997:166) and English (1996:228–229).

6. From *Too many songs by Tom Lehrer*, London: Eyre Methuen, 1981, 33–35.

7. For a clear and comprehensive account of how corpora are set up, see Stubbs (in press).

8. Alexander (1989) calls them "collocations of the month" (p. 18).

9. The London-Lund corpus "consists of nearly half a million running words" (Altenberg 1998:101–102).

10. Indeed, tracking discontinuous or variable formulaic sequences requires a flexible approach to measurement which cannot avoid also picking out nonformulaic material.

11. Bateson's *fused praxon* has a meaning that "is not derivable from its separate parts" (p. 62) and so it is effectively a morpheme with a complex structure. Thus, her differentiation is between complex and simple morphemes, the latter being indicative of the maximum level of flexibility in linguistic construction.

12. For discussion of the limitations of the TTR, see Perkins (1994:327f) and Malvern and Richards (1997).

13. George Grace (1981) proposes that the distinction between the message and its lexification is the most fundamental in language description; that is, it is more important than that between grammar and lexicon (pp. 23–24).

14. We may expect that in crafted writing (and possibly also in many kinds of speech) there will never be a total dominance of one means of expressing a common idea over all other possible means, because it is considered stylistically desirable to avoid the too-frequent use of the same words and expressions (see Chapter 4).

15. There might also be phonological cues (see later), though these are renownedly unreliable unless the hearer is confronted with a minimal pair, as Van Lancker, Canter and Terbeek's (1981) experiments, discussed later in this chapter, indicate.

16. This comment is not to be construed as a criticism of Butler's approach, which is not concerned with identifying patterns of form (or anything else), but only with "show[ing] that certain sequences of form are frequent in textual corpora". As such, "there is no requirement . . . even that sequences have a complete grammatical structure, and certainly no claims are made about them being stored or produced as units" (Chris Butler, personal communication).

17. If we are not familiar with it, the result will be mystification, followed by some hard pragmatic work to restore sense and relevance to the situation, as Kasper (1995) reports happened to her on first encountering *Is the Pope a Catholic?* (pp. 64–65).

18. Pawley and Syder (2000) do not entirely avoid the problem of circularity, whereby the formulaic sequence is defined as the fluent text between dysfluency features, and the dysfluency features are used to identify formulaic sequences. They rely on their intuition to police the external validity of the observed patterns (e.g., pp. 183, 188).

19. It is also worth noting that problems in the planning of the next utterance could create a hiatus well before the end of the preceding chunk, in which case the patterns of hesitation would still not be 'unprincipled', but they would certainly be much more difficult to describe.

20. However, Chris Butler (personal communication) has pointed out that "liaison involves the actual pronunciation of something that remains unpronounced otherwise ... and so the tendency away from liaison in colloquial speech could be seen as consistent with a principle of greater simplification, or less effort".

21. 'Fusion' is discussed in Chapter 6.

22. Technically speaking, the insertion of an isolated noun is arguably a case of 'code-mixing' (Malmkjaer 1991:62), but in the context of formulaic sequences there are no grounds for differentiating between inserted items by size and internal complexity, providing they *are* units.

23. This is Myers-Scotton's (1993) terminology: the 'matrix language' (ML) is the language which contributes the underlying morphosyntactic structure to the speaker's mixed language discourse, and the 'embedded language' (EL) is the other (effectively nondominant) language. According to Myers-Scotton's model, where constituents are mixed, the EL can only provide content morphemes, not structure morphemes.

24. The test must be whether there exist examples of code-switching in which the EL unit is *not* a grammatical constituent but can be reasonably regarded as a formulaic sequence. In a great many cases, it is impossible to tell the difference. For instance, Azuma's (1996) evidence of constituent completion before the language transition includes as examples the English phrases *about two hours, so many hills* and *it's so small* and the Japanese phrase *kuji-kara rokuji-made* 'from nine o'clock to six o'clock' (pp. 406–407). A reasonably liberal interpretation of formulaicity (such as the one used in this book) will also permit all of these as possible formulaic sequences, if only as frames with slots for the specific lexical material: *about NUMBER hours; so many N + PL; it's so ADJ; NUMBER-ji-kara NUMBER-ji-made*. However, both Backus and Azuma provide examples in which the inserted material appears to be formulaic but not a syntactic constituent. These include: *Mom, what happens if you barf on the siihen tietokoneen näppäilemisjuttuun* 'Mom, what happens if you barf on the computer keyboard?'; *Ich les' gerade eins, das handelt von einem alten second hand dealer and his son* 'I'm reading one at the moment about an old second hand dealer and his son' (Backus 1999:101); *My Japanese friend visited me. He's uh MBA no kurasu o totte ite*

'My Japanese friend visited me. He's taking a class for his MBA'; *Living in Austin is totemo ii keiken ni natteimasu* 'Living in Austin is a very good experience' (Azuma 1996:412). The combined evidence of the mixed code calques, which challenge Bachus's view, and these nonconstituent EL insertions, which challenge Azuma's, should make us cautious about believing that either account is able, at present, to capture the entire essence of what determines code-switching boundaries.

3. Pinning Down Formulaicity

1. A further problem is that what is formulaic for one person may not be for another, which makes generalization difficult (Erman & Warren 2000:53).
2. Sinclair (1991) also offers a kind of classification, but it is quite different in kind from the others, being based on observed frequencies of collocates rather than any higher level categorization. We shall not address this in the context of taxonomies.
3. These three approaches and the assumptions underlying them are compared in Wray (2000b).
4. Becker has further confused things by illustrating the sentence builder category with a metaphor.
5. For instance, their Figure 7 (p. 45) states that 'institutionalized expressions' are 'canonical', even though they have previously given as noncanonical the strings *what, me worry?*, *be that as it may* and *long time no see* (p. 40). The same happens with the 'sentence builders', which are 'canonical' in the figure but on p. 43 are "both canonical and non-canonical". Some of their judgements could also be questioned, such as terming *once upon a time* canonical (p. 40).
6. That is, from *vous* to *tu* (French), *Sie* to *du* (German), and so on.
7. Bateson (1975) illustrates this point with the string 'That man in the White House'. As a formulaic sequence this refers to the President of the United States, but as a novel string it could refer to any previously mentioned man currently in that building.
8. For comprehensive reviews of the idiom, see Makkai (1972), Wood (1986) and Moon (1998a:chap. 1). Fillmore et al. (1988) offer a useful basic subcategorization. For an exploration of the syntactic properties of idioms, see Williams (1994), and for a consideration of how idioms can be handled in a functional grammar framework, see Butler (1998).
9. In contrast to some accounts (e.g., Aphek & Tobin 1983:203), we shall keep a distinction between the terms *idiom* and *idiomatic*. The *idiom* is a specific type of turn of phrase with a nonliteral meaning (Irujo 1986:236), while we shall use *idiomatic* for the quality of language characteristic of turns of phrase that are commonly used by native speakers, as opposed to those grammatical sentences that a native speaker would not normally use (Pawley & Syder 1983). That is, *idiomatic* language derives from a facility in using the much wider spectrum of formulaic sequences, one subset of which is the idioms (Stubbs 1997:153).

10. Compare Hudson (1998:35). Joanette, Goulet and Hannequin (1990:185) examine this issue from the viewpoint of selective linguistic deficits.
11. Two of Howarth's examples are ambiguous. *Blow a fuse* is not meant in the sense of 'become very angry' and *under the table* is not intended to mean 'drunk'.
12. Care must be taken, however, for when Bolinger (1976) talks of "a vast continuum between morphology and syntax" (p. 2) he does not mean to describe a horizontal continuum between fixed and free forms, but rather a vertical one between syntax and phonology.
13. However, we shall take the opposite view in Chapter 14.

4. Patterns of Formulaicity in Normal Adult Language

1. Watkins (1992) attributes the long-term preservation of a formulaic sequence in oral culture to its significance in the culture as "something that matters" (p. 393).
2. Original source unknown.
3. Naturally, I am citing the version of "ibble obble" that I learned in my North London primary school playground in the 1960s, since this is the correct one!
4. BBC Radio 4's popular programme *Home Truths* featured, in July 2000, considerable listener discussion regarding the 'correct' response to the nonsense question "How many beans make five?" Proffered answers included "Two beans, a bean-and-a-half, half a bean and a bean", "Two whole beans, two half beans, a bean-and-a-half and half a bean", "Two beans, a bean, a bean-and-a-half and half a bean" and "One bean and a bean, two-and-a-half beans and half a bean" (and many more). These were characteristically prefaced by remarks like "My grandad taught me the answer . . .", "I was always brought up to understand . . .", "It's definitely . . .", and 'The correct version is . . .".
5. These contrasts are confirmed by their relative frequencies in the British National Corpus (Chris Butler, personal communication).
6. That is not to deny other factors. The discourse context places its own constraints on the apparently wide range of possible expressions (McCarthy 1998:69ff).
7. All of this notwithstanding, the phrasal versions also have the advantage of opening up possibilities for nominalization not available with the verb alone (e.g., *take a momentous decision; have a lovely, hot bath; give daddy a nice big kiss*) (Chris Butler, personal communication).
8. See Stubbs (1997) for examples from a German football commentator.
9. Kuiper also proposes this as a subsidiary function of formulaicity in auctions and sportscasting: it reduces the range of possible interpretations that the hearer has to consider (p. 90).
10. On the other hand, the unintentional use of a certain word or phrase more than once in close proximity is considered poor style (e.g., "Consider . . . 'When the *steamer* had raised *steam* she *steamed* out to sea'. This sentence jars on the ear. . . . Synonyms would help us over the difficulty. It is an obvious improvement to say 'When the vessel had raised steam she put out to sea'" (Joad 1939:110).

11. Goldman-Eisler was also investigating the relative fluency of the descriptive and interpretative parts of the commentaries, and found the latter to be less fluent.

12. Recent research (McCrone 1999; Musso et al. 1999; Raichle 1998) suggests that once the brain is familiar with a linguistic task, it is able to bypass the processing route that was used to learn it.

13. They actually report data from nine operators, but separate schemata are presented only for three.

14. If so, then the lexicon of words is not augmented *minimally* with useful pre-fabricated multiword strings, in the interests of providing just one low-effort way of delivering each run-of-the-mill message. It must be augmented by many times the minimum feasible amount.

15. An additional reason why we possess multiple expressions of the same message may be that they naturally accumulate as we deliberately spot strings that are formulaic in those who speak to us, and store them for future use. It will be argued in Chapter 5 that this accommodation of our own formulaic speech to that of the people around us is of central importance to the operation of successful interaction.

16. Compare the English *'Scuse fingers* when passing food using the hand.

17. Threats could as easily be placed in the top part of the table, since they have much in common with requests, commands and so on. It really does not matter for our present purposes just where they are placed, provided their role in manipulation is acknowledged.

18. Fortunately for Mr. Macey and the hapless couple, the law does not trust itself to formulaic sequences: "I held tight till I was by mysen wi' Mr. Drumlow, and then I out wi' everything . . . and he says, 'Pooh pooh, Macey, make yourself easy . . . it's neither the meaning nor the words – it's the regester does it – that's the glue' " (*Silas Marner*. London: Dent Everyman, 1906:66).

5. The Function of Formulaic Sequences: A Model

1. Although Bernstein is talking about ensuring that a message is sufficiently (but no more than sufficiently) elaborate for the hearer, this is clearly related to keeping the hearer's processing to a minimum.

2. Compare Segalowitz's (2001) development of MacWhinney's (1999:218ff) notion of 'affordances' in communication. Segalowitz proposes that linguistic constructions are perceived in terms of their ability to impact on other people in the achievement of the speaker's goals (pp. 17–18).

6. Patterns of Formulaicity in Child Language

1. As Peters (1977) points out, the child's early utterances may well be 'simple', but that does not mean they are necessarily short (p. 562).

2. Tomasello and Brooks (1999) call them "unparsed adult expressions".

3. Ellen lives in Scotland and traces of her accent are seen in her pronunciation of *little* with a 'dark l' in the second syllable, and *lane* and *dame* with a mid-high front monophthong.

4. Bates, Dale and Thal (1995) see unit size as a means of setting the analytic-holistic distinction aside: "it is possible that all children are essentially analytic in their approach to language, but the preferred size of units varies, so some children appear more holistic than others" (p. 132).

5. In Locke's (1999) view, early pointing and naming is not a function of the child's desire to communication thoughts, but of "want[ing] others to recognize that it knows and can say the names of things" (p. 383).

6. Bates et al. (1995:122) offer an overview of the differences found in research between referential and expressive learners, and the wider phenomenon of individual differences in first language acquisition is explored by Goldfield and Snow (1997) and Shore (1995).

7. This observation does not, of course, imply that their *later* use of morphemes is not analytically driven.

8. Compare 'field dependency' (see Wray 1992:87–88 for a brief account) and also Bernstein's (1972) 'restricted' and 'non-restricted' code, including his earlier formulation of these concepts, as 'public' and 'formal' language (Bernstein 1964).

9. As Locke (1999) points out, however, this does not mean that they learn language *in order* to communicate. Locke argues convincingly against such a teleological explanation of first language acquisition, and believes, rather, that "infants begin to talk for contemporaneous reasons that we do not know but should be trying to discover" (p. 378). In a similar vein, when Hirsh-Pasek and Golinkoff (1996:165) liken early language acquisition to watching a film in a language you don't know, they ask *not* whether it would be easier to learn the language with or without the visual input, but whether it would be easier to understand the film with or without the sound track. In other words, first language acquisition needs to be construed as a means for better understanding the world, rather than the world being a means for helping with language learning.

10. The very first stage of acquisition may be the child's storage of input strings, and Locke (1999) proposes that this is neither for the purpose of production nor comprehension of their content. Rather, it is a means of predicting the behaviour of caregivers: "when infants store utterances, they incorporate information about the speaker along with the individual speech sounds that comprise the words. . . . [A] primary consequence of storing vocal characteristics and utterances is the achievement of a behavioural prototype for each of [the child's] caregivers" (p. 382).

11. Of Foster's (1990) eight goals in the child's communicative schemata between ages 12 and 16 months (p. 39), seven are manipulations of others.

12. Hannah's mother notes that "at the time of the recording, Hannah's vocabulary was quite good. She could easily use sentences and was quite capable of letting you know what she wanted. *No* is a word I use quite a lot, so I have no doubt that she fully understood the meaning of the word. [On this occasion] I think that Hannah felt that I wanted her to do something that she didn't really want to do. . . . I think that she was saying that she didn't want to answer any of the questions that I was asking her. Hannah is very shy and stubborn and if she doesn't want to do something, she won't!" (personal communication).

13. They do this "through a combination of [the] distributional properties relative to prosodic phrase boundaries, and of [the] specific phonological properties" (p. 596), not through a pre-existing syntactic knowledge.
14. Stephen was acquiring Garo, an Indian language. Although raised bilingually, his knowledge of Garo was much more advanced than his English during the study. For this reason, Burling's study is treated here as an example of first language acquisition, and is not addressed in the second language acquisition chapter.
15. Gelman and Shatz (1977) have shown that even four year olds accommodate their speech when talking to two year olds (see also Barton & Tomasello 1994:121ff).

7. Formulaic Sequences in the First Language Acquisition Process: A Model

1. This contrasts, then, with the process of full analysis followed by relexicalization which Skehan (1996:90) favours for first language acquisition.
2. They are also somewhat vulnerable to phonological vagaries which may mean that native speakers are not sure of the precise form. Two examples are the phrase *off one's own bat* and *streets ahead* which are often heard as *off one's own back* and *streaks ahead*. This absolutely does not affect their usage, and it is only when one comes to write them that a new level of accuracy is required (see the discussion on the role of literacy in the development of the lexicon, later in this chapter).
3. Locke's model also has four phases, but the two schemata do not fully correspond. Locke's phases are: (1) prenatal, entailing vocal learning and using the SSC (see later); (2) 5–7 months, entailing utterance acquisition using the SSC; (3) 20–37 months, entailing analysis and computation, using the GAM (see later); (4) 3 years and over, entailing integration and elaboration, and using both SSC and GAM. Wray and Perkins's model excludes Locke's Phase 1; its own Phase 1 maps onto Locke's Phase 2, and its Phase 2 covers his Phases 3 and 4. Its own Phases 3 and 4 cover later childhood and adolescence. In essence, the focus of the two models is different, the emphasis in Wray and Perkins's model being the relationship between the early years of acquisition described by Locke and the later ones, which fall outside Locke's model. This difference reflects Wray & Perkins's concern with the entirety of the role of formulaic language rather than just its role in the acquisition of the analytic grammar. The larger time span tracks not only the rise in analytic activity noted by Locke (e.g., 1997:280, fig. 1) but also its subsequent decline.
4. Hallé and Boysson-Bardies (1994) found evidence of a receptive lexicon by 12 months, as witnessed by infants' preference for familiar over unfamiliar words.
5. An alternative formulation of this model could potentially discard the whole idea of the GAM, and rely on a more general process of pattern identification in the course of the needs-only analysis. However, if the GAM is construed as the catalyst to needs-only analysis, rather than as an access point to an innate universal grammar, then its existence is less theoretically biased.

6. "Studies have shown that early use of closed-class morphemes around 20 months of age is either *unrelated* or (depending on how it is measured) *negatively* correlated with grammatical productivity eight months later" (Bates & Goodman 1997:530).

7. Abkarian, Jones and West (1992) found that three-year-old children, who are newly into Phase 2, were better than five year olds at nonliteral interpretations of idioms. Thus, there seems to be a pattern in children of a preference for nonliteral, then literal, then nonliteral interpretations. This pattern is consistent with the model presented here.

8. Wray and Perkins (2000) suggest that "in phase 3, the SSC will frequently override the GAM in the case of frequently occurring items with a resultant gain in automaticity" (p. 20). If the SSC is seen as the agent of fusion, as this suggests, one might conclude that only strings with a socio-interactional function will be fused. As referential strings are also subject to fusion, this is potentially problematic. However, the problem is easily solved if the SSC is viewed as the *activator* of formulaic sequences for social interaction but not their *manager*. In this way, the process of fusion can be separated out, and put to work on all word strings, irrespective of their function. The socio-interactional ones are selected via the SSC, while referential ones are activated via the GAM, which simply retrieves them from the lexicon like single words, and fits them into slots in the discourse plan.

9. Children's make-believe games indicate that they do pick up a limited amount of certain types of "appropriate" talk from observation, however.

10. The transition from the predictable 'user-friendly' environment to the potentially unfriendly one of encounters with strangers may be eased by interaction with "other adults and children [i.e. the father and siblings] with whom they have an affective bond and with whom they have a fair amount of previous social experience" (Barton & Tomasello 1994:132; see also Fletcher 1994:1908–1909).

9. Patterns of Formulaicity in Children Using a Second Language

1. Oskaar (1977) mentions the early use of formulaic sequences in the acquisition of German by a boy aged 3;11, already bilingual in Estonian and Swedish. However, there is too little information for the case to be usefully included here.

2. In the following sections it has often been necessary to infer the function of utterances, and it is possible that in some cases a lack of context in the data has led to their purpose being misunderstood. The intention has been to read as little as possible into a usage, that is, assign it the function that seems most likely. Although it is also not always clear to whom an utterance was addressed, it can reasonably be assumed that the basic function is the same, even where, as with Karen for instance, many utterances are part of her make-believe play and were addressed to her dolls.

3. Karniol (1990) does not offer any clear examples from Karen of formulaic sequences based on group behaviour, but this could well be because they are not relevant to her own analysis.

4. Karniol goes on to note that up to half of her play at home involved this scenario, and that by three months into her L2 immersion, it was entirely conducted in the L2, even though this was linguistically extremely challenging for her.

5. The nature of the reporting of data from this family makes it impossible to separate off Inga for comparison with Virve, Karen and Takahiro.

6. Examples of Wong Fillmore's data are from the (1976) complete report unless otherwise stated.

7. As Bohn (1986) points out, Wong Fillmore only has data from set periods of observation, so there is no indication of what else the children were capable of at a given time.

8. Not being admitted to the children's social circle is the hardest blow that could befall our little girl. She understands the reason and takes measures to conceal, as quickly as possible, her ignorance of the language.

9. It would be misleading to suggest that group allegiances were only, or even primarily, linguistically defined, however. Yael, Etham and Nahla were bound by their allegiance to the group of girls, whose general class behaviour was quite different from that of the boys (Willett 1995:496).

10. Atsuko used a lot of input repetition at this stage (Rescorla & Okuda 1987:286).

11. He also copied a picture being drawn by the girl next to him, including writing her name on it (Wagner-Gough 1978:163).

12. Of course, not all formulaic sequences fall easily into a single functional category, nor should formulaicity be seen as the only means of fulfilling these agendas – novel language was also in use for these purposes.

10. Patterns of Formulaicity in Adults and Teenagers Using a Second Language

1. Since the greeting *see you* is not usefully viewed as a V + NP construction, doing this would have required a command of etymology rather than syntax.

2. Dechert (1983) resists a dual association between islands of reliability and prefabrication, since there is no logical reason for them to be wholly equivalent. However, he does note that "language production may be much less the result of creative construction processes than we have thought for a long time" (p. 184). He later adds that "[f]ormula-like linguistic units of various lengths and syntactic structures provide the material for building islands of reliability" (p. 193).

3. For explorations of the extent to which automatization can be measured, see Segalowitz and Segalowitz (1993). For indications that automatization leads to qualitative differences in neural circuitry, see Raichle (1998) and Musso et al. (1999).

4. . . . *ar gyfer gwaith a swyddfa, ysgol, coleg a chartref*: 'Guidelines on writing Welsh: for work and office, school, college and home'.

5. Another example is *Magu'r babi* 'Bringing up the baby' (Thomas 1997). This "handy phrasebook" (p. vii) is aimed at mothers who wish to raise their children as Welsh-speaking but who were not so-raised themselves. It lists

around 1,400 utterances gathered from recordings of Welsh-speaking mothers, covering contexts such as nappy changing, feeding, going for a walk, and, within these, speech acts such as warning of danger, reminding, encouraging and suggesting.

6. Cook (1994) also advocates the memorization of phrases even if they are not fully understood, and their use in 'intimate contexts' including talking to oneself. This use of language is, he argues, under-recognized as a feature of native speaker behaviour, but is "a source of comfort and an outlet for joy and exuberance, and a way of forming for ourselves and others an image of our own identity" (p. 138).

7. Henry (1996) also offers practical examples of how formulaic sequences can be taught, using pictograms and ideograms as mnemonics.

8. Task-based activities in pairs and groups, where the teacher does not preside, may have unintended consequences, however. The learners must establish a lingua franca that they can all cope with, and this will be matched to the least, not the most, proficient amongst them. And indeed, the whole notion of struggling to use an L2 when all the learners share the same L1 becomes bizarre when the activity is more important than the learning. Swain and Lapkin (1998) accept this, and argue that using the L1 for certain things during L2 tasks makes sense and is not disadvantageous to learning.

9. The eldest of Wong Fillmore's subjects, Juan (aged 8;0 at the end of the study), already seemed locked into a preference for explicit analysis over the simple use of formulaic sequences (1976:328), but this characteristic may be a feature of personality as much as a general maturational trait. In any case, while he was outshone by the others in that study, he should not be construed as an unsuccessful learner, since he was on track to achieve the same level of fluency and competence as the rest (Wong Fillmore 1979:227–228).

10. The existence of both the holistic and the analytic styles of learning, with the balance determined by age, context of learning, perceived need for the L2, and so on, could go some way to explaining the puzzling debate about whether vocabulary is best learned *in* or out of context (e.g., Nation 1982).

11. Formulaic Sequences in the Second Language Acquisition Process: A Model

1. The role of accommodation in the *adult* language learner is also discussed in Chapter 5.

2. It is nigh-on impossible to judge how the relative sizes of the three stores of unit types should be depicted. Sampling entries on four randomly selected pages of the *Chambers Dictionary* revealed a total of 3 bound morphemes, 119 monomorphemic words, 102 polymorphemic words and 62 multiword phrases. Such a survey is a blunt tool for our purposes, since a dictionary of this kind only lists some bound morphemes as separate items (e.g., -ology), and is highly selective about multiword phrases (largely restricting itself to idioms, phrasal verbs and compound nouns). In addition, of course, it is not

attempting to imply that any polymorphemic word or string is prefabricated. Nevertheless, the rough guidance that we gain from the dictionary plus our recognition that other kinds of multiword sequence exist, suggests that it is appropriate to depict the three types of unit as roughly equally represented in the native speaker's lexicon (Figure 11.1) (the bound morphemes and monomorphemic words being lumped together in this depiction). As for the detail of the figures, the aim is to illustrate typical patterns of operation, and only the main trends are shown. So the absence of arrows from, for instance, "morpheme" at the top of Figure 11.1, and from "word" and "morpheme" at the top Figure 11.2, does not necessarily mean that *no* instances of naturalistic input of those types contribute to lexical knowledge, only that it would be relatively unusual.

3. In line with the discussion of terminology in Chapter 1, 'formulaic word string' means a two or more words stored together as a prefabricated unit, and 'formulaic word' means a holistically stored polymorphemic word. Monomorphemic words may be seen as part of the 'morpheme' store (see Chapter 14 for further discussion of this 'layered' lexicon). All three kinds of unit are types of *formulaic sequence*.

4. This kind of learning has to be done piecemeal, since formulaic sequences are often not generalizable: knowing how to greet someone informally does not give you a head start in knowing how to greet someone formally, and knowing how to congratulate someone on his or her birthday will not necessarily be helpful when the occasion is a wedding.

5. These, along with any that *had* been learned whole, would tend to be overused, being relatively few in number (compare DeCock et al. 1998).

12. Patterns of Formulaicity in Aphasic Language

1. The fluent ones are Wernicke's, conduction and transcortical sensory aphasia (Buckingham & Kertesz 1974).

2. According to the definition in Chapter 1, the term *formulaic sequence* covers morphemes and words as well. In the interests of clarity, therefore, *formulaic word string* will be used for contrastive purposes. This term will occur mostly in discussions of form, where multiword strings are compared with single words. Since the literature, on the whole, speaks of *words* without distinguishing between those that are internally complex (polymorphemic) and those that are not, we shall not be able to make that distinction in the research review, though we shall do so in the model in Chapter 13. In the sections on function, it remains most appropriate to use the cover term *formulaic sequence*.

3. The # symbol represents a pause of more than 250 ms, and underlinings indicate words which Butterworth considers to be incorrect selections (paraphasias).

4. This sort of analysis seems equally applicable to other jargonaphasia data, such as, for instance, the output of the eight speakers (or rather the seven who produced recognizable words) described by Lecours et al. (1981). Of

these, case 6 (Mr. Y) is noted to feature "an overflow of coined expressions such as *Mon Dieu!, Bon sang!, N'est-ce pas?, Vous voyez, Qu'est-ce que vous voulez?*" (p. 29).

5. Always assuming that they *are* formulaic and that they are equally frequent in normal language.

6. Van Lancker (1987:88) reports that in a study in the 1920s, Henschen found that 63 out of 100 patients able to say only one word had, as that word, either *yes* or *no*.

7. However, once again, there turns out to be little value in differentiating between single-word and multiword dummy fillers, as their resemblance to something meaningful in their own right is secondary. Certainly, this is the view of Critchley (1970), Espir and Rose (1970) and Van Lancker (1987).

8. In *palilalia*, a symptom of Parkinson's disease, terminal phrases, words and syllables are involuntarily repeated (Van Lancker 1987:86).

9. Van Lancker (1987:51) also makes this point, but her example, *it's a small world*, is an unfortunate one. What she describes as the "complex proposition" of its meaning (*"people who know each other can coincidentally meet in the same place . . ."*) is really its customary pragmatic interpretation. A phrase like this really needs to be defined by its function: 'the thing that I say when I wish to signal that I have noticed a coincidence', just as *How do you do* is 'the thing I say when I meet someone for the first time in a formal setting'. Viewed this way, *it's a small world* is, after all, a nonreferential, nonpropositional expression, used for socio-interactional purposes.

10. Of course, caution is always required in any case where surgery is the result of longstanding condition, as this is likely to have caused an abnormal arrangement of functions.

11. Lecours et al. (1988) propose that "cerebral representation of language is more ambilateral in illiterates than it is in school-educated subjects, although left cerebral 'dominance' remains the rule in both" (p. 575). This pattern is precisely what our lexical model (see Chapters 13 and 14) would predict.

12. Dapretto, Hariri, Bialik and Bookheimer (1999) found evidence that the right hemisphere was involved only in prosody conveying emotional force, not in prosody conveying meaning (e.g., stress, intonation). However, Mayer et al. (1999) explain the difference in terms of the 'prosodic frame length': "prosodic features which require a short address frame (e.g., focused syllable) are lateralized differently than prosodic features requiring a long address frame (the whole intonational phrases for linguistic modus and paralinguistic affect). Prosodic frame length and not the linguistic/affective function is a basis of lateralization" (p. S1065).

13. These stages are not, of course, clear-cut transitions, but gradual.

13. Formulaic Sequences in Aphasia: A Model

1. This chapter separates the lexicon into different parts, each of which can contain formulaic sequences of different sizes and complexity: morphemes,

words and multiword strings. Because of this, the term *formulaic sequence* is problematic, since it is not defined to discriminate unit subtypes. As a result, in this chapter that term will be used only sparingly, and, in the pursuit of maximum clarity, we shall refer separately to *morphemes, polymorphemic* or *formulaic words* and (*formulaic*) *word strings* (see note 2 in Chapter 12, and the discussion of terminology in Chapter 1).

2. The prepositions which form part of a phrasal verb are not accessed from Column I, since they are prespecified as collocations of the verb. So the word *in* is accessed from the Column I part of the lexicon in the sentence *get in the car* (V PP) but from Column II, along with *bring*, in the sentence *bring in the washing* (V NP).

3. It is important to note that there is not a direct correspondence between Column V and expletive vocabulary. Expletives are not exclusively found in the context of reflexive expressions of emotion, any more than any other lexical unit must always serve the same function (for instance, *there's jam on the table* could be a referential description, a manipulative request or command, or a mnemonic for pin number 63235, based on the number of letters in each word). Swearwords can take direct referential roles based on their core meaning (e.g., *there's shit on the doorstep*), proform referential roles for particular effect (e.g., *the fucking fucker's fucked*), and a range of socio-interactional roles such as inciting the hearer to action and acting as a badge of group membership (Jay 1999:82). Although research does recognize this in principle (e.g., Jay 1999:135f), and evidence indicates that in aphasia only the automatic use of swearwords remains, not the propositional (ibid.:37–38, 87), accounts still tend to associate swearwords *directly* with subcortical processing, rather than recognizing the connection as indirect, via the function of emotional expression.

4. Holistic meanings are, therefore, entirely independent of componential ones, so we can sustain both metaphorical and literal meanings of the same phrase (e.g., *get the sack*), without even noticing that they are identical unless humour or curiosity invite us to scrutinize them. Similarly, phrasal verbs (e.g., *own up; take over*) are not, under normal circumstances, processed componentially.

5. Whether *bookshelf* is to be seen as mono- or bimorphemic is debatable, and this issue will be the focus of some discussion about the nature of lexical units, and the relationship between morphology and etymology, in Chapter 14.

6. The words may still be lodged in memory and just irretrievable (Goodglass & Wingfield 1997:4).

7. Even so-called verbal-fluency tasks are analytic, and entirely removed from real language processing for interactional purposes. Adcock, Calvert and Matthews (1999), for instance, administered three such tasks: generating words from letters, naming examples from hypernym categories (e.g., plants, animals), and creating verbs from nouns. Similarly, sentence comprehension tasks, despite their superiority over single word tasks as a representation of real language, still focus on a kind of testing that has nothing to do with genuine interaction. Meyer, Friederici and von Cramon's (1999) experi-

mental stimuli, for instance, were sentences containing pseudowords in place of content words.

8. As also from its phonetic shape: the most forceful swearwords in English begin and/or end with stop or fricative consonants (Crystal 1995:251).

9. While reflexive expressions of shock, pain, and the like are universal, the more 'lexicalized' ones, such as swearwords, must, historically, derive from other parts of the lexicon, since they are language, and indeed speech community, specific.

10. The term 'polyglot' is used here simply to avoid the much more loaded term 'bilingual'. Normally a polyglot speaks at least three languages, but we shall take the epithet here to refer to anyone who has knowledge of at least two. In this immediate context, we are also focussing on those who have learned their L2 after childhood, and probably in the foreign language classroom.

11. The relationship between the unit-size focus of Figures 11.1 and 11.2 and the functional focus of Figure 13.1 is clarified in Chapter 14.

12. The model predicts that the reverse could not occur, unless the individual's history of language use was such that L1 and L2 had switched roles, so that the lexical storage of the latter was L1-like, and that of the former was L2-like.

13. For a selection of original reports spanning the history of research into polyglot aphasia, see Paradis (1983), and for a comprehensive update, see Paradis (1995).

14. The Heteromorphic Distributed Lexicon

1. Compare Makkai (1972) on idioms that "lend themselves to incorrect decoding" versus those "subject to erroneous encoding" (p. 17), and discussion of this in Fillmore et al. (1988:504–505).

2. This observation is supported by cross-linguistic comparisons. Drazdauskiene (1981) notes that a great many expressions of several words in English translate as a single word in Lithuanian (e.g., *resiskia* 'it means', *zodziu* 'in a word', *atseit* 'as it were') (p. 59).

3. Wray (1996) reports 123 nonstandard additions or omissions of word breaks in a 173,000 word corpus of first year undergraduate essays, including *alot*, *afterall*, *aswell as*, *infact*, *can not*, *some what*, *stereo types*, *through out*, *up date* and *meaning less* (pp. 102ff). These examples indicate that knowing the correct spacing is no different from any other aspect of spelling, if the unit is formulaic. It is a matter of convention, and this changes over time, as witnessed by examples like *all right* versus *alright* (compare also Moon 1997:44–45; Sinclair 1998:1).

4. Marlsen-Wilson et al. (1994), for instance, argue for the morpheme as the base unit of the lexicon, but accept that some apparently polymorphemic words are actually "unanalyzed simple forms" (p. 31). Taking this position resolves the conflict between the language user's and the linguist's identification of the 'morpheme' and bars etymology from contributing to synchronic models (Lamb 1998:170). However, they reject the idea that the lexicon lists genuinely polymorphemic words or phrases.

5. There has been considerable discussion over the years about just what the lexicon has to list, and what can be generated (see Hendrick 1995 for an overview), but the fundamental position remains consistent: you list as little as the detail of your theoretical model will let you get away with. That is the essence of the contrast with what is proposed here.

6. See Pawley and Syder (1983:218–219) for additional discussion of this issue.

7. Jackendoff argues at length that a Chomskian framework needs to accommodate phrase-length lexical units. He shows that the existing machinery for handling irregular compound words can also handle such phrases (1997:chap. 7).

8. Compare Hanks (1987): "The distinction between the possible and the typical is of the greatest importance. It is possible, given a reasonably lively imagination, to use a particular word in any number of different ways. But when we ask how the word is typically used, rather than how it might possibly be used, we can generally discover a relatively small number of distinct patterns" (p. 121).

9. The problem extends when we consider some of the other meanings of *happily*, such as *Happily, it had stopped raining by then* ('fortunately') and *She was playing happily in a corner* ('quietly').

10. Lexicon V is independent of these concerns – see Chapter 13.

11. Although it will not be discussed further here, it may be noted that Functional Grammar also handles formulaic sequences in a convincing way (e.g., Butler 1998; Tucker 1998). For one overview of how formulaic sequences are accommodated in different grammatical theories, see Robinson (1986).

12. The details given here are taken, with permission, from Tuggy's paper "On the storage vs. complexity of complex linguistic structures", presented at the 5th International Cognitive Linguistics Conference, Amsterdam, July 1997.

13. The same fusion-based account of how large units get into the lexicon features in Bybee's (1998) model, the *emergent lexicon* (p. 421). This is another account which, in many other respects, mirrors the present one, by holding that "chunks of linguistic experience much larger than the analytic units of morpheme or even words are the usual units of storage and processing" (p. 421).

14. See, for instance, Sinclair (1998) on the meaning of *budge*.

15. We are thus provided with a solution to Bolinger's (1985) complaint that defining a word in isolation is like roughly uprooting a plant from a mass of others in a vegetable plot: the result is a 'damaged definition' (p. 69).

16. Caramazza (Chialant & Caramazza 1995) favours the flexibility of dual processing to account for morphological irregularities. However, in his model, the two types of processing operate simultaneously (p. 63), rather than strategically.

References

Aarts, J. 1991. Intuition-based and observation-based grammars. In K. Aijmer & B. Altenberg (eds.) *English corpus linguistics*. London, New York: Longman, 44–62.

Abkarian, G.G., Jones, A. & West, G. 1992. Young children's idiom comprehension: trying to get the picture. *Journal of Speech and Hearing Research* 35:580–587.

Adcock, J.E., Calvert, G.A. & Matthews, P.M. 1999. The determination of language dominance using verbal fluency tasks of short duration at high (3T) field. *Neuroimage* 9(6), part 2:S1039.

Aijmer, K. 1996. *Conversational routines in English*. London, New York: Longman.

Alajouanine, T. 1956. Verbal realization in aphasia. *Brain* 79(1):1–28.

Alexander, R.J. 1984. Fixed expressions in English: reference books and the teacher. *ELT Journal* 38(2):127–134.

Alexander, R.J. 1987. Problems in understanding and teaching idiomaticity in English. *Anglistik und Englischunterricht* 32:105–122.

Alexander, R.J. 1989. Fixed expressions, idioms and collocations revisited. In P. Meara (ed.) *Beyond words*. London: Centre for Information on Language & Teaching Research/British Association for Applied Linguistics, 15–24.

Allan, Q. 1998. Delexical verbs and degrees of desemanticization. *Word* 49(1): 1–17.

Altenberg, B. 1990. Speech as linear composition. In G. Caie, K. Haastrup, A.L. Jakobsen, J.E. Nielsen, J. Sevaldsen, H. Specht & A. Zettersten (eds.) *Proceedings from the Fourth Nordic Conference for English Studies, vol. 1*. Copenhagen: Dept of English, University of Copenhagen, 133–143.

Altenberg, B. 1993. Recurrent verb-complement constructions in the London-Lund Corpus. In J. Aarts, P. de Haan & N. Oostdijk (eds.) *English language corpora: design, analysis & exploitation*. Amsterdam: Rodopi, 227–245.

Altenberg, B. 1998. On the phraseology of spoken English: the evidence of recurrent word-combinations. In A. Cowie (ed.) *Phraseology: theory, analysis and applications*. Oxford: Clarendon Press, 101–122.

Ameka, F. 1987. A comparative analysis of linguistic routines in two languages: English & Ewe. *Journal of Pragmatics* 11:299–326.

Anglin, J.M. 1993. *Vocabulary development: a morphological analysis.* Monographs of the Society for Research in Child Development, series no. 238, vol. 58, no. 10. Chicago: University of Chicago Press.

Aphek, E. & Tobin, Y. 1983. Understanding idioms in first and second language acquisition. *Jyvaskyla Cross-language Studies* 9:203–224.

Austin, J.L. 1979/1996. Performative utterances. In J.O. Urmson & G.J. Warnock (eds.) *Philosophical papers* (3rd edition). Oxford: Oxford University Press, 233–252. Reprinted in A.P. Martinich (ed.) *The philosophy of language* (3rd edition). New York: Oxford University Press, 120–140.

Azuma, S. 1996. Speech production units among bilinguals. *Journal of Psycholinguistic Research* 25(3):397–416.

Backus, A. 1999. Evidence for lexical chunks in insertional codeswitching. In B. Brendemoen, E. Lanza & E. Ryen (eds.) *Language encounters across time and space.* Oslo: Novus Press, 93–109.

Bahns, J., Burmeister, H. & Vogel, T. 1986. The pragmatics of formulas in L2 learner speech: use and development. *Journal of Pragmatics* 10:693–723.

Barrett, M.D. 1994. Language acquisition: vocabulary. In R.E. Asher (ed.) *Encyclopedia of language & linguistics.* Oxford: Pergamon, 1927–1931.

Barton, D. 1985. Awareness of language units in adults & children. In A.W. Ellis (ed.) *Progress in the psychology of language, vol. 1.* Mahwah, NJ: Lawrence Erlbaum, 187–205.

Barton, M.E. & Tomasello, M. 1994. The rest of the family: the role of fathers & siblings in early language development. In C. Gallaway & B.J. Richards (eds.) *Input & interaction in language acquisition.* Cambridge: Cambridge University Press, 109–134.

Bates, E., Bretherton, I. & Snyder, L. 1988. *From first words to grammar.* Cambridge: Cambridge University Press.

Bates, E., Dale, P.S. & Thal, D. 1995. Individual differences and their implications for theories of language development. In P. Fletcher & B. MacWhinney (eds.) *The handbook of child language.* Oxford: Blackwell, 96–151.

Bates, E. & Goodman, J.C. 1997. On the inseparability of grammar and the lexicon: evidence from acquisition, aphasia and real-time processing. *Language and Cognitive Processes* 12(5/6):507–584.

Bates, E. & MacWhinney, B. 1987. Competition, variation & language learning. In B. MacWhinney (ed.) *Mechanisms of language acquisition.* Hillsdale, NJ: Lawrence Erlbaum, 157–193.

Bates, E., Marchman, V., Thal, D., Fenson, L., Dale, P., Reznick, J.S., Reilly, J. & Hartung, J. 1994. Developmental and stylistic variation in the composition of early vocabulary. In K. Perera, G. Collis & B. Richards (eds.) *Growing points in child language.* Cambridge: Cambridge University Press, 85–123.

Bateson, M.C. 1975. Linguistic models in the study of joint performances. In M.D. Kinkade, K.L. Hale & O. Werner (eds.) *Linguistics & anthropology, in honor of C.F. Voeglin.* Lisse: Peter de Ridder, 53–66.

Becker, J. 1975. The phrasal lexicon. Bolt Beranek & Newman Report no. 3081, AI Report no. 28. Reprinted in R. Shank & B.L. Nash-Webber (eds.) *Theo-*

retical issues in natural language processing. Cambridge, MA: Bolt Beranek & Newman, 60–63.

Beeman, M. & Chiarello, C. (eds.) 1998. *Right hemisphere language comprehension: perspectives from cognitive neuroscience.* Mahwah, NJ: Lawrence Erlbaum.

Beneke, J. 1981. Cultural monsters, mimicry and English as an international language. In R. Freudenstein, J. Beneke & H. Pönisch (eds.) *Language incorporated: teaching foreign languages in industry.* Oxford: Pergamon & Munich: Max Heber Verlag, 73–94.

Benson, M. 1985. Collocations & idioms. In R. Ilson (ed.) *Dictionaries, lexicography & language learning,* ELT Documents 120. Oxford: Pergamon, 61–68.

Benton, A.L. & Joynt, R.J. 1960. Early descriptions of aphasia. *Archives of Neurology* 3:109–126/205–222.

Bernac, P. 1976. *The interpretation of French song* (revised edition). London: Victor Gollancz.

Bernstein, B. 1964. Aspects of language and learning in the genesis of the social process. In D. Hymes (ed.) *Language in culture and society.* New York: Harper & Row, 251–260.

Bernstein, B. 1972. Social class, language and socialization. In P.P. Giglioli (ed.) *Language and social context.* Harmondsworth: Penguin, 157–178.

Biassou, N., Uftring, S., Chu, D. & Towle, V.L. 1999. The role of prefrontal cortex in visual language processing. *Neuroimage* 9(6), part 2:S1052.

Biber, D., Conrad, S. & Reppen, R. 1998. *Corpus linguistics: investigating language structure and use.* Cambridge: Cambridge University Press.

Biskup, D. 1992. L1 influence on learners' renderings of English collocations: a Polish/German empirical study. In P.J.L. Arnaud & H. Béjoint (eds.) *Vocabulary and applied linguistics.* Basingstoke: Macmillan, 85–93.

Blanken, G. & Marini, V. 1997. Where do lexical speech automatisms come from? *Journal of Neurolinguistics* 10(1):19–31.

Blanken, G., Wallesch, C.-W. & Papagno, C. 1990. Dissociations of language functions in aphasics with speech automatisms (recurring utterances). *Cortex* 26:41–63.

Bloom, L. 1973. *One word at a time: the use of single word utterances before syntax.* The Hague: Mouton.

Bloom, L., Hood, L. & Lightbown, P. 1978. Imitation in language development: if, when, & why. In L. Bloom (ed.) *Readings in language development.* New York: Wiley, 452–488.

Bloom, L., Lightbown, P. & Hood, L. 1975. *Structure and variation in child language.* Monographs of the Society for Research in Child Development, Series no. 160, vol. 40, no. 2. Chicago: University of Chicago Press.

Bloomfield, L. 1933. *Language.* London: Allen & Unwin.

Blumstein, S.E. 1988. Neurolinguistics: an overview of language-brain relations in aphasia. In F.J. Newmeyer (ed.) *Linguistics: the Cambridge survey. III. Language: psychological and biological aspects.* Cambridge: Cambridge University Press, 210–236.

Bohn, O.-S. 1986. Formulas, frame structures, and stereotypes in early syntactic development: some new evidence from L2 acquisition. *Linguistics* 24:185–202.

Bolander, M. 1989. Prefabs, patterns and rules in interaction? Formulaic speech in adult learners' L2 Swedish. In K. Hyltenstam & L.K. Obler (eds.) *Bilingualism across the lifespan*. Cambridge: Cambridge University Press, 73–86.

Bolinger, D. 1975. *Aspects of language* (2nd edition). New York: Harcourt Brace Jovanovich.

Bolinger, D. 1976. Meaning and memory. *Forum Linguisticum* 1:1–14.

Bolinger, D. 1985. Defining the indefinable. In R. Ilson (ed.) *Dictionaries, lexicography & language learning*. Oxford: Pergamon, 69–73.

Bouton, L.F. 1988. A cross-cultural study of ability to interpret implicatures in English. *World Englishes* 7(2):183–196.

Bower, G.H. 1969. Chunks as interference units in free recall. *Journal of Verbal Learning and Verbal Behavior* 8:610–613.

Bresnan, J. 1982a. *The mental representation of grammatical relations*. Cambridge, MA: MIT Press.

Bresnan, J. 1982b. Control and competition. *Linguistic Inquiry* 13(3):343–434.

Bretherton, I., McNew, S., Snyder, L. & Bates, E. 1983. Individual differences at 20 months: analytic and holistic strategies in language acquisition. *Journal of Child Language* 10:293–320.

Brown, G. 1990. *Listening to spoken English* (2nd edition). London & New York: Longman.

Brown, J.W. 1975. On the neural organization of language: thalamic and cortical relationships. *Brain and Language* 2:18–30.

Brown, R. 1973. *A first language*. London: Allen & Unwin.

Brown, R. & Hanlon, C. 1970. Derivational complexity & order of acquisition in child speech. In J.R. Hayes (ed.) *Cognition & the development of language*. New York: Wiley, 11–53.

Brownell, H. & Martino, G. 1998. Deficits in inference and social cognition: the effects of right hemisphere brain damage on discourse. In M. Beeman & C. Chiarello (eds.) *Right hemisphere language comprehension: perspectives from cognitive neuroscience*. Mahwah, NJ: Lawrence Erlbaum, 309–328.

Brownell, H., Potter, H.H., Bihrle, A.M. & Gardner, H. 1986. Inference deficits in right brain-damaged patients. *Brain and Language* 27:310–321.

Bruner, J. 1983. *Child's talk: learning to use language*. New York: Norton.

Buchanan, T., Lutz, K., Mirzazade, S., Specht, K., Shah, N.J., Zilles, K. & Jäncke, L. 1999. Recognition of emotional prosody and verbal components of spoken language: an fMRI study. *Neuroimage* 9(6), part 2:S1017.

Buckingham, H.W. 1981. Where do neologisms come from? In J.W. Brown (ed.) *Jargonaphasia*. New York: Academic Press, 39–62.

Buckingham, H.W. & Kertesz, A. 1974. A linguistic analysis of fluent aphasia. *Brain and Language* 1:43–62.

Burling, R. 1978. Language development of a Garo and English-speaking child. In E. Hatch (ed.) *Second language acquisition: a book of readings*. Rowley, MA: Newbury House, 54–75.

Butler, C.S. 1997. Repeated word combinations in spoken and written text: some implications for Functional Grammar. In C.S. Butler, J.H. Connolly, R.A. Gatward & R.M. Vismans (eds.) *A fund of ideas: recent developments in Functional Grammar*. Amsterdam: IFOTT, 60–77.

Butler, C.S. 1998. Multi-word lexical phenomena in functional grammar. *Revista Canaria de Estudios Ingeleses* 36:13–36.

Butler, C.S. 1999. Some possible contributions of corpus linguistics to the functional lexematic model. In M.J. Feu Guijarro & S. Molina Plaza (eds.) *Estudios funcionales sobre léxico, sintaxis y traducción. Un homenaje a Leocadio Martín Mingorance*. Cuenca: Universidad de Castilla La Mancha, 19–35.

Butterworth, B. 1979. Hesitation and the production of verbal paraphasias and neologisms in jargon aphasia. *Brain and Language* 8:133–161.

Butterworth, B. 1983. Lexical representation. In B. Butterworth (ed.) *Language production, vol. 2: development, writing and other processes*. New York: Academic Press, 257–294.

Butterworth, B. 1989. Lexical access in speech production. In W. Marslen-Wilson (ed.) *Lexical representation and process*. Cambridge, MA: MIT Press, 108–135.

Bybee, J. 1998. The emergent lexicon. *Chicago Linguistics Society* 34:421–435.

Bygate, M. 1988. Units of oral expression and language learning. *Applied Linguistics* 9(1):59–82.

Cacciari, C. & Levorato, M.C. 1989. How children understand idioms in discourse. *Journal of Child Language* 16:387–405.

Cameron, L. & Low, G. 1999. Metaphor. *Language Teaching* 32(2):77–96.

Caplan, D. 1987. *Neurolinguistics and linguistic aphasiology: an introduction*. Cambridge: Cambridge University Press.

Caramazza, A., Gordon, J., Zurif, E.B. & DeLuca, D. 1976. Right-hemispheric damage & verbal problem solving behavior. *Brain and Language* 3:41–46.

Carlisle, J.F. 1995. Morphological awareness and early reading achievement. In L.B. Feldman (ed.) *Morphological aspects of language processing*. Hillsdale, NJ: Lawrence Erlbaum, 189–209.

Carter, R. 1988. Vocabulary, cloze and discourse: an applied linguistic view. In R. Carter & M. McCarthy (eds.) *Vocabulary and language teaching*. Harlow: Longman, 161–180.

Chafe, W.L. 1968. Idiomaticity as an anomaly in the Chomskyan paradigm. *Foundations of Language* 4:109–127.

Chan, L.K.S. & Cole, P.G. 1986. Children's understanding of ironic utterances. In C. Pratt, A.F. Garton, W.E. Tunmer & A.R. Nesdale (eds.) *Research issues in child development*. Sydney: Allen & Unwin, 95–104.

Chernigovskaya, T.V. 1994. Cerebral lateralization for cognitive & linguistic abilities. In J. Wind, A. Jonker, R. Allott & L. Rolfe (eds.) *Studies in language origins, vol. 3*. Amsterdam: John Benjamins, 55–76.

Chialant, D. & Caramazza, A. 1995. Where is morphology and how is it processed? The case of written word recognition. In L.B. Feldman (ed.) *Morphological aspects of language processing*. Hillsdale, NJ: Lawrence Erlbaum, 55–76.

Chisanga, T. 1987. *An investigation into the form and function of educated English in Zambia as a possible indigenized non-native variety*. Unpublished D.Phil. thesis, University of York.

Chomsky, N. 1957. *Syntactic structures*. The Hague: Mouton.

Chomsky, N. 1965. *Aspects of the theory of syntax*. Cambridge, MA: MIT Press.

Christman, S.S. & Buckingham, H.W. 1991. Jargonaphasia. In C. Code (ed.) *The characteristics of aphasia*. Hove: Lawrence Erlbaum, 111–130.

Christophe, A., Guasti, T., Nespor, M., Dupoux, E. & Van Ooyen, B. 1997. Reflections on phonological bootstrapping: its role for lexical & syntactic acquisition. *Language and Cognitive Processes* 12(5/6):585–612.

Church, K.W. & Hanks, P. 1989. Word association norms, mutual information and lexicography. *Proceedings of 17th Annual Meeting of Association for Computational Linguistics*, 76–83.

Cicone, M., Gardner, H. & Winner, E. 1981. Understanding the psychology in psychological metaphors. *Journal of Child Language* 8:213–216.

Clahsen, H. 1984. The acquisition of German word order: a test case for cognitive approaches to L2 development. In R.W. Andersen (ed.) *Second languages: a cross-linguistic perspective*. Rowley, MA: Newbury House, 219–242.

Clark, E.V. 1995. Later lexical development & word formation. In P. Fletcher & B. MacWhinney (eds.) *The handbook of child language*. Oxford: Blackwell, 393–412.

Clark, R. 1974. Performing without competence. *Journal of Child Language* 1:1–10.

Clear, J. 1993. From Firth principles: computational tools for the study of collocation. In M. Baker, G. Francis & E. Tognini-Bonelli (eds.) *Text and technology: in honour of John Sinclair*. Philadelphia/Amsterdam: John Benjamins, 271–292.

Coates, R. 2000. Singular definite expressions with a unique denotatum and the limits of properhood. *Linguistics* 38(6):1161–1174.

Code, C. 1982a. Neurolinguistic analysis of recurrent utterances in aphasia. *Cortex* 18:141–152.

Code, C. 1982b. On the origins of recurrent utterances in aphasia. *Cortex* 18:161–164.

Code, C. 1987. *Language, aphasia, and the right hemisphere*. Chichester: John Wiley.

Code, C. 1991. Symptoms, syndromes, models: the nature of aphasia. In C. Code (ed.) *The characteristics of aphasia*. Hove: Lawrence Erlbaum, 1–22.

Code, C. 1994. Speech automatism production in aphasia. *Journal of Neurolinguistics* 8(2):135–148.

Code, C. 1997. Can the right hemisphere speak? *Brain and Language* 57:38–59.

Cook, G. 1994. Repetition and learning by heart: an aspect of intimate discourse, and its implications. *ELT Journal* 48(2):133–141.

Cook-Gumperz, J. 1977. Situated instructions: language socialization of school age children. In S. Ervin-Tripp & C. Mitchell-Kernan (eds.) *Child discourse*. New York: Academic Press, 103–121.

Cornell, A. 1999. Idioms: an approach to identifying major pitfalls for learners. *International Review of Applied Linguistics in Language Teaching* 31(1): 1–22.

Coulmas, F. 1979. On the sociolinguistic relevance of routine formulae. *Journal of Pragmatics* 3:239–266.

Coulmas, F. 1981. Introduction: conversational routine. In F. Coulmas (ed.) *Conversational routine*. The Hague: Mouton, 1–17.

Coulmas, F. 1994. Formulaic language. In R.E. Asher (ed.) *Encyclopedia of language & linguistics.* Oxford: Pergamon, 1292–1293.

Cowie, A.P. 1988. Stable and creative aspects of vocabulary use. In R. Carter & M. McCarthy (eds.) *Vocabulary and language teaching.* London, New York: Longman, 126–139.

Cowie, A.P. 1992. Multiword lexical units and communicative language teaching. In P.J.L. Arnaud & H. Béjoint (eds.) *Vocabulary and applied linguistics.* Basingstoke: Macmillan, 1–12.

Cowie, A.P. 1994. Phraseology. In R.E. Asher (ed.) *Encyclopedia of language & linguistics.* Oxford: Pergamon, 3168–3171.

Cowie, A.P. 1998. Phraseological dictionaries: some east-west comparisons. In A.P. Cowie (ed.) *Phraseology.* Oxford: Clarendon Press, 209–228.

Cowie, A.P. & Howarth, P. 1996. Phraseological competence and written proficiency. In G. Blue & R. Mitchell (eds.) *Language and education.* Clevedon: Multilingual Matters, 80–93.

Cowie, A.P. & Mackin, R. 1975. Index of nouns etc used in headphrases; index of nominalized forms. *Oxford dictionary of current idiomatic English, vol. 1: verbs with prepositions and particles.* London: Oxford University Press, 370–396.

Crick, F.H.C. 1979. Thinking about the brain. *Scientific American* 241:219–232; reprinted in *The Brain*, Scientific American special issue, 130–137.

Critchley, M. 1970. *Aphasiology and other aspects of language.* London: Edward Arnold.

Cruttenden, A. 1981. Item-learning and system-learning. *Journal of Psycholinguistic Research* 10(1):79–88.

Crystal, D. 1995. *The Cambridge encyclopedia of the English language.* Cambridge: Cambridge University Press.

Crystal, D. 1997. *The Cambridge encyclopedia of language* (2nd edition). Cambridge: Cambridge University Press.

Dapretto, M., Hariri, A., Bialik, M.H. & Bookheimer, S.Y. 1999. Cortical correlates of affective vs. linguistic prosody: an fMRI study. *Neuroimage* 9(6), part 2:S1054.

Dechert, H.W. 1983. How a story is done in a second language. In C. Faerch & G. Kasper (eds.) *Strategies in interlanguage communication.* New York: Longman, 175–195.

DeCock, S., Granger, S., Leech, G. & McEnery, T. 1998. An automated approach to the phrasicon of EFL learners. In S. Granger (ed.) *Learner English on computer.* London, New York: Addison Wesley Longman, 67–79.

Dell, G.S. 1986. A spreading-activation theory of retrieval in sentence production. *Psychological Review* 93:283–321.

Denès, P. 1914/1983. Contributions to the study of some aphasic phenomena. In M. Paradis (ed.) *Readings on aphasia in bilinguals and polyglots.* Montreal: Didier, 108–117.

DiSciullo, A.M. & Williams, E. 1987. *On the definition of word.* Cambridge, MA: MIT Press.

Dittmar, N. 1984. Semantic features of pidginized learner varieties of German. In R.W. Andersen (ed.) *Second languages: a cross-linguistic perspective.* Rowley, MA: Newbury House, 243–270.

Dogancay, S. 1990. Your eye is sparkling: formulaic expressions & routines in Turkish. *Penn Working Papers in Educational Linguistics* 6(2):49–65.

Drazdauskiene, M.-L. 1981. On stereotypes in conversation, their meaning & significance. In F. Coulmas (ed.) *Conversational routine*. The Hague: Mouton, 55–68.

Drescher, M. 1994. Für zukünftige Bewerbungen wünschen wir Ihnen mehr Erfolg: Zur Formelhaftigkeit von Absagebriefen. *Deutsche Sprache* 22(2): 117–137.

Dufon, M.A. 1995. The acquisition of gambits by classroom foreign learners of Indonesian. In M. Alves (ed.) *Papers from the 3rd annual meeting of the South-Eastern Asian Linguistics Society*. Arizona State University, 27–42.

Dyer, M.G. 1989. Comprehension and acquisition of figurative expressions with phrasal/lexical memory. *Metaphor and Symbolic Activity* 4(3):173–201.

Edwards, S. & Garman, M. 1991. Aphasia. In K. Malmkjaer (ed.) *The linguistics encyclopedia*. London, New York: Routledge, 16–20.

Edwards, S. & Knott, R. 1994. Assessing spontaneous language abilities of aphasic speakers. In D. Graddol & J. Swann (eds.) *Evaluating language*. Clevedon: Multilingual Matters, 91–101.

Eisenson, J. 1962. Language & intellectual modifications associated with right cerebral damage. *Language and Speech* 5:49–53.

Ellis, N.C. 1996. Sequencing in SLA: phonological memory, chunking and points of order. *Studies in Second Language Acquisition* 18:91–126.

Ellis, N.C. 1997. The epigenesis of language: acquisition as a sequence learning problem. In A. Ryan & A. Wray (eds.) *Evolving models of language*. Clevedon: Multilingual Matters, 41–57.

Ellis, N.C. & Schmidt, R. 1997. Morphological & longer-distance dependencies: laboratory research illuminating the A in SLA. *Studies in Second Language Acquisition* 19(2):145–171.

Ellis, N.C. & Sinclair, S.G. 1996. Working memory in the acquisition of vocabulary and syntax: putting language in good order. *Quarterly Journal of Experimental Psychology* 49A(1):234–250.

Ellis, R. 1984. Formulaic speech in early classroom second language development. In J. Handscombe, R.A. Orem & B.P. Taylor (eds.) *On TESOL '83*. Washington, DC: TESOL, 53–65.

Ellis, R. 1994. *The study of second language acquisition*. Oxford: Oxford University Press.

Ely, R. & Gleason, J.B. 1995. Socialization across contexts. In P. Fletcher & B. MacWhinney (eds.) *The handbook of child language*. Oxford: Blackwell, 251–270.

Emeneau, M.B. 1964. Oral poets of South India: the Todas. In D. Hymes (ed.) *Language in culture and society: a reader in linguistics and anthropology*. New York: Harper & Row, 330–343.

Encyclopedia Britannica. 1999. Standard edition. International version. CD-ROM.

Erman, B. & Warren, B. 2000. The idiom principle and the open choice principle. *Text* 20(1):29–62.

Espir, M.L.E. & Rose, F.C. 1970. *The basic neurology of speech*. Oxford & Edinburgh: Blackwell.

Eysenck, M.W. & Keane, M.T. 1995. *Cognitive psychology: a student's handbook* (3rd edition). Hillsdale, NJ: Lawrence Erlbaum.

Farghal, M. & Obiedat, H. 1995. Collocations: a neglected variable in EFL. *International Review of Applied Linguistics in Language Teaching* 33(4):315–331.

Ferguson, C.A. 1976. The structure & use of politeness formulas. *Language in Society* 5:137–151.

Fillmore, C.J. 1979. On fluency. In C.J. Fillmore, D. Kempler & S.-Y.W. Wang (eds.) *Individual differences in language ability & language behavior*. New York: Academic Press, 85–101.

Fillmore, C.J., Kay, P. & O'Connor, M.C. 1988. Regularity & idiomaticity in grammatical constructions: the case of 'let alone'. *Language* 64(3):501–538.

Firth, J.R. 1937/1964. *The tongues of men and speech*. London: Oxford University Press.

Firth, J.R. 1957/1968. A synopsis of linguistic theory, 1930–1955. *Studies in linguistic analysis: special volume of the Philological Society*. Oxford: Blackwell, 1–32. Reprinted in F.R. Palmer (ed.) *Selected papers of J.R. Firth 1952–59*. Harlow: Longman, 168–205.

Flavell, L. & Flavell, R. 1992. *Dictionary of idioms and their origins*. London: Kyle Cathie.

Fletcher, P. 1994. Language acquisition in the child. In R.E. Asher (ed.) *Encyclopedia of language & linguistics*. Oxford: Pergamon, 1903–1907.

Foster, P. 2001. Rules & routines: a consideration of their role in the task-based language production of native and non-native speakers. In M. Bygate, P. Skehan & M. Swain (eds.) *Researching pedagogic tasks: second language learning, teaching and testing*. London, New York: Longman, 75–94.

Foster, S.H. 1990. *The communicative competence of young children*. London, New York: Longman.

Fowler, A.E. & Liberman, I.Y. 1995. The role of phonology and orthography in morphological awareness. In L.B. Feldman (ed.) *Morphological aspects of language processing*. Hillsdale, NJ: Lawrence Erlbaum, 157–188.

Francis, G. 1993. A corpus-driven approach to grammar. In M. Baker, G. Francis & E. Tognini-Bonelli (eds.) *Text and technology: in honour of John Sinclair*. Philadelphia/Amsterdam: John Benjamins, 137–156.

Galloway, L. & Krashen, S.D. 1980. Cerebral organization in bilingualism and second language. In R.C. Scarcella & S.D. Krashen. *Research in second language acquisition: Selected papers of the Los Angeles 2nd Language Acquisition Research Forum*. Rowley, MA: Newbury House, 74–80.

Gardner, H. 1985. Loss of language. In V.P. Clark, P.A. Eschholz & A.F. Rosa (eds.) *Language: introductory readings* (4th edition). New York: St. Martin's Press, 184–195.

Gardner, H., Brownell, H.H., Wapner, W. & Michelow, D. 1983. Missing the point: the role of the right hemisphere in the processing of complex linguistic materials. In E. Perecman (ed.) *Cognitive processing in the right hemisphere*. New York: Academic Press, 169–191.

Gardner, H., Ling, P.K., Flamm, L. & Silverman, J. 1975. Comprehension & appreciation of humorous material following brain damage. *Brain* 98:399–412.

Garton, A. & Pratt, C. 1998. *Learning to be literate* (2nd edition). Oxford: Blackwell.

References

Garvey, C. 1977. Play with language & speech. In S. Ervin-Tripp & C. Mitchell-Kernan (eds.) *Child discourse*. New York: Academic Press, 27–47.

Gatbonton, E. & Segalowitz, N. 1988. Creative automatization: principles for promoting fluency within a communicative framework. *TESOL Quarterly* 22(3):473–492.

Gazzaniga, M.S. 1977. Consistency and diversity in brain organization. *Annals of the New York Academy of Sciences* 299:415–423.

Gazzaniga, M.S., Eliassen, J.C., Nisenson, L., Wessinger, M., Fendrich, R. & Baynes, K. 1996. Collaboration between the hemispheres of a callosotomy patient: emerging right hemisphere speech and the left hemisphere interpreter. *Brain* 119:1255–1262.

Gelman, R. & Shatz, M. 1977. Appropriate speech adjustments: the operation of conversational constraints on talk to two-year-olds. In M. Lewis & L.A. Rosenblum (eds.) *Interaction, conversation & the development of language*. New York: Wiley, 27–61.

Gerken, L. 1996. Prosody's role in language acquisition and adult parsing. *Journal of Psycholinguistic Research* 25(2):345–356.

Geschwind, N. 1979. Specializations of the human brain. *Scientific American* 240:158–168.

Gibbs, R.W., Jr. 1987. Linguistic factors in children's understanding of idioms. *Journal of Child Language* 14:569–586.

Gibbs, R.W., Jr. 1991. Semantic analyzability in children's understanding of idioms. *Journal of Speech & Hearing Research* 34:613–620.

Givón, T. 1989. *Mind, code and context*. Hillsdale, NJ: Lawrence Erlbaum.

Gleason, J.B. 1980. The acquisition of social speech routines & politeness formulas. In H. Giles, W.P. Robinson & P.M. Smith (eds.) *Language: social psychological perspectives*. Oxford: Pergamon, 21–27.

Gleason, J.B. & Weintraub, S. 1976. The acquisition of routines in child language. *Language in Society* 5:129–136.

Gleitman, L.R., Gleitman, H., Landau, B. & Wanner, E. 1988. Where learning begins: initial representations for language learning. In F.J. Newmeyer (ed.) *Linguistics: the Cambridge survey. III. Language: psychological and biological aspects*. Cambridge: Cambridge University Press, 150–193.

Goldfarb, R. & Halpern, H. 1991. Impairments of naming and word-finding. In C. Code (ed.) *The characteristics of aphasia*. Hove: Lawrence Erlbaum, 33–52.

Goldfield, B.A. & Snow, C.E. 1997. Individual differences: implications for the study of language acquisition. In J.B. Gleason (ed.) *The development of language* (4th edition). Boston: Allyn & Bacon, 317–347.

Goldman-Eisler, F. 1968. *Psycholinguistics: experiments in spontaneous speech*. London, New York: Academic Press.

Goldstein, K. 1948. *Language and language disturbances*. New York: Grune & Stratton.

Golinkoff, R.M. & Hirsh-Pasek, K. 1995. Reinterpreting children's sentence comprehension: toward a new framework. In P. Fletcher & B. MacWhinney (eds.) *Handbook of child language*. Oxford: Blackwell, 430–461.

Goodglass, H. 1993. *Understanding aphasia*. San Diego: Academic Press.

Goodglass, H. & Mayer, J. 1958. Agrammatism in aphasia. *Journal of Speech and Hearing Disorders* 23(1):99–111.

Goodglass, H. & Wingfield, A. 1997. Word-finding deficits in aphasia: brain-behavior relations and clinical symptomology. In H. Goodglass & A. Wingfield (eds.) *Anomia: neuroanatomical and cognitive correlates*. San Diego: Academic Press, 3–27.

Grace, G.W. 1981. *An essay on language*. Columbia, SC: Hornbeam.

Grace, G.W. 1995. Why I don't believe that language acquisition involves the construction of grammar. *Ethnolinguistic Notes* 4(1). *http://www2.hawaii.edu/~grace/*

Granger, S. 1998. Prefabricated patterns in advanced EFL writing: collocations and formulae. In A.P. Cowie (ed.) *Phraseology: theory, analysis and applications*. Oxford: Clarendon Press, 145–160.

Graybiel, A.M. 1998. The basal ganglia & chunking of action repertoires. *Neurobiology of Learning and Memory* 70:119–136.

Griffin, P. & Mehan, H. 1981. Sense & ritual in classroom discourse. In F. Coulmas (ed.) *Conversational routine*. The Hague: Mouton, 187–213.

Gross, R. 1996. *Psychology: the science of mind and behaviour* (3rd edition). London: Hodder & Stoughton.

Guillaume, P. 1927/1973. First stages of sentence formation in children's speech. In C.A. Ferguson & D.I. Slobin (eds.) 1973. *Studies in child language development*. New York: Holt, Rinehart & Winston, 522–541.

Haggo, D. & Kuiper, K. 1983. Review of *Conversational routine* by Coulmas (ed.) *Linguistics* 21:531–551.

Hakuta, K. 1974. Prefabricated patterns and the emergence of structure in second language acquisition. *Language Learning* 24(2):289–297.

Hakuta, K. 1976. A case study of a Japanese child learning English as a second language. *Language Learning* 26(2):321–351.

Hallé, P.A. & Boysson-Bardies, B. de. 1994. Emergence of an early receptive lexicon: infants' recognition of words. *Infant Behavior and Development* 17:119–129.

Halliday, M.A.K. 1975. *Learning how to mean*. London: Arnold.

Hanania, E.A.S. & Gradman, H.L. 1977. Acquisition of English structures: a case study of an adult native speaker of Arabic in an English-speaking environment. *Language Learning* 27(1):75–91.

Hanks, P. 1987. Definitions and explanations. In J.McH. Sinclair (ed.) *Looking up*. London: Collins, 116–136.

Harley, T.A. 1993. Phonological activation of semantic competitors during lexical access in speech production. *Language and Cognitive Processes* 8(3): 291–309.

Hatch, E., Peck, S. & Wagner-Gough, J. 1979. A look at process in child second-language acquisition. In E. Ochs & B.B. Schieffelin (eds.) *Developmental pragmatics*. New York: Academic Press, 269–278.

Head, H. 1926. *Aphasia and kindred speech disorders, vols. 1 & 2*. Cambridge: The University Press.

Hendrick, R. 1995. Morphosyntax. In G. Webelhuth (ed.) *Government and binding theory and the minimalist program*. Oxford: Blackwell, 297–347.

Henry, A. 1996. Natural chunks of language: teaching speech through speech. *English for Specific Purposes* 15(4):295–309.

Hickey, F. & Kuiper, K. 2000. 'A deep depression covers the South Tasman Sea': New Zealand Meteorological Office weather forecasts. In A. Bell & K. Kuiper (eds.) *New Zealand English*. Amsterdam: John Benjamins, 279–296.

Hickey, T. 1993. Identifying formulas in first language acquisition. *Journal of Child Language* 20:27–41.

Hinnenkamp, V. 1980. The refusal of second language learning in interethnic context. In H. Giles, W.P. Robinson & P.M. Smith (eds.) *Language: social psychological perspectives*. Oxford: Pergamon, 179–184.

Hirsh, K.W. & Funnell, E. 1995. Those old, familiar things: age of acquisition, familiarity and lexical access in progressive aphasia. *Journal of Neurolinguistics* 9(1):23–32.

Hirsh-Pasek, K. & Golinkoff, R.M. 1996. *The origins of grammar*. Cambridge, MA: MIT Press.

Hittmair-Delazer, M., Andree, B., Semenza, C., De Bleser, R. & Benke, T. 1994. Naming by German compounds. *Journal of Neurolinguistics* 8:27–41.

Hjelmslev, L. 1943/1969. Prolegomena to a theory of language (Transl. F.J. Whitfield). Madison: University of Wisconsin Press.

House, J. 1993. Toward a model for the analysis of inappropriate responses in native/nonnative interaction. In G. Kasper & S. Blum-Kulka (eds.) *Interlanguage pragmatics*. New York, Oxford: Oxford University Press, 161–183.

House, J. 1996. Developing pragmatic fluency in English as a foreign language. *Studies in Second Language Acquisition* 18:225–252.

Howarth, P. 1998a. Phraseology and second language proficiency. *Applied Linguistics* 19(1):24–44.

Howarth, P. 1998b. The phraseology of learners' academic writing. In A.P. Cowie (ed.) *Phraseology*. Oxford: Clarendon Press, 161–186.

Huang, J. & Hatch, E.M. 1978. A Chinese child's acquisition of English. In E.M. Hatch (ed.) *Second language acquisition: a book of readings*. Rowley, MA: Newbury House, 118–131.

Hudson, J. 1998. *Perspectives on fixedness: applied and theoretical*. Lund: Lund University Press.

Huebner, T. 1983. *A longitudinal analysis of the acquisition of English*. Ann Arbor, MI: Karoma.

Hughes, J.E. 1998. *Canllawiau ysgrifennu cymraeg*. Llandysul, Ceredigion: Welsh Language Board/Gomer.

Hughlings Jackson, J. 1866. Notes on the physiology and pathology of language. In J. Taylor (ed.) 1958. *Selected writings of John Hughlings Jackson, vol. 2*. London: Staples Press, 121–128.

Hughlings Jackson, J. 1874. On the nature of the duality of the brain. In J. Taylor (ed.) 1958. *Selected writings of John Hughlings Jackson, vol. 2*. London: Staples Press, 129–145.

Hunston, S. & Francis, G. 2000. *Pattern Grammar: a corpus-driven approach to the lexical grammar of English*. Amsterdam: John Benjamins.

Hymes, D.H. 1962/1968. The ethnography of speaking. In T. Gladwin & W.C. Sturtevant (eds.) *Anthropology & Human Behavior*. Washington, DC:

Anthropological Society of Washington, 13–53. Reprinted in J.A. Fishman (ed.) 1968. *Readings in the sociology of language.* The Hague/Paris: Mouton, 99–138.

Irujo, S. 1986. A piece of cake: learning and teaching idioms. *ELT Journal* 40(3):236–242.

Irujo, S. 1993. Steering clear: avoidance in the production of idioms. *International Review of Applied Linguistics in Language Teaching* 31(3):205–219.

Itoh, H. & Hatch, E. 1978. Second language acquisition: a case study. In E.M. Hatch (ed.) *Second language acquisition: a book of readings.* Rowley, MA: Newbury House, 76–88.

Jackendoff, R. 1997. *The architecture of the language faculty.* Cambridge, MA: MIT Press.

Jaffe, J. 1978. Parliamentary procedure and the brain. In A.W. Siegman & S. Feldstein (eds.) *Nonverbal behavior and communication.* Hillsdale, NJ: Lawrence Erlbaum, 55–66.

Jakobson, R. 1980/1990. Brain and language. *New York University Slavic Papers.* Columbus, OH: Slavica. Reprinted in L.R. Waugh & M. Monville-Burston (eds.) 1990. *On language: Roman Jakobson.* Cambridge, MA: Harvard University Press, 498–513.

Jaworski, A. 1990. The acquisition & perception of formulaic language & foreign language teaching. *Multilingua* 9(4):397–411.

Jay, T. 1999. *Why we curse: a neuro-psycho-social theory of speech.* Amsterdam: John Benjamins.

Jeremias, J.M.V. 1982. The 'social' component in the English classroom: semantic & pragmatic considerations. *Anglo-American Studies* 2(1): 63–73.

Jespersen, O. 1924/1976. Living grammar. In *The philosophy of grammar.* London: George Allen & Unwin, 17–29. Reprinted in D.D. Bornstein (ed.) 1976. *Readings in the theory of grammar.* Cambridge, MA: Winthrop Publishers, 82–93.

Joad, C.E.M. (ed.). 1939. *How to write, think and speak correctly.* London: Odhams Press.

Joanette, Y., Goulet, P. & Hannequin, D. 1990. *Right hemisphere and verbal communication.* New York: Springer-Verlag.

Kamhi, A.G. 1986. The elusive first word: the importance of the naming insight for the development of referential speech. *Journal of Child Language* 13:155–161.

Karniol, R. 1990. Second language acquisition via immersion in daycare. *Journal of Child Language* 17:147–170.

Kasper, G. 1995. Routine & indirection in interlanguage pragmatics. In L. Bouton & Y. Kachru (eds.) *Pragmatics & Language Learning Monograph*, series vol. 6, 59–78.

Keenan, E.O. 1977. Making it last: repetition in children's discourse. In S. Ervin-Tripp & C. Mitchell-Kernan (eds.) *Child discourse.* New York: Academic Press, 125–138.

Keller, E. 1981. Gambits: conversational strategy signals. In F. Coulmas (ed.) *Conversational routine.* The Hague: Mouton, 93–113.

Kenyeres, A. 1938. Comment une petite hongroise de sept ans apprend le français. *Archives de Psychologie* 26(104):321–366.

Kerbel, D. & Grunwell, P. 1997. Idioms in the classroom: an investigation of language unit and mainstream teachers' use of idioms. *Child Language Teaching and Therapy* 13:113–123.

Klein, W. & Perdue, C. 1992. *Utterance structure*. Amsterdam: John Benjamins.

Krashen, S. & Scarcella, R. 1978. On routines and patterns in language acquisition and performance. *Language Learning* 28(2):283–300.

Kuiper, K. 1991. The evolution of an oral tradition: race-calling in Canterbury, New Zealand. *Oral Tradition* 6(1):19–34.

Kuiper, K. 1996. *Smooth talkers: the linguistic performance of auctioneers and sportscasters*. Mahwah, NJ: Lawrence Erlbaum.

Kuiper, K. & Austin, P. 1990. They're off and racing now: the speech of the New Zealand race caller. In A. Bell & J. Holmes (eds.) *New Zealand ways of speaking English*, 195–220. Clevedon: Multilingual Matters, 195–220.

Kuiper, K. & Flindall, M. 2000. Social rituals, formulaic speech and small talk at the supermarket checkout. In J. Coupland (ed.) *Small talk*. London, New York: Longman, 183–207.

Kuiper, K. & Haggo, D. 1984. Livestock auctions, oral poetry, and ordinary language. *Language in Society* 13:205–234.

Kuiper, K. & Tan Gek Lin, D. 1989. Cultural congruence and conflict in the acquisition of formulae in a second language. In O. Garcia & R. Otheguy (eds.) *English across cultures: cultures across English*. Berlin: Mouton, 281–304.

Lamb, S.M. 1998. *Pathways of the brain*. Amsterdam: John Benjamins.

Langacker, R.W. 1986. An introduction to cognitive grammar. *Cognitive Science* 10:1–40.

Langacker, R.W. 1987. *Foundations of cognitive grammar, vol. I: theoretical prerequisites*. Stanford, CA: Stanford University Press.

Langacker, R.W. 1991. *Foundations of cognitive grammar, vol. II: descriptive application*. Stanford, CA: Stanford University Press.

Langacker, R.W. 1995. Cognitive grammar. In J. Verscheuren, J-O. Östman & J. Blommaert (eds.) *Handbook of pragmatics manual*. Amsterdam: John Benjamins, 105–111.

Larsen, B., Skinhøj, E. & Lassen, N.A. 1978. Variations in regional cortical blood flow in the right & left hemispheres during automatic speech. *Brain* 101:193–209.

Lattey, E. 1986. Pragmatic classification of idioms as an aid for the language learner. *International Review of Applied Linguistics in Language Teaching* 24(3):217–233.

Laver, J. 1981. Linguistic routines & politeness in greeting & parting. In F. Coulmas (ed.) *Conversational routine*. The Hague: Mouton, 289–304.

Lecours, A.R., L'Hermitte, F. & Bryans, B. 1983. *Aphasiology*. London: Ballière Tindall.

Lecours, A.R., Mehler, J. & Parente, M.A. 1988. Illiteracy and brain damage 3: a contribution to the study of speech and language disorders in illiterates with unilateral brain damage (initial testing). *Neuropsychologia* 26(4):575–589.

Lecours, A.R., Mehler, J., Parente, M.A., Caldeira, A., Cary, L., Castro, M.J., Dehaut, F., Degado, R., Gurd, J., Karmann, D., Jakubovitz, R., Osorio, Z., Cabral, L.S. & Junquiera, A.M.S. 1987. Illiteracy and brain damage 1: aphasia testing in culturally contrasted populations (control subjects). *Neuropsychologia* 25(1B):231–245.

Lecours, A.R., Osborn, E., Travis, S., Rouillon, F. & Lavallée-Huynh, G. 1981. Jargons. In J.W. Brown (ed.) *Jargonaphasia*. New York: Academic Press, 9–38.

Lennon, P. 1990. Investigating fluency in EFL: a quantitative approach. *Language Learning* 40(3):387–417.

Lennon, P. 2000. The lexical element in spoken second language fluency. In H. Riggenbach (ed.) *Perspectives on fluency*. Ann Arbor: University of Michigan Press, 25–42.

Leonard, C.L., Waters, G.S. & Caplan, D. 1997a. The use of contextual information by right brain-damaged individuals in the resolution of ambiguous pronouns. *Brain and Language* 57:309–342.

Leonard, C.L., Waters, G.S. & Caplan, D. 1997b. The use of contextual information related to general world knowledge by right brain-damaged individuals in pronoun resolution. *Brain and Language* 57:343–359.

Leopold, W.F. 1978. A child's learning of two languages. In E. Hatch (ed.) *Second language acquisition: a book of readings*. Rowley, MA: Newbury House, 23–32.

Le Page, R.B. & Tabouret-Keller, A. 1985. Acts of identity Cambridge: Cambridge University Press.

Levelt, W.J.M. 1989. *Speaking: from intention to articulation*. Cambridge, MA: MIT Press.

Levorato, M.C. & Cacciari, C. 1992. Children's comprehension and production of idioms: the role of context and familiarity. *Journal of Child Language* 19:415–433.

Lewis, M. 1993. *The lexical approach*. Hove: Teacher Training Publications.

Lewis, M. 1997. Pedagogical implications of the lexical approach. In J. Coady & T. Huckin (eds.) *Second language vocabulary acquisition*. Cambridge: Cambridge University Press, 255–270.

Lieven, E.V.M. 1978. Conversations between mothers and young children: individual differences and their possible implication for the study of language learning. In N. Waterson & C. Snow (eds.) *The development of communication*. Chichester: Wiley, 173–187.

Lieven, E.V.M. 1984. Interactional style and children's language learning. *Topics in Language Disorders*, Sept:15–23.

Lieven, E.V.M., Pine, J.M. & Barnes, H.D. 1992. Individual differences in early vocabulary development: redefining the referential-expressive distinction. *Journal of Child Language* 19:287–310.

Linnakylä, P. 1980. Hi superman: what is most functional English for a Finnish 5-yr-old. *Journal of Pragmatics* 4:367–392.

Locke, J. 1993. *The child's path to spoken language*. Cambridge, MA: Harvard University Press.

Locke, J. 1994. Gradual emergence of developmental language disorders. *Journal of Speech and Hearing Research* 37:608–616.

Locke, J. 1995. Development of the capacity for spoken language. In P. Fletcher & B. MacWhinney (eds.) *The handbook of child language*. Oxford: Blackwell, 278–302.

Locke, J. 1997. A theory of neurolinguistic development. *Brain and Language* 58:265–326.

Locke, J. 1999. Towards a biological science of language development. In M. Barrett (ed.) *The development of language*. Hove: Psychology Press, 373–395.

Lounsbury, F.G. 1963. Linguistics & psychology. In S. Koch (ed.) *Psychology: a study of science, vol. 6: investigations of man as socius*. New York: McGraw Hill, 552–582.

Luria, A.R. & Tsvetkova, L.S. 1970. The mechanism of 'dynamic aphasia'. In M. Bierwisch & K.E. Heidolph (eds.) *Progress in linguistics: a collection of papers*. The Hague: Mouton, 187–197.

Lyons, J. 1968. *Introduction to theoretical linguistics*. Cambridge: Cambridge University Press.

McCarthy, M. 1998. *Spoken language and applied linguistics*. Cambridge: Cambridge University Press.

McClelland, J.L. & Elman, J.L. 1986. The TRACE model of speech perception. *Cognitive Psychology* 18:1–86.

McCrone, J. 1999. States of mind. *New Scientist* 2178, 20th March:30–33.

McElduff, K. & Drummond, S.S. 1991. Communicative functions of automatic speech in non-fluent dysphasia. *Aphasiology* 5:265–278.

MacKay, D.M. 1951. In search of basic symbols. *Cybernetics: transactions of the 8th conference*, 181–221.

McLaughlin, B. 1978. *Second language acquisition in childhood*. Hillsdale, NJ: Lawrence Erlbaum.

McNeill, D. & McNeill, N.B. 1973. What does a child mean when he says 'no'? In C.A. Ferguson & D.I. Slobin (eds.) *Studies of child language acquisition*. New York: Holt, Rinehart & Winston, 619–627.

MacWhinney, B. 1999. The emergence of language from embodiment. In B. MacWhinney (ed.) *The emergence of language*. Mahwah, NJ: Lawrence Erlbaum, 213–256.

Mahootian, S. 1996. A competence model of codeswitching. In J. Arnold, R. Blake, B. Davidson, S. Schwenter & J. Solomon (eds.) *Sociolinguistic variation: data, theory & analysis*. Stanford, CA: Center for the Study of Language and Information, 387–399.

Makkai, A. 1972. *Idiom structure in English*. The Hague: Mouton.

Malinowski, B. 1923/1946. The problem of meaning in primitive languages. In C.K. Ogden & I.A. Richards. 1946. *The meaning of meaning* (8th edition). London: Kegan Paul, Trench, Trubner & Co. Supplement I, 296–336.

Malmkjaer, K. 1991. Bilingualism and multilingualism. In K. Malmkjaer (ed.) *The linguistics encyclopedia*. London: Routledge, 57–65.

Malvern, D.D. & Richards, B.J. 1997. A new measure of lexical diversity. In A. Ryan & A. Wray (eds.) *Evolving models of language*. Clevedon: Multilingual Matters, 58–71.

Manes, J. & Wolfson, N. 1981. The compliment formula. In F. Coulmas (ed.) *Conversational routine*. The Hague: Mouton, 116–132.

Marantz, A. 1995. The minimalist program. In G. Webelhuth (ed.) *Government and binding theory and the minimalist program*. Cambridge, MA: Blackwell, 349–382.

Marshall, R.C. 2000. Speech fluency and aphasia. In H. Riggenbach (ed.) *Perspectives on fluency*. Ann Arbor: University of Michigan Press, 74–88.

Marslen-Wilson, W.D. & Tyler, L.K. 1980. The temporal structure of spoken language understanding. *Cognition* 8:1–71.

Marslen-Wilson, W.D., Tyler, L.K., Waksler, R. & Older, L. 1994. Morphology and meaning in the English mental lexicon. *Psychological Review* 101(1):3–33.

Maslow, A.H. 1968. *Toward a psychology of being* (2nd edition). New York: D. Van Nostrand Company.

Mayer, J., Dogil, G., Ackermann, H., Erb, M., Grodd, W., Haider, H., Riecker, A. & Wildgruber, D. 1999. Prosody in speech perception. *Neuroimage* 9(6), part 2:S1065.

Meisel, J.M., Clahsen, H. & Pienemann, M. 1981. On determining developmental stages in natural second language acquisition. *Studies in Second Language Acquisition* 3(2):109–135.

Mel'čuk, I. 1998. Collocations and lexical functions. In A.P. Cowie (ed.) *Phraseology: theory, analysis and applications*. Oxford: Clarendon Press, 23–53.

Meyer, M., Friederici, A.D. & von Cramon, D.Y. 1999. Towards the cerebral organization of speech: event-related fMRI responses to syntax, semantics and phonology. *Neuroimage* 9(6), part 2:S1066.

Michaelis, L.A. & Lambrecht, K. 1996. Toward a construction-based theory of language function: the case of nominal extraposition. *Language* 72(2):215–247.

Miller, G.A. 1956. The magical number seven, plus or minus two: some limits on our capacity for processing information. *Psychological Review* 63(2):81–97.

Miller, G. & Chomsky, N. 1963. Finitary models of language users. In R.D. Luce, R.R. Bush & E. Galanter (eds.) *Handbook of mathematical psychology, vol. 2*. New York: Wiley, 421–491.

Milton, J. & Evans, V. 1998. *A good turn of phrase: advanced idiom practice*. Swansea: Express.

Mitchell, R. & Martin, C. 1997. Rote learning, creativity and 'understanding' in classroom foreign language teaching. *Language Teaching Research* 1(1):1–27.

Moon, R. 1992. Textual aspects of fixed expression in learners' dictionaries. In P.J.L. Arnaud & H. Béjoint (eds.) *Vocabulary & applied linguistics*. Basingstoke: Macmillan, 13–27.

Moon, R. 1997. Vocabulary connections: multi-word items in English. In N. Schmitt & M. McCarthy (eds.) *Vocabulary: description, acquisition and pedagogy*. Cambridge: Cambridge University Press, 40–63.

Moon, R. 1998a. *Fixed expressions and idioms in English*. Oxford: Clarendon Press.

Moon, R. 1998b. Frequencies and forms of phrasal lexemes in English. In A.P. Cowie (ed.) *Phraseology*. Oxford: Clarendon Press, 79–100.

Morton, J. 1969. Interaction of information in word recognition. *Psychological Review* 76:165–178.

Moscovitch, M. 1983. The linguistic and emotional functions of the normal right hemisphere. In E. Perecman (ed.) *Cognitive processing in the right hemisphere.* New York: Academic Press, 57–82.

Murdoch, B.E. 1996. The role of subcortical structures in language: clinico-neuroradiological studies of brain-damaged subjects. In B. Dodd, R. Campbell & L. Worrall (eds.) *Evaluating theories of language: evidence from disordered communication.* London: Whurr, 137–160.

Murphy, M.L. 2000. Knowledge *of* words versus knowledge *about* words: the conceptual basis of lexical relations. In B. Peeters (ed.) *The lexicon-encyclopedia interface.* Amsterdam: Elsevier, 317–348.

Musso, M., Weiller, C., Kiebel, S., Rijnties, M. & Müller, P. 1999. The ease of performance. *Neuroimage* 9(6), part 2:S1036.

Myers-Scotton, C. 1993. *Duelling languages: grammatical structure in codeswitching.* Oxford: Clarendon Press.

Myles, F., Hooper, J. & Mitchell, R. 1998. Rote or rule? Exploring the role of formulaic language in classroom foreign language learning. *Language Learning* 48(3):323–363.

Myles, F., Mitchell, R. & Hooper, J. 1999. Interrogative chunks in French L2: a basis for creative construction? *Studies in Second Language Acquisition* 21(1):49–80.

Nation, I.S.P. 1982. Beginning to learn foreign vocabulary: a review of the research. *Regional English Language Centre Journal* (Singapore) 14:14–36.

Nation, I.S.P. 1990. *Teaching and learning vocabulary.* Boston: Heinle & Heinle.

Nattinger, J.R. & DeCarrico, J.S. 1992. *Lexical phrases and language teaching.* Oxford: Oxford University Press.

Nelson, K. 1973. *Structure and strategy in learning to talk.* Monographs of the Society for Research in Child Development, seres no. 149, nos. 1–2.

Nelson, K. 1975. The nominal shift in semantic-syntactic development. *Cognitive Psychology* 7:461–479.

Nelson, K. 1981. Individual differences in language development: implications for development and language. *Developmental Psychology* 17(2):170–187.

Nespoulous, J-L., Code, C., Virbel, J. & Lecours, A.R. 1998. Hypotheses on the dissociation between 'referential' and 'modalizing' verbal behavior in aphasia. *Applied Psycholinguistics* 19:311–331.

Nickels, L. 1997. *Spoken word production and its breakdown in aphasia.* Hove, Sussex: Psychology Press.

Nippold, M.A. & Martin, S.T. 1989. Idiom interpretation in isolation versus context: a developmental study with adolescents. *Journal of Speech and Hearing Research* 32:59–66.

Obler, L.K., Centeno, J. & Eng, N. 1995. Bilingual and polyglot aphasia. In L. Menn, M. O'Connor, L.K. Obler & A. Holland (eds.) *Non-fluent aphasia in a multilingual world.* Amsterdam: John Benjamins, 132–143.

Ochs, E. & Schieffelin, B. 1995. The impact of language socialization on grammatical development. In P. Fletcher & B. MacWhinney (eds.) *The handbook of child language.* Oxford: Blackwell, 73–94.

Oelschlaeger, M.L. & Damico, J.S. 1998. Spontaneous verbal repetition: a social strategy in aphasic conversation. *Aphasiology* 12(11):971–988.

Opie, I. & Opie, P. 1959. *The lore & language of schoolchildren*. Oxford: Clarendon Press.

Opie, I. & Opie, P. 1969. *Children's games in street and playground*. Oxford: The Clarendon Press.

Oppenheim, N. 2000. The importance of recurrent sequences for nonnative speaker fluency and cognition. In H. Riggenbach (ed.) *Perspectives on fluency*. Ann Arbor: University of Michigan Press, 220–240.

Oskaar, E. 1977. On becoming trilingual. In C. Molony, H. Zobl & W. Stölting (eds.) *German in contact with other languages*. Kronberg: Scriptor Verlag, 296–306.

Pan, B.A. & Gleason, J.B. 1997. Semantic development: learning the meanings of words. In J.B. Gleason (ed.) *The development of language* (4th edition). Boston: Allyn & Bacon, 122–158.

Paradis, M. (ed.) 1983. *Readings on aphasia in bilinguals and polyglots*. Montreal: Didier.

Paradis, M. 1995. *Aspects of bilingual aphasia*. Oxford: Pergamon.

Pawley, A. 1985. On speech formulas and linguistic competence. *Lenguas Modernas* 12:84–104.

Pawley, A. 1986. Lexicalization. In D. Tannen & J.E. Alatis (eds.) *Language & linguistics: the interdependence of theory, data & application*. Georgetown University Round Table on Languages & Linguistics 1985, 98–120.

Pawley, A. 1991. How to talk cricket: on linguistic competence in a subject matter. In R. Blust (ed.) *Currents in Pacific linguistics: papers on Austronesian languages and ethnolinguistics in honour of George W. Grace*. Canberra: Pacific Linguistics C-117, 339–368.

Pawley, A. 1996. Grammarian's lexicon, lexicographer's lexicon: worlds apart. *KVHAA Konferenser* 36, 189–211.

Pawley, A. & Syder, F.H. 1983. Two puzzles for linguistic theory: nativelike selection and nativelike fluency. In J.C. Richards & R.W. Schmidt (eds.) *Language and communication*. New York: Longman, 191–226.

Pawley, A. & Syder, F.H. 2000. The one-clause-at-a-time hypothesis. In H. Riggenbach (ed.) *Perspectives on fluency*. Ann Arbor: University of Michigan Press, 163–199.

Perdue, C. (ed.) 1984. *Second language acquisition by adult immigrants: a field manual*. European Science Foundation. Rowley, MA: Newbury House.

Perdue, C. (ed.) 1993. *Adult language acquisition: cross-linguistic perspectives, vol. II: the results*. European Science Foundation. Cambridge: Cambridge University Press.

Perkins, M.R. 1994. Repetitiveness in language disorders: a new analytical procedure. *Clinical Linguistics & Phonetics* 8(4):321–336.

Perkins, M.R. 1999. Productivity and formulaicity in language development. In M. Garman, C. Letts, B. Richards, C. Schelletter & S. Edwards (eds.) *Issues in normal & disordered child language: from phonology to narrative*. Special Issue of The New Bulmershe Papers. Reading: University of Reading, 51–67.

Peters, A.M. 1977. Language learning strategies: does the whole equal the sum of the parts? *Language* 53(3):560–573.

Peters, A.M. 1983. *Units of language acquisition.* Cambridge: Cambridge University Press.

Peters, A.M. 1995. Strategies in the acquisition of syntax. In P. Fletcher & B. MacWhinney (eds.) *The handbook of child language.* Oxford: Blackwell, 462–482.

Pinker, S. 1994. *The language instinct.* Harmondworth: Penguin.

Plunkett, K. 1993. Lexical segmentation and vocabulary growth in early language acquisition. *Journal of Child Language* 20:43–60.

Poulin-Dubois, D., Graham, S. & Sippola, L. 1995. Early lexical development: the contribution of parental labelling and infants' categorization abilities. *Journal of Child Language* 22:325–343.

Raichle, M.E. 1998. The neural correlates of consciousness: an analysis of cognitive skill learning. *Philosophical Transactions of the Royal Society of London, Series B* 353:1889–1901.

Rampton, B. 1987. Stylistic variability and not speaking 'normal' English: some post-Labovian approaches and their implications for the study of interlanguage. In R. Ellis (ed.) *Second language acquisition in context.* Englewood Cliffs, NJ: Prentice-Hall, 47–58.

Raupach, M. 1984. Formulae in second language speech production. In H.W. Dechert, D. Möhle & M. Raupach (eds.) *Second language production.* Tübingen: Gunter Narr, 114–137.

Rehbein, J. 1987. Multiple formulae: aspects of Turkish migrant workers' German in intercultural communication. In K. Knapp, W. Enninger & A. Knapp-Potthoff (eds.) *Analysing intercultural communication.* Berlin: Mouton, 215–248.

Reis, A. & Castro-Caldas, A. 1997. Illiteracy: a cause for biased cognitive development. *Journal of the International Neuropsychological Society* 3:444–450.

Rescorla, L. & Okuda, S. 1987. Modular patterns in second language acquisition. *Applied Psycholinguistics* 8:281–308.

Robinson, P.J. 1986. Constituency or dependency in the units of language acquisition? An approach to describing the learner's analysis of formulae. *Linguisticae Investigationes* 10(2):417–437.

Russell, W.R. & Espir, M.L.E. 1961. *Traumatic aphasia: a study of aphasia in war wounds of the brain.* Oxford: Oxford University Press.

Salomon, E. 1914/1983. Motor aphasia with agrammatism and sensory agrammatic disturbances (excerpts). In M. Paradis (ed.) *Readings on aphasia in bilinguals and polyglots.* Montreal: Didier, 118–128.

Sampson, G. 1996. From centre embedding to corpus linguistics. In J. Thomas & M. Short (eds.) *Using corpora for language research.* London, New York: Longman, 14–26.

Saussure, F.De. 1916/1966. *Course in general linguistics.* New York: McGraw-Hill.

Scarcella, R. 1979. 'Watch up!': a study of verbal routines in adults second language performance. *Working Papers in Bilingualism* 19:79–88.

Schmidt, R.W. 1983. Interaction, acculturation, and the acquisition of communicative competence: a case study of an adult. In N. Wolfson & E. Judd (eds.) *Sociolinguistics and language acquisition.* Rowley, MA: Newbury House, 137–174.

Schmidt, R.W. 1993. Psychological mechanisms underlying second language fluency. *Studies in Second Language Acquisition* 14:357–385.

Schmidt, R.W. & Frota, S.N. 1986. Developing basic conversation ability in a second language: a case study of an adult learner of Portuguese. In R.R. Day (ed.) *Talking to learn: conversation in second language acquisition.* Cambridge, MA: Newbury House, 237–326.

Schneiderman, E.I., Murasugi, K.G. & Saddy, J.D. 1992. Story arrangement ability in right brain-damaged patients. *Brain and Language* 43:107–120.

Schumann, J.H. 1978a. *The pidginization process: a model for second language acquisition.* Rowley, MA: Newbury House.

Schumann, J.H. 1978b. Second language acquisition: the pidginization hypothesis. In E.M. Hatch (ed.) *Second language acquisition: a book of readings.* Rowley, MA: Newbury House, 256–271.

Scoresby-Jackson, R.E. 1867. Case of aphasia with right hemiplegia. *Edinburgh Medical Journal* 12(8):696–706.

Sebeok, T.A. 1964. The structure and content of Cheremis charms. In D. Hymes (ed.) *Language in culture and society: a reader in linguistics and anthropology.* New York: Harper & Row, 356–371.

Segalowitz, N. 1997. Individual differences in second language acquisition. In A.M.B. DeGroot & J.F. Kroll (eds.) *Tutorials in bilingualism: psycholinguistic perspectives.* Mahwah, NJ: Lawrence Erlbaum, 85–112.

Segalowitz, N. 2000. Automaticity and attentional skill in fluent performance. In H. Riggenbach (ed.) *Perspectives on fluency.* Ann Arbor: University of Michigan Press, 200–219.

Segalowitz, N. 2001. On the evolving connections between psychology and linguistics. *Annual Review of Applied Linguistics* 21.

Segalowitz, N. & Segalowitz, S. 1993. Skilled performance, practice, and the differentiation of speed-up from automatization effects: evidence from second language word recognition. *Applied Psycholinguistics* 14:369–385.

Semenza, C., Luzzati, C. & Carabella, S. 1997. Morphological representation of compound nouns: a study on Italian aphasic patients. *Journal of Neurolinguistics* 10:33–43.

Shapira, R.G. 1978. The non-learning of English: case study of an adult. In E.M. Hatch (ed.) *Second language acquisition: a book of readings.* Rowley, MA: Newbury House, 246–255.

Shore, C.M. 1995. *Individual differences in language development.* Thousand Oaks, CA: Sage.

Simon, H.A. 1974. How big is a chunk? *Science* 183:482–488.

Sinclair, J.McH. 1987. Collocation: a progress report. In R. Steele & T. Treadgold (eds.) *Essays in honour of Michael Halliday.* Amsterdam: John Benjamins, 319–331.

Sinclair, J.McH. 1991. *Corpus, concordance, collocation.* Oxford: Oxford University Press.

Sinclair, J.McH. 1998. The lexical item. In E. Weigand (ed.) *Contrastive lexical semantics.* Amsterdam: John Benjamins, 1–24.

Sinclair, J.McH. & Renouf, A. 1988. A lexical syllabus for language learning. In R. Carter & M. McCarthy (eds.) *Vocabulary and language teaching.* London, New York: Longman, 140–160.

Skehan, P. 1996. *A cognitive approach to language learning*. Oxford: Oxford University Press.

Smith, A. 1966. Speech and other functions after left (dominant) hemispherectomy. *Journal of Neurology, Neurosurgery and Psychiatry* 29:467–471.

Snow, C.E. 1978. Mothers' speech to children learning language. In L. Bloom (ed.) *Readings in language development*. New York: Wiley, 489–506.

Snow, C.E. 1979. The development of conversation between mothers & babies. In V. Lee (ed.) *Language development*. London: Croom Helm/Open University Press, 235–249.

Snow, C.E. 1981. The uses of imitation. *Journal of Child Language* 8:205–212.

Speedie, L.J., Wertman, E., Ta'ir, J. & Heilman, K.M. 1993. Disruption of automatic speech following a right basal ganglia lesion. *Neurology* 43:1768–1774.

Sperber, D. & Wilson, D. 1987/1996. Précis of *Relevance: communication and cognition*. *Brain and Behavioral Sciences* 10:697–754. Reprinted in H. Geirsson & M. Losonsky (eds.) 1996. *Readings in language and mind*. Cambridge, MA: Blackwell, 460–486.

Stanley, C. & Goodrich, P. 1991. *Spanish phrase book*. London: BBC Books.

Starkie, E. 1958. *Baudelaire*. New York: New Directions.

Stevick, E.W. 1989. *Success with foreign languages*. Hemel Hempstead: Prentice Hall.

Stubbs, M. 1993. British traditions in text analysis: from Firth to Sinclair. In M. Baker, G. Francis & E. Tognini-Bonelli (eds.) *Text and technology: in honour of John Sinclair*. Philadelphia/Amsterdam: John Benjamins, 1–33.

Stubbs, M. 1995. Collocations and cultural connotations of common words. *Linguistics and Education* 7(4), 379–390.

Stubbs, M. 1996. *Text and corpus analysis*. Oxford: Blackwell.

Stubbs, M. 1997. 'Eine Sprache idiomatisch sprechen': Computer, Korpora, kommunikative Kompetenz und Kultur. In K.J. Mattheier (ed.) *Norm und Variation*. Frankfurt am Main: Peter Lang, 151–167.

Stubbs, M. 2000. Using very large text collections to study semantic schemas: a research note. In C. Heffer & H. Sauntson (eds.) *Words in Context*. CD-ROM. Birmingham: University of Birmingham.

Stubbs, M. In press. *Words and phrases: studies in corpus semantics*. Oxford: Blackwell.

Swain, M. & Lapkin, S. 1998. Interaction & second language learning: two adolescent French immersion students working together. *The Modern Language Journal* 82(3):321–336.

Swinney, D.A. & Cutler, A. 1979. The access and processing of idiomatic expressions. *Journal of Verbal Learning and Verbal Behavior* 18:523–534.

Tager-Flusberg, H. 1994. Language acquisition: grammar. In R.E. Asher (ed.) *Encyclopedia of language & linguistics*. Oxford: Pergamon, 1918–1924.

Tager-Flusberg, H. & Calkins, S. 1990. Does imitation facilitate the acquisition of grammar? Evidence from a study of autistic, Down's syndrome & normal children. *Journal of Child Language* 17:591–606.

Tannen, D. & Öztek, P.C. 1981. Health to our mouths: formulaic expressions in Turkish and Greek. In F. Coulmas (ed.) *Conversational routine*. The Hague: Mouton, 37–54.

Thomas, S. (ed.) 1997. *Magu'r babi: speaking Welsh with children.* Cardiff: University of Wales Press.

Tippett, L.J., Glosser, G. & Farah, M.J. 1996. A category-specific naming impairment after temporal lobectomy. *Neuropsychologia* 34(2):139–146.

Tomasello, M. 1992. *First verbs: a case study of early grammatical development.* Cambridge: Cambridge University Press.

Tomasello, M. & Brooks, P.J. 1999. Early syntactic development: a construction grammar approach. In M. Barrett (ed.) *The development of language.* Hove: Psychology Press, 161–190.

Towell, R., Hawkins, R. & Bazergui, N. 1996. The development of fluency in advanced learners of French. *Applied Linguistics* 17(1):84–119.

Tucker, G.H. 1998. *The lexicogrammar of adjectives: a systemic functional approach to lexis.* London, New York: Cassell.

Van Lancker, D. 1987. Nonpropositional speech: neurolinguistic studies. In A.W. Ellis (ed.) *Progress in the psychology of language, vol. 3.* Hillsdale, NJ: Lawrence Erlbaum, 49–118.

Van Lancker, D. 1997. Rags to riches: our increasing appreciation of cognitive and communicative abilities of the human right cerebral hemisphere. *Brain and Language* 57:1–11.

Van Lancker, D. & Canter, G.J. 1981. Idiomatic versus literal interpretations of ditropically ambiguous sentences. *Journal of Speech and Hearing Research* 24:64–69.

Van Lancker, D., Canter, G.J. & Terbeek, D. 1981. Disambiguation of ditropic sentences: acoustic and phonetic cues. *Journal of Speech and Hearing Research* 24:330–335.

Van Lancker, D. & Cummings, J.L. 1999. Expletives: neurolinguistic and neurobehavioral perspectives on swearing. *Brain Research Reviews* 31:83–104.

Van Lancker, D. & Kempler, D. 1987. Comprehension of familiar phrases by left- but not by right-hemisphere damaged patients. *Brain and Language* 32:265–277.

Verstraten, L. 1992. Fixed phrases in monolingual learners' dictionaries. In P.J.L. Arnaud & H. Béjoint (eds.) *Vocabulary and applied linguistics.* Basingstoke: Macmillan, 28–40.

Vihman, M.M. 1982a. Formulas in first and second language acquisition. In L.K. Obler & L. Menn (eds.) *Exceptional language and linguistics.* New York: Academic Press, 261–284.

Vihman, M.M. 1982b. The acquisition of morphology by a bilingual child: a whole-word approach. *Applied Psycholinguistics* 3:141–160.

Vihman, M.M. & McLaughlin, B. 1982. Bilingualism and second language acquisition in preschool children. In C.J. Brainerd & M. Pressley (eds.) *Verbal processes in children: progress in cognitive development research.* New York: Springer Verlag, 35–58.

Wagner-Gough, J. 1978. Comparative studies in second language learning. In E.M. Hatch (ed.) *Second language acquisition: a book of readings.* Rowley, MA: Newbury House, 155–171.

Wales, R. & Coffey, G. 1986. On children's comprehension of metaphor. In C. Pratt, A.F. Garton, W.E. Tunmer & A.R. Nesdale (eds.) *Research issues in child development.* Sydney: Allen & Unwin, 81–94.

Watkins, C. 1992. The comparison of formulaic sequences. In E.C. Polome & W. Winter (eds.) *Reconstructing languages & cultures.* The Hague: Mouton, 391–418.

Webelhuth, G. 1995a. Introduction by the editor. In G. Webelhuth (ed.) *Government and binding theory and the minimalist program.* Cambridge, MA: Oxford University Press, 3–14.

Webelhuth, G. 1995b. X-bar theory and case theory. In G. Webelhuth (ed.) *Government and binding theory and the minimalist program.* Cambridge, MA: Oxford University Press, 15–95.

Weinert, R. 1995. The role of formulaic language in second language acquisition: a review. *Applied Linguistics* 16(2):180–205.

Weinreich, U. 1963. *Languages in contact* (2nd printing). The Hague: Mouton.

Weinreich, U. 1969. Problems in the analysis of idioms. In J. Puhvel (ed.) *Substance and structure of language.* Los Angeles: University of California Press, 23–81.

Weir, R.H. 1962. *Language in the crib.* The Hague: Mouton.

Wharry, C. 1996. *"I'm gonna preach it, amen": discourse functions of formulaic expressions in African American sermons.* Unpublished PhD thesis, Oklahoma State University.

Widdowson, H.G. 1989. Knowledge of language and ability for use. *Applied Linguistics* 10(2):128–137.

Widdowson, H.G. 1990. *Aspects of language teaching.* Oxford: Oxford University Press.

Wijnen, F., Krikhaar, E. & Den Os, E. 1994. The (non)realization of unstressed elements in children's utterances: evidence for a rhythmic constraint. In K. Perera, G. Collis & B. Richards (eds.) *Growing points in child language.* Cambridge: Cambridge University Press, 59–83.

Wildgruber, D., Pihan, H., Erb, M., Ackermann, H. & Grodd, W. 1999. Differential activation patterns during discrimination of affective prosody: influence of acoustics, emotional valence, accuracy, sex. *Neuroimage* 9(6), part 2:S1018.

Willett, J. 1995. Becoming first graders in an L2: an ethnographic study of L2 socialization. *TESOL Quarterly* 29(3):473–503.

Williams, E. 1994. Remarks on lexical knowledge. In L. Gleitman & B. Landau (eds.) *The acquisition of the lexicon.* Cambridge, MA: MIT Press, 7–34.

Willis, D. 1990. *The lexical syllabus.* London: Harper Collins.

Willis, D. 1999. Syllabus design & the pedagogic corpus. In J. Aitchison, H. Funk, R. Galisson, G. List, M.A. Mochet, C. O'Neil, C. Owen, W. Ulrich, G. Vigner & D. Willis *Vocabulary learning in a foreign language.* Fontenay Saint-Claud: ENS Editions, 115–148.

Winner, E. & Gardner, H. 1977. The comprehension of metaphor in brain-damaged patients. *Brain* 100:717–729.

Wong Fillmore, L. 1976. *The second time around: cognitive and social strategies in second language acquisition.* Unpublished PhD thesis, Stanford University.

Wong Fillmore, L. 1979. Individual differences in second language acquisition. In C.J. Fillmore, D. Kempler & S-Y.W. Wang (eds.) *Individual differences in language ability and language behavior*. New York: Academic Press, 203–228.

Wood, M.M. 1986. *A definition of idiom*. Bloomington, IN: Indiana University Linguistics Club.

Wray, A. 1992. *The focusing hypothesis: the theory of left hemisphere lateralized language re-examined*. Amsterdam: John Benjamins.

Wray, A. 1996. The occurrence of 'occurance' (and 'a lot' of other things 'aswell'): patterns of errors in undergraduate English. In G.M. Blue & R. Mitchell (eds.) *Language and education*. Clevedon: Multilingual Matters, 94–106.

Wray, A. 1998. Protolanguage as a holistic system for social interaction. *Language and Communication* 18:47–67.

Wray, A. 1999. Formulaic language in learners and native speakers. *Language Teaching* 32(1):213–231.

Wray, A. 2000a. Holistic utterances in protolanguage: the link from primates to humans. In C. Knight, M. Studdert-Kennedy & J. Hurford (eds.) *The evolutionary emergence of language*. Cambridge: Cambridge University Press, 285–302.

Wray, A. 2000b. Formulaic sequences in second language teaching: principles and practice. *Applied Linguistics* 21(4):463–489.

Wray, A. In press. Dual processing in protolanguage: performance without competence. In A. Wray (ed.) *The transition to language*. Oxford: Oxford University Press.

Wray, A. & Perkins, M.R. 2000. The functions of formulaic language: an integrated model. *Language and Communication* 20(1):1–28.

Yngve, V.H. 1961. The depth hypothesis. *12th symposium of applied mathematics: structure of language & its mathematical aspect*, 130–138.

Yorio, C.A. 1980. Conventionalized language forms and the development of communicative competence. *TESOL Quarterly* 14(4):433–442.

Yorio, C.A. 1989. Idiomaticity as an indicator of second language proficiency. In K. Hyltenstam & L.K. Obler (eds.) *Bilingualism across the lifespan*. Cambridge: Cambridge University Press, 55–72.

Zingeser, L. & Berndt, R.S. 1990. Retrieval of nouns and verbs in agrammatism and anomia. *Brain and Language* 39:14–32.

Index

accommodation, 85, 95, 99, 126, 203, 289, 291
age, 55–56, 102, 133–135, 145–146, 150, 158, 196–197, 241
agendas, 78, 99, 102, 118, 122, 124–126, 130, 145–148, Chap. 9, 182, 194, 212–213, 255
analysis, 7, 9, 18, 33–34, 56–59, 65, 101, 108, 114, 130–139, 146, 156, 188, 191, 193–194, 196–197, 200–201, 204, 209–210, 212, 232, 268, 274, 277, 294
analytic acquisition style, Chaps. 6–7
analytic language, 14–18, 35, 56, 123, 133
anomia, 218, 225–226, 230
aphasia, 46, 50, 112, 119, 154, Chaps. 12–13, 279
    polyglot, 256–257
    recovery from, 243–244, 261
apologizing, 53–54, 88, 192
appropriacy, 41, 46, 55, 73, 83, 87, 90–91, 102, 105, 110, 131, 143, 148, 171, 235, 292
articulation, 35, 37ff
    precision in, 35, 38, 111–113, 261
    rate, 35–37, 77, 111, 227
atomic lexicon, 265–273, 284
attention, 16–17, 62, 69, 72, 77, 81, 83, 95, 107, 183, 189, 193, 273, 284
attention-getting, 84, 88, 93, 95–96, 126, 157, 159, 165, 239
auctions, 76, 77–79, 100
automaticity, 16, 62, 211, 238–243, 273–274, 292
automatic language, 46, 49, 62, 154, 217, 239, 244, 250, 273; see also proceduralization
avoidance, 148, 165, 170, 183, 205, 255
'Away in a manger', 109

'Baa baa black sheep', 108
backchannel cues, 83–84
Baudelaire, 230
BBC Radio 4, 81, 288
birth order, 116–117

carers, role of, 108, 112, 115–118, 126, 128–129, 133, 136, 145, 153, 159
Chinese, 53, 147
circumlocutory expressions, 74–75
classifications, Chap. 3
classroom talk, 136–137, 177, 181, 200, 205
clause chaining, 16, 36, 190, 223
clinical data, 40, Chaps. 12–13
code-switching, 41–42
Cognitive Grammar, 10, 65, 273–275
coherence, 36, 222
collocation, 5–8, 25, 27, 30, 41, 46, 51–52, 62, 63, 73–74, 92, 130, 183, 185–186, 192, 201–202, 211, 250, 265, 271, 277, 283, 287, 297
commands, 90, 94, 96, 250
compliments, 47, 88
composites, 47, 54, 57, 61
compositionality, 4, 33–34, 36, 49, 51, 56, 57, 63, 121, 124, 129, 134, 137
compound nouns, 58, 74, 106, 229–230, 273, 295
comprehensible input, 129, 161
comprehension, 4, 12, 17, 33, 36, 93, 112, 135, 203, 227, 232–233, 236, 238, 240, 253, 254, 272
concreteness, 240–241, 277
Connectionism, 272
consonant weakening, 38
constituent boundaries, 26, 35–37, 41, 121, 245, 291

context, 13, 17–18, 29, 31, 55, 59, 73, 83, 88,
    111, 113, 116, 119, 121, 126, 135–137,
    153, 170–171, 204, 206, 209, 231, 241,
    248–250, 272, 275, 277, 279, 294
context dependency, 114, 248–257
continuum models, 34, 44, 52, 57, 62–65, 72,
    110, 186, 211, 250, 262
conversational routines, 7–8, 53, 90, 108,
    118, 131, 163–165, 182, 250–251, 279
corpus research, 7, 13–15, 21, 25–32, 51–52,
    54, 73–74, 184–186, 271, 275–277, 281
counting, 109, 220, 240, 242
creativity, 11–12, 14, 25, 45, 75, 101, 130,
    137, 148–149, 163, 169, 173, 183–184,
    186, 193–194, 196, 198, 201–202, 204,
    209–210, 218–220, 228, 245, 250–253,
    262–264, 269, 275; *see also* novelty
cricket, 76–77
critical period, 195–197, 212–213

declarative knowledge, 189, 243, 278
dictionaries, 28–29, 45–46, 61, 73, 145, 206,
    275, 294, 295
discourse management, 54, 85, 135, 181,
    200
discourse markers, 31–32, 53–54, 87, 93, 97,
    101, 177, 233
discourse structure, 36, 78, 87, 97, 101, 223,
    233, 241
dual systems, 14–15, 17, 272, 274, 278–279,
    299
dummy fillers: *see* fillers

education, 134, 159, 279, 280
    of parents, 116–117
embedding, 16, 28, 42, 51
Emergent Lexicon, 10, 299
emotional responses, 166, 177, 220,
    230–231, 235–236, 239, 241–242, 248,
    250, 255–257, 296, 297; *see also*
    reflexive expression
errors, 12, 17–18, 39–41, 137, 175–176,
    182–186, 199–200, 210, 212, 219–223,
    227, 277
Estonian, 157, 292
etymology, 33–34, 57, 132, 229, 265, 293,
    297, 298
evolution of language, 116, 241–242, 281,
    284
Ewe, 90
exclamations: *see* emotional responses
expediency, 255, 267–270
expletives: *see* emotional responses; sub-
    cortical processing; swearwords
expressive cognitive style, 114–116

false starts, 26, 36
fillers, 17, 49, 63, 83, 111–112, 119, 122, 167,
    177, 219

dummy, 112, 119, 228, 230–231, 235, 244,
    248, 254–255
Finnish, 41, 164, 268
first-born children, 116–117
first language acquisition, 39, Chaps. 6, 7,
    11
fixedness, 7, 31–32, 34, 50–52, 60, 62–65, 77,
    84–85, 91, 101, 128–129, 181, 184–185,
    202, 211, 219–225, 245–246, 250, 257,
    269, 275–276, 279
fluency, 7, 16–17, 35–37, 40, 69, 75–79,
    84–85, 95–96, 112, 119, 126, 134, 189,
    271, 279, 281, 284
    in aphasia, 219–225, 244–248, 257, 271,
    297
    in L2, 37, 145, 166, 167, 175, 189–190,
    211, 294
formulaic sequences
    in aphasia, Chaps. 12, 13
    boundaries of, 22, 27–28, 41–42
    in child language, Chaps. 6–7
    definition, 8–9, Chap. 3
    form, 31–32, 48–52
    function, 30–31, 47–48, 52–55, 58–59,
    63–65, Chaps. 4–5, 114–122, 131
    identification, Chap. 2, 184, 246
    in L2, Chaps. 8–11
    meaning, 56–59
    proportion in text, 28
    provenance, 59–61
    semi-fixed, 7, 9, 47–49, 53–54, 97, 221,
    223–224, 246, 275, 279, 287
    terms for, 9
fossilization, 33–34, 41, 49, 148, 184, 195,
    267
French, 37, 39, 137, 185, 187, 190, 196, 277
frequency, 13, 19, 23, 25–31, 52, 54, 73–74,
    105, 184–185, 226–227, 252, 270–271,
    276, 278, 285
'Frère Jacques', 109, 277
Functional Grammar, 10, 56, 299
function of utterance: *see* formulaic
    sequences: function
fusion, 41, 45, 59, 61, 84, 106–107, 117, 119,
    123, 126, 128, 135, 147, 153, 161, 163,
    165–166, 169, 177, 189, 246, 273, 299

GAM, 133–135
Gastarbeiter: *see* immigrant workers
gender, 86, 116, 156–157, 293
gender (noun), 188
German, 41, 55, 73, 83, 170, 181, 183, 228,
    229–230, 269, 285, 288, 292
gestalt language, 110–118, 122–124,
    133–134
gesture, 4, 78, 100, 118, 128, 166, 236, 255
gibberish, 45, 69, 154
grammatical analysis module (GAM),
    133–135

greeting, 7, 12, 54–56, 86–87, 117, 143, 158, 177, 181, 200, 220, 243, 293, 295
group membership, 90, 92, 154, 159–161, 163–164, 205, 250

habit, 5, 9, 55, 84–85, 250
'happy' and its derivatives, 270–271, 299
hearer, role of, 24–25, 36, 54, 55, 62–63, 79–91, 94–99, 126, 153–155, 164, 177, 195, 203, 210, 224, 231, 233, 250, 256, 279, 294
hesitation, 19, 26, 35–36, 77–78, 177, 223
heteromorphic distributed lexicon, Chap. 14
Hindi, 73
holistic language processing, 8, 11, 14–18, 24, 74–75, 79, 107, 110–112, 114–117, 123–124, 128, 133–135, 138, 183–184, 202, 232, 236, Chaps. 13–14, 294; *see also* gestalt language
horse-racing, 76–77
house of ill-repute, 267
humour, 24, 242, 297
hypercorrection, 156

identity, 48, 72, 101, 119, 169–170
    group, 76, 88–90, 92, 118, 126, 159
    individual, 88, 126, 148, 154–155, 164, 235, 294
    protection of, 170, 235
idiomaticity, 11–15, 20, 24–25, 29–30, 34, 53, 56, 72–74, 87, 92, 99, 101–102, 129, 143, 165, 167, 171, 176, 182–183, 191, 195, 206, 209–210, 212, 224, 261, 262–264, 272, 276, 285
idiom principle, 14, 62, 184, 276
idioms, 4, 8, 12–13, 15, 18, 20, 24, 28, 30, 31, 34, 38, 49–50, 56–58, 60, 62–63, 99, 130–132, 135, 182–183, 186, 193–194, 232–233, 242, 265–267, 278, 283, 287, 292, 295, 298
imageability, 240–241, 252
imitation, 92, 107–108, 111, 118–119, 124, 133, 143, 146–148, 153, 164, 166, 167–168, 176
immigrant workers, 172–175, 255
individual differences, 114, 134, 173–175, 192, 290
inference, 60, 81, 241–242
input, 32, 59–60
    impoverished, 99, 129
    in L1 acquisition, 106, 109, 115–116, 121, 131–132, 135, 290
institutionalised routines and expressions, 48, 53–54, 61, 108, 109–110, 117–118, 162–164, 182–183, 250, 251, 279
interactional function, 53, 114, 158, 181, 194, 203, 227, 238, 250–253, 279, 292, 297

interference, 41, 148, 181–183, 185
interlanguage, 176, 185, 199–201, 210
intonation, 35, 38, 54, 76–77, 79, 106, 111, 113, 117–119, 133, 135, 166, 168, 228, 230–231, 235, 244, 248, 254, 296
intuition, 13, 20–24, 27, 32, 38, 43, 73, 78–79, 183, 245, 276–277, 280, 286
involuntary utterances, 219, 242, 296
irony, 135
irregularity, 24, 49, 129–132, 137–138, 193, 210, 246, 261–268, 273, 278, 293
islands of reliability, 185, 293
isolation, 113, 117, 121, 122, 133, 138
'is the Pope a catholic?', 32–33
item-learning, 106
'it's a small world', 296

Japanese, 42, 55, 153, 286–287
jargonaphasia, 223–224, 227, 232, 295–296
jokes, 34, 84

L1 use in L2 context, 147–148, 153, 157, 161
language learners: *see* second language acquisition
learner types, 144–146
left hemisphere, 17, 134, 239, 240–241, 251–252, 284
    damage, 217, 232, 241–244, 251, 253–254
    processing, 234–238, 251, 257
lexicography: *see* dictionaries
lexicon
    native speaker, 12–13, 17, 30, 32–33, 42, 52, 59, 112–113, 119, 121, 128–135, 138, 207, Chaps. 12–14, 283
    non-native speaker, 208, Chap. 12
liaison, 39
linguistic 'dead end', 122
linguistic play, 34, 121–122, 126, 148, 155–157, 160, 167, 170, 293
literacy, 76, 134, 136–138, 194, 202, 203–206, 268, 279, 280, 296
literal meaning, 31, 33–35, 38, 49, 51, 56–58, 63, 66, 99, 129, 132, 135, 232–233, 238, 254, 292, 297
Lithuanian, 298

magic words, 109–110, 153, 162
make-believe, 156, 167, 292
manipulation, 87–91, 94–96, 101, 115, 118–119, 124–126, 153, 158–159, 161–163, 205, 248–252, 256, 290
maturation, 134–135, 195–198, 203, 294
measurements, 28–31, 36, 218, 236, 245, 293
mediacy, 239
memorized texts, 7, 40, 46, 49, 59, 62, 70–72, 75–76, 92, 96, 108–110, 114–115, 154, 156–157, 173, 176–177, 184, 190–193, 196, 200, 204–206, 217–220,

memorized texts (*cont.*)
225–226, 240, 246, 248, 250, 253–254,
284, 294; *see also* mnemonics;
playground rhymes; poetry;
quotations; rhymes; song
memory, 9–10, 16, 188–190, 242–243
short-term, 16, 87, 284
memory limitations, 16, 42, 76, 190
metaphor, 49–51, 56–58, 63, 74, 130, 135,
232, 241, 277, 297
mnemonics, 70, 95–96, 109, 219, 250, 253,
265, 279, 294
Montgomery, Field Marshall, 83
morpheme-equivalence, 265–269
morphemes, 9–10, 29, 42, 105–107,
112–113, 121, 134, 138, 202, 206, 245,
247, 250–251, 255, 257, 262–271, 285,
290, 292, 294, 295, 296–297, 299
motivation in L2 learning, 160–161, 167,
170, 191, 196–197, 256, 279
multiple representation, 15, 202, 230,
252–253, 256, 262, 268

names, 3–4, 60–61, 77, 283
naming, 117, 155, 167, 290
games 115, 155, 157, 167
insight, 113
tests, 227, 297–298
native-like language, 11, 13, 15, 99, 143,
146–148, 166, 171, 209–212
native speaker judges, 22–23, 73, 184
naturalistic L2 acquisition, 144–145, 148,
150–171, 172–176, 194–195, 199,
205–206, 295
needs-only analysis, 130–132, 138, 202, 274,
291
neologism, 227–228
'no', 119–120, 219, 244, 248, 254, 296
non-canonical form, 34, 129, 287
non-literal meaning, 34, 56, 99, 129, 132,
135
non-native speaker, 39–41, 53, 73, 90–100,
Chaps. 8–11
non-propositional language, 237–240
Nora, 100, 159–171, 197, 204–205
novelty, 11–18, 29, 31–35, 38, 45, 59, 62–65,
75–79, 94–97, 101, 107, 119, 126, 128,
134, 139, 166, 189, 190, 203–204, 218,
222, 245, 248–251, 262, 279, 281, 284;
see also creativity

obsolete vocabulary, 33, 131
one clause at a time constraint, 36, 190
open choice principle, 14, 52, 62
open class items, 7, 32, 37, 45, 50, 65, 176,
220–222, 245, 248
oral tradition, 75–76, 251, 288
overuse, 181, 184–185

paralinguistic abilities, 241–243, 252
paraphasia, 227–230, 237, 295
passivization, 49, 50, 261
Pattern Grammar, 10, 275–276, 278
pauses, 19, 35–37, 49, 85, 111, 189, 190, 223
performatives, 90–91
phonological cues, 31, 35, 225
phonological form, 35–39
phonological indistinctness, 108, 117, 124,
173, 222, 227
phrasal verb, 30, 295, 297
phrasebooks, 191, 294
pitch, 35, 111
place-holders: *see* fillers
planning, 16, 36, 75, 184, 190, 211, 286
play, 148, 150–153, 155–156, 160, 168, 170,
293
playground rhymes, 71, 288
poetry, 12, 75–76, 209, 219, 284
politeness routines and formulas, 88–90,
94–96, 109–110, 158, 162
pragmatics, 11, 17–18, 31, 33, 51, 55–56,
58–60, 108, 113, 129, 133, 135, 206,
235, 241–242, 248, 254, 278, 286,
296
preaching, 83–84
proceduralization, 37, 126, 189, 190, 211,
274
processing
effort, 15–18, 25, Chap. 4, 99, 101, 107,
126, 198, 250, 254, 278
limitations, 16, 18, 42, 75, 107, 112
load, 69, 75, 91, 97, 128, 205
pressures, 15–17, 75, 77, 79, 97, 174–175,
277
route, 289
shortcuts, Chap. 4, 94, 97, 101, 106,
119–122, 126, 188, 198, 205, 210, 233,
235, 251, 256, 261, 269, 279
speed, 16, 84–85, 284
proforms, 17, 223, 230–231, 250, 254; *see
also* pronouns
promotion of self, 95–96, 98, 101, 118–127,
145, 154, 158, 165–166, 175, 195, 253,
255–256, 258, 279, 281
pronouns, 31–32, 50, 114, 115–116, 187,
222, 241
propositional language, 238–239
prosodic features, 121, 241, 296
proverbs, 24, 49, 56, 63, 71

quotations, 49–50, 70–72, 248

'rain check', 60
ratio measures, 28–29, 37, 218
Real Word Recurrent Utterances, 239
referential cognitive style, 114–117
referential language, 50, 54, 96–97, 113,

130, 134–136, 166, 187, 204, 223, 227, 248–250, 279, 297
reflexive expression, 248, 250, 256–257, 262, 297, 298
regularity, 10, 14, 33–34, 49–51, 57–58, 63, 121, 128–132, 138, 193, 210, 218, 246, 253, 261–267, 273, 278–279
rehearsal, 155, 176, 184, 192, 253
repetition, 19, 28–29, 34, 36, 38, 76, 83–87, 93, 107–108, 129–130, 154–155, 167–170, 173, 177, 189, 190, 192, 204, 217, 219–220, 226, 228, 231, 242, 272, 288, 293, 296
   partial, 85–86, 155, 168–169
requesting, 53, 63, 88, 94–96, 107, 116–118, 145, 155, 250, 289
rhymes, 7, 40, 46, 49, 59, 70, 72, 108–110, 117–118, 128, 131, 225–226, 248; see also *playground rhymes*
rhythm, 38, 70, 75–77, 113, 117, 168
right hemisphere, 17, 134, 233–235, 237–244, 248, 251–252, 254–255, 257, 284
ritual, 55, 84, 90–91, 109, 170, 220
role play, 160, 167
Russian, 53, 73

second language acquisition, 21–22, 40–41, 99–100, 114, Chaps. 8–11, 256, 279
   adult and teenage, 145–146, 148–149, Chap. 10, 201, 205–206
   young children, 150–157, 203–204
   older children, 151–152, 157–171, 204–205
second language teaching, 38, 188, 191–197, 280
segmentation, 38, 113, 115, 117, 121–122, 138, 148, 156, 168–169, 171, 173, 176, 187–188, 193, 262, 264–267, 269, 273–274, 277
selective impairment, 226–227
self-promotion: *see* promotion of self
semantic paraphasia, 228–230
semantic transparency, 3–4, 24, 33–34, 56, 63, 193–194, 253, 264
semi-fixed frames: *see* formulaic sequences
semi-preconstructed phrases: *see* formulaic sequences
sentence boundaries, 26, 35, 36
sentence builders: see formulaic sequences
sentence chaining, 16
serial lists: *see* memorized texts
sermons, 83–84
shared knowledge, 20–25, 71
shipping forecast, 79–81
Silas Marner, 91, 289
silent period, 166
Singaporean English, 147

social hierarchy, place in, 90, 110, 126
social integration, 90, 118, 148, 154, 157, 160, 163, 169–171, 175, 235
socio-interactional bubble, 135–137, 204
song, 63, 70, 75, 108–110, 117–118, 128, 130–131, 154, 164, 219–220, 225–226, 242–244, 248, 254
specialization in social cognition (SSC), 133
speech act, 88, 110, 191, 234
speech community, role of, 8, 20, 24, 58, 61–63, 72–75, 85, 96, 99, 101, 129, 143, 267
speech rate, 37, 76–77
sports commentaries, 27, 76–77, 288
SSC, 133
strategies, 98, 126, 144, Chap. 9, 176, 186, 195, 205, 222, 236, 271, 280
   compensatory, 173, 183, 195, 204, 235–236, 243, 251, 253–255, 258
   processing, 14–15, 36, 106–107, 112–113, 121–122, 132–135, 173, 190, 271–272, 274, 279–280, 299
stress (phonological), 37–38, 49, 108–109, 113, 228, 261, 296
stressful situations, 52, 195–196
style, 83–84, 288
sub-cortical processing, 242–243, 248, 250, 255–257
supermarket checkouts, 86–87
swearwords, 230, 239, 242–244, 248, 250, 255, 256, 297, 298
system-learning, 106

task-based language teaching, 193, 212, 294
taxonomies, Chap. 3
teenage, 135, 205–206; *see also* second language acquisition: adult and teenage
testing, 225, 227, 232, 236, 248, 253, 271, 280
'too big a piece', 130
Tourette syndrome, 242
translation, 55, 166, 182–183, 298
Turkish, 90, 268–269
two systems: *see* dual systems
type-token ratio, 29, 218, 285

underanalysed strings, 106–113, 122–124
unit of acquisition, 112–113
unit size, 212, 290
Universal Grammar, 129, 291
unrandomness, 14
utterance length, 189, 219

vagueness, 184, 230–231
variability, 48–51
verbal stereotypy, 231–232, 244

vocabulary acquisition (L1), 114–117, 123–124, 131, 133–134, 137, 294
vowel reduction, 38

'wanna', 156, 169
'watch your bag', 252–253
'way', 29
weather forecasts, 79–83, 93
Welsh, 191, 293, 294

Wernicke's aphasia, 218, 221–223, 227–229, 295
word breaks, 137, 264, 298
word class, 226, 240
word-finding difficulties, 222, 225–227
written language, 27, 35, 84, 137–138, 228, 285

'yes', 217, 219, 244, 248, 254, 296

Printed in the United States
119581LV00002B/67-69/A